HOAX

HOAX

THE POPISH PLOT THAT NEVER WAS

VICTOR STATER

YALE UNIVERSITY PRESS
NEW HAVEN AND LONDON

For information about this and other Yale University Press publications, please contact:
U.S. Office: sales.press@yale.edu   yalebooks.com
Europe Office: sales@yaleup.co.uk   yalebooks.co.uk

Set in Adobe Garamond Pro by IDSUK (DataConnection) Ltd
Printed in Great Britain by TJ Books, Padstow, Cornwall

Library of Congress Control Number: 2022934812

ISBN 978-0-300-12380-7

A catalogue record for this book is available from the British Library.

10 9 8 7 6 5 4 3 2 1

For my favourite kings,
Charles and Henry

CONTENTS

PLATES

1. Titus Oates, by Cornelius Nicolas Schurtz, 1678–79. © National Portrait Gallery, London.
2. William Staley dragged to Tyburn, by William Fairthorne, 1678–79. © National Portrait Gallery, London.
3. The 'murder' of Sir Edmund Godfrey, after Francis Barlow, 1679. © National Portrait Gallery, London.
4. A 'Godfrey dagger', 1678. Courtesy of Lambeth Palace Library.
5. Silver medal, 1678. © Trustees of the British Museum.
6. 'Captain' William Bedloe, by unknown, 1679. © National Portrait Gallery, London.
7. The Old Bailey. FALKENSTEINFOTO / Alamy Stock Photo.
8. Sir William Scroggs, after John Michael Wright, c. 1678. © National Portrait Gallery, London.
9. Charles II and his queen, Catherine of Braganza, by unknown, c. 1662. © National Portrait Gallery, London.
10. Anthony Ashley Cooper, after John Greenhill, c. 1672–73. © National Portrait Gallery, London.
11. James, duke of York, by Henri Gascar, c. 1673. Royal Museums Greenwich. © National Maritime Museum, Greenwich, London.
12. Anti-Catholic demonstration, London, by unknown, 1679. EB65 A100 680s4, Houghton Library, Harvard University.
13. Titus Oates and the Devil, by unknown, c. 1680. The History Collection / Alamy Stock Photo.
14. Stove tile, by Jan Ariens Van Hamme, 1680. © Victoria and Albert Museum, London.
15. Reliquary of Oliver Plunket. Photo by David Iliff, 2015. License: CC BY-SA 3.0.
16. Titus Oates in the pillory, May 1685, after Robert White, 1685. Royal Collection Trust / © Her Majesty Queen Elizabeth II 2022.

INTRODUCTION

People can believe preposterous things. In our own century many believe that a paedophile ring has seized control of the American government. Others are convinced that the Kremlin succeeded in electing a president of the United States who was an intelligence asset to them. In the last century some people believed that the British royal family had murdered Diana, Princess of Wales, in 1997, and that the 'Elders of Zion' plotted world domination for Jewry. It has always been so. Believing conspiracy theories is part of human nature, and believers are not necessarily stupid. We credit the preposterous because it often confirms our own bias; it is easy to believe that an enemy is an unprincipled conspirator. We often do not stop to examine the presumptions of the like-minded, and we too often refuse to accept the rational explanations of those who disagree with us.

This book tells the story of one of the most preposterous – and consequential – conspiracy theories of all time. It threatened a renewal of civil war in Britain, but in the end it ushered in a new political model instead of war: two political parties competing, more or less peacefully, for power. The story is one of ruthless opportunism, naivety, cruelty and astonishing self-sacrifice.

In the summer of 1678 a half-mad English clergyman with an obsessive hatred of Jesuits met a shifty vagabond with a past so full of misdeeds and scandal that showing his remarkably ugly face in public was an act of courage. The clergyman was Israel Tonge and the vagabond was Titus Oates. The two of them concocted a story intended to gain them notoriety, and, with luck, a living. There was, they claimed, a diabolical conspiracy, led by prominent Catholics, both lay and clerical, to kill King Charles II.

The plot they described in its first iteration involved the king's assassination, followed by a Catholic uprising. There would be elaborations, but this was the original outline of their story, and it was enough to spark a political crisis and send many wholly innocent people to their death. Why did this incredible story have such an impact? Neither Tonge nor Oates exuded credibility – though Oates at least made up for that with a grating self-confidence that might have passed for credibility in some quarters. In the beginning the conspirators had trouble gaining attention – but happily for them (and disastrously for many others) events turned in their favour in the late summer and early autumn of 1678.

Political tensions had been growing in England for years. The joy that had greeted the restored monarchy in 1660 had curdled by the mid-1670s. King Charles was good-natured, indolent and fickle, more interested in a quiet life pursuing his pleasures – some of dubious morality. Power shifted into and out of the hands of a cast of characters whose ambitions often outweighed their talents. In matters of religion Charles sought to ease tensions between former supporters of Cromwell's regime, who tended to lean towards Puritanism, and the High Church Anglicanism dear to Royalists. Twice, in 1662 and 1672, he tried to remove penalties against those who chose to worship outside the Church of England. The strong opposition these indulgences provoked meant that both were quickly withdrawn. Some detected a growing Catholic influence at court, a real danger for Charles, and more crucially, for his brother James, the heir apparent.

More than a century after Henry VIII broke with Rome, anti-Catholicism remained a powerful force in Protestant England. Yet Charles, after spending years in exile under the protection of his Catholic cousin Louis XIV, remained on good terms with him. Many English Protestants feared Louis even more than the pope. Charles had married a Catholic and several of his influential mistresses were Catholic. Worst of all, the king's brother James, duke of York, had converted to Catholicism by the early 1670s. As it became increasingly clear that Queen Catherine would bear no children, Protestants feared that the throne would pass to James and a Catholic dynasty would henceforth rule England.

This was the context within which Oates and Tonge emerged with their tale of popish skulduggery. What allowed the wild stories about assassinations and royal ambushes to spiral out of control was a combination of coincidence – the death of a London magistrate, the discovery of some mysterious letters, and unexpected revelations about the size of London's Catholic underground – and politics. For a number of high-ranking politicians seized upon the plot as a tool to advance their own personal interests. The Lord Treasurer, Thomas, earl of Danby, hoped he might exploit the plot to build support within a Parliament that had become increasingly fractious. But more important than Danby was Anthony, earl of Shaftesbury. An unscrupulous opportunist – in this he and

Oates were born partners – he had during the course of his life served – quite ably – Charles I, Oliver Cromwell and Charles II. He had been a central part of the king's government in the early 1670s, but had been ousted from power by Danby. The 'little earl', as Shaftesbury was called because of his short stature, intended to use the plot to return to the centre of power, perhaps even to displace James, for whom he had an abiding loathing.

Charles II's apparent weaknesses played an important part in the unfolding of the plot. The king was, though historians have rarely noted it, Britain's first 'modern' monarch. He pursued an interest in the emerging scientific revolution, chartering the Royal Society and spending time tinkering in his own chemical laboratory. His foreign policy was less dynastic than cognizant of a national interest defined by international trade and empire, hence his two wars against Europe's leading trading power, the Dutch Republic. He wore his religion lightly, as his attempts to indulge dissenters showed. At home he supported and fostered commerce, appointing a council of trade and plantations and supporting the malign work of the Royal Africa Company. In this work Charles's modernity manifests itself most notably in his politics. The plot forced the king to respond politically and he did so with a strikingly modern attitude: he became, in effect, the leader of a political party. Using the power of patronage, sponsoring favourable propaganda, and through the use of his own personal charm – 'campaigning' before the public at civic banquets – he strove to repel the determined attacks of his political enemies.

Few expected that Charles could or would respond to a political crisis with fortitude or determination. And what came to be known as the 'Popish Plot' created a crisis, for by the late autumn of 1678 it had developed into a struggle over the succession. James became a target of the plotters, who hoped to remove him from the succession. Much of the further development of the plot revolved around this struggle. By 1681 the kingdom was hopelessly divided between exclusionists – committed to James's destruction and 'Yorkists' who maintained his right to the throne. The 'Whigs', so-called by their enemies, who compared them to Scottish radicals of the same name, squared off against the 'Tories', dubbed by their enemies after the Catholic bandits infesting the Irish countryside. The Whigs had no qualms whatever about inflating the public's fear of Catholicism, and by extension of James. Sending innocent people to their death did not bother them – and eventually it would not bother many Tories either.

This book tells the story of the Popish Plot from the moment of its unfolding. It does so with very close attention to the chronology of events and to the actions and statements – many of them under oath – of the main participants. It is a narrative rather than an analytic account of the plot. Although the tale is based on years of research in the archives and printed sources, notes are kept to a minimum to allow readers to absorb themselves in the story without distraction. It is crucial for understanding this 'preposterous' story that readers experience the fear, loathing, blind prejudice and outright lying that took place in the eventful three years that changed the course of British history.

The plot was crucial as a political catalyst; it enabled the formation of what would become a two-party political system. It triggered an explosion of political propaganda, giving rise to a partisan press that has been an enduring feature of Anglo-American political life ever since. No one knew it at the time, but this form of political competition would become an essential element of politics throughout the English-speaking world. Party politics were born in an atmosphere of cruelty and injustice: politicians, particularly Whigs, sacrificed innocent lives in the pursuit of their goals. It was an ugly process. But crucially, it provided a framework for competition that would actually lessen the chances of civil war in a nation where political passions had already triggered one just three and a half decades earlier. And it all started because of the squalid ambitions of one very bad man: Titus Oates.

PROLOGUE
THE DEATH OF WILLIAM STALEY
NOVEMBER 1678

William Staley was the first victim, though he would certainly not be the last. He lived with his father, John, and sister near Covent Garden, where he worked in the family trade as a goldsmith. The Staleys were prosperous, if not fabulously rich – goldsmithing was a profitable, if risky trade. The risks lay not so much in the fashioning of gold into luxurious household ornaments and jewellery as in a more recent sideline: banking. The Staleys, like other, much richer families, took deposits from customers. Their premises were secure; they were well versed in the art and science of precious metals and jewels; it made sense for them to offer this facility for clients. Trusting that their deposits would be readily available on demand – and not subject to the danger of casual housebreakers or dishonest servants – wealthy ladies and gentlemen carried their bags of gold to be locked up in the strong chests and cellars of the goldsmiths. Goldsmiths earned a profit by loaning out some of their deposits, usually charging substantial rates of interest. As long as everyone remained honest, and unforeseen disasters could be avoided, the arrangement was quite satisfactory.

The Staleys prospered in this way; but while always subject to the usual risks of the business, they added one more: they were Roman Catholic. Catholics, despised by many of their neighbours, and subject to a wide range of discriminatory laws, preferred to keep their private affairs – especially their money affairs – within the faith. A Catholic goldsmith could be expected to protect his co-religionists' secrets. For there were many of these, especially among wealthy Catholics. Assets that might be subject to seizure under a variety of discriminatory laws were hidden behind phalanxes of trustees and complicated blind trusts. John Staley knew how these things were done, and he knew to whom to turn when a new trust or new arrangements were needed. For wealthy Catholics, dealing with the Staleys was a comfort. Moreover, it gave them a ready-made set of customers, whose loyalty could be relied upon.

John Staley had earned a good reputation; he had well-placed, influential friends, Catholic and Protestant alike. He lived in a fashionable part of town, close to wealthy families who frequently needed his services, and made a good living. In due course his son William would take over the business. In 1678 William was probably in his twenties. He had been educated abroad, in a Jesuit school that catered to the families of English Catholics hoping to keep their faith strong from one generation to the next. The practice was strictly illegal: Parliament had long ago outlawed it, but the government rarely enforced the statute. As a result, William spent much of his youth in Europe, travelling in France and Italy, where he learned the languages – good preparation for the family banking business. After his return he settled down to help his father.

In mid-November 1678 the business that had sustained the Staleys was threatened by one of those dreaded unforeseen events: widespread rumours of a Catholic political conspiracy. Catholics were, not surprisingly, nervous, and many rushed to secure the wealth they had left in the Staleys' hands. Something of an undercover run – for Catholics did not care to let everyone know they were fearful – had begun. On 14 November, William and one of his customers, an elderly Italian named Benjamin Fromante, were in the Black Lion cookshop, close to Covent Garden. While they were speaking together, at about 11 a.m., three men walked into the shop and ordered pots of ale and slices of roast beef. Shops like the Black Lion were the fast-food restaurants of their day; they were ubiquitous and always had some hearty fare available at any time: roast or boiled meat being favourite choices. As the three men awaited their meal, their attention was drawn to the two men in the next room, some seven or eight feet away. The fact that they spoke in animated French was eye-opening. Many of the latest rumours and tales of Catholic skulduggery involved mysterious French agents, and so the customers immediately pricked up their ears – and what they heard (or thought they heard) astounded them. The old man was saying that the English king persecuted the people of God. The younger man agreed, and passionately stamping his foot on the floor, called Charles II 'a great heretick', and clapping his hand upon his chest, said 'I myself will kill him!'

In the atmosphere of suspicion and panic that had been rapidly building in London over the previous weeks, these words shocked the witnesses – or two of them, at any rate, since one, Philip Garret, knew no French, though the others, Captain William Carstairs and Alexander Sutherland, did. Carstairs in particular was outraged and determined not to allow the episode to pass. Shortly after overhearing the remarks, the two unknown 'Frenchmen' disappeared into the streets. Carstairs did not know who they were, but he quickly sent a servant after the two men to follow them. He soon learned that one of the two had been followed to the home of John Staley, goldsmith. It was Staley's son William. Carstairs and his friends had no intention of allowing a dangerous 'Papist' to run free after threatening the king's life.

Without a warrant from a justice of the peace, Carstairs could not accost William – even in the atmosphere of alarm created by rumoured Catholic plots. Legal forms must be maintained. Early the next morning, Sutherland turned up at the Staley shop posing as a customer in the market for a jewelled button. Unfortunately this dodge had little effect; William said that they had no such articles in stock, and Sutherland would be better off seeking out a jeweller at the Royal Exchange, the centre of that trade. Sutherland's aim was to keep William occupied until Carstairs could return with a warrant and a constable, but his gambit having failed, he was forced to leave the shop. Fifteen minutes later Sutherland returned, with a new ploy: would William join him at the nearby Crossed Keys tavern? An 'honourable person' wanted to speak with him. Hoping, no doubt, that he was about to meet a wealthy potential customer, William agreed. At the Crossed Keys he met a man – either Carstairs or Gifford – who proceeded to give him a glass of wine (several it seems – between 8 a.m. and 11, according to the tavern keeper, these gentlemen consumed five bottles) and 'a great many ceremonies'. And so the trap was sprung, baited by free wine and an order of roast beef – the latter of which was never consumed.

At about 11 a.m. a constable arrived bearing a warrant for William's arrest. It had taken more than two hours to find someone with the proper authority; in the end the witnesses had to go all the way to Whitehall, where they obtained the signature of the Secretary of State himself, Sir Joseph Williamson, and another magistrate, Sir Gilbert Gerard. Carstairs and his friends now accused William of treason and presented him with a written account of what they had heard the day before. William denied everything: 'I do not understand you! I am innocent! You must not put any bubble on me!' The bewildered Staley was carried off to jail, first in the Gatehouse prison, a jail attached to Westminster Abbey, and then, the next day, he was moved to Newgate. This at least, unlike the decrepit Gatehouse, was a new building, designed by Sir Christopher Wren in the aftermath of the Great Fire of 1666.

When one of the Staley maids arrived at the Cross Keys later in the morning, sent by John, now anxious about his son, she found him gone and learned of his arrest.

When the seventeenth-century criminal law cranked into gear it moved swiftly. Gilbert Burnet, Bishop of Salisbury, knew William's accusers, 'profligate wretches'; Carstairs was a professional informer not above extortion. Burnet sent word to the Attorney General and Lord Keeper in an attempt to forestall the prosecution. 'I wished they would not rush too hastily to the taking men's lives upon such testimonies.'[1] But he found the minister's minds made up; the Attorney General accused Burnet of trying to curry favour at court and pressed on with preparations for a quick trial.

On 20 November, William was arraigned on a charge of high treason in the court of King's Bench in Westminster Hall. Sir William Scroggs, Lord Chief Justice, would preside, and when the arraignment was finished, Scroggs licensed Robert Pawlet, a London printer, to publish an official account of the trial set for the following day. William's predicament was not his alone – word of his arrest had spread to his customers, some of whom panicked, fearing the loss of their money. The law was clear: convicted traitors forfeited all their property to the Crown and no one wanted their own assets swept away with whatever William might have. After he was returned to Newgate, William received a visit from two gentlemen who pressed him to sign a document that would prevent the loss of their £1,000 investment. How the dejected young man received these visitors can easily be imagined.

The following morning, Thursday, Staley was brought once again to Westminster Hall. He would have been familiar with the place – the principal common law courts all met in this ancient barn of a building and it housed a wide array of booksellers and peddlers of all sorts. Dealers in money like William would have been in and out of the Hall constantly, and he might well have stopped to hear the occasional interesting, or notorious, criminal case. The courts conducted their business in the open – King's Bench cases being heard at one end of the large open room. But now it was William's turn to be notorious, and there was a large audience waiting to watch the trial.

The crier called the court to order, Justice Scroggs assumed his seat overlooking the crowd, and the proceedings began. The first task was to empanel a jury. This case was a particularly important one, being prosecuted by no other than Sir Cresswell Levinz, the king's Attorney General. Therefore, the jurors would be more substantial characters than men who might be chosen in a run-of-the-mill felony prosecution. Twelve were seated, and they were indeed substantial: five were knights and seven esquires. Some might have known William or his family; several lived barely a stone's throw away from the Staleys. Sir Philip Matthews and Sir Richard Blake, a prominent surgeon, both lived very near Covent Garden. William had the right to challenge jurors, but he allowed all the gentlemen called to be seated – perhaps he thought his family's respectable reputation might work to his advantage among some of his near neighbours.

William's indictment was read and the Attorney General, who had had perhaps three or four days to prepare his case, began. Staley had threatened the king's life, a clear violation of the treason statute that Parliament passed in 1663: he had, as the law required, spoken 'advisedly and maliciously' and there were witnesses to prove his words. Staley's rage against the king was founded, Levinz said, in his religion and spurred on by his anger over the effect that tales of Catholic plots was having on his business. William's Jesuit education prepared him for acting the assassin, for the Order had been steeped in treachery and murder from its foundation.

Then followed the Crown's principal witnesses: Carstairs, Sutherland and Garret. The first two recounted what they had heard in the Black Lion; Garret, not understanding French, affirmed their account, though he could not testify to William's precise words. After the prosecution finished its questions, William was given an opportunity to interrogate the witnesses, though he did not shake their stories. One Catholic version of the proceedings says that Staley claimed his accusers had attempted to extort £200 from him before calling a constable, though this fact does not appear in the authorized account of the trial.[2] Staley argued that the witnesses must have misunderstood his French – he had been talking of the French king, and moreover had never threatened to kill any king at all, but rather himself.

This latter claim prompted an intervention from Justice Scroggs on the bench: 'Would you kill yourself because you said the King of France was a great heretic?' It is easy to imagine that this question was put in a less than sympathetic manner. In theory, criminal defendants were not allowed legal counsel because the judge played that role – in practice, as in this case, that was far from true. William claimed that he and Fromante had in fact been comparing England and France – and condemning Louis XIV as a tyrant (though not, he said, a heretic – he had never used that word). Moreover, 'I have been thought a person of some intelligence and some understanding in the world.' Would such a person speak treasonous words in public before a crowd of strangers? He then reiterated his claim that he had been talking of suicide, not regicide. Once again Scroggs interjected a hostile comment: 'What Jesuit taught you this trick? It is like one of them, it is the art and interest of a Jesuit so to do.'

A key part of William's defence would have been the testimony of Benjamin Fromante – but he was not in the court. Another handicap defendants faced was that they, unlike the Crown, could not compel a witness to testify. We cannot know why Fromante was not present – but the Attorney General did have a written statement from him. This he gave to William, and asked him if he wished to enter it in evidence in his defence. Curiously, William did not – evidently Fromante's statement did not seem to be helpful. The fact that it was apparently procured by the prosecution perhaps makes William's response less than surprising.

Staley called one witness – a Protestant gentleman who remained nameless in the printed account of the trial. He had on many occasions heard William say positive, loyal things about Charles II, and bitter negatives about the Jesuits. William had expressed horror about the alleged Catholic plot on everyone's lips as well. But the witness had not been present at the Black Lion on 14 November and therefore could not say anything about the actual words William had spoken.

Here again Scroggs placed his thumb on the scale of justice, belittling the witnesses' testimony, 'That is when he (Staley) spoke to a Protestant.' The evidence having been presented, it was the judge's turn to sum up for the jury. He was no less biased in his summation than he had been during the presentation of the case. After bitterly attacking the principles of the Society of Jesus, he dwelt on Staley's calling the king a 'great heretick'. 'When a papist once hath made a man a heretique, there is no scruple to murther him. Whosoever is not of their perswasion are hereticks, and whoever are hereticks may be murthered, if the pope commands it, for then they may become saints in heaven . . . Therefore [speaking to the jury] discharge your consciences as you ought to do, if guilty you shall do well to begin with this man, for perchance it may be a terror to the rest.'

The jurors, without leaving their places, returned a guilty verdict almost immediately.

With the verdict rendered, the final act of the courtroom drama played out. William was asked, 'What have you to say for yourself wherefore the court should not proceed to judgment against you?'

'I have nothing to say.'

Justice Scroggs then pronounced judgement, '. . . you seem instead of being sorrowful, to be obstinate. Between God and your conscience be it, I have nothing to do with it. It is my duty to pronounce judgment upon you, which is this: you shall return to the prison, from thence be drawn to the place of execution, where you shall be hanged by the neck, cut down alive, your quarters shall be severed and disposed of as the King shall think fit, and your bowels burnt, and so the Lord have mercy on your soul.'

And so William returned to Newgate to await his end, which was not long in coming. His execution was set for Tuesday 26 November. In the five days remaining to him he was visited by his father and sister, who no doubt offered what comfort they could – and who were also concerned about the whereabouts of some of their customers' money and jewels. The Anglican chaplain at Newgate, Samuel Smith, prayed with William – but had no luck converting him to Protestantism. On his last day, William told Smith that he was reconciled to death, but he was worried that the pain of his execution might spur him to curse 'or use any unchristian word'.

Dressed in a sober – and expensive – black suit, a fashionable periwig and silk stockings, William was tied around the chest to a straw-covered sledge drawn by four horses. He looked around him at the huge crowd of onlookers as the horses dragged him to Tyburn. It would have taken some time, as the distance was over a mile and the way crowded with people. He was surrounded by a large number of constables and watchmen, for fear of a rescue attempt – but none happened. He mounted the scaffold and spoke his last words and 'seemed willing to extenuate his guilt, by alleging he had no treasonous intention'. The executioner's grisly work began. It ended with him lifting William's bloody heart high above the thick crowd and shouting, 'Here is the heart of a traitor!'

William's gory remains were heaped upon the sledge – the need for the straw was now apparent – and returned to town. At some point, the family had used its influence and obtained one small (very small) mercy from the Crown. William's remains were returned to them and he was allowed Christian burial, rather than the customary humiliation of a public display of the head and quarters on the city gates or London bridge.

Within hours of William's death, London's printers were busily composing accounts of his trial and execution, including one luridly illustrated broadside ballad, 'Treason Justly Punished':

O stay, and lend an ear
You Loyal subjects all
And by this story you shall hear
Behold a traitor's fall.

Was William Staley really guilty of treason? Perhaps – he might have made threatening comments about Charles II, whose government he might have held responsible for the panicked withdrawals being made by his customers. Or perhaps, threatened with financial ruin, he really was talking of suicide. More likely he was the victim of the unscrupulous Carstairs, who saw him as a potential meal ticket for a time. We will never know. But another question arises: Why did the Crown see fit to prosecute a young man of good family and reputation when worse things were said about the king and his government on a daily basis? And why make the case such a high priority, assigning it to the Attorney General?

The answer seems clear. The government was losing control: fears of Catholic conspiracies were rampant, rumour and charges of treason emerging at all hands, and the government's political enemies were beginning to exploit those fears for their own ends. When Bishop Burnet protested that Carstairs was a perjured villain, Lord Shaftesbury, leading the charge against Lord Treasurer Danby, said 'We must support the evidence, and that all those who undermined the credit of the witnesses were to be looked on as public enemies.' The case against William Staley was necessary because it demonstrated that the king's ministers were doing something. William was sacrificed – innocent or guilty made no difference – because he was available and Catholic. His trial was evidence that the government was in charge, and was capable of defending the king and defeating the Papists.[3] Only time would tell whether this impression would endure.

ONE

POLITICS AND POPERY
1675 TO SUMMER 1678

In early February 1678 some of London's booksellers began stocking a new title, one that would have an explosive impact on English politics. *An Account of the Growth of Popery and Arbitrary Government in England* bore no author's name on its title page, and its Amsterdam imprint was false – a transparent attempt to avoid responsibility for a highly inflammatory book. The anonymous author of this tract was Andrew Marvell. An accomplished poet and Member of Parliament (he represented the Yorkshire port of Hull in the Commons), Marvell, fifty-six, had grown increasingly disenchanted with Charles II and his ministers. A former official in Oliver Cromwell's administration, he had accepted the Restoration but remained sympathetic to the Old Cause – and was especially sympathetic towards Protestant dissenters.[1]

At some point in 1677 – there were rumours afoot that someone was writing about a Catholic conspiracy that summer – Marvell decided that he would publish an assault upon those responsible for what he believed was England's drift into dangerous political waters.[2] His first sentence made his object clear: 'There has now been for diverse years, a design been carried on, to change the lawfull government of England into an absolute tyranny, and to convert the established Protestant religion into down-right popery . . .'[3] The key tool used by the conspirators was corruption – especially the buying off of MPs with grants of offices and pensions. The government controlled the votes of at least one-third of the House of Commons, and Marvell argued that the mere prospect of reward might tempt another third to advance the grand conspiracy.[4] These machinations were carried out with the support and financial aid of Louis XIV's France, Europe's most aggressive Catholic power. The French king, Marvell and people like him believed, intended to create a 'universal monarchy' and was scheming behind the scenes to advance his cause, liberally distributing gold coins, many of which were Louis d'or – bearing the Sun King's portrait, an unmistakable display of regal power. In the months before Marvell wrote his account, the English government's actions were secretly coordinated with France: 'For all things betwixt England and France moved with that punctual regularity, that it was like the harmony of the spheres, so consonant with themselves, although we cannot hear the musick.'[5]

Nowhere in his book does Marvell actually identify the conspirators – naming names would create even more difficulty for himself – but, as with the place of publication, his readers would have no trouble identifying their leader. 'But if anyone delight in the chase, he is an ill woodsman that knows not the size of the beast by the proportion of the excrement.'[6] This could mean only one man: Thomas Osborne, earl of Danby, the Lord Treasurer and the king's principal minister.

For the opposition Danby was the key target. He had, since his first appointment as Lord Treasurer in 1673, gradually built a formidable political faction, one that gradually denied other ambitious politicians the fruits of office. Part of Marvell's bitterness was personal. He and Danby came from Yorkshire, and both had been connected with the grandest of their home county's grandees, George, second duke of Buckingham. Danby had outgrown the connection, and in fact had done much to undermine the duke's political standing. Marvell, while at times bemused by Buckingham's flighty nature – sometimes, for instance, favouring a French alliance, while at others insisting upon toleration for Protestant dissenters – stuck with his old friend and patron.

Lord Treasurer Danby was a deft player of parliamentary politics, and Marvell was quite correct that he used the Crown's patronage as a tool to advance his interests. Liberal applications of cash from the Exchequer for 'secret service' worked persuasive miracles among members of Parliament. Between 1676 and 1679 as much as £300,000 was devoted to 'secret service'.[7] Some of this money went for the ordinary work of foreign espionage, but a great deal of it ended up in the hands of venal politicians. But Danby's success was not all about venality: much of his support was principled (even some of those occupying profitable office had principles!). He cultivated that part of the political spectrum best described as 'Royalist Anglicans': those who combined fear and loathing for the dissenters whom they blamed for the civil war and regicide with contempt for popery and France. Royalist Anglicans formed the backbone of the House of Commons: they could be motivated as much by hatred of religious nonconformity, or disdain for the 'superstition and mummery' of Catholics, as by a pension.

By the beginning of 1678, Danby had played his cards skilfully; there was no question that he was, after King Charles himself, the dominant political force in the land. But his very success drew increasingly hostile opposition – and not merely from backbench Parliamentarians like Marvell. The Lord Treasurer's enemies ran the gamut from dissenting hedge preachers who railed against him in farm lanes and barns to dukes – Buckingham being only the most flamboyant. Dissenters hated Danby, Catholics loathed him – but he clung onto the Royalist Anglican centre and survived.

Survival, however, was becoming ever more difficult. Fending off bitter attacks in Parliament, the corrosive sniping of scribblers and pamphleteers, and the more subtle manoeuvres of French diplomats, by the time Marvell's book came out Danby was walking a tightrope. Complicating his situation was the fact that his master the king was, at best, an inconstant ally.

Charles II had entered the thirtieth year of his reign by January 1678 – officially, at any rate, since the eleven years between his father's execution and his restoration 'counted'. The republic and commonwealth so despised by Cavalier Royalist Anglicans had never been a legitimate government. Although in 1660 Parliament had actually made it illegal to 'disquiet or trouble' Charles I's former enemies in an 'Act of Oblivion', one could hardly describe most Cavaliers as oblivious to their old foes. Curiously, one of the few people who took the principle of oblivion with some seriousness was the king himself. On this score Charles and his Lord Treasurer did not see fully eye to eye. All too often the king would undercut Danby's persecutory instincts by pardoning jailed Quakers or Baptists, and he persisted in dealing with those who sneered at the established Church, not least Buckingham.

A more significant difference of opinion between Charles and Danby was their approach to France. Danby intended to capitalize on fears of French aggression – he could rally support among Royalist Anglicans and possibly even lure away part of the anti-Catholic opposition with a firmly anti-French foreign policy. The trouble was that Charles was not nearly anti-French enough to suit his minister – or most of his people, for that matter. The king's relationship with France was a complicated one. He was bound to France by blood: his mother was Louis XIV's aunt, and his favourite sister had married Louis's younger brother, so they were both brothers-in-law and first cousins. While in exile Charles had depended upon French support to maintain his phantom court. But since the Restoration the course of Anglo-French affairs had never run smoothly, whatever Marvell said about harmonious spheres. The two kingdoms warred in the mid-1660s and England concluded an anti-French alliance with Sweden and the Dutch in 1668. But Charles was ambivalent about France – Louis's continental ambitions alarmed him at times, but they also offered opportunities. French power might add weight to Charles's own, particularly in his relationship to England's other main rival: the Dutch Republic. In 1678 Danby was pushing to renew war with France, but Charles was more interested in cultivating Louis's friendship as a counter to the Dutch.

It was in the midst of these complicated realities that Marvell's book appeared, and the precariousness of Danby's situation explains the fury that greeted its publication. The law required books and pamphlets to be licensed by government authority – either by the bishop of London or, more commonly, by the Surveyor of the Press, an officer appointed by the Secretary of State. The Surveyor had broad powers to search for seditious literature and arrest those responsible for it, and in the case of *Growth of Popery* those powers would be exercised with considerable vigour.

Sir Roger L'Estrange had been Surveyor of the Press since 1662 and had earned a reputation as a dogged enemy of the unlicensed press. Although he was already in his early sixties in 1678 – an age at which most seventeenth-century Englishmen were retired or dead – L'Estrange had the energy of a youth. When he was not dashing about London harassing printers, he was writing himself. He authored at least 130 books and pamphlets – not counting an unknown number of anonymous pieces that have yet to be firmly ascribed to him. As the nemesis of seditious printers – especially dissenters or those who sympathized with the 'Good Old Cause' of Oliver Cromwell – he was feared and hated by many. John Bunyan called him 'Mr. Filth' and others nicknamed L'Estrange things like 'the Devil's bloodhound' and, rather more colourfully, 'Old Crackfart'. The nickname that characterized him best, however, was 'Towzer', a common name for the fierce dogs used in blood sports like bear-baiting.[8]

L'Estrange led the pursuit of those who produced *Growth of Popery*, but he was certainly not the only person involved. Authorities turned London upside down hunting for the printer and author of the book. Sir Joseph Williamson, who as Secretary of State had the chief responsibility for the manhunt, issued a warrant on 19 February for a city-wide search for copies of the book and ordered the arrest of anyone involved in its production.

While Williamson and L'Estrange could call on substantial resources in their search, the problem was that London was a big city, and the printing trade was widespread. In the mid-1660s there were over 600 bookshops in London, and as many printers. The Worshipful Company of Stationers, the official printer's guild, had several thousand members. Finding the right printer was harder because the trade had at best an ambivalent relationship to clandestine publication. The Stationers' Company were charged with assisting the Surveyor of the Press – they provided the manpower for searches and had the power to punish members who published forbidden material. Only the trade in under-the-counter books was highly lucrative – pornographic books like *The School of Venus* (translated, naturally, from the French) sold at a handsome mark-up, as did seditious political works such as *Growth of Popery*. More than a few of the stationers who manned the search parties directed by L'Estrange had probably already sold copies of the book themselves.

Obstacles notwithstanding, however, by 1 March the government was on the scent. William Leach, a stationer, told Secretary Williamson that a man named Samuel Packer had brought him a copy of *Growth of Popery* early in February and asked him to have it bound. Leach knew Packer, who he said was a clerk at one of London's jails, the Poultry Compter. And if Leach told the truth – not by any means entirely likely – Packer behaved suspiciously, attempting to keep the title of the book concealed. Leach, no doubt testing Williamson's patience, claimed that he had barely looked at the book and had no idea what was in it, but he agreed to do the work.

Packer wisely fled his job and went into hiding, prompting the government to further widen its net with an offer of a reward. The 21 March edition of the *London Gazette*, the government's official newspaper, offered a £50 reward for information about anyone involved in producing the book and another £100 for whoever brought the manuscript to press (presumably the author or someone who knew the author). Sweetening the deal, it offered to allow any printer who turned in one of his fellows the opportunity to open his own print shop.[9]

L'Estrange hoped that Packer would lead him to the author, but the wily clerk was difficult to run down. He kept in touch with his wife through intermediaries, sending small sums of money to her and sending his daughter Nannie his love. He assured his wife that he had support – what he did was 'not without advice'. Although the manhunt was terrifying, 'they apprehend some and imprison some every day, even on the most frivolous suppositions', but he was sure that the pursuit would eventually run out of steam: 'As soon as their rage is a little over,' he wrote to his wife, 'I will send for thee to meet me.'[10] But he reckoned without the determination of 'Towzer' – and by 12 July he had at last been run to earth.

Packer was brought before Secretary Williamson and closely examined. His explanations were, at best, lame – he had no idea where his copy of *Growth of Popery* came from – it had mysteriously appeared on his chair one day, and though he admitted taking it for binding, he claimed that he had not looked beyond the title page. As for his disappearance and time spent on the run, that, he said, had nothing to do with seditious literature; he was fleeing his creditors. Sir Joseph knew better, because he had copies of several of Packer's letters to his wife, which contained no mention of creditors, but plenty of comment about the search for the printers of Marvell's book.[11]

Unfortunately for L'Estrange, seizing Samuel Packer proved to be a dead end. He did not reveal the author of *Growth of Popery*, and even if he had Towzer's triumph would have been short lived – on 16 August 1678 Andrew Marvell died of a fever. L'Estrange kept looking for Marvell's accomplices into late August – he was sure that one of them was the Widow Brewster, who L'Estrange had encountered before. He urged Williamson to bring her in for questioning so that the broader network of seditious writers and publishers might be wrapped up. He feared that with Marvell gone, '. . . probably she will cast the whole upon Mr. Marvell, who is lately dead, and there the inquiry ends'.[12] L'Estrange was right; the pursuit fizzled out, frustrating the Surveyor of the Press and leaving a number of informers wondering if they would ever be paid the rewards offered to them (given the track record of Charles II's Exchequer, they had much to worry about). In any case, by then the government had more important matters to deal with.

Although the campaign to root out Marvell and his confederates was not particularly successful, the Crown launched an assault on another front. L'Estrange put on his propagandist hat, and in between ransacking printers' cellars and stationers' shops, he found time to turn out an answer to Marvell, *An Account of the Growth of Knavery, Under the Pretended Fears of Arbitrary Government and Popery.* Admitting that the anonymous author was 'a great master of words', L'Estrange proceeded to challenge Marvell's argument and proposed a theory of his own: the *Growth of Popery* was part of a long-standing plot to overthrow the monarchy. Marvell's tactic of raising the spectre of Catholic treason was effective, but L'Estrange's strategy, conjuring the demons of revolution and regicide, was powerful too. He dwelt upon the parallels between 1641 and 1677. Back then, Charles I's enemies had gained the upper hand in Parliament and plunged the kingdom into civil war; now, an opposition, also based in Parliament, made similar claims about the threat to liberty represented by the

Court. The result would be calamity, as in the 1640s: 'Overthrowing the government, under the colour of a zeal to support it, and instead of setting us right in our religious and civil liberties, they left us neither church, nor law, nor King, nor Parliament, nor properties, nor freedoms. Behold the blessed reformation, and remember the outcries against tyranny, popery, and evil counselors, were the foundation of it.'[13]

These arguments, elaborated on, expanded, revised and reiterated endlessly in the next several years, dominated politics. They entrenched divisions and increased distrust, and heightened a growing sense of crisis. Incidentally, they fattened the purses of printers and gave a living to many hack writers, who cheerfully stoked the flames of political controversy. The furor over *The Growth of Popery and Arbitrary Government* encapsulates the widening political divide of the mid- to late 1670s between those who feared rampant popery and those terrified of a resurgent republicanism. It also illustrates the fragility of Lord Treasurer Danby's control over the situation: although he still dominated the ministry, he found himself looking constantly over both shoulders – on the one side at a vigorous and determined set of opponents in Parliament, and on the other at Charles II, whose determination to support his Lord Treasurer was suspect at best.

Danby's tactics – catering to the prejudices and desires of Royalist Anglicans, combined with the judicious employment of patronage – created a solid, if at times precarious, position in Parliament. His opponents believed that the best way to break the ministry's grip on power was to wipe the parliamentary slate clean by a dissolution of Parliament followed by new elections. But calling a new Parliament was the king's prerogative, and as long as Danby successfully conducted the king's business, Charles had no reason to take the political leap in the dark that new elections entailed. So the objective of the opposition was to obstruct, as far as possible, the king's business. Eventually, they reasoned, Charles, whose loyalty to his ministers was notoriously weak, would abandon Danby and turn to politicians who could make progress on his agenda. Those politicians would be, they were sure, themselves: primarily a group of aristocrats in the House of Lords, the two most important of whom were the duke of Buckingham and the earl of Shaftesbury.

For contemporaries, George Villiers, second duke of Buckingham, was a towering figure. Buckingham was two years older than the king and had known him since infancy. His father, a favourite of Charles I, Lord High Admiral, and the most powerful man in England after the king himself, had been assassinated when George was only five months old, and a grief-stricken king took on the responsibility of raising the fatherless infant. The result was that Buckingham had already been resident in the royal nursery for over a year when the infant Prince Charles was born in 1630. So the relationship between Charles II and Buckingham stretched quite literally from the cradle to the grave (the duke outlived the king by a little more than two years). Charles found Buckingham to be both exasperating and – for most of his life – indispensable. The king forgave George over and over again; in 1667 the duke went to the Tower for casting Charles's horoscope. This was a treasonable offence, because it involved imagining the king's death. Within a month of his arrest, Charles had released him, restored him to his offices and allowed him to assume an important role in his counsels. A year later, the duke fought a spectacular duel that resulted in the death of the earl of Shrewsbury, whose wife Buckingham had seduced. The duke insouciantly moved his victim's widow into his own London house, where the couple set up housekeeping to widespread scandal. Not surprisingly, the duchess objected to this humiliation, saying she would not live under the same roof. Her husband callously replied, 'Why madam, I did think so, and therefore have ordered your coach to be ready to carry you to your father's.'[14]

Buckingham was a man of colossal appetites, sexual and otherwise. He spent recklessly on building, art, furniture and clothes; he generously hosted a vast array of clients, friends and hangers-on. He had inherited one of England's greatest estates, but by the 1670s the only way he kept his creditors at bay was by mortgaging land (and in many cases, remortgaging already encumbered property). He was also perfectly happy to accept bagfuls of French gold, furtively delivered by diplomats, or collected in person on trips across the Channel.[15]

Buckingham's fame was enhanced by his skills as a playwright and poet. His social and political satire *The Rehearsal*, first performed on the London stage in 1671, became a theatrical standard, being performed several hundred times over the next century. The duke was impossible to ignore and as a leader of Danby's principal opponents he represented a serious threat: his fame, not to mention his unique relationship with the king, made him a challenge that the Lord Treasurer could well have lived without.

But ultimately Buckingham was more tinsel than substance: glittering and brilliant, but flighty, unstable and frequently unfocused, jumping from enthusiasm to enthusiasm. As a leader of the ministries' enemies he was problematic at best. The real steel behind the opposition, however, was his ally and fellow aristocrat

Anthony Ashley Cooper, earl of Shaftesbury. Whereas Buckingham had been raised in the royal nursery and was a duke from infancy, Shaftesbury had a much longer journey. Born in 1621, the son of a Dorset gentleman, Anthony Ashley Cooper was orphaned by the time he was ten, and he was raised by guardians – who took advantage of their ward, plundering his estate to the tune of thousands of pounds. But what remained was more than enough for the young gentleman to cut a handsome figure in his county – and financial constraints certainly did nothing to rein in his ambition, which was prodigious from an early age.

Shaftesbury's political career began early; he was elected to Parliament for the first time in the spring of 1640, still only eighteen. This proved an abortive start for the young MP, however, as the session abruptly ended in dissolution after less than a month, when Charles I and his parliamentary opponents deadlocked. When those relations finally degenerated into civil war, Cooper hesitated, but ultimately he sided with the king. In 1643, some months after the fighting had begun, he raised a regiment of infantry and a troop of cavalry at his own expense. His military service was troubled; his superiors worried about his youth and military inexperience (he had none to speak of). His delayed adherence to the king's cause also concerned them – how committed was he, they wondered? They had good reason to worry; in February 1644, less than a year after his debut as a royalist commander, Cooper suddenly resigned and presented himself to Parliament, assuring members that he believed the king to be a threat to the religion and liberty of the people. Evidently this was good enough for the Parliamentarians, who fined him £500 (a very modest sum, given the size of his estate – and one which, moreover, was never collected). Testimony of Parliament's favour was not long in coming; Cooper was soon dispatched to the field in command of an infantry brigade and appointed the gaudy title of 'field marshal general'. Yet his talents were really not military; a diminutive man, Cooper's health was fragile and the rigours of the field did not suit him. He gave up his command in the spring of 1645, barely a year after his appointment.

In fact, Cooper's real talents – and his ambitions – were political. For the remainder of the civil wars he took an active part in local government. Following Charles I's execution in January 1649, Cooper moved ever closer to the centre of power in the new regime, becoming an MP and, by the summer of 1653, a member of the Council of State, the inner circle of government. His relationship with the Lord Protector, Oliver Cromwell, broke down in late 1654 – either because Cromwell refused to allow him to marry one of his daughters or due to reservations about Cromwell's tendency towards despotism. Cooper remained on the political sideline until after the Protector died in September 1658, after which he re-emerged, playing a central role in the chaotic last months of the Interregnum regime. Although he had rejected several quiet attempts to gain his allegiance to the exiled Charles II, by early 1660 he was distancing himself from the revolutionary regime. In January he was angling for lodgings in the palace of Whitehall – where a restored monarch would almost certainly set up residence.[16] He so far succeeded in this that by May 1660 he was among the dozen prominent men who travelled to the Netherlands with an invitation to Charles for his return.

Cooper's star ascended further after the king's return from exile. Charles granted him a pardon for his previous disloyalty and appointed him to his Privy Council, whose members were the king's closest advisors. In April 1661 he was raised to the peerage as Baron Ashley (and, a decade later, promoted to the rank of earl). The same year he became Chancellor of the Exchequer. In 1663 Charles named him, with seven others, as one of the proprietors of the newly founded colony of Carolina. With the help of his physician-philosopher John Locke, he created a constitution for the colony that demonstrated a strong bent towards aristocratic (rather than monarchical) government. Cooper never visited his domain and its form of government remained more theoretical than real. Philosophical services aside, Locke kept his patient alive by inserting a catheter into Shaftesbury's side to drain a liver abscess (witty enemies would call the earl 'Tapski'). By the early 1670s he was considered one of the Crown's leading ministers, rising to the kingdom's highest office, the Lord Chancellorship. But the earl occupied this height for only a brief time, just short of a year. His relationship with the king had frayed, partly because of his attempts to persuade Charles to divorce the childless Queen Catherine and his strong hostility towards Charles's heir apparent, James, duke of York. Moreover, the king suspected that Shaftesbury was involved in intrigues with Scottish malcontents and the Dutch. On this, he might well have been correct, at least with regard to the Scots. On 9 November 1673, Charles dismissed Shaftesbury from his office as Lord Chancellor – though he cushioned the blow with yet another royal pardon (his third).

Shaftesbury out of office proved to be a formidable enemy to anyone who was in – as he put it shortly after his dismissal, 'It is only laying down my gown, and putting on my sword.'[17] Although the diminutive, frail earl hardly fit the image of a warrior, he proved himself highly capable at political organization. A meticulous strategist, he compiled elaborate lists of MPs, sorting them into two main categories: a 'w' denoted 'worthy'; a 'v', 'vile' (with qualifiers – some members got two or even three 'w's or 'v's, depending upon their worthiness or vileness). He lost no opportunity to disrupt or delay the ministry's agenda in Parliament. In May 1675 he stirred up a dispute between the two houses of Parliament – over a technical question about the House of Lords' judicial authority – that brought legislative progress to a grinding halt and threatened to deprive the king of essential revenue. Charles was forced to adjourn, or prorogue, Parliament in November to allow tempers to cool.

This prorogation lasted almost sixteen months, a frustrating period for the earl, who was thereby denied a platform for his cause. Shaftesbury recognized that Danby, as Lord Treasurer and the king's principal minister, had considerable advantages: using the king's power to prorogue Parliament and the rewards in the Crown's gift, he could expect to continue his grasp on power. The goal for Shaftesbury was the end of the current Parliament and the summoning of another. A new Parliament, he hoped, would not prove as docile as the current one, which had been sitting since 1661. But dissolving Parliament was the king's prerogative, and neither Charles nor Danby intended to play into the opposition's hands. Hence the earl's repeated attempts to obstruct the king's business in both houses – if Charles faced fiscal disaster caused by an obstructive legislature, perhaps he would give in and call new elections.

But neither Charles nor Danby would cooperate, and when Parliament at last reassembled after its long adjournment in February 1677, Shaftesbury was no closer to success. But during the months he waited to regain his parliamentary soapbox, he crafted a new strategy: if the king would not dissolve Parliament, Shaftesbury and his allies would do it for him. This would be accomplished by recourse to the statute book. Like the Bible, parliamentary statutes could be mined for laws forbidding or, as in this case, requiring virtually anything. According to two 300-year-old statutes passed in the reign of Edward III, Parliaments were to be held at least once a year – and, because the long prorogation had extended well beyond a year, the old Parliament had legally ceased to exist. A new Parliament must be summoned.

On 15 February the king opened the new session, delivering a speech from the throne to both houses. Many complained that Charles was, at best, an indifferent public speaker – he tended to read his text in a monotone without looking up at his audience. Referring to another speech, Samuel Pepys said: 'His speech was very plain, nothing at all of spirit in it, nor spoke with any; but rather on the contrary, imperfectly, repeating many times in his words, though he read all . . .'[18] On this occasion, whatever his delivery was like, Charles shrewdly twisted the opposition's ear: '. . . let all men judge who is for arbitrary government, they that foment such differences as tend to dissolve all Parliaments; or I, that would preserve this and all Parliaments from being made useless by such dissentions.'[19]

But the opposition was not to be deterred; no sooner had the king left and the two houses assembled in their own chambers, than George Villiers, the duke of Buckingham, rose to his feet to say that according to Edward III's laws, Parliament was no more. Typically, Buckingham made his argument with the rude wit he was renowned for: 'Statutes are not like women, for they are not one jot the worse for being old.'[20] No doubt even some of the reverend bishops, all members of the Lords, listening to the debate, indulged in a guffaw. In this Buckingham was immediately supported by Shaftesbury, who took up the duke's arguments and elaborated on them. In the end, this bold effort backfired. The Lord Treasurer was well prepared, for the parliament-is-dissolved theme had been circulating in London for some weeks before the session began. It was immediately apparent that support for this idea was very weak, and when Danby's cousin and ally Lord Frescheville spoke it was to demand that Buckingham, Shaftesbury and two of their supporters, the earl of Salisbury and Lord Wharton, be called to the bar of the house to apologize for daring to attack the validity of the current Parliament. A vote to order the four peers to withdraw from the House passed with a solid majority against them – 53 to 30. And to Danby's great satisfaction all four lords were ordered to be imprisoned in the Tower of London, there to remain until they offered a satisfactory apology and retracted their inflammatory claims about Parliament's supposed dissolution.[21]

Imprisonment in the Tower was, for a peer, generally a tolerable situation – rank did indeed have its privileges. Shaftesbury had comfortable quarters. He was allowed his own cook (his request was taken by many as an insinuation that 'someone' might poison him); his needs were attended to by his own servants and his wife was allowed free access. He was permitted visitors, with the Lord Treasurer's permission – but Danby was careful to keep his prisoners separated. He now had his most dangerous enemy exactly where he wanted him; Shaftesbury had overplayed his hand and would pay the price. It was undoubtedly a great advantage for the government to keep the little earl off the floor of the House of Lords – what he lacked in stature he more than made up for in rhetorical skill.

The result was the most successful session of Parliament, from the government's perspective, in several years. The Commons voted a generous supply for the king: £700,000 – more than double the amount it had granted Charles in 1675. The jailed nobles remained in the Tower for the rest of Parliament's session, though Wharton and Salisbury were granted several weeks' leave before their final release. Buckingham remained imprisoned until August, and Shaftesbury, who stubbornly refused to admit that he was wrong, was still in the Tower when he sued for release on bail in the court of King's Bench. This gambit had the positive effect of putting Shaftesbury's case before the public, and it certainly solidified his standing as a leading opponent of Danby's government. But the downside was that the judges declined to overrule an order of the House of Lords – and that the king viewed the earl's continued defiance as a serious affront. The result was his continued confinement in the Tower, and under stricter conditions – Charles personally reviewed the list of Shaftesbury's permitted visitors, and cut it back dramatically. It was thus that the former Lord Chancellor spent the next seven months in prison – able to keep up with political developments, but frustratingly unable to participate in them.

Finally, with Marvell's incendiary pamphlet making the rounds and a new session of Parliament about to begin, Shaftesbury decided that he would at last submit. He offered a full apology for his offences, read a statement of contrition before the House and, to Danby's chagrin, was restored to his seat. From 27 February 1678, then, the government's most determined enemy was once again free to pursue ministerial game. Was it a coincidence that the same day Shaftesbury returned to the Lords, a bill 'For suppressing popery' was read for the first time?[22] Using Marvell's themes – 'Popery!', 'Arbitrary government!' – he set out to harry the ministry without mercy. The remainder of the session would not be a happy time for the earl of Danby.

Shaftesbury would exploit every opportunity to undermine the ministry, negotiating with anyone who might serve his purpose, including French diplomats and the duke of York. For one whose professed fear of popery was so great, the earl had chosen some very strange bedfellows.[23] But the ends justified the means; both Louis XIV and the duke were alarmed at Danby's anti-French policies. The Lord Treasurer was pushing for war, in order to forestall the French conquest of the Spanish Netherlands – a prospect that in early 1678 seemed near at hand. The conquest of the Spanish Netherlands represented a dire threat to the Protestant Dutch, and Danby hoped to ward this off. Shaftesbury and the

Sun King, then, occupied the same ground, hoping for the overthrow of Danby's government.

But this common interest by no means reduced the opposition's alarmism about the Catholic threat – on the contrary, French advances in the Low Countries were seen as part and parcel of an international conspiracy, whose tentacles stretched from Rome through Paris, and increasingly, into England. The impact of Marvell's pamphlet – and the vigorous response it provoked from the government – demonstrates the power of anti-Catholic rhetoric at this moment.

What, then, were English Protestants so afraid of? By the late 1670s there should not have been a Catholic community in England at all. The old faith had been, after all, legislated out of existence generations before. The Elizabethan Act of Uniformity, passed in 1559, was the first in a long series of attempts to root out popery from the land. It provided penalties that were by comparison to later statutes almost benign – fines of only one shilling for failing to attend the Church of England's regular services. But the hope that English Catholics – called 'recusants' – would abandon their faith to avoid fines of less than £3 annually faded quickly. Harsher laws followed, made harsher still as international tensions between Protestants and Catholics grew. By the time of James I's accession in 1603, English law made life as a Catholic theoretically impossible. Traditional elements of Catholic devotion were criminalized – the possession of rosaries, missals or Catholic prayer books was forbidden. Printing or selling Catholic books was a crime, and magistrates had the authority to raid homes and businesses to search for these items. Fines for non-attendance at church were now ruinously high (£20 per month was levied on recusants, with still other fines imposed for keeping recusant servants or wives). Those too poor to pay the fines were to be banished from the realm and executed if they returned. The law required infants to be baptized with Protestant rites; it forbade Catholic education for children, at home or abroad; it demanded Protestant wedding ceremonies; it insisted that all burials be performed using the Protestant Book of Common Prayer. Catholics were denied access to the universities and the professions. Refusing to swear the oaths of supremacy and allegiance, drawn up specifically to prevent a Catholic from taking them in good conscience, could, on a second conviction, result in life imprisonment and loss of goods. Converting, impoverishing or banishing the Catholic laity was the final goal of these statutes, but the Crown's plans for Catholic clergy were even less generous: here the aim was death. Any Englishman ordained a Roman priest abroad was subject to the death penalty, as was anyone who converted a layperson or who introduced a papal brief into the realm.[24]

The statute book was reinforced by a plethora of royal proclamations. Among other things, these ordered the expulsion of Catholic clergy and the punishment of those sheltering them. They enjoined the capture and execution of missionaries; they imposed martial law upon those possessing popish books, established commissions to hunt down priests, forbade the education of children in Catholic schools abroad and threatened recusants with disinheritance for sending money for the support of students abroad.[25]

But the frequent iteration of these proclamations, and the increasing severity of parliamentary statutes, suggests that there was a wide gap between the theoretical extinction of popery in England and the practical reality. In fact, of course, Roman Catholicism continued to exist despite every expedient the Crown employed against it. It is difficult to say exactly how many Catholics there were at the Restoration; for obvious reasons most recusants preferred to keep out of the public eye. London probably had the largest number of papists in England; there were several Catholic chapels available for worship (though technically natives were forbidden to attend them) – those of the French and Spanish ambassadors were perennially well attended, as was Queen Catherine's. Many of those who attended mass in these venues were merely sightseers; Pepys attended the queen's chapel out of curiosity on 21 September 1662, for example.[26] John Evelyn went to the Catholic chapel at Somerset House a decade later 'to see the fopperies of the Papists'. There he was fascinated – and rather appalled by – a life-sized tableau of the Last Supper in wax.[27] But even without the tourists there were hundreds, probably thousands, of recusants in the capital alone. The province of Canterbury had a Catholic population of perhaps 15,000 adults; the province of York had significant concentrations of recusants as well, especially in Lancashire and Durham. Wales and the Marches also had substantial communities – particularly in Monmouthshire and Staffordshire. A best guess for the whole kingdom during Charles II's reign is around 60,000–70,000 recusants, not much more than one per cent of the English population.[28]

Socially, English recusants ran the gamut from the queen and duke of York down to humble servants and tradesmen. In the provinces Catholic gentry tended to patronize and shelter recusant tenants and servants; the roll call of popish gentry families is familiar: Gage and Shelley, Petre and Howard, Montague and Vaux. For generations they had kept the old faith alive through their perseverance and sacrifice, sheltering priests, educating children and guarding the assets of the Church.[29] In the city the diversity among Catholics was remarkable: surviving recusant rolls from the period list a wide range of occupations. There were Catholic musicians, artists, carpenters, silversmiths, stonecutters, bookbinders, barbers, cheesemongers, perfumers, bakers, button makers, joiners, tailors, cordwainers, ironmongers and schoolmasters (the last in spite of legal prohibition).[30] Adding in church papists (Catholics who occasionally attended Protestant services) and those who managed to avoid conviction would no doubt add substantially to the list. In the city, then, as well as in some parts of the country, Catholics were ubiquitous in the Restoration.

Counting lay Catholics is exceptionally difficult, and enumerating clergy is not much easier. Priests frequently employed pseudonyms, disguised themselves as stewards or tutors and moved frequently from place to place, so identifying them accurately often poses problems. The big picture is relatively clear: there were, in the late 1660s, about 230 secular priests in England. Distributed across the kingdom, usually living in the homes of gentry families, they were loosely directed by a dean.[31] Periodic calls for the appointment of a bishop generated controversy among recusants, lay and clerical, and Rome preferred to avoid the complications that direct episcopal authority might generate.[32] In addition to the secular clergy, there were Benedictines, Franciscans, Dominicans, Carmelites and Jesuits. There were more regulars in England than seculars. Probably the most important of these, in both numbers and influence, were the Jesuits. Jesuit numbers in England peaked in 1678 – there were 128 brothers serving in the kingdom then, about two dozen of whom lived in London.[33] There were eighty Benedictines and fifty-five Franciscans in about 1670.[34] Contemporary Protestants worried that Catholicism was on the rise. The king himself admitted in 1663 that his 'lenity and condescension' towards Catholics had led to increasing numbers of Roman clergy arriving in England.[35] There is plenty of evidence demonstrating considerable self-confidence and hope for some kind of toleration among English recusants in the 1660s and 1670s.[36]

Catholic hopes rose dramatically with the restoration of the monarchy; recusants had tied themselves to the Stuart cause from early on, and while some Catholic individuals had made their peace with the Interregnum – Solomon Swale, MP, for example, married the daughter of one of Cromwell's generals – most were like the marquess of Worcester, who had virtually ruined himself financially in support of the king.[37] Recusants hoped that the liberty of conscience the king promised immediately before his restoration in the Declaration of Breda would apply to themselves as much as to Protestant dissenters. With this in mind, they greeted Charles's return to London enthusiastically. Allegedly, some were quite sure that the king would reward them for their support; Mary Pressicks, a London seamstress, told the informer Robert Bolron that Charles had promised '. . . to bring in their religion if ever he enjoyed his own again, and that it was upon hopes thereof, whilst the troubles were here in England, that so many of that religion did venture their lives and estates for his majesty'.[38] Recusants and Catholic clergy alike presented the king with several testimonies of their joy at his return and assurances of their loyalty. Lord Arundell of Wardour, representing Catholic peers, petitioned the Crown on behalf of laymen, while the Benedictines and secular clergy also presented loyal addresses.[39] These pleas were well received, and sparked tentative negotiations aimed at relaxing some of the penal laws. Lord Stafford, a prominent Catholic peer, recalled discussions with a 'great lord' – presumably Lord Chancellor Clarendon, the then leading minister of state – about the possibility of an indulgence for Catholics. Clarendon encouraged Stafford to present a concrete proposal, about which Stafford 'had greate hopes'. Some said that these proposals would be accompanied by a payment of £100,000.[40] These negotiations proved abortive. In July 1660, John Evelyn noted that he heard Sir Samuel Tuke, a Catholic convert, deliver a plea to the Lords for toleration. Tuke spoke several other times to the same purpose, though he was never as successful as he hoped.[41] In the summer of 1661 the House of Lords debated a variety of proposals for Catholic relief, strongly supported by the Catholic Lord Arundell of Wardour, and the earl of Bristol, and, behind the scenes, the king. The climate seemed favourable; even strong opponents of repealing any of the penal laws like Lord Wharton accepted that the laws might be loosely enforced. In the end, despite Charles's sympathies, and his generosity to individual papists, nothing formal was done to relieve Roman Catholics.

Yet it would be a mistake to assume that the failure of these attempts to reduce the impact of the penal laws led to renewed persecution. In fact, over the next decade and a half what emerged was more like de facto toleration of popery, and not simply from the Court. During these years English Roman Catholics enjoyed a period of relative security such as they had not seen for decades. Historians (and Whig politicians) have frequently pointed their fingers at Charles II and his ministers; it is certainly true that the king, at any rate, and some of his advisors, preferred to leave recusants alone. But there is more to the story than that. After all, as the king himself pointed out to the House of Commons, enforcing the laws against popery required the cooperation of magistrates – something there was very little of in these years. In 1670, responding to complaints about 'the growth of popery' from the Commons, Charles said, 'I will not be wanting to let all of my subjects see, that no care can be greater than my own, in the effectual suppressing of popery: and it shall be your faults, if in your several countries the laws be not effectually executed against the growth of it.'[42]

The increasing clamour about popery from the early 1670s, rising from some in and some out of Parliament, should not obscure the fact that the urgency of the threat seems to have motivated relatively few. All over the country recusants practised their faith with little or no interference from the authorities. Presentations of recusants before Quarter sessions in the Thames Valley, for example, were a thing of the past after the Restoration.[43] Exchequer accounts tell the same story: from 1660 to 1672 the Crown collected only a token £147 15s 7d in recusancy fines. Even after the earl of Danby began emphasizing the popish threat as a means to solidify parliamentary support from 1674, there were few provincial takers for persecution. The bishops advised Danby that new laws were unnecessary, if only those currently on the books were enforced. But the penal laws continued to be a dead letter; in 1675 a grand total of £78 5s 6d came to the Treasury, followed the next year by an improved, but still insignificant, £535.

Catholic confidence grew in this atmosphere of benign neglect. Recusants had nurtured their faith clandestinely for a century, developing a range of strategies designed to protect them from hostile scrutiny. Catholics could not hope to remain entirely invisible, of course, and there had been moments in the past when accidents, or the vigour of the authorities, revealed hidden depths. In 1623, for example, Londoners were astonished to learn details of the extent of the Jesuit mission in their midst, when a nondescript brick building in Blackfriars suddenly collapsed into the street. Inside a Jesuit priest had been saying mass to 300 worshippers, of whom dozens were killed – to the grim satisfaction of some Protestants who believed in divine judgement.[44] But such accidents happened only rarely, and so most people lived their lives in blissful ignorance of the extent of the popery in their midst. This was as most Catholics wanted it; they had ample reason to fear drawing attention to themselves. During the first fifteen years of the Restoration, however, some recusants began relaxing their guard.

Lord Thomas Howard, for example, took John Evelyn on a tour of his mother's country home: 'My lord leading me about the house, made no scruple of shewing me all the *Latebrae* & hiding places for the popish priests, & where they said masse . . .' Howard's blithe revelations came on 25 August 1678 – less than a month before news of the supposed Popish Plot broke.[45]

Trusting in the protection of powerful patrons like the marquis of Worcester, Welsh recusants openly undertook pilgrimages to shrines sacred to Catholics, and in some places like Abergavenny, papists outnumbered Anglicans at Sunday services.[46] The ostentatious conduct of some London Catholics has already been noted. Drawing both the curious and faithful alike, Catholic chapels in London probably attracted as many Protestants as were repelled by popish 'fopperies'. Certainly there was a continuing trickle of converts to Rome, probably hundreds annually. While these were more than likely overbalanced by apostasies, few, Catholic or Protestant, seemed to pay much attention to that side of the religious equation. One Catholic litany in use during the period prayed God 'That Thou wouldst mercifully hasten the Conversion of England, Scotland, and Ireland, from the infection of heresy and infidelity.'[47] The Court of King's Bench convicted Friar William Burnet for converting a Protestant in December 1674, reflecting both the continuing hopes of Catholics for the growth of their faith and Protestants' increased anxiety about the same thing. Condemned to die under an Elizabethan statute, the king reprieved Burnet.[48] Nevertheless, hopeful expressions about Catholicism's prospects may be found repeatedly during this period. In May 1676, when drawing up instructions governing the use of a bequest, the Catholic vicar general in London referred confidently to the period 'after the restauration of catholique religion'.[49] Edward Colman, the duchess of York's secretary, was at the same time predicting the same eventuality to Catholic correspondents on the continent.[50]

Roman Catholic printers and booksellers were increasingly active in London, publishing and selling their wares. Catholic literature became the stock-in-trade of even Protestant booksellers, and the occasional spasm of persecution made little dent in the trade. In the summer of 1676, for example, Bishop Compton of London raided a Catholic bookshop and confiscated a missal allegedly written by Colman. But prominent popish printers went about their business without any let-up; Nathaniel Thompson, for example, continued to churn out materials despite complaints about his activities.[51]

Faithful Catholics continued to bequeath property to the Church, which developed effective ways to disguise its administration. They used a number of

London attorneys, like Richard Langhorne of the Middle Temple, to craft trusts and conveyances.[52] They also continued supporting Catholic schools, both at home and on the continent, with their (illegal) donations. Recusant youth like William Staley travelled to St Omer, Douai, Valladolid and Rome for their education, continuing a long-standing (and again, illegal) tradition. Numbers of English students remained steady through this period. These students provided many of the missionary clergy, but even when they did not, they continued to support the faith as laymen. Francis and Michael Trappes, for example, young gentlemen from Yorkshire, were typical – neither had a religious vocation, but they did take advantage of their time abroad by (among other things) collecting (illegal) religious medals, books and other trinkets with which to ply their female relatives.[53]

A telling example of the increasing self-confidence of Restoration Catholicism, and its remarkable ability to defend its interests, is the case of *Gerard v. Biddulph*, heard in the Court of Exchequer in 1667–68. On the face of it, the dispute was over lands dedicated to 'superstitious uses' – that is, devoted to the support of Catholicism. Elizabethan statute made it illegal for anyone to hold property, real or personal, in trust for Catholics.[54] Proof of such an arrangement would require forfeiting the property to the Crown. The law encouraged prosecutions by awarding half the value of seizures to the informer. Nevertheless, it appears that very few actions were brought under the law, so *Gerard v. Biddulph* was rather unusual. It was in fact even more unusual than it appeared.

In 1638, John Worthington, SJ, rector of the clandestine Jesuit college of St Aloysius in Cheshire and Lancashire, had £1,000 to invest. Obviously he could not act openly, and so he worked through surrogates. John Biddulph, ostensibly acting for himself (though in reality as trustee for the college), bought an annuity of £80 from Thomas Gerard, a prominent recusant gentleman. The money came from rents collected on the manor of Ince, Lancashire, part of the Gerard estate. For almost thirty years Biddulph collected the money and handed it over to the Jesuits. Eventually, however, Biddulph passed from the scene, and his heir balked at continuing the arrangement – he intended to keep the money for himself. After all, he must have figured, the investment had officially been made by his father. How could the Jesuits argue otherwise? If they did so they would reveal themselves acting contrary to the law, and the annuity would be forfeit in any case. The younger Biddulph must have congratulated himself upon a very neat piece of work. The annuity still had well over 900 years to run (its original term was for

1,000 years), so his descendants could reckon on a handsome return on his sharp practice. But Biddulph had not reckoned on the ingenuity of Jesuit lawyers.

Faced with the possible loss of a substantial part of their income, the Jesuits of St Aloysius acted. They engineered Biddulph's prosecution – accusing him of holding land in trust for Catholics! The society's agent was Sir Richard Gerard, himself a Catholic with court connections. He complained to the Exchequer that Biddulph's annuity had been dedicated to superstitious uses (as indeed it had, at least until recently). A commission duly appeared in Lancashire and heard testimony proving the truth of the charge, and the court seized the annuity. As the prosecutor, Sir Richard received half of the proceeds – but thanks to his friends at court he was granted the whole of it. This he promptly began paying over to the Jesuits.[55]

The Jesuits used the same tactics in 1671 when one of their own, Friar John Travers, apostasized and attempted to make off with property worth over £2,000.[56] Travers failed, and was forced to return his ill-gotten gains to the society's (incognito) trustees. These cases suggest that the famed subtlety of the Jesuit Order was not wholly mythical: using laws expressly designed to starve them of resources, to in fact defend and even recover them once lost, was no mean feat. It also illustrates the growing confidence that many Restoration recusants had about their place in English society. They could not, of course, claim liberty of conscience, or rest assured that persecution was entirely a thing of the past. But by the early 1670s many dared hope that the worst might be over.

Some recusants worried that their co-religionists displayed too much enthusiasm. In January 1667, for example, Henry Howard, who as heir to the duke of Norfolk was perhaps the most prominent non-royal recusant in England, feared that letters from his friend William Leslie, a Scottish priest, might be misinterpreted. Although Leslie's letters mostly concerned the internal politics of the English college in Rome, Howard urged more circumspection: 'I have been very near beshitting myself lest some of your letters should have been opened and racked to a wrong sense.'[57] Howard's caution proved all too prescient; just such careless language brought Edward Colman to the gallows a decade later, guilty of over-enthusiasm for his religion, if nothing else.

The increasing boldness of Catholics certainly did not go unnoticed. In February 1663, in his speech from the throne opening the new session of Parliament, the king addressed concerns spawned by the December Declaration of Indulgence:

The Truth is, I am in My Nature an Enemy to all Severity for Religion and Conscience, how mistaken soever it be, when it extends to Capital and Sanguinary Punishments . . . I hope I shall not need to warn any here not to infer from thence, that I mean to favour Popery. I must confess to you, there are many of that Profession, who, having served My Father and Myself very well, may fairly hope for some Part in that Indulgence I would willingly afford to others, who dissent from us. But . . . I am far from meaning by this, a Toleration or Qualifying them thereby to hold any Offices or Places of Trust in the Government; nay, further, I desire some Laws may be made, to hinder the Growth and Progress of their Doctrine.[58]

The king might well have succeeded in allaying the concerns of many with a proclamation ordering the departure of Catholic clergy from the realm in April.[59] It is noteworthy that enforcement of this expulsion, left in the hands of local authorities, seems to have been a dead letter.

The Great Fire of 1666 attracted fresh attention to the presence of Catholics in the kingdom. Opinions were divided about how and why the conflagration began; the well-informed (such as the king and Privy Council) believed that the blaze was accidental. Many, however, identified human agency – but responsibility was hotly debated. Some suspected Protestant dissenters in league with the Dutch, some papists. Charles issued a proclamation ordering the execution of the penal laws, responding to parliamentary complaints, again without any noticeable increase in local action.[60] It is noteworthy that in the country at large, recusancy prosecutions remained quite infrequent, and many, if not all, Catholics seemed to fear no impending persecution. Even the Jesuits, traditional whipping boy of anti-Catholic rhetoric, continued to hold regular meetings (albeit under careful security) right through the 1670s.[61]

But from 1671 concerns about popery resonated more broadly. French aggression in Europe combined with anxiety about Catholicism at court and the apparent growth of recusancy in the country brought traditional fears back to the fore. Anti-Catholic ballads and short, crude, polemic sold briskly.[62] Ballads such as *A Rare Example of a Vertuous Maid in Paris, Who Was by Her Own Mother Procured to be Put in Prison, Thinking Thereby to Compel Her to Popery, But She Continued to the End, and Finished Her Life in the Fire* (London, 1674) appeared along with pamphlets such as *A Protestant Catechism for Little Children, or Plain Scripture Against Popery* (London, 1673) and *A True Relation from Germany, of a*

Protestant Shepherd's Killing a Counterfeit Devil that Would Have Perverted Him to Popery (London, 1676). The publication of popular literature of this sort suggests an increasingly uneasy public.

A significant measure of public concern was the first Test Act, passed in 1673. The Test Act was preceded by Charles's unpopular Declaration of Indulgence. Intended to attract dissenters' support for war with Holland by allowing freedom of worship, it was taken by many to be a step towards tolerating Catholicism. The Act required all office holders to swear the oaths of allegiance and supremacy acknowledging the king as head of the Church. It also required office holders to deny the Catholic doctrine of transubstantiation and required them to take communion in the Church of England within three months. The Test Act flushed several high-ranking Catholics out of hiding, most notably, of course, the duke of York, but also Lord Treasurer Thomas Clifford. Further cause for concern emerged as French aggression continued, along with domestic evidence of Catholic self-confidence. The tone of parliamentary debate over popery sharpened; in 1675 the Commons again considered a bill intended to reverse Catholic gains, and the king once more issued a proclamation expelling priests.[63] The English were finally beginning to catch fleeting glimpses of the shadowy depths of popery, finding that, apparently, Catholicism had enjoyed its decade or more of de facto toleration by growing more influential and, many thought, more dangerous.

Rising fears did little to quicken persecution in the provinces, but some Catholics were wary of an increasingly hostile climate.[64] The triennial meeting of the Jesuit mission, held in London in April 1678, was preceded by urgent warnings enjoining secrecy. The Jesuits, worried about the possibility of discovery, abbreviated their meeting from three days to one.[65] As they met in the duke of York's lodgings, prudence seemed eminently justified. The indefatigable efforts by Shaftesbury and the opposition to fan the flames of anti-Catholicism, further fuelled by fears of 'arbitrary government', were making headway.

As the spring session of Parliament drew to a close, Danby worked hard to keep control of affairs. In early June he arranged a meeting between the king and a group of loyal MPs, where no doubt they discussed plans to counter the opposition. On 20 June, Charles prorogued Parliament until November, giving the ministry breathing space – and denying Shaftesbury the oxygen of parliamentary mischief-making. The coming session would test both sides – and in dramatic, wholly unexpected ways.

In the meantime, the propaganda war raged on. One anonymous pro-government pamphlet ridiculed the opposition's anti-Catholic fearmongering:

> Prithee, as soon as thou canst, send me over some *Hand-Granadoes*, I mean some pretty quaint *stories* to throw among the people. Popery is as good a topick, as ever; it holds out admirably well. This morning a man brought me a dozen of Stories to sell; and at least nine or ten of 'em were on that subject. But I refused 'em all for improbable, save only one, which was of 50 Priests in a Cave in *Wales*, which he offered to prove out of the *Old Testament* . . .[66]

The hand grenades were about to start falling, fast and thick.

— TWO —
HAND 'GRANADOES'
SUMMER 1678

The London parish of St Giles-without-Cripplegate – so called because the church stood just outside the ancient city wall – survived the devastation of the Great Fire of 1666, and consequently in 1678 looked very much as it had for the previous century. A warren of narrow lanes and courts, houses were packed closely together, upper stories leaning forward towards the middle of the street, reducing even further the fickle sunlight of the 'little ice age'. Rich and poor alike lived in these streets – other parts of London, especially the western suburbs and some of the burned-over neighbourhoods, were beginning to become segregated by class. But in Fig Tree Court, to take one example of many, there were ten houses ranging from Christopher Berry's, who was taxed on only three hearths, to the grandest, Sir Richard Barker's, who paid tax on no fewer than sixteen.[1] We do not know who Berry was, or his occupation – he was most likely a modest tradesman or artisan, typical of many Londoners. But we know a good deal more about Barker, and it was in his substantial city home at Fig Tree Court that what would soon be called 'the Popish Plot' was born.

Barker was a physician, and a well-known one at that. Of obscure origins, he had by 1660 come to be a force in London's medical world. Seventeenth-century doctors were a cantankerous lot – there had been important progress in some ways; William Harvey's painstaking experimentation had revealed the heart's vital role in the circulatory system before the civil wars. But long-standing disputes had split doctors into warring camps, especially between the Galenists – those who took the early Greek physician's theories as the fundamental starting point for all medical theory – and the 'chemists'. These latter were doctors who hoped to advance upon Galen's ideas through the use of chemistry. Barker was firmly on the side of the chemists, and this might have been an element of his professional success. Charles II cultivated an interest in experimental chemistry, and he maintained a fully equipped laboratory at Whitehall. By 1673, Barker had won an appointment as one of the king's doctors-in-ordinary and a knighthood. Although the appointment did not come with a regular salary – not that this mattered much; salaried royal doctors frequently went unpaid anyway – it did give him contacts at court. One of these was the king's lab assistant, Christopher Kirkby, who would play a minor but crucial part in the unfolding drama.

Sir Richard's medical career was a fairly distinguished one; he published a number of treatises on various subjects, and he must have had a thriving practice. Certainly it was prominent enough to draw the attention of the London College of Physicians, which prosecuted him more than once for practising without proper qualifications. But his interests were not solely medical and scientific. He was also highly sensitive to the threat of popery; he had long-standing connections to supporters of the republican 'Good Old Cause', and had made his anti-Catholicism plain to all. It was this anti-Catholic prejudice that probably led him to offer shelter in his capacious home to a rather peculiar cast of characters.

From about 1675, Barker had sheltered the Reverend Israel Tonge, a clergyman who had been burned out of his home parish in the Great Fire. Tonge had had a distinguished career, but had suffered a series of reverses that left him vulnerable and adrift. The son of a Yorkshire clergyman, Israel had studied at Oxford, where he received a Bachelor's degree in 1643. Although an ordained clergyman, teaching occupied most of his early career and he earned a solid reputation for his pedagogical methods. That reputation enabled him, in 1648, to return to Oxford and take up a position on the faculty. He was awarded a Master's degree the same year, followed in 1656 by a Doctorate of Theology. Now married, with a son bearing his wife's maiden name (Simpson), Tonge had reached the pinnacle of his career.

In 1657, Tonge took up a fellowship at New College, Durham, a plum position. This was an ambitious attempt on the part of Oliver Cromwell to establish a new university, one that would provide higher education for the first time in the north of England. Tonge was one of the first two faculty members named, and he must have relished the opportunity to create a rival to the ancient universities in Oxford and Cambridge. He set about recruiting new faculty and taught Latin grammar to the students. Unfortunately, the college proved short-lived. Neither of the two established universities welcomed the competition, but, more importantly, New College's crucial patron, the Lord Protector, died in September 1658, leaving the institution friendless in the corridors of power. It closed the following year, leaving Tonge jobless. He returned to teaching, taking a position at a girl's school in suburban Islington, north of London. This would have been a serious comedown for one of the founders of England's newest (though sadly defunct) institutions of higher learning.

Teaching at this level was miserably paid – one Islington school of the time paid two pence per student per week. That meant an income of perhaps £20 a year – not much more than a common labourer would have made.[2] But soon another opportunity arose: in the spring of 1660 the newly installed governor of the English-held port of Dunkirk, Colonel Edward Harley, appointed Tonge chaplain to the garrison there. The pay would hardly have been grand, but certainly more than he made school-mastering suburban girls. But like his still-born career in Durham, this position also proved a short one. Harley, who had supported the Restoration, was nevertheless not especially well-suited to his office, mostly because of his deep-dyed Puritanism – something that made governing a city full of Catholics problematic. Forced to resign in May 1661, Harley was compensated with a knighthood but little else. His patron gone, Tonge too departed the continent, this time, fortunately, with a small country parish rectory to support him, the gift of Colonel Harley.

Tonge might have travelled to the wilds of Herefordshire, on the Welsh border, to minister to his parishioners, but if so, he had moved back to London by the summer of 1666, where he took up the rectory of a small city parish, St Mary's Staining, an eleventh-century church in Oat Lane, not far from Sir Richard Barker's Fig Court mansion. Once again, Tonge was dogged by ill-luck – having barely settled into his new living, on Sunday 2 September the Great Fire broke out in a baker's shop in Pudding Lane, and by Tuesday his church and home were gone, along with thousands of other structures.

This latest disaster led Israel to take up another offer overseas – a chaplaincy to the king's garrison in the North African port of Tangier. Part of the dowry that Catherine of Braganza had brought to the king, the port was an expensive millstone, absorbing huge sums of money for its defence. It was a hot, unhealthy and depressingly dull place to be. The English occupiers spent most of their time cooped up behind the city walls, complaining about the food, the weather and one another. Constantly besieged by the hostile local population, taking a position there was no less a sign of desperation than teaching girls in Islington – and a far more dangerous occupation. This occupied Tonge for about two years, after which he made his way back once again to London – some said he had been dismissed for sowing dissension among the troops.[3] In any case, by the early 1670s he was on the loose in the capital, full of grievances and bitterness about all of his failures since the Restoration.

It was at some point during these unhappy years that Tonge made Sir Richard Barker's acquaintance – perhaps through their shared interest in things chemical, their hatred of Catholics, or both. In any event, Barker rescued Tonge; evidently, he bought the right to appoint the rector of a small country parish from its lay owner in 1676, and gave the living to his protégé. Avon Dassett, Warwickshire, was a very small place not far from Stratford-upon-Avon, whose income must have been trifling – and which in any case Tonge claimed his enemies had withheld from him. Once again a country parish found its spiritual care sacrificed for the interests of a lay patron – a common state of affairs in the seventeenth-century Church of England.

Given the Reverend Tonge's increasingly erratic behaviour and mental state, the Warwickshire locals might in fact have been fortunate that they never saw their rector. Barker's support gave him the freedom to indulge his increasingly manic obsession with Catholicism – and especially the Society of Jesus. His principal work at this time was translating from the French a long book attacking the Jesuits. Originally written by Nicholas Perrault, *The Jesuits Morals* comprised nearly 400 pages of turgid prose.[4] Tonge had trouble finding a publisher, not surprising considering the nature of the work. Unlike the snappy invective against the Jesuits that flew off the shelves of London booksellers at this time – *An Account of the Bloody Massacre in Ireland Acted by the Instigation of the Jesuits* or *The Jesuits Manner of Consecrating Both the Persons and Weapons Imploy'd for the Murdering Kings and Princes* to name but two – Tonge's labours produced a volume practically guaranteed to bury anti-Catholic fervour under a heap of convoluted scholasticism. But he blamed his failure in the market on the Jesuits themselves. They were so threatened by his work, Tonge believed, that they would stop at nothing to prevent it. He was no less certain that they would happily assassinate him, such was his notoriety as an opponent of popery. But he declared himself determined to continue his necessary work, despite the odds: 'It's ill writeing in a storm when the ship heaves & setts & knocks and sometimes makes the writers teeth chatter in his head, and when there is cause to drop more tears from the writer's eye then ink from his pen.'[5]

Sir Richard was hardly one to discourage his client's paranoia, paranoid as he was himself. But he was joined far more effectively by yet another of the motley collection of waifs and strays who orbited around the big house in Fig Tree Court.

This new character was Titus Oates, destined to be the most significant player in the coming tragedy.[6] A twenty-eight-year-old born in the tiny county of Rutland, he had, like Tonge, led a remarkable life, but one in which success seemed always just beyond his reach. The grandson of a Church of England minister, his father also pursued a religious vocation, although his was not, at least originally, in the Anglican Church. Oates's father Samuel was an itinerant Baptist preacher who in the 1650s became chaplain in the regiment of Colonel Thomas Pride, the radical whose purge of the Long Parliament had made possible the trial and execution of Charles I. The elder Oates spent most of the Interregnum sheltering under the protection of his patron, who, when he was not busy suppressing popular entertainments such as cock-fighting, bear-baiting, fencing and 'prophaneness', was piling up a considerable fortune. Buying former royalist and Crown property at knock-down prices, Pride flourished. Unhappily for Samuel, however, the colonel died in 1658. In any event, the Restoration would have ended any help coming from that quarter; as it was the Pride family lost its property and barely avoided having their father's body exhumed and publicly hanged like Cromwell's.[7]

Under the circumstances Samuel Oates's earlier radicalism bore rethinking, and he and his family conformed to the Church of England. When the king returned to his throne in May 1660, hundreds of parishes in England stood vacant – either abandoned by their Interregnum incumbents, or vacant for other reasons. Bishops and patrons were, under the circumstances, not always very particular about whom they appointed to those vacancies. Titus's mother was a Hastings girl, so there was a family connection, and in this fashion her husband became rector of All Saint's, an imposing fourteenth-century church in the famous port town.[8] Titus, then eleven or twelve, had never been baptized, a fault his father rectified in November 1660 – easily done, since the baptismal font stood handily in his own church.

Apart from the gift of baptism, though, Oates senior seems to have been a less than affectionate father. And Titus was no prodigy, in looks or appearance. Perhaps part of the child's problem was his appearance – he had a broad, abnormally flat face with an unfortunately jutting lower jaw. He would have been the target of more than the usual schoolyard mockery, and he showed no great ability to defend himself, verbally or otherwise. His earliest education remains a blank – probably at home, as the family was so unsettled in the years before arriving in Hastings. His first real independent foray into the wider world came when he was fifteen, and sent to London as a student at the Merchant

Taylors School. Located in a subdivided old aristocratic mansion once belonging to the fifteenth-century dukes of Suffolk, the school, founded in 1561, provided an education for sons of members of the company, or those connected with them. Hastings's Member of Parliament, Nicholas Delves, was a merchant tailor who in 1664 got Titus a place as a free scholar – that is, a scholarship, requiring only the payment of an entrance fee. William Smith, his tutor, later claimed that Titus cheated him out of even this, and so within a few months he was expelled from school – not for the last time.

Back to Hastings Oates went, enrolling in a local school for a time before heading for Cambridge, where in 1667 he enrolled at Gonville and Caius College. Here the pattern was repeated: failure and if not expulsion, resignation. Next came a stint at St John's College, Cambridge, ending the same way. In this case he was apparently accused of cheating a tailor out of the value of some clothing he had ordered and denying his crime by an oath sworn on a Bible.[9] He left the university without a degree in 1669 – although he always falsely claimed to have earned one. For Oates, even early in life, lies came easily.

Intellectual (and moral) failures notwithstanding, by 1670, non-existent degree in hand, Titus had been ordained by the bishop of Ely (not far from Cambridge) and received a licence to preach from the bishop of London. In fact he had earned something of a reputation as a preacher, having absorbed a measure of his father's flamboyant radical style. This might have brought him to the attention of Sir George Moore, patron of the living of Bobbing, Kent, a small parish about forty miles southeast of London. On 13 March 1673, Titus took up his first real cure of souls, 780 acres of not-very-productive agricultural land and a few hundred residents. As a parish priest Oates was no more successful than he had been as a student. Rampant complaints about his behaviour – drunkenness and homosexuality headed the list of offences – soon alienated his flock and he was forced to resign. He returned to Hastings, where his father employed him as his curate at All Saints.

In Oates's mind this was a mere stopgap; Titus intended to take over as master of the local school. It was inconvenient that the position was already taken, occupied by William Parker. But Parker could be removed if he were unfit for his post – so in April 1675, Titus accused him of pederasty. The resulting scandal would see Parker out, and himself in (though in point of fact Oates himself had been suspected of the same crime). But the plan proved less than foolproof: the charges convinced no one, and Titus instead found himself charged with perjury.

At this point Oates fled Hastings and somehow got himself an appointment as a naval chaplain. At the time shipboard ministers were hard to find, and the Admiralty was not very particular about who served – Oates's appointment being solid evidence of the fact. He went aboard the 34-gun warship *Adventure*. Three decades old, the *Adventure* was not one of the Royal Navy's prestige ships, but as chaplain Titus would have the status of an officer, though not much else. The pay was low (and often in arrears) and the respect offered by 200 or so profane seamen not much higher. Nevertheless, the post at least offered escape from his legal troubles, and soon he was on his way to Tangier – a port which had, if anything, become even less attractive since Israel Tonge had left it several years earlier.

Like Tonge, Titus had no desire for a long-term stay in North Africa; it was a convenient, if exceptionally uncomfortable, place to lie low until his Hastings troubles blew over. But discretion was never one of his talents, and Oates was soon again in trouble over charges of homosexuality. He left the navy under his usual cloud. He was in London by 1676 – safe, for now, from his perjury accusation, but weighed down by a poor reputation. And he lacked any secure way to earn a living. Finding a new parish church seemed unlikely – even if one were found, given his troubles it was perhaps best to maintain a low profile for some time to come. While drifting around London at this time, he frequented the company of actors – hardly suitable companions for an upstanding minister of the Church of England. But then Titus was hardly upstanding. One of his friends was Matthew Medbourne, a well-known member of the Duke's Company of players, one of London's two main theatres (the other being the King's Company). It was perhaps fitting that Medbourne was in the Duke's Company, though, because he was a Catholic, like the theatre's patron. He also had a reputation as a dissolute and, at times, violent man – just the sort one might expect Titus to consort with.[10]

Medbourne's faith gave him connections to London's Catholic networks, particularly the sort of Catholics who frequented the theatres: the well-born and wealthy. One of those was Henry Howard, the presumptive heir of England's senior Catholic peer, Thomas, fifth duke of Norfolk. Thomas had been insane for years by 1676 (he died the following year), so Henry had for some time occupied a prominent place in England's Catholic community – and his theatrical interests were more than merely artistic. He had lived with an actress, Jane Bickerton, for years, and in fact married her shortly after succeeding to his dukedom, to the fury of his legitimate children by his first wife. As a high-ranking nobleman and one of great wealth – his income in the early 1670s was said to be £25,000, a staggering sum – he had a huge household. Many of those who served him were Catholics, but more than a few were Protestants, and he employed a chaplain for them as well as his own Catholic confessors. In 1676 the post was vacant, and it went to Titus Oates. This was ideal for Titus, if not for Howard's servants. As a private chaplain he escaped the attention of the regular hierarchy of the Church of England – no need to worry much about officious bishops and bureaucrats poking into his affairs. And as the Protestant chaplain to a Catholic master, there was not much worry about being scrutinized too closely. Howard would never pop into one of Titus's services or ask him for his (heretical) Protestant theological opinions. A better situation could hardly be imagined for a person of Oates's peculiar qualifications. He settled into Howard's huge thirty-hearth mansion in the Strand, with every chance of coasting along indefinitely in a comfortable billet.

But Oates was a stranger to coasting, just as he evidently found it impossible to control himself. A story from about this time has him delivering one of his theatrical sermons as a guest preacher. He spent a good part of his time in the pulpit denouncing John Calvin and all of his works, to the outrage of some of the congregation, who complained bitterly to the incumbent who had invited him.[11] Whether or not it was this sort of irritation, roistering around the city in the company of actors like Medbourne, or some other, less savoury offence, within a few months Oates was once again unemployed. And by this time the spectre of unemployability loomed – his Protestant copybook was definitively blotted. To fail as a naval chaplain was a tall order; to fail as a rector, a curate, a schoolmaster (though that failure was more or less embryonic), and as private chaplain to a patron who never actually attended his services, was, in sum, failure of a quite spectacular degree.

Having begun life worshipping as a Baptist, and then moving opportunistically into the Church of England, it could have been no serious strain for Oates to take the next step: the Church of Rome. His time in Howard's service had given him some knowledge of London's Catholics, and while it would be unadvisable to turn to those in Lord Howard's direct orbit (they knew him too well), there might perhaps be others – others less informed, or perhaps more open to Oates's style of blandishment – who might be called upon. And in March 1677 he had found just the man: Father Berry, whose alias (a trick employed by many Catholic clergy to throw off pursuit) was Hutchinson. Father Berry was originally in

Anglican orders, though subsequently he converted to Catholicism, joining the Jesuits (and sometime later returning to the Church of England). Bishop Burnet knew him, and described him as a 'weak and light-headed man', but one who was nevertheless 'sincere and devout'. This was just the sort of holy innocent Titus needed, and the Jesuit received Oates into the faith, little knowing the consequences of his act. Oates used his status as a convert to beg small sums of money from the Catholic clergy; he was given a small allowance of about nine pence a day – hardly enough for even a poor man to survive on, barely £1 a month. This he supplemented by cadging a shilling here and there from other acquaintances, including Berry.[12]

Although his conversion gave Titus a new set of marks for his various frauds, he still led a hand-to-mouth existence. He ingratiated himself with some of the Catholics in and around Somerset House, where Queen Catherine's household was based. He supplemented small loans and alms from there with petty theft from the Catholic chapel, but he no doubt resented his position. After all he had been in the service of a soon-to-be duke, had held the king's commission in the Royal Navy and possessed a Bachelor's degree (so he said) from Cambridge. For a man who was 'proud and haughty' such a life rankled deeply.

It was at about this time – the spring of 1677 – that Oates seems to have met Israel Tonge, probably through his father, who now lived in London and who had resumed his dissenting connections, including with Sir Richard Barker. Titus and Israel could swap stories about the miseries of Tangier, the harshness of fate and the devilries of the Jesuits – in Israel's case, their role in obstructing his work, and in Titus's the short rations and contempt they imposed upon him. Titus, with his inside, if rather superficial, knowledge of London's Catholic underground, could egg the older man on and feed his fantasies, all the while working him for loans. Moreover, Israel's connections with the wealthy Sir Richard opened vistas of more easy pickings. Titus would certainly have noted the physician's generosity to both his father and the Reverend Tonge. He might possibly have the satisfaction of profitably working both ends of the religious spectrum if he played his cards correctly.

Titus seems to have offered to help Tonge in his anti-Jesuit crusade by giving him inside information about the Order, and possibly helping him in the production of more anti-Jesuit polemic. The main trouble, however, was that as a recent Catholic convert he was hardly at the heart of the London mission. He knew some of the important figures in London's Catholic community by sight, and he had dealt personally with some others – though most of these interactions probably involved little more than forelock-tugging in return for handouts. But fortune smiled upon Titus (or turned against the Society of Jesus, for the effect was the same) in April, when he was introduced to Father Richard Strange, the Provincial, or head, of London's Jesuits. Presenting himself as a former Anglican minister who had seen the truth of Rome and, as a consequence, renounced a rich benefice, Titus persuaded Strange to sponsor his education on the continent. It was not unusual for the Jesuits to recruit new members from among their English flock, though for the most part the men who went to one of the Jesuit colleges in Europe from England were much younger than Titus, and from families whose Catholicism was of long standing. What means Titus used to win Strange over are unknown, but they might testify to his guile. Or perhaps, as Burnet said Father Berry told him, sending Titus to Europe was merely a ploy to get him out of London, where he had made himself increasingly obnoxious.[13]

At all events, by the beginning of June 1677, Oates had arrived in Valladolid, Spain. Founded by the English Jesuit Robert Persons with Philip II's support in 1589, the English College was a mainstay of English Catholicism. It educated young Englishmen for the priesthood, and sent them back home to labour for England's conversion. With a chapel dominated by a mutilated statue of the Virgin Mary and infant Jesus (la Vulnerata – the Wounded One), desecrated in an English raid on Spain in 1596, the college had been deeply involved in supporting Catholic goals – or, for Protestants, Catholic treason – in England. It had already provided almost two dozen martyrs, priests executed by the English state for their alleged treason. It is unlikely that Titus intended to emulate them. But Valladolid offered a refuge, an environment that was agreeably all-male (and young male at that), and which might afford him some inside information he could put to good use later.

At Valladolid Titus, who called himself Titus Ambrose, was a student of religion and philosophy, at least formally. The college's authorities quickly found that their new student was a serious problem, 'not constant in the faith', which was putting it mildly.[14] Within a month he had been expelled. But Oates was never one to pass up opportunities. His time at the college gave him a fund of inside information about the Catholic mission in England, and it also, serendipitously, initiated a crucial relationship for the future. Sometime shortly before Titus was invited to leave the college, he made the acquaintance of a pair of English brothers, William and James Bedloe. These two had just arrived from the

Spanish university town of Salamanca, where they had been pretending to be an English lord and his servant on a continental tour. In fact, they were both dedicated con artists and horse thieves, on the run from English justice – and now wanted in Salamanca. The brothers met Titus, who generously offered to buy them a meal, which they repaid by stealing a sum of money from him and disappearing. But Oates must have been impressed by their boldness, because when their paths crossed again in London, William and Titus made common cause.[15]

Perhaps his encounter with the Bedloes gave Titus the idea of a further embellishment of his fraudulent academic qualifications. From this time forward he claimed that the University of Salamanca had awarded him a doctoral degree. 'I was admitted doctor of divinity at the said University of Salamanca, and did all the exercises for the said degree that was required of me.'[16] With this grand addition to his résumé – but no further Spanish prospects – Oates returned once again to London. He soon reappeared at the door of Father Strange, begging charity and claiming he had left Valladolid because of his inability to abide the haughty ways of the Spanish. Strange, either hoping to get rid of Oates or sympathizing with him, gave him another chance. This time he would try his hand in the Low Countries, at the Jesuit college of St Omer in Flanders. Like Valladolid, this school was founded by Father Robert Persons and its mission was to educate English Catholic youth. Oates was considerably older than most of the students enrolled there, and his experience at the college was typically disastrous. In December 1677 he enrolled under the name 'Samson Lucy' (his mother's Christian name was Lucy) and immediately became a problem. A decade older than even the oldest students, from the beginning he set a bad example, and he was a lazy, bad-tempered, blaspheming and highly unpopular student. He bullied his fellow scholars but was sycophantic towards the schoolmasters, begging their forgiveness 'with whining faces, great exterior submission, and sober protestations' when caught in his various misdeeds.[17]

Within a few weeks the exasperated Fathers of St Omer were looking for an opportunity to rid themselves of the 'new boy'. When Oates professed an earnest desire to join the Jesuits, Father Richard Ashby, the school's rector, arranged for him to attend a nearby Jesuit seminary – if not as a formal postulant, then as a kind of test run for a commitment to the Order. This experiment lasted a matter of days in December 1677; Titus was very soon back in St Omer, a failure all over again. Oates would never have survived the rigorous training the Society imposed upon its postulants – even if he had the intellect required (highly doubtful), he most assuredly did not have the selfless dedication that the Order demanded. But it is not likely that Oates had any serious intention of becoming a Jesuit; what he was probably after was information. Remembering his discussions with Israel Tonge, he would have known that even a few days in a Jesuit seminary would fill in awkward gaps in his knowledge.

Following his reconnoitre of the seminary, Oates returned to St Omer, where he remained until June 1678, by which time Father Ashby finally lost patience. By July, Titus had been expelled once again and was back in London, penniless. Having thoroughly alienated London's Catholics and the Jesuit mission, he turned to Tonge, renewing his acquaintance and offering much more than general anti-Jesuit polemic. He had been, he assured Israel, admitted to the deepest secrets of the Order; he had served as a courier bearing secret messages to and from the continent; and he had gained the Jesuits' trust. Titus told Tonge that the Jesuits particularly hated Israel for his valiant work against them. Indeed – now setting his hook deep by flattering Tonge's considerable vanity – the Order's leaders had commissioned him, Titus said, to assassinate Israel for a reward of £50.

Tonge needed no persuasion to believe everything Oates told him; it was self-evident to him that the Jesuits conspired against all that was good and targeted anyone who dared expose them. He embraced Titus and urged him to set down all he knew about these awful plans. Later, Israel's son remembered that Oates and his father rented lodgings in Vauxhall, at the time a quiet suburb across the Thames from the city. There, in a house belonging to a bell-founder named Lambert, Oates began crafting the first of his 'granadoes'.[18] He produced a list of forty-three points (later expanded to over eighty) outlining a Jesuit conspiracy against the Stuarts stretching all the way back to 1639. The civil wars and regicide were laid to their charge, as was the Great Fire. The next step was to assassinate the king in order to provoke civil war and to inspire French intervention. Louis XIV would then dominate England, which would be re-Catholicized and turned over to the tender mercies of the Society of Jesus.[19]

Having crafted this bombshell, Oates and Tonge (who of course believed every one of Oates's charges) next had to figure out where to throw it. The obvious way to attract official attention was to go straight to the king himself. In the 1670s access to the Court and the king was far easier than it would be today; Charles II did not exist within a cocoon of bodyguards and high security. In fact, the king was unusually accessible, even for his time: he regularly attended the theatre in public; he took daily walks, unguarded, in St James's Park adjacent to his palace at

Whitehall; and he often presided over public ceremonies open to anyone. But this openness was not absolute; Tonge still needed an introduction. And here it was the Barker connection that proved crucial. With his connections at court as a royal physician and chemist, the necessary intermediary might be found.

But Tonge was anxious to protect Titus's identity – after all, having a spy among the Jesuits was of great value, and if the fathers knew that Oates had betrayed them, not only would his utility be destroyed, but his life would be in danger. How, then, to proceed? First, on 11 August 1678, Oates left his articles 'under the wainscot at the farther end of Sir Richard Barker's house . . . neare to the Doctor's [i.e. Tonge's] chamber, where he tooke them up'. But Israel decided that he would further shield Oates by pretending that his information came to him anonymously. He told Titus to recopy his charges, but this time 'in the Greeke character rather than his owne hand'.[20]

Primed 'granadoe' now in hand, Tonge used Barker to contact Christopher Kirkby. Kirkby was a minor figure at court, who sometimes assisted the king in his various amateur chemistry experiments. Tonge met Kirkby, who promised that he could get Israel a private audience with the king. Going to the palace on the evening of 12 August, Kirkby awaited an opportunity to take the king aside – but was frustrated by the fact that at no point was Charles out of the immediate company of his brother James, duke of York. Kirkby returned to Barker's house and he and Tonge devised a second plan: Kirkby would wait for Charles to emerge the next morning for his regular walk in the park, and tell him then.

The next day, Tuesday 13 August, Kirkby was ready and waiting for Charles. As the king moved towards the stairs leading to the park, Kirkby presented him Oates's charges, which he scanned as he went down. At the foot of the stairs, Charles turned to Kirkby and asked what he had to say. And so the grenade exploded: Kirkby breathlessly explained that 'his majesties enemies had a designe against his life, & therefore [Kirkby] desired his Majestie to keepe himself close in the midst of his company, for he did not know but that he might be in danger in that very walke'. Charles asked how, and Kirkby said 'by shot'. Apparently not much worried by this dramatic information, Charles sallied forth on his walk, telling Kirkby to wait behind and that they would talk when he returned.

Charles's insouciance about the possibility of assassination was typical; this was by no means the first time such threats had come to him. Less than a month before, he and his brother had personally interrogated a suspect connected to the infamous Colonel Thomas Blood, who had stolen the Crown Jewels and attempted to kidnap the Lord Lieutenant of Ireland, the duke of Ormond.[21] Kirkby's excited appearance notwithstanding, news such as this would not delay Charles's accustomed jaunt in the park. In any event, as his panting courtiers could have told any would-be assassin, simply keeping up with Charles as he strode briskly through the park would make fumbling with pistols or muskets a considerable challenge.

At length Charles returned and spoke with Kirkby in his bedchamber, asking him to tell his story. Kirkby said that a friend (not naming Tonge) had told him yesterday of a conspiracy, and he asked permission to bring his informant in for a private audience. Charles told them to return that evening at eight, and Kirkby took his leave. Kirkby, with Tonge now in tow, returned at the appointed hour, having come up the Thames in a boat, landing at the Privy Stairs on the riverbank. Here the king's personal servant, William Chiffinch, who was intimately acquainted with backstairs intrigue at court, discreetly brought the king's guests to the 'red room'. This room, near the king's bedchamber, could be accessed easily without drawing much attention to a visitor's identity, quite handy for meetings with mistresses, politicians or, as in this case, informants with secret information.

Once in Charles's presence, the king quizzed Tonge: How did he get his information? Who was involved in this conspiracy? What were the plotters' intentions? Israel answered these questions elliptically – he claimed that the information came from someone within the Jesuit mission, but he could not say who. Tonge offered to keep Charles abreast of the plot in weekly private meetings.

Charles evidently found the prospect of weekly meetings with this odd man less than enticing, and a hint of royal scepticism soon became evident. Saying that his informant's lengthy charge sheet was 'tedious', Charles wanted Tonge to briefly summarize their content – which Tonge proceeded to do, though hardly briefly. Charles wanted to know who among the plotters were figures of 'quality', that is, the important ones. At this point Israel named only two: Lord Petre and Queen Catherine's personal physician, Sir George Wakeman. Both of these men were Catholics, but Charles thought that neither was a likely assassin. Petre was fifty-two and an active member of the House of Lords, but otherwise he had had no very significant political role. Wakeman, Charles told Tonge, 'was a simple man and poor but had allways the reputation of an honest man'.[22] To the king's mounting impatience, Israel related a complicated story weaving together fantastic plans for regicide, civil war, uprisings in Ireland and a French invasion. Later, Charles told Bishop Burnet that Tonge had told him 'a long thread of many passages, all tending to the taking away of his life', which he 'knew not what it could amount to'.[23]

Unimpressed by the urgency of Israel's tale, Charles decided that he would fob the earnest doctor off on his Lord Treasurer, Danby. Charles planned to go to Windsor the following morning, and he clearly had no intention of worrying himself over this farrago of mysterious information. Towards the end of the interview, Kirkby frantically signalled Israel – the duke of York was approaching down the Privy Gallery that led to the 'red room'. Tonge made a hasty departure, but James apparently caught a glimpse of him as he left. Asking his brother the king who he had been with, Charles simply said 'it was a base business' and left it at that.[24] The king, at this point, apparently did not want to involve James – not that Charles distrusted his brother's loyalty, but rather his political instincts. In this he was, as events would show, absolutely correct.

The following day Charles, accompanied by his brother and much of the Court, travelled to Windsor. Charles enjoyed spending time there in the summer, fishing, hunting and toying with his dogs and mistresses. Queen Catherine, by now reconciled to her husband's peccadillos, amused herself with picnics on the castle grounds. At Windsor, Charles could get away from political intrigue in the capital – though of course wherever the Court was, intrigue followed. At least in this instance, the problem of Israel Tonge and his conspiracy remained in the capital, squarely in the lap of the Lord Treasurer.

Lord Danby had a great deal on his mind in mid-August 1678. In less than a month his daughter Bridget was due to marry Charles, earl of Plymouth, one of the king's illegitimate sons. This connection to the royal family was welcome, but it generated legal and logistical headaches, as the celebrations – and more importantly the details of marriage settlements and dowry – were negotiated. In public affairs, the newest session of Parliament was due to open in a couple of weeks, and Danby was not yet fully prepared. He had already put off the session from early August to the end of the month, and he now persuaded the king to delay the session until early October. These repeated postponements caused some grumbling outside Parliament, though it is doubtful that most members were anxious to convene in the midst of a hot Westminster summer. October would suit most of them fine, and it would give the Lord Treasurer more time to line up his supporters and wrong-foot his opponents. Recently things had gone fairly well; the parliamentary opposition had been on the defensive in the session that had ended in July. But Danby knew that complacency could be fatal; as the publication of *The Growth of Popery* had shown, his enemies had no intention of giving up. With Shaftesbury and Buckingham in the van, they would come to Parliament intent upon making Danby's life as difficult as possible.

This was the state of affairs on Wednesday 14 August, when Tonge and Kirkby turned up at the Lord Treasurer's residence at 9 a.m., ready to repeat their story. Danby kept the pair waiting for hours, not actually admitting them until four in the afternoon. In the meantime his prospective son-in-law Plymouth had brought the papers that Tonge had presented the day before to the king. Tonge then launched into his tale, taking care to keep Oates's name out of it. He implicated several plotters, notably Thomas Pickering, John Keynes and John Grove, all Jesuits, who intended to murder the king, waylaying him out of doors with pistols loaded with silver bullets. In the event that this attack failed, Wakeman would be ready to dispatch Charles with poison.

Danby professed to be 'of the greatest concerne in the world' and he questioned Tonge closely. He asked about 'Honest William' Grove and Thomas Pickering, who Tonge told him were to ambush the king as he walked in St James's Park. Danby wanted to know where they lived so that they might be arrested quickly – but Israel said he did not know their lodging place. However, he continued, they were often in the park, so if Danby sent some men with him he could point them out.[25] The story that Tonge told undoubtedly fitted the Lord Treasurer's typical Protestant anti-Catholicism – but it offered him something else as well: a convenient rallying cry for the upcoming session of Parliament. Ever since gaining high office Danby had pursued an anti-Catholic policy – one that at times put him at odds not only with the duke of York, but at times the king as well. But this might be an opportunity; it was obvious that public unease about popery had grown notably in recent months, and it was equally obvious that Shaftesbury and the opposition intended to use that concern to undermine the ministry. Why not seize control of Shaftesbury's stick and use it against him? He was known, for example, to be friendly with Lord Petre. If Danby could pose as a determined investigator of the plot, the distraction might complicate the opposition's plans.

So Danby called in a servant, Mr Lloyd, and instructed him to do all he could to assist the Reverend Tonge in the apprehension of the accused. Israel, with Lloyd's assistance, then began a concerted effort to track down the accused Jesuits. Tonge ran into difficulties, for his quarry had apparently gone to earth and was nowhere to be found. For the next two weeks, while the Court was at Windsor and with Danby increasingly preoccupied by his daughter's upcoming wedding, our sleuth got nowhere. The king's scepticism grew as Tonge's excuses for missing the assassins lengthened. On one occasion, for example, a group of assassins apparently cancelled an attempt on Charles at Windsor because one of their horses was 'slipt in the shoulder'. Charles continued to insist that the matter be kept quiet – publicizing the plot would 'alarm all England and put thoughts of killing [Charles], into people's heads, who had no such thoughts before'.[26] Moreover, Danby's interest in the affair seemed to be waning. Oates's 'granadoe' appeared in danger of fizzling out altogether.

Under the circumstances, Tonge and Oates (who remained unknown to Danby and the Court for another two weeks) conferred and devised a plan to relight their fuse. Danby had been pressing them for more written evidence implicating specific plotters. Hoping to satisfy him, on 30 August they produced five forged letters, supposedly from some of the Jesuit plotters, detailing various elements of the conspiracy. 'Like the whole Iliad inside a nut, the entire story of the plot was contained in summary form: that Scotland was ready, that Ireland was tense with expectation of revolution; that he must beware of four assassins who had made up their mind to kill the king, etc.'[27] These they put together in a packet addressed to Father Thomas Bedingfield, the duke of York's confessor at Windsor. They told the Lord Treasurer that he could intercept these letters at the London post office – but in fact before that could happen they had already been delivered to Bedingfield. Opening the packet, Father Thomas found letters from four Jesuits: Whitbread, Fenwick, Ireland and Blundel, all of whom he knew personally, and another by one Father Fogarty, apparently an Irish priest who was a stranger. Bedingfield was mystified; all of the letters contained information about a treasonable conspiracy – but none of the handwriting resembled that of his friends.

This accident in fact worked greatly to Tonge and Oates's advantage. Bedingfield immediately took the letters to his master. Now James, who had heretofore no hint of any alleged assassination plot, was in the know. He of course was well acquainted with many members of London's Catholic mission; the previous April he had allowed the Jesuits to conduct a meeting (a 'consult') of all their members in his own lodgings at St James's Palace. It seemed perfectly plain to him that there was a conspiracy afoot to implicate Catholics in general and himself in particular in treason. He also suspected that Danby was using these obviously bogus charges in order to distract the parliamentary opposition at the expense of himself and his co-religionists. Bringing the letters to his brother the king, he demanded a full investigation be made, once again proving his political maladroitness to Charles, who believed that the less said publicly about all of this the better. The granadoe's fuse sputtered back to life.[28]

Danby came down to Windsor from London to see the letters, and debate over how to proceed continued over the next couple of weeks. James pressed hard for the information to be presented before the Privy Council, and Tonge relentlessly pushed for action. Titus had a problem now that the London Jesuits knew about the letters – Israel had urged him to continue collecting inside information, but Oates, who of course had been shunned by the Jesuits for some time, needed an excuse to 'break' with them. Turning to his ever-fruitful imagination, Titus told Israel that the duke of York had recognized him from a fleeting glimpse he had when they spoke to the king at court in August, and James had therefore blown Oates's cover. Titus said that on 4 September, Father Thomas Whitbread, now leader of the Jesuit mission, had allegedly summoned him. When Oates arrived at Whitbread's lodgings, he had furiously accused Titus of betraying their plot, and assaulted him with a stick.[29]

The next day, this time accompanied by the chastened (though strangely unmarked) Oates, Tonge returned to Secretary Williamson's office to urge pursuit of the conspirators. Williamson, no stranger to informers peddling tales of intrigue (a major part of his work involved dealing with secret-service matters), was beginning to have doubts about the entire affair. Tonge had had several weeks to round up the alleged conspirators but got nowhere. The letters received by Bedingfield increased the king's scepticism, and of course infuriated James. Despite Danby's desire to make something of all this, the secretary plainly hoped to unload these troublesome suitors on someone else. Williamson, a practised bureaucrat, suggested that the pair convey their information to a London magistrate, who could take an official deposition. Israel was disgruntled by his reception, 'finding a rude repulse and noe admission there', but took the secretary's advice.[30] By speaking to a magistrate, details of the plot would be entered officially into the record. The idea appealed to Tonge and Oates, convenient as it was for Williamson, who would thereby get them out of his office. Israel and Titus were beginning to suspect that their bombshell would be snuffed out before exploding, thanks to Whitehall foot-dragging.

On Thursday 5 September, Tonge appeared before Sir Edmund Berry Godfrey, a justice of the peace for Middlesex. Sir Edmund heard Tonge reluctantly, but finally agreed to take his deposition the next day, with Titus Oates in attendance. Oates made a greater impression on Sir Edmund than Tonge, whose mental stability seemed dubious. But Titus was a very different sort: apparently level-headed and full of circumstantial detail. Unlike Tonge the day before, he named names – the Jesuits named in Bedingfield's letters, and other prominent members of the London mission. He mentioned Edward Colman, who Godfrey knew had been the secretary to the Catholic duchess of York. Oates seemed to have a thorough grasp of the details of the plot, which the magistrate, still reluctant, proceeded to take down. When Titus accused the Jesuits of having orchestrated a fire that burned much of Southwark, London's south bank suburb, in May 1676, the magistrate took notice; he himself had heroically tackled many of the problems arising from the Great Fire a decade before.

Once Oates and Tonge had finished their fantastic story, Sir Edmund had to decide what to do. The pair had indeed left a 'granadoe' sputtering in his lap. He knew some of the figures Oates identified, notably Colman – and later he might even have sent him a warning. For all of his rigour as a justice of the peace, Godfrey had maintained cordial relations with both Catholics and Protestant dissenters. Like the king, he saw no good in religious persecution and had never vigorously enforced the laws against religious nonconformity. But if he did warn Colman, he opened himself up to a very serious charge: misprision of treason. Concealing treason was a felony, punishable by forfeiture of all property and life imprisonment. Clearly Godfrey was troubled by what he had learned; becoming entangled in such an intrigue offered no upside that he could see. He had several sessions with Oates and Tonge over the next days as they elaborated details about the conspiracy. But Sir Edmund was uncharacteristically hesitant to pursue their charges.

Faced again with what seemed to be official reluctance, Tonge kept trying. He made several more attempts to speak with Danby, and Kirkby once more tried to intervene with the king. But interest in their revelations continued to wane; Danby told Tonge that the king and duke were convinced the Bedingfield letters were forgeries and that the whole plot was a contrivance. On 19 September, Israel decided to hang about Bridget Osborne's wedding to the earl of Plymouth; both Charles and James attended, and he hoped to speak to the king. No luck. Still, Tonge laboured on, turning next to Henry Compton, bishop of London. Two fruitless interviews with the bishop led him to try another prelate. On Thursday 26 September he called on Bishop Burnet, telling him about the plot. Burnet was nonplussed; he had known Tonge for some time and had never had much confidence in his sanity. The tale that Israel unfolded, involving a plan by a Jesuit named Coniers to stab the king (details that never actually appeared in the later charges drawn up by Oates), seemed fantastic. But like Godfrey, Burnet worried that either there was some truth in it or there was some dark plan to lure him into a misprision charge. He shared the information with his friend the Reverend William Lloyd, asking his advice. 'Go to the Privy Council,' was the reply.

The Council, composed of some dozen of the most important men in the kingdom, including Danby, the duke of York and other high officers of state such as the Lord Chancellor, was the obvious body to deal with such serious charges – and of course James had been trying to get the information before it for some time. He was about to get his wish.

Oates and Tonge produced a lengthy list of charges to lay against the Catholics – the original forty-three points had, by late September, grown to eighty-one. In a letter to Danby dated 21 September, Tonge requested a formal hearing before the Council, and asked that a committee be appointed to investigate the affair, even attempting to veto the appointment of two councillors, Secretary Williamson and Lord Finch, who Tonge said had been overly sympathetic to Catholics as Lord Chancellor.[31] Yet even after weeks of shuttling back and forth between the Lord Treasurer, various bishops, Secretary Williamson and Sir Edmund Godfrey, nothing was happening. Williamson's notes of a Privy Council meeting on 25 September say nothing at all about the plot; the council discussed the upcoming session of Parliament, foreign affairs and matters of colonial trade.[32] Tonge was verging on despair and considering the drastic step of making his charges public.

But at last the combination of pressure from James, Danby and Tonge himself led to action. On Friday 27 September the Privy Council was informed of the existence of a plot, and Williamson ordered Tonge's appearance for interrogation. He arrived at court too late in the evening for a hearing, and Robert Southwell, the clerk of the council, instructed Tonge to return in the morning, leaving his long list of popish plans behind. The next morning the privy councillors assembled in the council chamber at Whitehall, a few steps from the elaborate laboratory that Charles frequently pottered about in with Christopher Kirkby. The king presided, which was not unusual, but his scepticism was obvious. He had resisted acting for weeks, despite the combined pressure from his brother James and Danby, to say nothing of the frantic lobbying by Tonge. Just how happy he was to launch an investigation at this point might be guessed – he was against it, but by now something had to be done. Rumours of the plot were leaking out and soon would be public.

Tonge entered the council chamber and knelt before Charles, presenting him with a petition asking for a royal pardon for any crimes they might have committed while investigating the conspiracy. Along with this he handed over a list of plotters with information about their lodgings. Lord Chancellor Finch asked Tonge to relate his story and present his evidence. Tonge claimed that all he knew came to him through Oates – who was not present – prompting Charles to ask, most likely with some impatience, who this Mr Oates was. Tonge then related a highly edited version of Titus's recent life, and his assurances of his friend's reliability. At this point Charles had had more than enough of Dr Tonge. He had delayed his departure to the horse races at Newmarket, some sixty-five miles north of London, and all of this talk of scheming assassins and silver bullets bored him. The king left the council to carry on in his absence.

This was a serious mistake. Had he remained, Charles might well have cooled the ardour to investigate among some of the members, particularly Danby. But as he left the palace, anxious for the delights of the turf, a messenger went out calling for Titus Oates's presence before the council that afternoon. The members would hear for themselves what Oates had to say without the ramblings of Israel Tonge intervening.

Titus's appearance was, as always, striking. Dressed in the black gown of an Anglican clergyman, he exuded gravity and reliability. Once fairly started he ploughed through his eighty-one charges in astonishing detail, reciting many of them exactly as worded in his affidavit. Councillors, a number of whom were predisposed to be sceptical, were impressed 'by the excellency of his memory' in spite of themselves, and others were overwhelmed by the sheer volume of information that Titus laid before them.[33] Sir Richard Southwell, one of those present, reflected the ambivalence that some felt: 'Itt went on for 2 or 3 hour very doubtfull as to his credit, thoe the board, in a question of the king's safety and to see his [Oates's] prodigious memory and unexpected answers at severall turns, were in great pain and surprise.'[34]

Oates testified that he was present at the Jesuit 'consult' held at a London tavern in April 1678, where the brothers decided to assassinate the king. The plan left nothing to chance: Charles was to be ambushed and shot (with silver bullets), failing which he was to be ambushed and stabbed by Irish assassins (armed with specially manufactured daggers), failing which he was to be poisoned by Sir George Wakeman. Wakeman was to be offered up to £15,000 to do the deed – though an effort was to be made to get the job done for a cut-rate £10,000. The assassination would signal a massive Catholic uprising in England, Scotland and Ireland, led by several Catholic peers. The Lord General of this popish army was to be Lord Belasyse, a distinguished Royalist veteran of the civil wars, but who, in his mid-sixties, was in poor health and hardly up to the rigours of military command. Oates provided lists of Catholics who would, at the Pope's command, be installed as bishops and officers of state – Lord Arundell of Wardour, who had lobbied the king for toleration for English Catholics, was to be the new Lord Chancellor. Philip, Cardinal Howard (the duke of Norfolk's brother), was to be Archbishop of Canterbury, and Edward Colman the new Secretary of State. In fact, of course, while the Jesuits were meeting in London, Titus had been wandering around Europe compiling his disastrous record as a Catholic student. The 'consult', which had indeed taken place, was held in the duke of York's rooms at St James's rather than a tavern – a fact that if generally known would have made James very uncomfortable indeed.[35]

A tricky moment came when the Bedingfield letters were brought forward – folded so that the signatures might not be seen, Oates was asked to identify their authors. Without a mistake, he identified all of them – of course as he had in fact written them himself in the first place, his achievement was not as remarkable as some in the room thought. When challenged upon some of the letters' details – some misspellings, the dissimilarity of some of the supposed plotters' handwriting – he was prepared. Demonstrating an unflappability that would serve him very well in the months to come, Titus brazened it out. Jesuits, he said, were trained to write disguised hands. Furthermore, they frequently deliberately misspelled words and names in order to disguise their identity. Apparently no one thought to ask how writing 'Harcot' for 'Harcourt' or 'Bennigfield' for 'Bedingfield' disguised anything much at all. Nor did anyone comment on other anomalies – three of the letters being written on the same type of thin watermarked paper, two others also on the same sort of heavier stock with the same watermark.[36] Quite the contrary, Council Clerk Southwell later said that this performance did more than anything else to convince most of the members of the truth of Oates's charges.

Having heard Titus out, the Privy Council issued warrants for the arrest of several Jesuits: Grove, Pickering and Whitbread, and Oates himself led the party of messengers in pursuit. Titus knew where his quarry might be found, and most of them were rounded up that night. Tonge later complained that the arrests were negligently done. Oates was only accompanied by council messengers, low-ranking officers who had no discretion in the performance of their duties. Oates had 'noe secretary, nor Clerke of the Council, nor Justice of the Peace, nor person of quality who might supply the defects of the warrants'. These shambling proceedings resulted in the loss of important evidence: documents were left behind and even Father Grove's pistols, 'in their cases hanging on the wall without enquireing whether they were . . . charged with silver bullets'.[37]

More arrests followed, including Edward Colman and Sir George Wakeman. Colman was brought before the Privy Council for questioning, followed by Sir George. Oates was present at both examinations, and he gave a detailed account of their involvement in the conspiracy. Asked if he recognized the prisoners, Titus at first claimed he had never seen either of them – but hastily changed his tune when he learned who they were. Once again an element of doubt crept in, and once again Oates faced it down. He redoubled his accusations, providing still more circumstantial detail – Colman was in contact with Louis XIV, for example, and Wakeman had already been paid a large sum of money on account for murdering Charles. Besides, Oates said, he had not recognized Colman because his eyes were dazzled by the candlelight in the council chamber. Councillors relaxed their guard again.

For most of the next two weeks Oates, who was rapidly becoming the dominant partner among the informers, led officers in pursuit of plotters and evidence. Colman's lodgings were thoroughly searched, and though no recent papers were found, a sheaf of letters written in 1675 to and from Louis XIV's confessor turned up. Waverers in the council had to admit that this was a worrisome find, and one which bolstered Oates's credibility. And yet there remained doubt. Writing to his son-in-law (and nephew) the Prince of Orange on 1 October, James mentioned 'a pretended plot, which makes great noise here', while his brother the king continued to doubt. At one point during this period, for example, Charles asked Oates to describe the Spanish Catholic Prince Don Juan, who supposedly had brokered Wakeman's fee. Oates obliged: he was dark, tall and lean. Titus had of course seen many Spaniards as he whiled away the days at Valladolid, and no doubt this description would have applied to a good many of them. Unfortunately, Don Juan was a Habsburg, and he looked like many others of his race: short, fat and fair. Charles could not help but laugh, and his trust in 'Doctor' Oates (as he was now calling himself) sank still further.

For all of Charles's disbelief, the fact was that Oates and Tonge's 'granadoe' had exploded before the Privy Council and persuaded many of its members, making, as the duke of York put it, 'a great noise'. But this was as nothing compared to the next explosion. On Saturday 12 October, Sir Edmund Berry Godfrey vanished.

THREE

GODFREY DAYS
SEPTEMBER–OCTOBER 1678

'Some very honourable friends' had suggested to Israel Tonge that Sir Edmund Berry Godfrey was the right magistrate to take his deposition. On 5 September, Tonge went to see him at his home in the West End parish of St Martin-in-the-Fields. Secretary Williamson, anxious to get Tonge out of his office, was no doubt pleased. And Godfrey was a natural choice. He was well known at court and in London as a magistrate who took his duties exceptionally seriously. Originally from Kent, he was fifty-seven years old and had been a justice of the peace since the Restoration. A prominent dealer in coal and firewood, he had earned his reputation for his exemplary behaviour during the 1665 plague epidemic in London. Unlike most of the rest of the capital's authorities – from the king down – Godfrey had remained steadfastly in the city as one in five of its inhabitants died of the Black Death. The calamity wiped out whole families, decimated entire neighbourhoods and left administrative chaos in its wake. The final death toll was some 100,000 victims – and Godfrey was one of the very few magistrates on the scene, dealing with abandoned property, orphaned children, stray animals and thousands and thousands of corpses. His standing increased still further the following year, as he helped organize efforts to fight and recover from the Great Fire.

In the aftermath of the fire, the king knighted Sir Edmund and awarded him silver plate worth £200. In the years since, Godfrey had been a constant presence carrying out his magisterial duties. Unmarried and childless, he devoted a great deal of his time to investigating crime and pursuing criminals – once even chasing a suspect into a plague-stricken house. His reputation as a dogged pursuant of wrongdoing overshadowed a somewhat eccentric personality. Rather hard of hearing, he led a solitary life enlivened by few friends; many said he was gloomy and melancholy – not surprising for someone partially deaf who spent a great deal of time dealing with the dark side of human nature. He would prowl the streets and alleys of the city alone after dark looking for malefactors and was known for the stern sentences he inflicted upon the guilty. In any case, it was to Sir Edmund that Tonge repaired following his abortive visit to Secretary Williamson.

As was his wont, Tonge was cryptic and elusive in his first interview with the justice, informing Godfrey that he had vital information about a dangerous plot. The justice tried to elicit specifics – but found Tonge less than forthcoming. Eventually, Godfrey agreed to see Tonge again the following day, Friday 6 September. What he must have thought about his strange caller and his mysterious information can be imagined – there was good reason to be sceptical, but it was nevertheless Godfrey's duty to investigate. The following day Israel returned, this time with Titus Oates. Titus had hastily moved into Israel's lodgings the day before, convinced, he said, that the Jesuits were plotting his murder. Whether this was true or not, it was certainly convenient; the men could plan their next moves more easily, and of course Titus could sponge off his friend.

Oates later recalled that Sir Edmund seemed frightened by the burden his revelations represented. In his customary crude fashion Titus said that Godfrey was 'a cowardly rascal, for when I went with my depositions to him he was so frighted that I believe he beshit himself, for there was such a stink I could hardly stay in the room'.[1] Godfrey had been friendly with Edward Colman, now jailed in Newgate prison on a charge of treason. Colman had in fact visited him the day before Titus's first examination before the Privy Council. It can be assumed that Colman said something to his friend about the rumours of a Catholic plot; Tonge and Oates had sworn their deposition before Sir Edmund three weeks earlier. In the meantime, Godfrey had wrestled with what to do with the information. Word was beginning to spread; within a few days of the council's first examinations of the informers, Thomas Barnes, one of Secretary Williamson's regular correspondents, passed on some of the stories he was hearing in London. 'Some say 'tis worse and deeper laid than the Powder Plot and give out that many thousands are concerned.'[2] On 8 October the duke of Monmouth, the king's eldest bastard son and Lord Lieutenant of the East Riding of Yorkshire, ordered his deputies there to search for hidden stockpiles of weapons in Catholic homes.[3] Monmouth, an ally of the earl of Shaftesbury, might well have been deliberately attempting to heighten tension in advance of the imminent parliamentary session. But whatever his motives, the rapid spread of the news of a conspiracy left Sir Edmund Godfrey open to charges that he had concealed a dangerous plot.

At the time, people who saw Sir Edmund thought he seemed gloomy and distracted. One of these was Mary Gibbon, an old friend of the magistrate. Sir Edmund had visited her that week, and, as she later testified, he had been upset and agitated – worried that he might be in trouble over Oates's depositions. After all, he had done little or nothing to pursue the charges they contained in the several weeks since he took them – apart from giving his friend Colman a heads-up. But now Colman was in jail, accused of treason. Would Godfrey follow, accused of covering up the plot? Bishop Burnet, encountering him in the street, said the justice was 'apprehensive and unnerved' and in a conversation about state affairs 'he said he believed he himself should be knocked on the head'.[4] Much would be made of this last comment later. Something was clearly bothering Godfrey. On Friday 11 October his servant Judith Pamphlin saw him looking depressed, burning papers.

The next day he left home as usual, at about 10 a.m. Early that afternoon someone saw him near St Clements, a church in the Strand not far from his home. It was the last time anyone saw him alive. Godfrey was a man of regular – not to say rigid – habits, and when he failed to return home that night his servants were troubled. Their first thought was that their master had been called to attend on his elderly mother, who lived in Hammersmith, a short distance west of London. On Sunday, however, he had still not come home. This clearly was something to worry about. Henry Moor, Godfrey's clerk, got in touch with his brothers Benjamin and Michael. They lived in the city and perhaps they knew where their brother was. In fact, the Godfreys, who Bishop Burnet said 'were not acquainted with his affairs', had no idea where Edmund was.[5] But they asked Moor to keep quiet at least until Monday, and told him they would begin a search. Meanwhile, Sir Edmund's servants went to the homes of various people who they hoped might have information.

On Monday the search continued. The Godfrey brothers themselves visited Mrs Gibbon and asked her about their brother – not, interestingly, where he might be, but rather what his mood had been at their last meeting. When Mary told them that Sir Edmund had been disturbed, Michael 'lifted up his eyes and hands and said Lord we are undone, what shall we doe!'[6] Following this rather peculiar exchange, the Godfreys went to visit the Lord Chancellor, Lord Finch. Sir Edmund was missing, they said, and furthermore they feared that Catholics involved in the plot might have murdered him. Finch found the idea faintly preposterous, and in any case Sir Edmund had only been gone a couple of days. He related this exchange later that day to fellow privy councillors and they likewise found nothing very alarming in the story. Benjamin and Michael returned to the Chancellor's to air their concerns and Finch, puzzled and annoyed by their persistence, told them to bring their worries to the Privy Council – which they soon did.

But by the end of the day, no doubt in some measure because the Godfrey brothers wanted it to, word of Sir Edmund's disappearance had spread rapidly through London. The excitement was heightened by the rumour of foul play. London was already beginning to fill up with Members of Parliament for the session due to open the following Monday, 21 October. The capital's taverns and coffee houses hummed with the news of the strange disappearance – and some politicians sensed opportunity. Rumours of a Catholic conspiracy were already circulating widely through the country – though so far hard evidence remained elusive. Perhaps Godfrey's vanishing was connected? His brothers believed – or pretended to believe – that it was. Politicians eager to derail the Lord Treasurer's agenda were no less anxious to believe in a popish threat. And so by Wednesday all London was agog at the news of the missing magistrate. Rumours flew, and anti-Catholic feeling rose ever higher. Godfrey had been run through with a sword, some customers at a London bookshop were told by a pair of mysterious Scotsmen. Another man, Richard Whitehall, heard that Godfrey had been murdered the previous Sunday or Monday.[7] At the same time different stories asserting that Sir Edmund had been seen alive in various places competed with the rumours of murder. The Catholic duke of Norfolk industriously spread a story – which the privy councillors found highly amusing – that the unmarried Godfrey had eloped with an elderly widow.

King Charles and his brother returned to London the same day. The king maintained his attitude of aloof scepticism, despite the rapidly spreading anxiety over Godfrey's disappearance. The search continued and the Godfrey brothers once again turned up at Whitehall to press the Privy Council for action: they wanted a proclamation calling for information about Sir Edmund's disappearance. A royal proclamation would greatly elevate the importance of the affair, putting the full weight of the Crown behind the search. Sir Robert Southwell, whose unhappy job was dealing with the agitated brothers in the council chamber, fended them off, believing that a full official hue and cry was premature. They left angry, accusing Southwell of obstruction.

The next day, Thursday 17 October, was overcast and at times rainy. William Bromwell and John Waters walked together late in the afternoon near Primrose Hill, an area well beyond the streets of the city. The hill was popular in the summer as a place to take the air, and it offered a spectacular view of London to anyone who climbed the 200-odd feet to its summit. But by mid-October the crowds were mostly gone, and on a wet day it would have been a lonely place. The men spotted something on the ground at the bottom of the hill – a pair of gloves, scabbard and walking stick. Assuming these items belonged to someone who had stepped into the bushes to answer the call of nature, they continued on to a nearby tavern, the White House.

The White House was not a particularly salubrious hostelry in the best of times, and on a rainy late afternoon in October it must have presented a dismal prospect to the walkers. But it was more or less dry, more or less warm, and it at least offered the prospect of alcoholic comfort. John Rawson the tavern keeper was probably not terribly busy when the two men came in, and so had time to chat about their discovery in the field nearby. Rawson, who earned a precarious living even when the summer walkers came in from town, saw an opportunity now in the off-season. He could retrieve these items; their owner might come to claim them, which could result in a reward. Or he might not, in which case Rawson could keep the stuff or sell it in London's lively market in second-hand goods.

The tavern keeper offered Bromwell and Waters a shilling each in bar credit if they would take him back to where they saw the goods. They agreed, and although it was getting dark, they sallied forth into the gloom – Rawson anticipating a potential windfall and the other two the pleasure that a shilling's worth of ale or wine would provide – about twelve pints of the former or three or four of the latter. This expedition had promise for everyone. A few minutes' walk brought them back to the scene. There were the items: gloves, scabbard and sword belt, and the stick. Bending down to retrieve them Rawson was startled to see, face down in a ditch, a man's body. Protruding from his back by some seven or eight inches was a sword blade.

The three men ran to fetch a constable, and they soon returned, accompanied by a number of other excited neighbours. The dead man was fully dressed but for a missing cravat; his hat and periwig were caught in some bushes bordering the ditch. Two men clambered down into the ditch and turned the body over. One of them immediately recognized the face staring up at him: Sir Edmund Godfrey had been found at last.

Sir Edmund's body was carried back to the White House and the constable, John Brown, emptied his pockets, finding two rings, one of which had a diamond, and a significant amount of money, about £20 in gold and silver coin. He was also wearing another ring on a finger. Clearly robbery had not been a motive in this particular death.

In the event of a suspicious death – which this most emphatically was – the county coroner was obliged to summon a jury and hold an inquest. Given the lateness of the hour, Sir Edmund's body was left under guard in the tavern and the coroner, John Cooper, prepared to open an inquiry the next day. Not surprisingly, this inquest turned into a circus. In addition to Cooper, the Middlesex coroner and his jury of a dozen local residents, the White House was jammed with spectators anxious to witness the proceedings. Among them were the Godfrey brothers, who brought with them the coroner of the borough of Westminster. A tussle ensued over which coroner should preside, ultimately resolved in Cooper's favour – the body was clearly not found in Westminster. Two surgeons, Zachary Skillarne and Nicholas Cambridge, were present and also in the crowd were a father and son duo named Chase who were royal apothecaries. Lord Danby's interests were watched over by his sergeant-at-arms, Mr Ramsey. The first order of business – after dealing with the attempted takeover by the intruder from Westminster – was to view the place where the body was found. Mr Cooper and the jurors, jostled by a vast crowd of onlookers, made their way to the site. Given the number of spectators who had trampled over the area, it is not surprising that this field trip yielded little evidence, but the jurors did note that the ditch where Godfrey lay was dry and there was no sign of blood.

Returning to the tavern, Sir Edmund's body was stripped and examined. The surgeons noted two wounds, one about an inch deep, ending at a rib, and the other transfixing the body from just below the left breast to the back. These wounds, the doctors believed, were inflicted after death, because of the lack of blood either on the sword found in the body or upon the clothing. Additionally, the doctors noted signs of bruising on the body's upper torso. Many observers took this as evidence of violence, though in fact it might well have been post-mortem lividity – the settling of blood in the body as Godfrey lay face down in the ditch. Although Michael and Benjamin Godfrey protested, the body was opened up, revealing the beginnings of decomposition of which there was no outward sign. This decay led to the conclusion that Sir Edmund had been dead four or five days – that is, since the previous Saturday or Sunday. Around

Godfrey's neck was a distinct mark – evidence of some sort of ligature. This, all agreed, was the cause of death.

The jurors now considered their verdict. This would be a matter of great significance: personally, for the Godfrey family, and politically, for the effect that verdict would have on the credibility of Titus Oates's conspiracy. Two possible verdicts, death by accident or act of God, were never considered. This left two other choices: homicide or suicide. The jurors deadlocked on this point, some leaning towards murder – committed by persons unknown, though everyone seemed determined to pin the blame on Catholics – and others to suicide. There had been testimony regarding Sir Edmund's depressed state of mind in the days before his disappearance, and some thought this suggested he might have done away with himself. The Godfrey family strongly resisted a suicide verdict, and not simply for the stigma attached. Suicides were denied Christian burial – their bodies often unceremoniously dumped in a hole dug at a crossroads. More important than this humiliation, suicide was a felony, and the property of a felon was forfeit to the Crown. Sir Edmund was a childless, unmarried man of substantial means. His brothers and sisters were his principal heirs. Much was at stake for them personally.

But the jury was not wholly persuaded that murder was the right verdict, and wrangling continued until the coroner finally called a halt to the proceeding, adjourning to the next morning. The court reassembled on Saturday 19 October. This time barman Rawson lost out on his windfall: the court met in a larger tavern, the Rose and Crown, in the parish of St Giles. Reassembling in the midst of an even larger company than the day before, the jury heard a number of other witnesses testifying to Sir Edmund's movements in the days before he died. But the jurors continued to struggle over the verdict, sitting far into the evening. Finally, at around midnight, they made their decision. Sir Edmund Godfrey had been murdered.[8]

What really happened to Godfrey? At this distance in time a definitive answer to the question will probably never be found. But Alan Marshall, who has examined the mystery in minute detail, convincingly argues that Sir Edmund's brothers successfully covered up his suicide. In doing so they saved his estate for the family – but they launched Titus Oates and a raft of other informers onto a high road to success in the process. And they also condemned many others to judicial murder.

The Godfrey brothers were not the only ones with a vested interest in a murder finding. With a new session of Parliament looming, the ministry's opponents were anxious to exploit the coroner's finding. Writing on the first day of the inquest to his son-in-law the prince of Orange, the duke of York reported the discovery of Godfrey's body and said 'This makes a great noise and is laid against the Catholics also, but without any reason for it, for he [Sir Edmund] was known to be far from an enemy to them. All these things happening together will cause, I am afraid, a great flame in the Parliament, when they meet on Monday, for those disaffected to the government will inflame all things as much as they can.'[9] Never known for his political acumen, James was on this occasion absolutely correct.

Lord Danby did what he could in the brief time available to him to brace himself. On Sunday 20 October the government issued a proclamation seeking information about 'the barbarous and inhumane' murder of Edmund Godfrey. The proclamation promised a £500 reward for the murderer's capture as well as a pardon to any conspirators giving evidence against their fellows. The reward was a very tempting offer – it was money enough for a gentleman to live handsomely for a year, or to keep a tradesman comfortable for a decade. There would be no shortage of people seeking to claim the prize.

The Lord Treasurer walked the tightest of ropes. The king's Catholic and Francophile brother James disliked Danby's anti-papist sentiments, while many others were deeply suspicious of him, fearing that he intended to make Charles II absolute. Fortunately for Danby, the king remained confident that his Lord Treasurer would continue mustering the votes needed to supply the Court with money to pursue its life and policies – frivolous though they sometimes were.

On the eve of the session Danby still hoped that Oates's plot might be used to strengthen his position. In the preceding weeks he had taken steps to ensure the attendance of army officers, invariably reliable supporters of the ministry, and shored up the Crown's finances raising money by borrowing against anticipated revenue. Vigorously pursuing the plot would boost Danby's reputation as a solid Protestant. James later wrote that Danby intended to 'pass for a pillar of the church and ward the blow which he foresaw was falling on his shoulders'. But he did not account for the possibility that he might be out-shouted in his anti-Catholicism. Shaftesbury said 'Let the Treasurer cry as loud as he pleases against Popery, and think to put himself at the head of the Plot; I will cry a note louder and soon take his place.'[10]

Although many members of both houses had not yet arrived in London, Parliament opened on schedule. The king, in his robes of state and suffering under the weight of the crown, almost five pounds of 22-carat gold and gems, sat on his throne in the chamber of the House of Lords. Before him sat in strict order of rank, fifty-two (of some 130 eligible) temporal peers of the realm, also clad in their bright red parliamentary robes. The spiritual peers, of whom only nine were present, including the Archbishop of Canterbury, William Sancroft, represented the established Church, while the Lord Chancellor and judges perched on their red wool-stuffed cushions in the middle of the chamber. Beyond the bar of the House – a railing that separated their lordships from commoners – crowded members of the Commons, led by their speaker, Sir Edward Seymour.

The acoustics of the House of Lords were bad; hardly improved by the old tapestries depicting the defeat of the Spanish Armada hung around the walls. The crowd of peers and MPs fidgeted and muttered, making it still more difficult to hear the king as he began his speech from the throne. King Charles was never known for his oratory, typically mumbling indistinctly and indifferently from his throne. On this occasion, dramatic though it was in the midst of the terrifying details of the plot, he ran true to form. Charles read from a piece of paper in front of him, and many MPs caught virtually none of his words. This hardly mattered, for Charles had virtually nothing to say about what they wanted to hear most: the conspiracy to assassinate him and overthrow Protestantism. In a speech that lasted perhaps two and a half minutes, Charles referred only briefly to the plot: '. . . I have been informed of a design against my person by the Jesuits, of which I will forbear any opinion, lest I may seem to say too much or too little, But I will leave the matter to the law, and in the meantime, will take as much care as I can . . .'[11]

This was hardly what MPs wanted to hear. Charles seemed far less concerned than many members felt he should be, and his reference to unnamed 'others' who plotted with foreigners might have meant politicians intriguing with the French or Dutch ambassadors. Charles knew very well that certain prominent opponents of the ministry engaged in just such scheming, and he was probably more concerned about the threat they represented than those warned of by Tonge and Oates.

Adding a plea for more money (no speech from the throne was complete without it), Charles left the chamber. Following his address, speaking from his uncomfortable woolsack below the throne, was Lord Finch, the Lord Chancellor. Finch presided over the Lords when it was in session and the High Court of Chancery when it was not. Distinguished by his very prominent nose, he was an accomplished lawyer and stalwart supporter of Danby's ministry. Shaftesbury hated him – Finch had replaced the earl when the king sacked him as Chancellor in 1675 – and the speech that Finch now delivered did nothing to change his opinion.

Finch, like the king, downplayed the plot, though at somewhat greater length. Stressing the uncertainty of foreign affairs, he urged members to provide money for the army and navy. He did not arrive at the matter of the plot until his eighteenth paragraph, where he echoed the king, denouncing those who 'meddle with matters of state and Parliament, and carry on their pernicious designs by a most dangerous correspondency with foreign nations'. More important, Finch argued, was the need to support the government, to trust the Court and to provide vital tax revenues. In closing he fired a parting shot at those in the audience he knew would soon be working to exploit the plot for their own ends: '. . . that which is to be infinitely lamented is that malicious men too begin to work upon this occasion, and are in no small hopes to raise a storm that nothing shall be able to allay'.[12]

Lord Chancellor Finch was an astute forecaster. His ten-minute speech finished, MPs trooped back to their own dingy chamber in St Stephen's chapel, a short walk away. Both houses of Parliament inhabited ancient buildings acquired haphazardly and with nothing remotely resembling a plan. St Stephen's, completed in the year of the Black Death in 1348, was now where MPs debated. Whitewashed walls, remnants of Reformation-era iconoclasm, could hardly disguise the original purpose of the building. The Speaker's chair stood on the steps of the former altar and members sat on benches on either side of the room, the area once occupied by the choir. When the House divided, members voted by exiting through the doors of the former choir screen – 'no's to the left, 'aye's to the right. When every member was present, the chapel was seriously overcrowded, but on this particular day that was less of a problem. Many members were still travelling to London from their homes around the country. But the passionate interest in Oates's revelations ensured that soon places on the benches would be at a premium.

The Commons appointed two committees, one charged with finding ways to assure the king's safety, and another to investigate both the plot and the presumed murder of Sir Edmund Godfrey. Membership of these committees largely overlapped, and they were ordered to meet at the same time and place, 3 p.m. in the Speaker's Chamber. Members included several prominent allies of the Court, such as Sir Edward Dering ('doubly vile', according to Shaftesbury), but they were outnumbered by its opponents.[13] Danby's hope to use the plot as a tool to strengthen his ministry was unravelling before the first day of the session ended.

In the Lords the first impulse was to call for divine assistance, to be expected in a body where some of the most diligent members were bishops. Their lordships asked the king to declare a 'Solemn day of fasting and humiliation' for God's help, 'to pray Him to bring to light, more and more, all secret machinations against Your Majesty and Your Kingdom'. More consequently, at least in the temporal world, they also asked Charles to furnish them with copies of documents relating to the plot, 'that we may use our utmost endeavours to serve Your Majesty as is our bounden duty and allegiance'.[14] It was probably quite clear to some peers that 'utmost endeavours' would also include an attempt to wrest investigation of the plot away from Danby and the Privy Council. The investigation might serve admirably as a weapon aimed at the Lord Treasurer.

The next day, the Lords reassembled at their usual ten o'clock starting time – the Commons started work at eight o'clock. The king and his brother were both there, and Charles agreed to provide the Lords with papers relating to the plot – a fateful concession on his part. He also agreed to consider their request for a fast, promising to deliver an answer that afternoon. At 3 p.m. Charles awaited the arrival of both houses of Parliament, seated on his throne in the Banqueting House. This was a convenient venue for such a meeting – large enough to accommodate both houses (if everyone turned up, a sizable body of perhaps 700 peers and MPs), and grand enough to allow the king to shine. Moreover, the building was on Charles's turf, a part of the complex of buildings that made up the Palace of Whitehall. It was completed in 1622, designed by the famous architect Inigo Jones and used for court entertainments. Rubens, celebrating the Stuart dynasty, had decorated its ceilings with a magnificent set of paintings. The central painting depicted Charles's grandfather, a rather nervous-looking James I, being hoisted towards heaven by angels. Here Charles now waited for the Parliamentarians to make the ten-minute walk up from Westminster. The king had time to contemplate the complex meaning of this site, for while it memorably celebrated his family, it also recalled the Stuarts' greatest calamity. Almost exactly thirty years earlier, the king's father, Charles I, had walked through the hall, beneath those paintings, and stepped out of the central window onto the scaffold where he was executed. The vision of his father's apotheosis was one of the last things Charles I saw, and as his son sat beneath those same images he must have thought about the fine line separating political opposition from treason.

For the moment though, Charles needed to play the role of gracious sovereign. Before the crowd of peers and MPs he granted Parliament's request, announcing a national day of fasting and prayer for 13 November. Members then trooped out, many no doubt headed for nearby taverns and alehouses, swapping rumours about conspiracies and plots, ready to resume work the next day.

Most of the coming week focused on Parliament's continuing investigation and the build-up to the funeral of Sir Edmund Godfrey, scheduled for Halloween, on Thursday. Both fronts were winners for Shaftesbury, who missed no opportunity to encourage alarm both inside Parliament and out. On Monday Oates arrived with a dramatic statement that he feared a possible reprise of Guy Fawkes's treason in 1605. The Commons ordered a thorough search of spaces beneath Parliament, and the Lords forbade the storage of any flammable material nearby. The search revealed nothing, temporarily laying to rest fears of being blown to bits or roasted in a popish bonfire, but it kept members anxious and nourished the atmosphere of crisis. Meanwhile, both houses continued to hear Oates's further elaborations of his story, and to consider evidence from the interrogation of Catholic prisoners.

On Thursday all of London's attention was fixed upon the spectacle of Sir Edmund Godfrey's funeral. For two days before the ceremony the body lay in state at Bridewell, on the eastern side of the city. Formerly a royal palace, Bridewell was now a jail and hospital, providing plenty of space for viewing a celebrated corpse. Sir Edmund's brother Michael Godfrey arranged the funeral, though some said it was Shaftesbury's idea to leave Sir Edmund's sword where it had been found, transfixed in the martyr's breast.[15] Even as final details were arranged, enterprising Londoners sought to cash in on the crime of the year. London cutlers sold 3,000 'Godfrey daggers' in a single day – including one with a gilded handle that someone sent to the duke of York.[16] Hack writers churned out bad (and worse) verse. When the body – which must have been embalmed, given that Sir Edmund had been dead for three and a half weeks – went on display, Benjamin Harris, a printer with a shop near the Exchange, was ready with *An elegie on the Right Worshipful Sir Edmond-Bury Godfrey, Knight*. Decorated with typical memento mori – skulls, crossbones and the like – it displayed a sure grip of the coroner's findings, if not much poetic skill:

> Methinks I see him as first he stood
> With his pale body newly streak'd with blood
> With gaping wounds like mouths, which called for woe
> And home revenge, on those who made him so:
> With bruised neck, and cheek, and battered chin;

And breast as black as his vile butchers' sin:
But with a soul more innocent and gay
Than new born lilies in the midst of May.

The printers of these works no doubt had plenty of copies to hand at Godfrey's visitation, providing an entertaining way to pass the time until visitors could pass the coffin. Licensed the day after the funeral, yet another poet published *The Proclamation Promoted, or an Hue and Cry and Inquisition After Treason and Blood: Upon the Inhumane and Horrid Murder of that Noble Knight, Impartial Justice of Peace and Zealous Protestant Sir Edmond Berry Godfry of Westminster.* Hinting at the text to come, the author subtitled this gem *An Hasty Poem.* This elegy had a political edge, and urged bloodthirsty vengeance on Catholics:

Ye Lords and Commons joyn your speedy votes,
A pack of bloodhounds threaten all your throats.
And if their Treason be not understood,
Expect to be dissolved in your own blood.
O vote that every Papist (high and low)
To martyred Godfry's corps in person go
And laying hand upon his wounded brest,
By oath and curse his ignorance protest.
But oh the atheism of that monstrous crew,
Whose Holy Father can all bonds undo:
Whose bretheren put away the heaviest oaths;
Who fear no heaven or Hell, but laugh at both . . .
O vote each sign post shall a gibbet be,
And hang a traytor upon every tree.
Yet we'le find wood enough for Bone-fire piles
T'inlighten and inflame our Brittish Isles
Upon th'approaching fifth November night,
And make incendiaries curse the light.

By calling on Parliament to exterminate Catholics 'high and low', this author advanced Shaftesbury's case, shifting responsibility for prosecuting the plotters away from king and council. Nor would anyone have been confused about whom to include among the 'high' Catholics: James, duke of York.

The flood of overheated verse in the days surrounding the funeral merely whetted the public appetite for the spectacle. The main event was, of course, the funeral itself. It was, as the family and interested politicians like Shaftesbury intended, designed to be a first-class affair. There would have been very few as elaborate all year. The funeral procession formed up at Bridewell. Leading the body was a phalanx of seventy-two clergymen all in their canonical robes, walking two by two. The body followed, borne by eight justices of the peace, all knights. The Lord Mayor and the entire corps of London's aldermen followed them, after which came an immense train of over 1,000 nobles and 'worthy gentlemen'.

The streets would have been packed with spectators eager to see the coffin and the high-ranking mourners making their slow way to Sir Edmund's parish church, St Martin-in-the-Fields. The church – not the same as the elegant neoclassical building so well known today – dated from the reign of Henry VIII, and it could accommodate a substantial crowd. The parish was one of London's most populous, and its rector, Dr William Lloyd, was a familiar and popular preacher. He was used to preaching to a full house, but this occasion must have given even the most experienced minister pause. There was certainly a full house – overfull. The family, led by Sir Edmund's two brothers, would have been in the forefront, but the rest of the church was crowded with peers, Members of Parliament, gentlemen and women 'of quality', and the cream of the city's merchant oligarchy – obtaining a seat in the midst of this multitude was a coup.

Dr Lloyd preached the sermon. He had known Sir Edmund well, and he had been one of the first to view the body after its discovery. In print the sermon (which of course was printed within days – in multiple editions) amounted to a little over forty pages, and would probably have taken two hours or more to deliver. He took his text from the second book of Samuel: 'And the king lamented over Abner, and said "Died Abner as a fool dieth?" Thy hands were not bound, nor thy feet put into fetters: as a man falleth before wicked men, so fellest thou. And all the people wept again over him.' Dr Lloyd knew his work. First he called on God to avenge Sir Edmund's death and then lauded his many virtues, 'O my friends! I [speaking as Godfrey] spent my life in serving you. It was my business to do justice and shew mercy. See what I had for it, insnared and butchered by wicked men against justice and without mercy.' He created a picture of his victim that could not but move the audience: 'My poor mangled macerated body must be thrown out to birds and beasts . . .' Later the reverend returned to the magnitude of the crime: 'But perhaps never any was murthered as he was, so treacherously and basely, and with such bloody and barbarous cruelty.' He speculated luridly on Sir Edmund's final hours: 'God knows where they kept him . . . Ah poor soul! How many comfortless hours did he reckon in the merciless trap where they kept him? How many insulting words, how many reproaches did he hear? What racks, what bodily tortures might he probably suffer?'

The Reverend Lloyd dismissed rumours of suicide: 'For the melancholy that was observed in our friend, I think none that knew him ever thought it distraction [insanity], or anything tending in that way, but a thoughtfulness sometimes, that proceeded from the intricacy and multiplicity of business.' The Godfrey brothers seated in the pews must have been well pleased by these remarks, just as Shaftesbury and his friends were satisfied when Dr Lloyd laid the blame for Sir Edmund's death on the Jesuits: 'They hold it lawful to kill men that would prejudice them or their religion.' Moreover, he tied the 'murder' to Oates's plot, a key issue: 'That it was their interest to kill him, 'tis manifest, if they had any design against the government . . . But that is the interest of their sect, and of their church, to subvert the government; and that they for their parts design it now at this present, I think this 'tis so palpable . . . that I should but lose time in proving it.' For good measure he blamed the Jesuits for the Great Fire, harping on a theme lovingly fostered by the opposition. The reverend thanked God for discovering the plot, by implication making Titus Oates and Israel Tonge divine instruments protecting England from popish treason. 'God still deliver us from your bloody hands! Keep England from your bloody religion!'[17]

As the coffin was borne to the grave and the crowd dispersed, many of the principal actors in this drama had reason to be pleased. The Godfrey brothers could be proud of their martyred loved one; Shaftesbury, Oates and Tonge saw that Godfrey's death was now recognized as positive proof for the existence of their plot; Dr Lloyd emerged with enhanced standing in the Church – within two years he would be a bishop. The booksellers profited from doggerel elegies and copies of the funeral sermon; souvenir makers sold medals with Godfrey's image. One of these showed a pair of hands in the act of strangling Sir Edmund and combined the face of the Devil with the Pope. Another manufactured daggers depicting a skull and the words MEMENTO GODFREY CAESUS OCTO 12 on one side of its sharp blade and PRO RELIGIONE PROTESTANT on the other. There was something for everyone (Protestant) in Sir Edmund's passing.

But for some the circus surrounding Sir Edmund's death would be the start of the final act of their lives.

— FOUR —
THE INVESTIGATION
AUTUMN 1678

On Wednesday 23 October the Lords created a committee to examine papers turned over by the king about the plot, also charging it to investigate Godfrey's murder. The House gave it authority to summon witnesses and examine them on oath, and to subpoena documents. Like most committees in both houses, membership was broad: service on committees was more a matter of personal interest than anything else. Members volunteered and were taken on, though usually – and especially in this case – a handful of active members dominated the committee's work. Forty-eight temporal peers and seven bishops served, including such pro-court stalwarts as York, Danby and Charles's cousin Prince Rupert. There were even several Catholics included, like Lords Petre and Arundell of Trerice. But from the beginning, the lead was taken by Shaftesbury and a handful of his closest allies, such as the earl of Essex, who had dedicated themselves to overthrowing Danby long before.[1] This body became the primary engine driving the plot forward, and it would succeed in creating a political crisis worse than any since the civil war.

That day in the Commons the House began work on a new bill that would deprive Catholic peers of their seats in the Lords. Catholics had been barred from the Commons since 1673, but the Lords had hitherto resisted this drastic measure. The current crisis represented an ideal opportunity for anti-Catholic MPs, and the bill was hastily read and scheduled for a second reading the next day. That accomplished, the House turned to the plot. Members ordered Titus Oates and Michael Godfrey, Sir Edmund's brother, to appear. Godfrey was to testify about the depositions his brother took from Oates and Israel Tonge, but the attention of the House was undoubtedly focused on Oates, now making his first appearance before them.

After appointing a sermon for 5 November to mark the Gunpowder Plot, the House called for Oates and Godfrey, who was ordered to bring his brother's papers. Titus came in and stood at the bar of the House – the first time many members had seen him, though of course by now everyone knew (or thought they knew) who he was. Titus was apparently blessed with the king's confidence, for the Crown had provided his lodgings in Whitehall Palace and a generous weekly pension. Oates's credibility, bolstered by his solemn appearance in the gown of a Doctor of Divinity, grew as he launched into his tale. Speaking in his accustomed booming voice ('like a flawed organ pipe')[2] he began relating his story. Building on what he had already told the Privy Council, he added more detail. There was a secret Benedictine residence at the Savoy, near the queen's Somerset House lodgings. Orders duly went out for a raid; the monks were to be arrested and their quarters thoroughly searched. Nightfall would see another group of hapless Catholics jammed into the overcrowded cells of Newgate. But this was only the beginning. Oates was still talking when time to adjourn for the day came, and he was instructed to return in the morning.[3]

On Thursday 24 October, following a hasty second reading of the new Test Bill, the Commons took a step that must have seemed ominous to the Court. Members resolved to address the king, asking him to take better care of his person, to increase security at court and 'give order, that the cities of London and Westminster, and parts adjacent, may, during the time of sitting of the Parliament, be secured and guarded by the militia'.[4] Asking specifically for militia protection made a statement: Charles already had troops in arms who could easily have provided sufficient security. The Commons address suggested a serious lack of trust in the king. This request could not but raise alarming memories of 1641 and 1642 when Charles I had struggled with Parliament over control of the militia – the immediate prelude to open civil war.

Having sufficiently alarmed the Court with this address, the House turned to the pursuit of Sir Edmund Godfrey's killers. A witness, Mr Mulys, testified that he had encountered a distressed Sir Edmund in St James's Park five or six days before his disappearance. 'Some great men,' he had told Mulys, 'blame me for not having done my duty and I am threatened by others and very great ones too for having done too much.'[5] The allusion to 'very great ones' opposing investigation of the conspiracy was clearly intended to suggest Danby and the duke of York. Another witness quoted Godfrey saying, 'I believe I shall be the first martyr.'

Oates then returned to the bar naming more names. This time his principal victim was Richard Langhorne, a barrister of the Middle Temple. Implicating Langhorne was a shrewd move by Titus; he had for years been a trusted advisor to the Catholic community, and had played a crucial role in its business affairs. He had arranged trusts and real-estate deals that funded much of the Jesuit mission in England – all of which were illegal, of course, and which had to be arranged with great care to avoid disclosure. If anyone could reveal the inner workings of English Catholicism it was Langhorne.[6] He had been jailed since the first wave of arrests led by Titus in early October – Oates knew him because he had met his son, a student in Valladolid, and had carried letters between them.[7]

Parliamentarians interrogated other suspects as well. The committee examining Edward Colman in Newgate prison received little satisfaction from him: he denied any assassination plot, even after an offer of a pardon and a reward for information. But the information he did volunteer was alarming enough for members already on edge. Colman admitted that he 'had been guilty of many follies' and that he had corresponded with French Catholics – including Louis XIV's confessor, Father François de La Chaise. He had solicited French money to advance the Catholic cause in England and conducted – without, he said, informing his master the duke – a one-man diplomatic mission with foreign Catholics. While Colman denied the truth of Oates's allegations, he hardly cleared himself – or, more to the point, the duke of York – of suspicions.

The investigation soon brought accusations against members of the upper House. Soon after the peers began their session, on Saturday 26 October, with both the king and his brother the duke of York present, William, Viscount Stafford, rose and declared that Lord Chief Justice Scroggs had issued a warrant for his arrest. Taking a member of the House of Lords was no small matter – their lordships often reacted with fury even when their menial servants were locked up for minor offences. Scroggs then explained that the night before he had received a letter from the Speaker of the Commons accusing Stafford, a Catholic, and four other recusant peers, of treason. Along with the earl of Powis and Lords Petre, Belasyse and Arundell of Wardour, Stafford had been accused by Oates of complicity in the plot – Titus identified each of them as being assigned leadership positions in the forthcoming popish regime. The clerk read Oates's deposition against the five, and though Stafford passionately denied the charges, he offered to surrender himself to Scroggs's custody. Powis and Arundell had already surrendered and were being held in the Gatehouse prison, hard by Westminster. Lord Petre was arrested the following day.

It was a solemn moment; unlike the far larger Commons, peers knew one another well, were often bound by ties of kinship and most had been acquainted all their lives. For five of their number to be accused of conspiring murderous treason was shocking. The king and duke of York looked on as Oates's deposition accusing the peers was read to the House. Stafford replied with a vigorous denial of the charges, then left the chamber to place himself in Scroggs's custody. It was the last time he would ever stand in the House of Lords a free man.[8]

That day the Commons was treated to a rambling monologue from Israel Tonge, pinning the blame for the Great Fire of 1666 on the Jesuits. Already being eclipsed by his fellow informer Oates, Tonge succeeded in wresting some attention back by outlining in lurid detail the Catholic arson attack. It was already a byword among many that the Great Fire had been deliberately set by papists, so this tale received an uncritical hearing. Tonge was manifestly not a stable man, but his story fit popular prejudices so well that anything short of raving delusions would have been convincing to most members.[9] It demonstrated the long-standing malevolence of the Jesuit Order – part of a chain of outrages extending back to the Irish rebellion of 1641, the assassination of the French king Henri IV in 1610, the Gunpowder Plot of 1605 and the Spanish Armada of 1588.

That afternoon both houses joined to ask the king to issue a proclamation expelling all Catholics from London and ordered the search and seizure of Catholic books, as well as the arrest of James Thompson, a well-known Catholic printer. Having accomplished all this, the Lords committee repaired to Newgate to interview Colman. The following day London's pulpits rang with denunciations of the plot, calls for vengeance on Godfrey's alleged murderers and thanksgivings for having escaped yet another bloodthirsty scheme of the Jesuits.

Messengers fanned out across London, armed with warrants to search for Catholic clergy and incriminating documents. Among the first victims were the six Benedictine monks serving the queen's chapel at Somerset House. They lived quietly nearby, within the old Savoy hospital complex, and had occupied those lodgings since the king's return from exile.[10] Until this moment they had enjoyed a measure of royal favour, for one of them, Father John Huddleston, had saved Charles's life after his defeat at Cromwell's hands in the battle of Worcester in 1651. Charles supported the monks with generous pensions of £100 a year and covered many of their expenses.[11] Father John continued to enjoy Charles's personal protection, but he could not shelter the others from the storm descending upon them; parliamentary messengers ransacked their quarters and hauled all the monks they found to the cells of Newgate. Luckily the ongoing round-up of Catholic clergy made the monks wary enough to have burned many of their papers, including lists of lay supporters.

The Privy Council's pursuit of the plotters had been vigorous, and it continued, but Parliament's pursuit soon overshadowed it. Parliamentarians, motivated by a sincerely held fear of Popish Plotting or manipulated by politicians advancing personal agendas, were far more aggressive. And Oates was just getting started. Having boomed away until the end of the day's business, he promised still greater revelations the next day. After ordering all MPs who were Middlesex magistrates to cooperate with Oates by issuing warrants for arrests and searches of the homes of those he had accused, the House adjourned, with Titus scheduled to appear before them again the next day.

In his next instalment Oates revealed details about an important part of the Catholic underground: its legal and financial infrastructure. The principal target was Richard Langhorne, who Oates had had arrested nearly a month before. Langhorne had made a successful career arranging the legal affairs of English Catholics. Although he outwardly conformed to the Church of England, he educated his children in Catholic schools abroad, and was probably a closeted Catholic himself.[12] Oates had picked his victim because he was aware of his Jesuit connections – though there was also a personal connection. After his expulsion of the Jesuit college in Valladolid, Oates had delivered the elder Langhorne a letter from his son Charles, a student there. That connection proved to be highly dangerous – ultimately fatal – for the lawyer. Oates knew where he lived, and he might well have worried that Langhorne knew, or could find out, the details of his expulsion for 'great moral offenses', presumably pederasty.

Oates's charges against Langhorne inspired the Plot committee to order a close examination of his voluminous papers. These documents revealed an intricate but hidden Catholic world: there were trusts providing income to support Catholic clergy, sales and purchases of land, transactions designed to hide Catholic property and income. Preposterous though many of Titus's allegations were, the genuine existence of this secret world did a great deal to persuade many in Parliament and outside it that the popish threat was acute. The Plot committees in both houses spent countless hours poring over these documents, convinced that they went far towards proving the reality of the plot.

In the following week London was treated to a series of spectacles highlighting the kingdom's fraught condition. On Tuesday 29 October, Londoners enjoyed the pageantry of the Lord Mayor's Show – the annual inauguration of a new mayor of the City. Each of London's livery companies spent freely to celebrate their own contributions to the City and the show symbolized London's wealth, magnificence and unity. This year's mayor was Sir James Edwards, and his company – the Worshipful Company of Grocers – was determined to shine. Assembling at their hall in the heart of the city, at 7 a.m., liverymen dressed in their finest robes ('faced with budg' – lamb's wool) and their hoods, joined by fifty gentlemen ushers in velvet coats and golden collars, processed through the streets to Goldsmiths' Hall. No one could miss their coming, for over fifty trumpeters and a couple of dozen drummers blared and banged their way past hordes of spectators.[13] The new mayor then embarked on an elaborate gilded barge and made his way upriver to Westminster Hall, where he took an oath of allegiance to the king and government beneath the thirteenth-century hammer-beam roof. Returning to the city by water and greeted by a military salute from London's militia, Sir James led the parade down Cheapside, the broadest of the city's streets, and was treated to a series of pageants.

The first of these was characteristic: a stage decorated with a painted camel, 'so curiously carved and exquisitely gilded that it appeareth like a live animal in a hide of massy gold'. This spectacle was presided over by an African boy (possibly genuine, more likely in blackface) 'habited in an Indian robe of divers colour, a wreath of various coloured feathers on his black and wooly head'.[14] The boy threw a variety of grocer's wares to the audience. Scrambling for raisins, dates, almonds and nutmegs, spectators probably paid little attention to the speech of Fidelity, gaudily dressed in a golden breastplate, and helmet, armed with a silver lance and golden sword – and oddly, a silver truncheon. The new Lord Mayor listened benignly as Fidelity extolled the virtues of good government, loyalty, constancy, justice and union. Amid the rhetoric of unity and peace, however, there were hints that all was not altogether as it should be. Part of the performance included a song sung by 'a stout planter with a voice like a trumpet, [who] distendeth his copious chops':

> For London's great grocers we labour and work
> No plots against princes in our heads do lurk.
> We plant, set, and sow, likewise for the physician,
> But plant no rebellion and sow no sedition.[15]

The final words of the day's celebration suggested that London stood at a threshold:

Since Union and concord bring plenty and peace,
And amity is the kind cause of increase:
Let love from division our fancy's release,
And all our dissensions ever cease.[16]

The new Lord Mayor and his subjects straggled home after a long day of feasting – and drinking – but we may doubt that these high-sounding sentiments lasted much longer than their hangovers.

The next morning's spectacle unfolded in the House of Lords. With both the king and the duke of York present, and before a very full House, Titus Oates made his first appearance. Dressed in black clerical garb, he made an impressive appearance. In a speech that could have given the earl of Shaftesbury no comfort, Oates came to James's rescue. Shaftesbury's report of Colman's interrogation had implicated the duke in Colman's machinations, but now Oates appeared to contradict him. In his usual style – one reason was never as good as six – Oates told the lords that he believed York was innocent because the Jesuits had counterfeited the seals of both James and his wife, and used them to create forged letters. Furthermore, Oates claimed to have overheard Jesuits in Ghent saying that James had not been informed of the plot because they feared he loved Charles too much. He also saw a letter written to Father Nicholas Blundell declaring that the order 'longed to see the Duke trepanned' (knocked on the head). Oates also said that the so-called Bedingfield letters – the ones he and Tonge had forged in August – were part of a ploy designed to implicate the duke in the conspiracy, an attempt that went wrong when James handed the letters to the Privy Council rather than concealing them. Having reported all of this Oates withdrew and was ordered to return the next day to give a full account of his knowledge of the plot.[17]

Oates's attempt to mollify James is clear evidence that at this point he was not working with the earl of Shaftesbury and the opposition. The 'little lord' was as determined to attack the duke of York as he was Lord Treasurer Danby. Shaftesbury had in the spring proposed to work with James to topple Danby, whose anti-French policies irritated the duke. But the offer was rejected and so the earl widened his sights and targeted both the heir presumptive and the Treasurer.[18]

Although the duke of York might have taken some comfort in Oates's declaration, the investigation continued unabated. The Lords committee to investigate the plot was already working feverishly. John Dolben, bishop of Rochester, was nominally chairman of the group, but the well-fed prelate was not sufficiently anti-Catholic to satisfy the most active members, notably Shaftesbury and Essex. His role devolved into making perfunctory reports to the House, while Shaftesbury and his allies did the real work. An early example of this came on Saturday night, when Shaftesbury, Essex and their loyal supporter the earl of Clarendon descended on Newgate to question Edward Colman.

Armed with copies of his letters to Father de La Chaise, Louis XIV's confessor, Shaftesbury had high hopes for this interrogation. Colman had, after all, written of his confidence that all three British kingdoms would soon become Catholic – but these letters were now over three years old, and the committee believed that there were probably others of more recent date. These might have been destroyed – an assertion that soon became established as truth – though it did not explain why Colman had failed to burn all of his papers. In any event, under questioning perhaps Colman would reveal more secrets about a Catholic conspiracy.

The Lords were disappointed. Colman admitted he had indeed written the letters, and that 'he had been guilty of a great many follies', but he denied any involvement with an assassination plot. Even the offer of a pardon left him unmoved. To the committee's annoyance, Colman distanced himself from the duke of York, asserting that his letters to Father de La Chaise were written without the duke's knowledge.[19] The committee got nowhere with several other prisoners in Newgate, who were interviewed at the same time. Priests Thomas Jennison, Edward Petre and William Ireland, 'all obstinately deny' any knowledge of a plot – even when offered both a pardon and a hefty reward for information.[20]

The following day Oates returned to the bar of the Lords, ready to repeat his entire story. The tale that he told varied little from what he had presented to the Privy Council and the Commons. It was vintage Oates: a methodical, point-by-point account (eighty-one in all) swarming with precise dates, names and places. Titus described a diabolical plan involving nearly one hundred Catholic clergy and an array of laymen, including, of course, the now-jailed five 'Popish lords'. In addition to assassinating King Charles ('the fatal blow shall be delivered to the Black Boy at Whitehall with all speed'), the Jesuits were responsible for unrest in Ireland and rebellion in Scotland. They planned to disrupt England's relations with Spain and the Holy Roman Empire; they planned to subvert children by bribing their parents to teach them Catholicism; they intended to engineer the dissolution of Parliament. Charles would be shot by 'Irish ruffians'. Or poisoned by his doctor. Or stabbed (with a carefully described knife: a foot-long blade with a six-inch haft, bought for ten shillings from 'the Old Cutler in Russell Street'). In the process, Oates credited Catholics with both the Great Fire of London and several lesser blazes in recent years, including a massive fire that destroyed much of Southwark in 1676. Back in 1666 fifty or sixty Irishmen using 700 'fireballs' had spread the fire. These arsonists industriously looted homes as they went, netting an impressive haul in jewellery and plate – 'there was 1,000 carats in diamonds' alone, and thousands of pounds of other loot.[21]

Oates provided details about the Catholic mission in England, particularly London, most of it highly exaggerated but all designed to alarm his audience at the sinister presence among them. The London Jesuits, he said, had secreted away £100,000 in cash and property, bringing in £60,000 a year in rents. These figures were grossly inflated; the Society did in fact own some property (through carefully concealed deeds and trusts), but its portfolio was extremely modest.[22] They were moneylenders as well, offering loans at 50 per cent interest. Jesuits had infiltrated many of London's trades: merchants, tobacconists, goldsmiths, scriveners and others, and they used these tradesmen to secretly gather information about Protestants – learning details of their wealth and estates to use for the Society's advantage. They employed spies to lurk at Westminster, picking up parliamentary news and gossip, bribing clerks for information. Jesuits were everywhere, and when the assassination took place, they would be ready with thousands of supporters all over Britain, ready to snuff out the Protestant religion. The rebels would use 40,000 'black bills' (edged weapons like halberds) stockpiled for the purpose.

Presumably stunned by the mass of detail, most peers seem to have taken all that Oates said at face value. But it could not have been comfortable listening for some, especially King Charles and his brother. Titus seems to have relished reporting a variety of slanders directed at the sovereign and his family. One Jesuit claimed that Charles I was 'a heretic and bastard, and his father was Queen Anne's [James I's wife, Anne of Denmark] tailor'; Charles II himself was 'given to drinking and whoring', and his speeches were ridiculed by seminarians at St Omer. He was 'the fool at Whitehall'. The duke of York fared somewhat better. Oates carefully avoided implicating James directly, noting several times that the plotters did not trust the duke. 'What if the Duke should prove slippery?' Oates said he had asked two Jesuits named Edward Neville and Thomas Fermour in the library at St Omer (Titus always tethered his lies to such specific details). They supposedly replied, 'His passport was ready, whenever he should appear to fail them.'[23]

The oration lasted a full six hours – with a break for lunch – and Oates must have exhausted the peers as much as himself. Finished at last, the House dismissed Oates briefly and then brought him back to answer a pointed question: 'if there be particular Persons concerned, of what Quality soever they be, the House expected he should name them. But he named none, but those he had mentioned in his Narrative; nor could name no other Person.'[24] In doing so, Oates definitively ruled out the duke of York as a suspect. For the present.

Before departing from the house Oates requested a guard to defend him from attack, and the House obliged, tasking the king's bastard son the duke of Monmouth with keeping the reverend safe. Furthermore, Oates complained about the quality of his lodgings in Whitehall – they were 'underground'. While it seems unlikely that he was in fact assigned to a palace cellar, one suspects that the king had no desire to make his guest any more comfortable than necessary. Finally, the Lords asked Danby, as Lord Treasurer, to ensure that he had enough money 'for his necessaries'.[25]

The following day Parliament increased the pressure on the government. Its charges were typical of the random malice that Titus employed. Mr Moore was a seller of popish books; Dennis Glisson, a schoolmaster, 'did install ill principles into children'. In Glisson's case, Oates threw red meat in the direction of MPs with a university education. The schoolmaster, he alleged, had said 'there is no learning in Cambridge, and nothing but debauchery in Oxford'. That both of these statements were not far from the truth did not seem to matter. One man, Mark Preston, Oates accused of being a Catholic priest. Preston denied the charge, pointing out that he was a married man with children. A Mr Smith had reportedly 'spoken very unseemly words against the king's person'.[26] In each of these cases, Oates was building the general impression that Catholics were everywhere in London. But the charges were either hearsay – Oates did not himself have direct information about either Smith or Glisson – or disappointingly weak. The threat represented by sellers of Catholic books seemed remote, at best. And Preston easily refuted Oates's charge. Still, coming as they did the day after Godfrey's burial, they helped sustain the panicked atmosphere in Parliament.

At the end of the day, both houses joined in a resolution, '*Resolved*, That, upon the Evidence that has already appeared to this House, this House is of opinion that there has been, and still is, a damnable and hellish Plot contrived and carried on by the Popish Recusants, for the assassinating and murdering the King, and for subverting the Government, and rooting out and destroying the Protestant Religion.' The vote was unanimous in both chambers.[27]

Shaftesbury was now ready to step up his campaign against the duke of York, trying to tie the duke's close associate and client, Samuel Pepys, to the Godfrey murder. The Lords committee arrested Pepys's clerk, Samuel Atkins, and accused him of being an accomplice in the crime. In the meantime, the earl launched a more direct assault on the duke of York. In Saturday's session of the Lords, Shaftesbury proposed an address to the king, asking that James be removed from both the Court and the Council. Despite Oates's testimony three days earlier exonerating the duke, Shaftesbury intended to cast suspicion on York. For the moment, in the absence of hard evidence, the peers stood by the heir apparent. The motion was rejected, but it made a significant impact at Whitehall. When the Privy Council met on Sunday, the subject was discussed in detail. Secretary Williamson's sketchy notes suggest the king's determination to defend his brother. 'No division between the brothers. No harm to him.' Charles believed that a political conspiracy was afoot: 'We talk of designs. Pray God this be not a design to put division between the king and his brother.' How, in any event, could James be prohibited from communicating with his brother? If James went into exile, would that not simply make him desperate? Is it not safer to keep him at court, where he could be influenced by loyal subjects? The king reminded the Council of his father's last instruction to him: 'The message from the last king to the now king. Never to suffer any division between the king and his brothers.'[28]

When Parliament assembled on Monday morning, the duke's enemies resumed the attack. William Russell, the earl of Bedford's son and a loyal follower of Shaftesbury, moved an address to the king, asking that James 'be removed from the king's presence and councils'. This was exactly what the Lords had rejected on Saturday, but the Commons contained a larger contingent of James's enemies. There is no doubt but that the motion was coordinated by Shaftesbury, and in the debate which followed the opposition fuelled the Commons' fear and hatred of popery.[29] Sir Thomas Meres's contribution was typical of the anti-Catholic rhetoric the opposition employed: 'the Papists take scripture from us; they take sense from us in transubstantiation . . . Popery sets up another government, *imperium in imperio*, it is against the interest of the nation ! . . We are satisfied, both lords and commons, that there is a plot. Let us do our part. If this be not done, farewell any attempts to preserve the Protestant religion!'[30] 'I believe popery is a confederacy against God, and against the kingdom!' said Sir Philip Warwick.[31] Opposition MPs argued that James obstructed anti-Catholic legislation by his presence in the Lords, and that his Catholicism encouraged conspiracy. Sir Robert Sawyer said, 'For the duke to depart from that religion his father signed with his blood! I can assign no other cause for this dismal attempt that has been discovered, but the hopes the papists have of the duke's religion.'[32] Most of the speakers took care to avoid treating the duke too harshly, but some were much less respectful. William Sacheverell, one of the MPs most reliably hostile to James and the ministry, commented ominously, 'I wonder . . . whether the king and the Parliament may not dispose of the succession to the crown?'[33] This radical solution to the problem of a Catholic heir soon would become an essential part of the opposition's programme, and clearly Sacheverell was testing the waters.

James's defenders rehearsed the arguments sketched out in Sunday's Privy Council meeting. The royal brothers would still communicate, even if James were banished. Keeping him close would ensure his continuing loyalty, while sending him abroad might encourage plotting. Solicitor General Winnington argued that removing James from court singled him out unjustly, for he had done nothing unlawful: '. . . shall the king's brother be in a worse capacity than the meanest subject?' Sir George Downing, Parliament's only Harvard graduate, agreed: 'You begin with punishment, before examination. Do not do that to the king's brother which you would not have done to another.'[34] Lawrence Hyde, brother of James's deceased first wife, raised the topic of separation: 'The two sons of the martyred king, the only surviving sons, now to be torn from one another by such a parliament as this!'[35]

In the end, the debate ended inconclusively, and in fact while it was going on James rendered the discussion moot. At the king's request, he announced to the Lords his intention of withdrawing from public business. It seems likely that Shaftesbury took this more as a sign of weakness than a gracious concession, and he increased the pressure. He had many potential weapons at hand: Oates, Atkins and other prisoners in Newgate, the most important of whom was Edward Colman, who he was squeezing hard for information. And who knew what other informers might emerge in search of the £500 reward offered for information into the plot?

First, however, both houses of Parliament took a break to indulge in an annual ritual made all the more important by Oates's revelations: the anniversary of the discovery of the Gunpowder Plot of 1605. Naturally, this offered a golden opportunity for Catholic bashing, and both houses indulged with relish. Each House heard a sermon – as did virtually every parish in the land – on the subject.

The Lords assembled in Westminster Abbey. Surrounded by the tombs of kings and high-ranking nobles (Buckingham's father, for example, assassinated in 1629, resided in an elaborate tomb near the graves of Elizabeth I and Henry VII), they heard a sermon from Thomas Lamplugh, bishop of Exeter. Lamplugh was not much of a scholar, and he had no great reputation as a preacher – this sermon was the only work he ever published – but he had no trouble generating some two hours' worth of anti-Catholic invective. Papists, he warned, were everywhere and capable of anything: 'They can compile legends, geld authors, stab kings, blow up Parliaments, convert infidels by killing thousands, and sending them up martyrs in fiery chariots into heaven. They can set the Devil on work about God's business.'[36]

The House of Commons jammed itself into the much smaller and less grand church of St Margaret's, a stone's throw from the abbey. Their preacher was John Tillotson, dean of Canterbury and a future archbishop. Tillotson was a popular preacher and was known for his cordial relations with Protestant dissenters, thus making him more generally sympathetic to opposition MPs. And he could abuse Catholics with the best. He took as his text the same verses Lamplugh used, from chapter nine of Luke's Gospel, 'But he turned, and rebuked them, and said Ye know not what manner of spirit ye are of. For the son of man is not come to destroy men's lives, but to save them.' In another two-hour-plus stem-winder, he expanded on the evils of popery. Was the Pope antichrist? He was not sure, 'but however that be, I challenge antichrist himself whoever he be, and whenever he comes, to do worse and wickeder things'.[37] Of the failed Gunpowder Plot he said 'the horrid bloody design of this day [5 November], such a mystery of iniquity, such a masterpiece of villainy, as eye had not seen, nor ear heard, nor ever before entered into the heart of man. So prodigiously barbarous as it is not to be paralleled in all the voluminous records of time from the foundation of the world!'[38] He referred to the current conspiracy, 'A dangerous plot, deeply laid, secretly carried on, and that stumbles at nothing that lies in their way; not at the very life of the king himself, though a prince of so much clemency and mercy.'[39]

Probably millions of Anglicans heard similar messages in England's thousands of parish churches and cathedrals that day, keeping the national terror of popery at a high pitch. But not every parson sang from the same hymnal. Some parishioners heard an interesting sample of the divisions growing beneath the surface of England's anti-popery on 5 November. Not far from Westminster was the city parish of St Sepulchre's, the largest parish church in the City. It stood very near the Old Bailey, where the alleged plotters would be tried, and was a near neighbour to Newgate. In fact, the parish clerk had the ghoulish task of ringing a handbell outside the cell of condemned prisoners the night before their execution. He repeated these lines:

All you that in the condemned hold do lie
Prepare you, for tomorrow you shall die:
Watch all, and pray, the hour is drawing near
That you before the Almighty must appear
Examine well yourselves, in time repent
That you may not to eternal flames be sent
And when St Sepulchre's bell tomorrow tolls
The lord have mercy on your souls
Past twelve o'clock![40]

The preacher at St Sepulchre's on Gunpowder Day was Aaron Baker, an Oxford-educated clergyman. Interestingly, he dedicated the sermon to John Tillotson, a favourite of Shaftesbury and his friends. The dean apparently urged its publication. Unlike Parliament's preachers, Baker took a very different text for his subject: 'And one told David, saying, Achitophel is among the conspirators with Absalom, and David said O Lord, I pray thee, turn the counsel of Achitophel into foolishness' (2 Samuel 15:31). This story involved the rebellion of David's son, Absalom (perhaps a stand-in for the duke of Monmouth?), a rebellion enabled by 'Achitophel, that state Machiavel'.[41] Well before the poet laureate John Dryden brilliantly used the same story in his devastating satire against Shaftesbury, Baker made the same connection, although nowhere does he explicitly mention the earl. He did take time to lambast the 'bloody and murtherous Papists' who 'never bogling at, nor making any conscience of driving on their projects and wicked self ends under the vizard and pretence of religion'.[42] But he targeted others – those who would create political faction: 'As we must shun faction and rebellion, so must we avoid all occasions conducing thereunto, and especially mark those that cause them, that are the chief actors and ringleaders in them.'[43] He denounced the many 'seditious pamphlets and scandalous libels that have of late years stolen out into print, to rob our governors ecclesiastical and civil of their reputation . . . that they may sooner ripen the people for a rebellion . . .'[44] While Baker flailed the Gunpowder Plotters in no uncertain terms, he had virtually nothing to say about the new plot. Rather, he warned against 'others mutinying against their rulers, detracting from the worth of their good deeds, and amplifying and aggravating their bad'.[45] Baker certainly did not reject the plot's reality – almost no one did at this point – but his sermon does reflect a growing concern among some that it might be used to undermine the monarchy. The fault lines dating to the civil war had by no means disappeared.

Improved, if not exhausted, by this annual festival of anti-popery, Parliament resumed its work the next day. In the Commons the opposition, led by Sacheverell, proposed that Colman's letters be published. This would serve to keep the plot in the news, ensuring its continued utility in advancing the opposition's plans. Government supporters opposed the idea, no doubt for this very reason. Secretary of State Sir William Coventry quite correctly pointed out that the letters made no mention of any of Oates's plot: 'Will you print those letters, and nothing in them appear of murdering the king's person? Will you therefore lay a plaster where there is no sore, and leave the sore raw?'[46] But opposition members insisted. Sir John Coventry (a nephew of Shaftesbury's and the Secretary) vehemently pronounced: 'If these letters cannot be printed, let us have a bill to bring in popery . . . I think whoever is against printing has either taken money for his vote, or is popishly affected.'[47] This was ironic given that a number of the proposers, like Sacheverell, were on the French payroll. The squabble about Colman's letters went unresolved.

And now a new informer emerged. This was William Bedloe, who on 30 October had written to the secretaries of state from Bristol, claiming to have information about the plot. The following day he sent another letter, tantalizing the government with his knowledge. 'By the last post I gave you an account of a great part of this horrid design, that it lay in my hands to discover some of the parties who have no small part in it and some whose power is too great to be concealed any longer.' He was willing to come to London secretly (at the Crown's expense) to reveal what he 'dare not trust to a letter'.[48] Secretary Coventry responded on 2 November, asking Bedloe to come to the capital. Bedloe travelled the hundred-odd miles remarkably quickly – he appeared before the king and Privy Council on Thursday 7 November.[49]

The man in the council chamber was a good-looking person in his late twenties, with an air of sincerity and a voice that carried conviction. He was emphatically not sincere, however, and later it would be clear that virtually every word he said was a lie. In this he had long experience, despite his relative youth. Born in south Wales, he had been raised in Bristol, where he received enough education to pass himself off as a gentleman. By the time he was in his late teens or early twenties, he had left his mother's home and was living by his wits in London. He dabbled in various petty frauds, was jailed for a time and, like Oates, received some support from the London Catholic community. In fact, he and Oates probably knew one another; both served in different noble Catholic households during this period – a very narrow world in which everyone knew everyone else. By 1677, Bedloe had made London too hot to hold him and, accompanied by his brother James, took himself off to the continent.

Bedloe travelled about Europe under a variety of false names – Captain Williams was one, though he preferred to use an aristocratic alias ('Lord Gerard', 'Lord Cornwallis', 'Lord Newport' – what the actual owners of these titles must have thought about this effrontery has unfortunately gone unrecorded). The brothers left a trail of unpaid bills, petty thefts and swindles wherever they went, even indulging in the occasional horse theft. A speciality of the pair was defrauding exiled English Catholic clergy: £175 from a priest in Paris (as 'Cornwallis'); £125 from another in Rouen. Moving on to Spain they finagled £250 from an English merchant in the port of Bilbao. By late 1677 they found themselves arrested and jailed in Valladolid, Spain, where they turned for help to an English expatriate currently 'studying' at the English Jesuit college there: Titus Oates. In a rare display of good nature, probably owing to their prior London connection, Titus came to their aid, providing the brothers with help after they wrangled their release from jail. This assistance Bedloe repaid by stealing £2 10s from his benefactor (Titus was always hard up), and leaving him stuck with a tavern bill. Having worn out his welcome in Spain, Bedloe returned to England and by late October was in Bristol once again.[50]

Word of the plot came to Bristol, and Bedloe, searching for new targets, heard of the £500 reward offered by the king for information regarding Godfrey's death. He boasted to a woman that he would have the reward, promising her a diamond ring if he won it.[51] In this one supposes he was no more sincere than any other promise he made in life. But the prospect of a large sum of money, and who knew what other opportunities, was alluring. After all his old victim Oates was now famous with a royal pension and rooms in Whitehall Palace. Bedloe's letters to the secretaries of state exuded secrecy and skulduggery, but in Bristol before his departure he boasted openly of his information.

This was the man who now appeared before the Privy Council claiming to know details of Godfrey's death. He certainly did not, but Bedloe's London experience gave him some familiarity with the city's Catholic community; he could name names. And while he was not as facile a liar as Oates, his affect was actually rather more credible. Well-spoken and gentleman-like (Oates was neither), on the surface he seemed plausible. No doubt the king (to say nothing of his brother) saw Bedloe as another opportunist, and some on the Council did likewise – Secretary Coventry, for example – but the reaction at court was barely relevant at this point.

In his testimony before the king, Bedloe told of 40,000 Spanish Catholics planning to rendezvous at Santiago de Compostela, disguised as pilgrims. From there they would launch an invasion of England, where a Catholic uprising would overthrow Protestantism. As Bishop Burnet wryly put it, 'This was looked on as very extravagant.'[52] He also said, the king later recalled, nothing significant about Oates's plot. But when he turned to Godfrey's death, he told a detailed story, claiming to have been a witness. Bedloe's testimony had to be passed on to Parliament; if not, the opposition, who already accused ministers of 'stifling' the evidence, would explode.

Bedloe's value to Shaftesbury was immense – here was a witness who could corroborate Oates's story. Until now, the latter's only real support had come from Israel Tonge. As Roger L'Estrange scornfully said of Tonge and Oates, 'Dr. Tonge was hardly ever without a plot in his head, and a pen in his hand. The one (Tonge) bred the maggots, the other (Oates) vented them.'[53] But now in Bedloe there was someone who, unlike Tonge, seemed to have a firm grasp of reality. On Friday 8 November, Bedloe made his debut at the bar of the Lords. This version of his tale varied considerably from what he told the king the day before. He had been converted to Catholicism by the Jesuits, and so knew much of their plots. Four men had murdered Sir Edmund Berry Godfrey at Somerset House, where the queen had a set of lodgings and her personal chapel. Two of the murderers, Charles Walsh and one Father Lefevre, were Jesuits; the other two, unnamed, were laymen, one a servant of Lord Belasyse and the other a servant working in the chapel. They first attempted to smother Godfrey between a pair of pillows, but he revived and so was finished off with a cravat around his throat. Bedloe was not present for the murder, but Lefevre had told him the grisly details. Bedloe's part involved disposing of the body. He was offered the fantastic sum of 2,000 guineas (enough money to live as a gentleman for a decade or more) for his help. Godfrey's corpse was for two days after his death shuffled from room to room in Somerset House, until finally it was removed in a sedan chair on Monday 14 October.

Bedloe said that he did not participate in this, thus missing his big payday – but he learned further details from the murderers afterwards. Lord Belasyse arranged the murder, and the other peers whom Oates had already accused were also involved.

Whether Bedloe had colluded with Oates or Shaftesbury is unknown; the king certainly thought so. He told Burnet that none of the charges Bedloe laid against Lord Belasyse, for example, had figured in his testimony before the Privy Council. Charles believed that overnight Bedloe had colluded with someone to align his story with Oates's. This was quite likely. But when asked directly if he knew Titus, Bedloe said that he did not – one more lie among all the rest. He asked for permission to withdraw from the House and for time to write out his story at greater length. This he was allowed to do. The privilege would be fatal for a number of innocent members of London's Catholic community.

The excitement generated by Bedloe's information gave further impetus to the opposition's campaign against Catholics, especially the most prominent Catholic in the kingdom: James, duke of York. Shaftesbury's motion to remove James from his brother's presence had failed, but the duke's voluntary withdrawal on Monday suggested that further pressure might force Charles to change his mind. He had, after all, yielded to parliamentary pressure before. Two weeks earlier the Commons had almost passed a new Test Bill, requiring all members of the House of Lords to swear oaths denouncing popery. This bill would deprive Catholic peers of their seats, and of course that included James. Many peers had misgivings about denying nobles what most believed to be their birthright, but Bedloe's charges added even more urgency to the case. The king realized that something must be done to slow the momentum building against his brother.

Saturday morning, 9 November, with the duke of York sitting at his side, Charles summoned both houses before him. He spoke for about two minutes. First complimenting both houses for the 'extraordinary care' they had taken for his safety, he then assured them 'I am as ready to join with you in all the ways and means that may establish a firm security of the Protestant religion as your hearts could wish.' Coming to the central point, he said 'whatsoever reasonable bills you shall present to make you safe in the reign of any successor . . . shall find from me a ready concurrence'. The possibility of limitations placed on a Catholic successor (obviously James) was a bold concession, designed to blunt the force of Shaftesbury's assault on the duke. But Charles qualified his offer – he would not allow any bill that tampered with James's right to the Crown. 'So as they tend not

to impeach the right of succession, nor the descent of the crown in the true line
...'[54] When he had finished, Charles left the chamber, followed by the
Commoners. Both houses then offered motions thanking the king for his speech,
and asked him to allow its publication.

Back in their own chamber, the Commons debated Charles's speech. Few
would have been surprised that the first member on his feet was William Sacheverell,
who had a few days before hinted that Parliament could alter the succession.
Charles's offer was hardly satisfactory: 'I desire to know whether the conditions in
the King's speech are not to tie our hands so fast, that we can do nothing for the
King's safety, or the Protestant religion.' He was, in fact, not a little contemptuous
of the royal offer: 'I am one of those of opinion not to accept of a rattle, to keep us
quiet.'[55] Courtiers gamely played up Charles's sincerity (never an easy task where
he was concerned): 'The King's heart was never more open than in this business,'
said Secretary Williamson. Opposition MPs succeeded in watering down the
House's thanks to the king, not mentioning his proffered concessions, but blandly
thanking Charles 'for the gracious expressions in his speech'.[56] They then turned to
the pursuit of random Catholics in London, including one M. Tortereaux, 'very
aged and infirm', formerly carver at Queen Henrietta Maria's table, who as one MP
said 'has not brains enough to be a plotter'. But anti-popery demanded its victims
regardless of their capacity. 'I see these people have advocates,' sneered Sir Nicholas
Carew; Colonel Birch asked 'is this a time to excuse papists, and talk of Carvers to
the Queen Mother? Let him take the oaths or go to jail.'

While MPs elaborated ways to persecute elderly recusants, William Bedloe
polished his story. On 10 November he came to the bar of the Commons in an
unusual Sunday sitting and read his newest account, adding a variety of details
left out earlier – such as a Catholic scheme to attack the important Yorkshire
port of Hull. The next day he returned to the Lords where he offered still more
details, followed by a closed session with Shaftesbury's committee. An awkward
moment came when one of those he accused in Godfrey's death, Thomas
Plessington, a servant of Lord Belasyse, appeared, and Bedloe admitted he had
never seen him before.[57]

But this embarrassment did nothing to shake his credibility for Shaftesbury
and his committee. They did their best to bolster their current star witness. The
following day Lord Winchester reported from the committee to his fellow peers,
taking special care to praise Bedloe's trustworthiness. The committee 'did conjure
William Bedloe to speak nothing but truth. And he did, in the presence of God,

as he should answer for it at the day of Judgment ... And the lords are of opinion that he hath been very exact in his testimony, in not accusing any one further than he had perfect memory of, and of what he knows of his knowledge, or from the mouths of others.'[58] There followed Bedloe's most elaborate account yet. In general terms the story was much the same; he had been offered the vast sum of £4,000 to assist in Godfrey's murder. Even though he avoided the actual murder, the ringleader, Father Lefevre, inexplicably offered Bedloe another huge reward – £2,000 – to help move the body. In the course of this testimony, no doubt with the encouragement of Shaftesbury, he incriminated Samuel Atkins, who he said was one of those charged with moving Godfrey's corpse. Confronted by Atkins, Bedloe hedged, 'He is in all things very like the person he saw in the room with Sir Edmundbury Godfrey's dead body, and he doth verily believe it was him that owned himself to be Mr. Pepys's clerk ... he cannot positively swear to it, but he doth verily believe him to be that man.'[59] William Bedloe's 'perfect memory', then, was perhaps not quite so perfect after all.

Bedloe did his best to promote Lord Belasyse – in whose household he might have served – as the lay leader of the plot. But he cast a broad net: 'There was not a Roman Catholic in England, of any quality or credit, but was acquainted with this design of the papists, and had received the Sacrament from their father confessors, to be secret and assistant in the carrying of it on.' Finally, in an extravagant instance of lily-gilding, he claimed that a French army was poised to seize the Channel islands of Jersey and Guernsey.[60]

Lord Winchester also read several depositions relating to Bedloe's information, one of which was about Pepys's clerk Atkins. Among these, though, were two more, one from Henry Berry (a porter at Somerset House, soon himself to be a victim of the informers) and another from an officer in the king's foot guards, Captain Hawley. Neither man had anything to say about Godfrey's death – but they were told on the weekend of the magistrate's disappearance to admit no one to Somerset House 'for that the Queen desired to be private'.[61] Neither of these depositions were particularly useful as props for Bedloe's story. But they do suggest that Shaftesbury was laying the groundwork for an escalation of his attack.

FIVE

KNAVISH TRICKS: ATTACKING QUEEN CATHERINE, THE TEST ACT AND THE FALL OF LORD DANBY
NOVEMBER–DECEMBER 1678

The day after Bedloe's performance in the Lords and the planting of a seed of doubt about the queen, Catherine of Braganza, Titus Oates requested an audience with King Charles. The king saw him, accompanied by both secretaries of state, Williamson and Coventry. Oates clearly intended to continue operations against the queen, but he proceeded gingerly, confining himself to general information about her connections with London's Jesuits. He said that while he had never seen a letter from the queen to any individual Jesuit, he had read letters from them to her. These letters expressed the Order's gratitude for money donated for the English mission's support. He specifically mentioned a £4,000 gift, and he named two Jesuits frequently in the queen's company, De Abuceda and Emmanuel, 'He thinks, does not swear it.' As ever, Oates embellished his account with specific-sounding detail – in return for her £4,000, Catherine received '500 masses, 650 pair of beads (rosaries), 1,150 mortifications'.[1] He was not clear about exactly what a 'mortification' was, but clearly it involved some sort of popish superstition. Titus was carefully vague – he did not say that Catherine's gift to the Order was connected in any way to the plot, and he also avoided connecting De Abuceda and Emmanuel to the conspiracy, 'he dare not say they have any [part in] the plot'.[2]

It seems likely that Charles knew exactly what this trial balloon foretold. If not, the House of Commons provided further clarification the next day, 14 November. MPs demanded that all of Queen Catherine's Catholic servants be dismissed, excepting only those specifically covered in her marriage treaty. Courtiers pointed out that only a handful of Catholics served at Whitehall. Sir William Coventry, MP for Great Yarmouth, said 'Are not seventeen, or twelve, enough to do a mischief that seventeen hundred years cannot repair? They that have the keys of the king's lodgings, and access to his person, by their attendance, are they not enough to let in more?'[3] The House then passed an address to

Charles – its second – asking that all of Catherine's servants take the oaths of allegiance and supremacy. Next came William Bedloe. At the bar, he added a couple of details about the plan to attack the Channel Islands, and further incriminated Lord Belasyse and his confessor, Father Conyers. But the real point of Bedloe's appearance lay in his demand for a broader royal pardon than the one he had. The king had already pardoned him for any crimes connected to Godfrey's death, but Bedloe said 'I confess that I have been a great rogue to the king, and my country, and that if I had not been so I could not have revealed what I have done.'[4] The first half of this statement was perhaps the only truthful thing he had said since his arrival in London. The crucial statement followed: 'I will not bring more matter to endanger myself, till I have the king's pardon, because I have something to say against a great person near the king, and great things.'[5]

A 'great person near the king' was obviously the queen. The hints offered over the previous few days – the depositions and Oates's statements to Charles – pointed in that direction. Now Bedloe's cryptic remark further heightened suspicion. Who was behind this intrigue? It is not hard to detect the subtle hand of the earl of Shaftesbury. He had advocated a royal divorce more than once; dragging the queen into the plot was another way to accomplish the same end.[6] In fact, the queen's fate was of little interest to Shaftesbury – like his attempts to embroil Samuel Pepys and his clerk in the plot, the true target was always James, duke of York. Getting rid of Catherine opened the prospect of Charles's remarriage and his fathering a legal heir. This scheme represented a new avenue towards the same destination.

On Monday 18 November, Bedloe renewed the attack, demanding a fuller pardon before he would reveal further information about his mysterious 'great person'. Then he went on to accuse a variety of other Catholics, including Lord Brudenell, heir to the earl of Cardigan, and Lord Carrington. Carrington's sister was a Catholic nun in France, a brother was a Jesuit, and he himself had donated generously to a variety of Catholic causes.[7] Inexplicably Oates had left him out of his tales, but he was clearly a ripe target for Bedloe. Carrington had supposedly offered £5,000 and a body of troops to support the Catholic uprising; Brudenell likewise promised to support the rebellion. Both men soon found themselves jailed. MPs then debated ways to secure those whom Bedloe accused, and out of this came a suggestion most alarming to the Court. Papists, Mr Sacheverell said, should have their horses confiscated to prevent flight. Sir Eliab Harvey, one of Sacheverell's reliable allies (and also a recipient of French bribes), put in that the Catholics 'generally now have extraordinary horses, four or five more than ordinary'.[8] From seizing horses the discussion turned to searches for arms, and then Sir Gilbert Gerard, MP for Northallerton, broadened the discussion: 'The king is in greater danger than ever; the Papists are universally in the plot [after all "Captain" Bedloe has just said so]. This is not the way, to take their horses from them; they are all gone – I move that an address be made to the king that he command at least half of the militia of England to be in readiness, till we are in some measure secure from the papists.'[9] Thomas Bennett, Shaftesbury's loyal servant, then suggested raising the militia and disbanding Charles's regular troops. Finally, opposition MPs argued for a bill that would put one-third of England's militia in the field to guard against a Catholic uprising. This proposal could only have been received in Whitehall with the gravest concern. Civil war had broken out in England in 1642 after Parliament seized control of the militia by passing an ordinance. Here was the opposition – not government ministers – advocating something that looked very similar.

No sooner had this dangerous suggestion been made than Sacheverell rose and launched an attack on one of the Crown's most important servants in the Commons, Sir Joseph Williamson. Sir Joseph had joined the king's service as an undersecretary in the summer of 1660 and by 1674 he had become a knight, privy councillor and Secretary of State. He was an exceptionally important royal servant – his administrative efficiency was considerable and he was especially good at providing intelligence and information to the ministry. The king relied upon him to get the Crown's business done in the Commons. Ponderous and not a little officious, his parliamentary talent was for organization rather than forensics. One of Williamson's useful traits was delivering speeches so dull that he could empty the chamber within minutes. This was a valuable skill, making it easier to get the government's policies through a thinly attended House.[10]

But now the secretary's debating skills would be put to the test. Sacheverell waved a document and proclaimed 'I have a letter in my hand, that gives an account of several popish officers that have received commissions since the house sat down, and several commissions were signed by a member of this house, a secretary of state! . . . If this be true, all you can do for your safety is to no purpose – sixty commissions to popish officers have been signed since the 20th of October!'[11] Sacheverell could not have hit upon a better way to undermine trust in the king's regular forces – and to add pressure for the mobilization of the reliably Protestant militia. And there was the added benefit of ruining one of the king's most effective servants.

Williamson defended himself as best he could. The king had commissioned the officers in question (the king signed the commissions of every officer in the army), and he had countersigned them as he was bound to do. The duke of Monmouth, currently being groomed by Shaftesbury as James's replacement as heir to the throne, had himself recommended these officers. But Williamson had to admit that he had indeed signed the infamous documents, and further that he had dispensed with the requirement that the officers swear the oaths of supremacy and allegiance. Most recognized the king's power to dispense individuals from statutes in some situations, but for the hapless Williamson this was the wrong occasion on which to have done so. MPs flailed him: Sir Francis Drake said, 'It appears plainly, that the secretary . . . has given out warrants, contrary to law . . . and in this time of danger, when the king's life is concerned – I would have him withdraw, that you may consider what to do with him!' Gilbert Gerard, who began the mischief about the militia earlier in the day, followed with 'I am sorry . . . that I must see a minister of state, who should be a bulwark against popery, sign commissions and dispensations to popish officers. If you allow that the king can do no wrong, there is an end of the government; it is the ministers that do the wrong – you can do no less than send Williamson to the Tower – and that is my motion!'[12] Williamson's defence was feeble at best, and he got very little assistance from his fellow ministers. Secretary Coventry and Sir John Ernly, the Chancellor of the Exchequer, both mitigated Williamson's offence by claiming that the press of business at court ensured that not every document presented to a secretary could be inspected closely. Sir Christopher Musgrave, one of the ministry's allies, agreed that Williamson might not have realized what he had signed, and moreover had not originated the appointments. This rally died after another member commented, 'If Williamson signed what he knew, he was a knave, if he signed what he knew not, he was a fool.'[13] The secretary soon left Westminster under guard, headed for the Tower.

The secretary's imprisonment ended within hours; King Charles ordered his immediate release, and he summoned the Commons to the Banqueting House the next day. There he sharply reproved the House for its action, and explained why he had commissioned the Catholic officers. Afterwards the Commons voted to address the king, asking him to keep Williamson jailed. Some of the louder opponents of government wanted him impeached, a procedure that might end in capital punishment.[14] Charles ignored the address, and there was no impeachment. Yet the opposition succeeded in removing an effective minister from Parliament. After his release Williamson avoided the House, and a few months later resigned as Secretary of State. The loss of Sir Joseph's services was quite significant; the king's right to name his own servants without reference to Parliament was a fundamental royal prerogative, and forcing Williamson's resignation undermined Charles's authority.

As the opposition pursued the plot and strove to undermine the ministry, work continued on Shaftesbury's other anti-York vehicle, the Test Bill, which would deny Catholic peers their seats in the Lords. The Commons passed the bill within a week of the session's opening, but the Lords had been working on it very slowly. Many peers believed that their seats in the House were a part of their patrimony. Depriving any noble lord of his seat in the House, even a Catholic, seemed an affront to honour and property – a step many hesitated to take. The Commons were increasingly exasperated by what they saw as foot-dragging in the upper House, and they sent message after message urging its passage. On 20 November the bill at last passed the upper House. But the Lords added a crucial amendment to the Commons bill: an exemption for James, duke of York. This had come only after the duke had made a personal plea. As Bishop Burnet, an eyewitness, reported it, 'He spoke on that occasion with great earnestness, and with tears in his eyes. He said he was now to cast himself upon their favour in the greatest concern he could have in this world. He spoke much of his duty to the king, and of his zeal for the nation, and solemnly protested that whatever his religion might be, it should only be a private thing between God and his own soul, and that no effect of it should ever appear in the government. The proviso was carried for him by a few voices.'[15]

Before sending the bill down to the Commons for final passage, James and six other peers, all Catholics, entered a solemn protest against it. Action now shifted to the lower House, where the opposition did everything in its power to reject James's proviso. MPs debated the amended bill long and passionately, beginning with those supporting his exemption. Secretary Coventry led the way, arguing that rejecting the proviso would in effect force James into exile. 'You have the greatest matter before you that ever was in this house ... The danger of disturbance of religion is one of the most pernicious apprehensions imaginable. If this prince should go into another place, it must cost you a standing army to bring him home again.' Sir Allen Apsley argued that depriving James of his seat was rank ingratitude for 'the Duke's valor and exposing himself for the honour of the nation'. Sir William Killegrew broke down and wept over the prospect of separating the royal bothers. Several argued that James would be driven to desperation if the exemption failed, others that excluding him from the king's presence was both unjust and impractical. Sir John Birkenhead said, 'To make a law that the king shall not go to his brother, I understand it not . . . Do you think that the king will give his consent to this bill, to restrain himself thus? Cannot the king go to see Mr. Colman [now awaiting trial for treason] if he will? And not go to see his brother! You here will make a law, that the duke shall be removed from the king's presence. Whither shall he go? Into the country? Or will you force him beyond sea? . . . Drive him into French hands . . . For God's sake, pass this proviso!'[16]

Opponents of the proviso remained silent through this intense display of loyalty to the duke, and a number of members shouted for the question to be called. Some opponents might have wanted to avoid a public declaration of their anti-Yorkist views. But William Sacheverell knew that he, at any rate, had no friends at court. The first opponent of the proviso to speak, he offered a thoroughly disingenuous argument: 'I wonder, why, when the preservation of the king's person is the case, the duke should be excepted. I would gladly know how these gentlemen know that the duke is a recusant, and will not take the oaths nor the test?' Of course no one in the room had any doubt but that James was indeed a recusant, and if the proviso were rejected he would lose his parliamentary seat as well as his place in the king's counsel.[17]

Sir Thomas Meres joined Sacheverell, 'On the one side, the reason against the proviso is prudence and safety. On the other, civility, gratitude, and compliment. I would be on the civil side, were not the safety of the nation concerned. No doubt but that Sir Edmundbury Godfrey was civil to go to Somerset House, and he was civil to Mr Colman to compare notes with him. But he lost his life by it.' Sir Philip Warwick hinted at excluding James from the succession: 'I would rather consider that a popish successor may not be, but a Protestant of our own religion.' Passions rose as the debate continued. Raucous cries for calling the question competed with shouts of 'Colman's letters!' from the duke's opponents. Sir Thomas Lee raised the spectacle of gentlemen losing their former monastic lands in a Catholic England, and worse, the proviso would 'pile up faggots to fire Protestants and we will need nothing but setting them on fire . . . is not this proviso enough to raise all the people in rebellion?'[18]

It was at last time to call the question, and this revealed the extent of the divisions emerging in Parliament – and the kingdom as well. Parliamentary procedure revolved around a presumption of consensus. It was crucial to avoid, whenever possible, conflict. Very often decisions were made '*nem con*', that is, unanimously. This was the ideal, for it meant that there were no losers. To lose an important vote was not simply a matter of policy – it was in fact a matter of honour. The loser felt disrespected, and that was a slur on a gentleman's honour. Honour was priceless, and a gentleman's first duty was to defend it. The swords that gentlemen carried everywhere they went were not articles of fashion; they were the final guarantor of a man's honour. House rules requiring members to hang their swords up before entering the chamber were not symbolic. They were necessary to ensure that violence remained out of doors.

When unanimity could not be achieved, the Speaker's duty was to call for a voice vote, and he decided which side won: decision by decibels. Voice votes were a way to defuse some of the potential consequences of losing – individuals did not need to identify themselves with one side or the other; their individual decision was lost in the general shout. But sometimes – quite rarely – the voice vote was inconclusive. Then the House must divide – members crowded out of the chamber and then returned, the 'aye's to the left, the 'no's to the right. They were counted as they filed back in by tellers – usually two MPs on each side. A division forced members to identify themselves and could easily lead to open conflict.[19]

This is precisely what happened in the House of Commons on 21 November. The question of whether to accept the Lords exemption could only be resolved by a division – the first of this parliamentary session, evidence of their rarity. Not surprisingly the House was quite full, with over 300 members packed into an inadequate space. MPs shuffled slowly out of the chamber, jostling one another as they made their way into the lobby, and after the long debate tensions were high. Sir Jonathan Trelawney, a strong supporter of the duke (in fact one of the two tellers for the 'aye' side), ended up near a strong opponent of the proviso, John Ash. Trelawney was the picture of the royalist Anglican – his family had sacrificed a great deal for Charles I and he had no fondness for dissenters. Ash, on the other hand, came from a Presbyterian family that had sided with Parliament during the civil wars. Bringing these two men so close together at this moment certainly risked an explosion. In due course, the fireworks began. An opposition MP, Colonel Birch, provided the catalyst, commenting that if the duke's exemption passed, full religious toleration might just as well be introduced. Trelawney replied, 'No I never was for that', and Ash said, 'I am not for popery', insinuating that Sir Jonathan was. 'Nor I for Presbytery,' Trelawney replied.

Further insults flew, 'Rebel!' shouted Trelawney. 'Rascal!' responded Ash. Finally, Trelawney swung, striking Ash a hefty blow to the head. Other MPs intervened and separated the men, ending the brawl. Had this occurred outside Parliament, in all likelihood swords would have been drawn and serious injury or death the result. As it was, the fight demonstrated the wisdom of making divisions as rare as possible.[20]

This drama concluded, the voting resumed. Trelawney, joined by Lawrence Hyde, brother of James's deceased first wife, counted for the 'aye's. Sacheverell and Thomas Bennett, Shaftesbury's loyal client, for the 'no's. The result: 158 'aye's and 156 'no's.[21] It was the narrowest of victories, but nevertheless a decisive defeat for Shaftesbury. Only one of the Catholics who sat in the Lords was his real target: James, duke of York. The others were few in number and had little influence; some rarely attended the House at all. In the rabidly anti-papist atmosphere, even conscientious Catholic peers were safer at home. And of course half a dozen were imprisoned in the Tower of London. Shaftesbury had failed to destroy the duke this way, but he had other methods in mind.

Shaftesbury now turned up the heat on Queen Catherine. A hint of what would come might be seen in a confrontation in the Privy Garden at Whitehall on Friday 22 November. A favourite place for courtiers to take the air, with well-kept walks, statuary and fruit trees, it was private and only steps away from the Council chamber. Walking there that day Lord Treasurer Danby encountered Titus Oates, the king's unwelcome lodger. Since he had taken up residence in the palace, Oates frequently sauntered throughout it, alternately bragging to and bullying those he passed. On this occasion Danby had had too much of the insufferable scourge of popery and lost his temper, saying that he hoped Oates 'would be hanged within a month'.[22] Oates's willingness to confront Danby in the palace suggests that he was preparing to burn his bridges with the Court.

This he did, in spectacular fashion, two days later. Titus requested an audience with King Charles on Sunday 24 November. There, with Secretaries Coventry and Williamson present along with the king, Oates accused Queen Catherine of involvement in the assassination plot. The previous July, he claimed, he had seen letters to and from Sir George Wakeman, Catherine's Catholic doctor, implicating her. Furthermore, he said, he had been present at a 'consult' between Catherine and several others, among whom were two Jesuits, where she agreed to Charles's murder by poison. Charles, whose opinion of Oates and his story had never been high, was infuriated at this attempt to drag his wife into the plot. He ordered

Oates to be placed under guard, denied access to any visitors and ordered that his papers be seized. All of this reflected the king's growing conviction that Oates was coordinating his acts with Shaftesbury and the opposition. Isolating Oates would prevent further collusion, and his papers might reveal evidence supporting Charles's theory.

Replacing the queen was not a new idea, but this gambit threatened to remove Catherine not just from court, but from the living world. Henry VIII had executed two wives who fell afoul of faction, and there was no reason to think that a third royal queen might not follow the same path. Certainly Shaftesbury would have no compunction about sacrificing Queen Catherine if it would allow Charles to remarry and father a legitimate heir. The diarist John Evelyn thought that Oates acted 'to gratifie some, who would have been glad His majestie should have married a more frutifull lady'.[23] King Charles had different ideas. 'They think I have a mind to a new wife, but for all that, I will not see an innocent woman abused.'[24] He also told Bishop Burnet that Catherine 'was a weak woman, and had some disagreeable humors, but was not capable of a wicked thing, and considering his faultiness towards her in other things, he thought it a horrid thing to abandon her'.[25]

Catherine of Braganza had already been abused, by her faithless husband, whose affairs he flaunted before her, completely unconcerned about her feelings. Yet the royal couple had come to a satisfactory arrangement. The queen knew that she could not compete with her husband's favourite mistresses – she was short, had a prominent overbite and, as Pepys wrote when he met her for the first time, 'she be not very charming'.[26] Unfortunately, she also proved unable to provide an heir. She conceived two, or possibly three times, but none of her pregnancies went to term. The last was in 1669, nearly a decade earlier, when she miscarried after being frightened by one of the king's pets – a fox that apparently leapt on her and ran across her face.

But Charles bore with the disappointment of a childless marriage (after all there were plenty of other children, by his mistresses, upon whom he could dote). Catherine, in turn, reconciled herself to Charles's infidelities. Despite his affairs, he was kind to his wife, allowed her to live more or less as she pleased, and by 1678 the couple had a companionable, if not uxorious, relationship. It was strong enough to survive the attack orchestrated by Shaftesbury. But the earl pressed forward; he never abandoned the belief that Charles II was at heart too weak to resist pressure, if it was great enough. In any case, even if the king refused to divorce and remarry, there was always the possibility of a treason charge.

Now that Oates had lobbed his bombshell, what would happen? The king called an emergency meeting of the Privy Council. At 6 p.m. the next day, Monday 25 November, the Council gathered to hear Oates's story. The councillors carefully examined Oates over the course of two days, meeting all day on the Tuesday. On oath (not that this ever meant anything to him), Titus repeated his charges of the day before, and answered the obviously sceptical questions of the Lords. According to Williamson's notes, Oates was asked when and where he had seen the queen, though his answers were vague. He said he had seen a letter from Sir George Wakeman to a Jesuit named Thimbleby. Along with advice concerning Thimbleby's bad digestion – the doctor recommended mineral water – Wakeman casually threw in that he had agreed, at the queen's urging, to poison Charles. Late last July, 'not on a Sunday, but some other day of solemnity', he had been summoned to Somerset House 'by a messenger, one Sir Robert or Sir Richard, a person of ordinary stature, a nimble man, about 44 or 45', but who he could not otherwise identify. Arriving with unnamed Jesuits, Oates overheard the queen agreeing to Charles's murder – though he said he was in an outer room, and not present first-hand. Oates said that he was joined in the outer room by three or four Jesuits. Despite all the ears present, Oates claimed that he was the only person who heard anything said in the other room, 'being curious'.

Councillors asked Oates why he had waited so long to charge the queen? Moreover, had he not only recently said that he had named every 'great person' connected with the plot? His answer to this very good question was particularly lame: 'by persons of quality, he understood members of the House of Lords'. The queen was not a member of the Lords, and therefore, by this standard not a 'great person'. Asked if he knew William Bedloe – some councillors suspected that the two informers compared notes – elicited another weak response: 'It's like he may have seen him, but did not know him by that name. If he did see him, he went by the name of Wilkins. If he ever saw him it was in Spain.'[27] The Privy Council clearly found this new information not credible – but for Oates, this was not important. King Charles and his courtiers did not believe him. No matter. There were plenty who would.

It probably came as no surprise to Charles that William Bedloe wasted no time climbing aboard Oates's newest bandwagon. On Wednesday 27 November, having spent the morning perjuring himself in Edward Colman's trial, Bedloe vented more lies, directed at the queen, in the evening. Before the king and Council he swore that on May 11 he had attended a 'consultation' at Somerset House. Present were Lord Belasyse, Lord Powis, Colman and several priests, as well as the queen. Afterwards, Colman told Bedloe, 'They made the Queen weep with the proposition of taking off the king, but at last she consented to it.'[28] As he spoke, Shaftesbury's committee was preparing for the next day's drama in Westminster.

Action began in the Commons. Captain Bedloe arrived at the bar. Ushers locked the doors of the House to keep unwanted listeners out, and Bedloe rehearsed his new story. He told of the Somerset House meeting, adding that among those attending were two men, 'who, by the respect that was given them, I believe were persons of quality'.[29] He then told of being sent to Douai with a message about the state of the conspiracy. 'Father Stapleton opened the letter, and by it understood that all went well in England, and that at last they had brought the Queen to consent.' Finally, at the end of his testimony, Bedloe outdid even Oates in his audacity: 'Only I have this more to say of the persons of quality that had their backs towards me; they were the duke of York and the duke of Norfolk.'[30] Ordered to put his testimony in writing, he then withdrew, returning shortly with a document that the Speaker read to the House, 'and Bedloe owned every word of it to be true as the gospel'.[31]

Oates took Bedloe's place at the bar. He loudly complained about his situation at Whitehall: 'I have an unjust restraint upon me, and my papers have been taken from me . . . I cannot speak with my friends . . . my pockets have been picked, and I will charge that man that did it with felony.' Opposition MPs believed 'some great persons' intended to suppress Oates's testimony. Mr Williams, one of several voluble Welshmen of that name, said 'Pen ink and paper to be forbidden a man is an extraordinary restraint! What! Is it to prevent discovery of the plot? If this be true, it must be from great men, it may be too big for him.' In what must have been music to Titus's ears, Sir Thomas Clarges suggested a large reward: 'I would have £200,000 given him . . . He cannot be too well rewarded. I would have you address the king for his liberty, and an honorable maintenance for him.'[32] Oates aroused the sympathy of the House – or at least that of opposition MPs. Sir Thomas Meres said with unconscious irony, 'After both king and kingdom have had so great a deliverance by Mr. Oates's discovery, that he should be used like a rogue for it, at the Lords' bar!'[33]

Back at the bar, Oates resumed his complaint. 'My servants were sent away, and the Yeomen of the Guard were smoking tobacco in my chamber. My own friends were denied access to me, and forbid to speak to me, unless in the presence of one of the clerks of the council.' Finally, he used his supposed knowledge of the plot as leverage: 'Till I have my liberty, if I suffer ten thousand deaths, I will not open my mouth and farther of what I know.'[34] He withdrew again. Sir John Ernly spoke up for the Court: 'What restraint Mr. Oates had, was in order to his safety, for his person and papers.' It is unlikely that even Ernly believed this; certainly Colonel Titus did not. 'We are told that this restraint is for Mr Oates's safety, for his father must not speak with him. I know not the meaning of that, unless they apprehend danger that his father should cut his throat. Deprived of his pen! That is but an ill instrument to make himself away with. I know not what disease Oates has to be cured of, by smoking him with tobacco.'[35]

Speaker Seymour asked Oates 'what method will you propose, yourself, if you be discharged of your guards, and go from Whitehall, for your security for giving evidence, and of your person?' Oates feared for his life at Whitehall, 'I am in some danger of being poisoned, as I was before of being stabbed. My treason [his failure until now to accuse the queen] is not so great, as in the person that I now discover.' Knowing that his bridges to the Court were well and truly burned, Oates wanted out of the palace. 'I desire I may provide my own lodgings, near the House . . . My fortune would be better if I should not discover any further, but I will endeavor to save three kingdoms.'[36]

His appeal made, Oates again left the chamber, whereupon the House resolved to address the king for his release and the provision of a weekly allowance. Additionally, they wanted Oates's pardon extended to cover his misprison of treason. Now that Titus had the formal backing of the Commons, he could expand his attack on Queen Catherine. Returning to the chamber once again, Titus spoke, 'I do accuse the Queen for conspiring the death of the king, and contriving how to compass it.'[37] The story he told differed from his testimony before the Privy Council – he made Queen Catherine look worse. He first became aware of Catherine's role in the conspiracy, he said, when he saw a letter from Sir George Wakeman to a Jesuit named Richard Thimbleby the previous May. In this letter Wakeman wrote that the queen had enlisted him to poison Charles. Later, in July, at Somerset House, Oates said 'I heard the Queen then say She would no longer endure the affronts she had received, but would revenge the violation of her bed.'[38] After saying that he would recognize the room where the meeting occurred if he saw it, Oates finished.

Debate followed, in which some opposition MPs favoured an immediate impeachment – that is, a treason charge – against the queen. But the sense of the House rested with Colonel Birch, who said 'I do not think we are ready yet for impeaching the Queen . . .' although that qualifying 'yet' was ominous. What he proposed instead was that the queen and every other Catholic, whether high-ranking courtier or menial servant, be removed from Whitehall. The House composed an address and sent it to the Lords for their concurrence: '. . . having received informations, by several witnesses, of a most desperate and traitorous design and conspiracy against the life of your most sacred Majesty, wherein, to our great astonishment, the Queen is particularly charged and accused . . .' Parliament did 'most humbly beseech your majesty, that the Queen, and all her family, and all papists, and reputed or suspected papists, be forthwith removed from your majesty's court'.[39] In the Lords this address received a cool reception – though ironically it did generate heat. Arguing against it, the earl of Clarendon (another of the first duchess of York's brothers) provoked the marquis of Winchester, one of Shaftesbury's chief lieutenants, to proclaim 'He lies! He lies!' One of James's friends commented, 'if he had the lie given him he would stab him as gave it'.[40] Lord Chancellor Finch, presiding over the debate, rebuked Winchester and the House ordered both peers to reconcile. The marquis apologized, though bad feeling remained. The Chancellor's intervention might have forestalled a duel. Perhaps hoping to reduce tension in the House, Finch put further debate of the address off until the next day.

The chance to sleep on their differences made little difference, judging from the atmosphere in Parliament when it assembled on Friday 29 November. Both Oates and Bedloe appeared before the Lords, ready for a reprise of the previous day's performance in the Commons. With both King Charles and his brother looking on, they rehearsed their stories. Oates, as the senior rogue, began with another declamation about his house arrest at Whitehall. He 'prayed that the restraint might be taken off, that he might be enabled to give his evidence more cheerfully'.[41] Oates repeated yesterday's story, though this time peers peppered him with sharp questions – did he recognize Dr Wakeman's handwriting? No, he said, but the Jesuit Thimbleby told him the letter he saw was Sir George's. Why had he not accused Catherine in earlier testimony before the Lords? 'It was because the Queen was the wife of the king's bosom, and he had not then acquainted the king with it, and therefore thought not fit to mention it before a public council.'[42] His story remained much as it had been the previous day, though this time he named the Jesuits who had attended the Somerset House meeting: William Harcourt, John Keynes, Basil Longworth and John Fenwick. He attributed the same words to Catherine about her marital humiliations, but added another motive for Charles's murder from her mouth, to 'assist in propagating the Catholic religion'.[43] He repeated some of his earlier inventions – the hundreds of rosaries, masses and 'mortifications' he had mentioned two weeks earlier, for example.

The Lords were a tougher audience than the Commons, and some shook Oates with their questions. Asked again about why he said nothing about Catherine's involvement in the plot between July and November, the best Oates could come up with was because 'the Queen was not to act till all other practices [ambushes in the park, silver bullet sniping, etc.] failed, and that then she was to have further notice'.[44] Another peer asked him why he had said nothing about Wakeman's involvement in his first examination before the Privy Council – a neglect that allowed the sinister doctor to remain at liberty, presumably a danger to the king, for weeks. One might wonder how many lords found Oates's answer credible; he '. . . had attended the council so long, that he was ready to faint, and that the weakness of his body so confounded his memory, that he forgot to mention that letter'.[45] Bishop Burnet, listening, thought Oates's performance less than convincing: this 'took off much from Oates's credit'.[46] It did not help when, in the company of the earls of Ossory and Bridgewater, Oates failed to identify the room at Somerset House in which Catherine had supposedly met the Jesuits.

Although some in the audience panned Oates's performance, Bedloe had yet to take the stage. He was next. Repeating his earlier story, Bedloe focused on the alleged meeting at Somerset House in the spring of 1678. He accused the same men, and swore that he had seen the queen there. This time, however, the dukes of York and Norfolk became 'two other persons of quality, but [he] did not see their faces'.[47] Asked whether he knew Oates, he sang from the same hymnal as Titus: their paths had crossed briefly in Spain. He admitted that the previous year he had been jailed in the Marshalsea prison 'for his brother's debts' (not likely), and that London Jesuits had charitably maintained him. Bedloe finished by declaring that he knew of no others involved in the plot but those he had already accused. He seems to have held up rather better than Oates under this interrogation, though in the end a majority of the lords remained unpersuaded.

After their informants had left the chamber, the Commons address for the queen's banishment came to the floor, 'and, after a long debate' the Chancellor put the question: 'Whether to agree with the House of Commons in this address?' Their lordships overwhelmingly answered 'no'. Only eleven (of 88 present) voted for the motion and just three peers entered a formal dissent: Shaftesbury, the earl of Clare and lord Paget.[48] Clare was one of Shaftesbury's 'thrice worthy' stalwarts, raised in a Presbyterian family, while Paget was a political novice, having entered the House only a week before. The fact that there were so few dissenters, and that apart from Shaftesbury they had little political clout, suggests that support for the queen in the upper House was significant.

The next morning King Charles, crowned and in his ermine-trimmed robes, mounted his throne in the House of Lords. Before him the peers, also bedecked in ermine and scarlet, and as many MPs as would fit in the chamber, waited. The business awaiting the king consisted of two bills that Parliament had passed in the previous few days: the Test and Militia bills. Charles addressed the Test first. Using the Norman French phrase that English monarchs had employed for centuries, he said 'Le roi le vault' ('The king wills it'): the bill was now an Act. Next, the Militia. This time Charles used a different Norman phrase: 'Le roi a advisera' ('The king will consider it'): a circumlocution meaning a veto. Then came one of his laconic speeches – not much more than ninety seconds long, but significant nevertheless. The king rejected the Militia Bill, '. . . because it puts out of my power the militia for so many days. If it had been but half an hour, I would not have consented to it, because of the ill consequences it may have hereafter, the militia being wholly in the crown, and . . . I shall employ them as I think fit and necessary for the safety of myself and the kingdom.'[49] Charles expressed doubts about the Test even as he passed it: 'I have passed the other bill, which is of great importance, of which there may be ill consequences hereafter. But I am willing to oblige them who have thought it fitting at this time, and I hope that they will be careful to give me due satisfaction for the future.'[50]

The Test Act, the only statute passed in the entire parliamentary session, went into effect immediately. Peers lined up to swear the oaths of allegiance and supremacy and those Catholics present spoke their last words in Parliament. Lord Audley, whose family ruined itself defending the royalist cause in the civil wars, took his leave with such eloquence that the House instructed Lord Chancellor Finch to recommend him to the king 'for his favor and grace, considering his ancient descent, and the great actions done by his ancestors in France in former times, and the small estate and fortune left to his family by reason of his fortune spent in that service by his ancestors'.[51] Roman Catholic peers did not return to the House of Lords for another 150 years.

While the opposition could point to the Test Act as a victory, in reality the session so far was a bitter disappointment. The king and his principal minister the Lord Treasurer gave some ground: they offered rewards for information about the plot, issued proclamations ordering Catholics out of London and arrested more than a few Catholics accused by informers. But on key issues, Charles and Danby stood firm. James's exemption from the Test was paramount, but the rejection of the Militia Bill hinted at hitherto unrecognized steel in Charles's spine. Bishop Burnet warned the king that 'some of them hoped, when that bill passed into law, they would be more masters, and that the militia would not separate [disband] till all the demands of the two houses should be granted'.[52] The king took this advice to heart, as his speech from the throne shows. And Charles's unexpectedly firm defence of his queen undercut Shaftesbury's belief in the king's weakness.

But the earl assured himself that continued pressure would eventually work: the king would abandon his minister, his wife and finally his brother. Charles was too indolent and inconstant to hold out against determined opponents. The earl of Shaftesbury was nothing if not determined. By the end of November 1678 he had not yet achieved his ends. The attack on James had failed. The accusations against the queen seemed ineffective. The attempt to seize control of the militia dead-ended in a royal veto. There were minor successes; Oates and Bedloe's stories had raised an anti-Catholic storm throughout the kingdom. Their testimony convicted James's former servant Edward Colman of treason, and dozens of Catholics filled the cells of Newgate and other prisons. Aided by an active and dedicated cohort of allies in both houses, Shaftesbury chipped away at Parliament's trust for the king and Danby. The perjuries of Oates and Bedloe helped keep that distrust alive, and with the help of his fellow committee members, the earl intended to further erode confidence in the Court.

The first two months of the session demonstrated the fertility of Shaftesbury's mind; when one strategy failed he soon developed a new one. He was, said Robert Southwell, 'the great giant that speaks to all, and they say with strange freedom and admirable eloquence'.[53] As December began, after the setbacks of late November, Shaftesbury prepared for another round. This time he would prove to be rather more successful. The new target would be Danby. The Lord Treasurer had over the previous year displayed a remarkable ability to cling to power, whatever the opposition threw at him. It had done everything in its power to force Parliament's dissolution, hoping to undermine his position. If he failed to get the king's business through Parliament, Shaftesbury thought, Charles would discard him, as he had done to many ministers before. And that would open the way for new counsels. But Danby proved resilient. With a narrow face that put people in mind of a ferret, he also had a ferret's cunning. He used the patronage of office to build support, awarding pensions and sinecures in return for service in Parliament. He could dispense money directly from the Treasury for 'secret service', and he did so. The current session of Parliament tested Danby's machine like no other, yet by the end of November he remained in control, if only barely.

In fact, the plot's momentum seemed on the wane. During the first two weeks of December there were several days in which Parliament's business hardly touched on the plot at all. And there were hints – not widespread, to be sure – that doubts about the conspiracy were growing. On 9 December, Secretary Williamson received a letter from Henry Layton, a Yorkshire gentleman: 'On the breaking . . . of the great Popish Plot the crack and noise filled us with great visions and apparitions of armed men assembled and riding by night, on which strong, strict watches were set, the militia drawn out, popish houses searched . . . but [I] could not find truth in any of these reports, nor person nor thing of danger met with, nor arms of danger nor ammunition in any popish house.' In Layton's view, false rumours 'were the very *preludium* to the late successful rebellion'. Tales of imminent French and Spanish invasions – such as those retailed in Oates's and Bedloe's fantasies – swirled through the Yorkshire countryside and many local dissenters gave them immediate credit. Layton advised Williamson to ensure that local leadership be placed unequivocally in the hands of men of 'royal and episcopal inclinations'.[54] For Layton, and for a growing number of others, the plot was beginning to look like a Trojan horse for disloyal elements, bent on undermining the monarchy and the established Church.

These were promising developments for Danby and the Court. But the opposition still had a trick up its sleeve: the new member of the House of Commons for the city of Northampton, Ralph Montagu. The forty-year-old son of Lord Montagu had since the Restoration been an active courtier, holding a number of offices and sinecures – a member of the Privy Council, he was also Queen Catherine's master of horse, in charge of her stables for thirteen years. It was a lucrative office, and one he could fill in absentia – convenient, because he served the king as an ambassador to France on two occasions, from 1669 to 1672, and most recently from 1676 to 1678. Montagu was no stranger to trouble; Charles had sent him to the Tower once for challenging the duke of Buckingham to a duel following a shoving match in the queen's drawing room. But it was in his second tour of duty in Paris that Montagu really blotted his copybook.

Montagu, like many (perhaps most) Restoration-era aristocrats, was a ladies' man. By no means an Adonis – his portraits reveal a jowly man whose full-bottomed wig did nothing to conceal an arrogant attitude – he did have charm when required. When it came to fashionable women, in fact, he seems to have been quite irresistible. While in France he began an affair with the king's former mistress, the duchess of Cleveland. The duchess, whose once passionate affair with Charles withered after he became enamoured of the French-born Louise, duchess of Portsmouth, had moved to France in 1676. This relationship ended with great bitterness in 1678 when Cleveland learned that her lover had eloped with her seventeen-year-old daughter Anne, countess of Sussex. Anne was staying in a Paris convent following a scandalous, possibly lesbian, relationship with another of Charles's mistresses, Hortense Mancini. Evidently Montagu exercised his considerable charm on the daughter as well as the mother. Cleveland wrote a furious letter to Charles, Anne's acknowledged father – though she might in fact have been the earl of Chesterfield's child. She passionately denounced Montagu for seducing her daughter, 'I am so much afflicted that I can hardly write this for crying, to see a child that I doted on as I did on her, should make me so ill a return, and join with the worst of men to ruin me.'[55] She also told Charles that his ambassador held him and his brother the duke of York in contempt, 'he has several times told me that in his heart he despised you and your brother, and for his part he wished with all his heart, that the Parliament would send you both to travel, for you were a dull governable fool, and the duke a willful fool'.[56]

This affair – or rather affairs – had doomed Montagu as a courtier. He had, however, a plan. If King Charles turned against him, the fruits of office were gone, as were his ambitions for further advancement. He had in fact recently schemed to purchase Secretary Coventry's office for £10,000 – an offer ultimately blocked by Danby, who had another man in mind for the place. In July 1678, Montagu abruptly returned to England, abandoning his post without royal permission. Charles dismissed him from the Privy Council and all his offices and refused the now ex-courtier's requests for an audience. The Court's enmity could be dangerous and Montagu knew that he might need protection – this he achieved to some degree when in September one of Northampton's MPs died, leaving a vacancy. The Montagu family had long-standing ties with Northamptonshire, and so Ralph announced his intention to stand. Danby threw a last-minute candidate into the fight, but Montagu intended to win come what may. Reportedly spending no less than £1,000 on ale for the voters, he was elected in a beery landslide.[57]

A seat in the Commons would be the ideal place from which to launch his attack on the Lord Treasurer, who Montagu held responsible for his loss of favour. On 24 October, just after the start of the new session, Montagu met secretly with Paul Barillon, the French ambassador. In return for 100,000 écus (about £40,000 – an enormous sum), he would guarantee Danby's overthrow within six months. He would be revenged for the Treasurer's interference, and profit handsomely in the bargain. Barillon agreed – prudently offering to pay half up front, the rest later.[58] With this promise in his pocket, the member for Northampton awaited his opportunity.

As ambassador, Montagu received many letters from Danby (and other ministers). These he carefully kept, knowing that they contained sensitive information about King Charles's diplomacy, and particularly about his frequent attempts to wheedle money out of his French cousin. Of course, if the truth were known, wheedling money from Louis XIV was something of a national pastime. But given the atmosphere of alarm over the plot, details of Charles's secret diplomacy would be explosive. Fully aware of the hostages to fortune Montagu held, Danby resolved to act first: with Charles's permission he ordered his papers seized. Montagu, Danby claimed, had while in Paris communicated with the papal nuncio in France without authorization (which was in fact quite true, although the correspondence was mostly innocent). With the papers in his hands, Danby could remove his own letters and destroy them. But he acted too late. Montagu had removed the most dangerous of Danby's letters and hidden them; the searchers came up with little more than scrap paper. The drama was now underway.

On Thursday 19 December, Sir John Ernly, Chancellor of the Exchequer, read a message in Parliament from the king: 'that his majesty, having received information that his late Ambassador in France, Mr Montagu, a member of this house, had held several private conferences with the Pope's nuncio there, has, to the end that he may discover the truth of the matter, given order for the seizing of Mr Montagu's papers'.[59] Opposition MPs – some of whom were themselves on the French payroll – immediately defended Montagu, insinuating that Danby intended to frame him.

At last Montagu himself rose to his feet. 'I believe that the seizing my cabinets and papers was to get into their hands some letters of great consequence, that I have to produce, of the designs of a great minster of state.'[60] William Harbord, member for Dartmouth (and Versailles, for he too received French backhanders), assured the House that Montagu's letters 'will open your eyes, and though too late to cure the evil, yet they will tell you who to proceed against . . .'[61] Some recommended that Montagu's papers be brought to the House and revealed the next day, but others wanted immediate action: 'I know not whether we shall be here tomorrow morning or no. It may be we shall all be clapped up [jailed] by tomorrow,' said Sir Nicholas Carew.[62] Sir John Lowther threw in the threat of murder, 'For ought I know, Montagu might be served as Sir Edmundbury Godfrey was . . . I move therefore to have the papers sent for now.'[63]

Then followed a carefully contrived drama, intended to bring members to the edge of their seats. Opposition leaders clearly knew what Montagu intended to reveal: 'I believe, it will appear by those papers, that the war with France was pretended, for the sake of an army, and that a great man carried on the interest of an army and popery, and Montagu gives you the convenience of this discovery,' said Lord Cavendish, heir to the earl of Devonshire and Shaftesbury's close ally.[64] Lord Russell, also 'thrice worthy' in Shaftesbury's eyes, avowed that Montagu had already revealed the paper's contents to him and that he could produce copies immediately. Harbord left the chamber and returned with a locked box. The key was safely at Whitehall, in the hands of the ministry – but London had many locksmiths. The House summoned one, and he soon opened the box. Montagu rose, papers in hand, ready to do his worst.

With crocodile tears flowing, he said, 'I am sorry that so great a minister has brought this guilt upon himself. It was my intention (making reflections upon [Parliament's] apprehensions of a standing army) to have acquainted Mr Secretary Coventry with the papers. I will now only tell you, that the king has been as much deluded as the Dutch or Spain, and you have been deluded too by this great minister . . .'[65] He then read out two of Danby's letters, one dated 16 January and the other 25 March 1678. At the time, the king's policy – one strongly supported by Danby – was to threaten war against France, in alliance with Spain and the Dutch Republic. Louis XIV's constant aggressive behaviour towards Charles's allies threatened England's interests, and furthermore Danby intended to use hostility towards France to bolster his support in Parliament. French-bashing was ever popular among the nation's salons (even those secretly taking French bribes). But Charles II and Louis XIV were, after all, cousins. Indeed, Charles was half French; his mother had been a French princess. His favourite sister (now alas dead) had married Louis XIV's only brother Philippe, duc d'Orléans. Louis XIV welcomed and supported (not lavishly, it is true) Charles during his exile. The king went along with Danby's plan but his commitment to open war was dubious.

While Charles was willing to fight France (he had already done so in the 1660s), he was also perfectly prepared to negotiate a deal. His cousin was the richest monarch in Europe, why should Charles not benefit? After all, more than a few of his own subjects already had. This was where Montagu's letters came in. Written by Charles's command – one of them contained, in the royal hand, 'This letter is writ by my order. C.R.' – they offered Louis peace in return for cash. Charles promised to stand his army down and continue the peace for six million livres a year over three years. He also offered to keep Parliament, a perennial thorn in Louis's side, in abeyance for the same period.[66]

As intended, Montagu's reading of this letter left the House thunderstruck. Total silence descended upon the chamber as members weighed the import of Danby's letter. Unsurprisingly, one of the contrivers of the ambush, Shaftesbury's proxy Thomas Bennett, was the first to speak. 'I wonder the house sits so silent when they see themselves sold for six millions of livres to the French!'[67] It might be noted that Bennett himself was a downright bargain, as his French subsidy was a mere few hundred pounds. But of course most members knew nothing of Bennett's arrangement with ambassador Barillon, and he continued, 'Now we see who has played all this game, who has repeated all the sharp answers to our addresses . . . I would impeach the treasurer of high treason!'[68]

William Harbord laid it on particularly thick, 'I hope now gentlemen's eyes are open, by the design on foot to destroy our government and our liberties. I believe if the house will command Mr Montagu he will tell you more now. But I would not press it now upon him, because poisoning and stabbing are in use. Therefore I would not examine him farther now, but let him reserve himself till the matter comes to trial before the Lords.' Doing his best to revive the panic that Oates had created and which now had begun to wane, Harbord went on, 'I protest, I am afraid that the king will be murdered every night! A peer, and an intimate of this earl's [Danby] said "There would be a change in the government in a year." He [remaining vague about who "He" might be] has poisons both liquid and in powders. But I would ask Montagu no more questions now, but have an impeachment drawn up, and I doubt not but that this great man will have condign punishment . . .'[69]

Danby's friends defended him as best they could. Harbord's invention of a mysterious poisoner gave them an opening. Sir Henry Goodricke, a Yorkshire neighbour of Danby's, spoke for his friend first: 'We now come upon impeachment of a noble peer, who deserves well of the nation, and I assure you, has promoted the Protestant religion, and has honor for the government. I put Harbord upon it, that all the evidence against him may be produced, and make it out who converses with this nobleman, that has "the poisons" he mentions. For the king's security, I would have the persons named.'[70] Harbord, alarmed that his attack on Danby might be derailed by his off-the-cuff creation, replied rather feebly that King Charles was already aware of the identity of the mysterious poisoner, and soon enough the attack on Danby returned to its track. John Knight, MP for Bristol, laid blame for the nation's crisis at Danby's feet. 'This army raised for a French war, and so many hundred thousand pounds given for that purpose, and yet we had no war! Money given to disband the army, and that not done! The Popish Plot discovered at that time! And all runs parallel. Take such evil counsellors from the king that have done these things, and he, and his posterity, and we all shall flourish; else we shall be destroyed. I move for impeachment!'[71] Sir Thomas Higgins, one of York's allies in the House, offered perhaps the most cogent defence of the Lord Treasurer: 'So great a minister of the king to be impeached! I desire to see better reasons than have yet been offered . . . One thing that is objected against him, "His treating of peace with the king of France". It seems by the letter that the conditions were for an honorable peace, and why should any man be ashamed of it? For it is a very ordinary thing for kings to get money from one another . . . and there is no ground of this accusation of treason against this lord. And another thing that concerns the safety of the king's person, "A friend of this lord's that has poisons." This concerns us all. Let us not go out of the house till this person be known.'[72]

Harbord rather desperately claimed that focusing on the unnamed poisoner diverted attention from the real issue: Danby's letters. In the process, however, he could not resist further gilding his poisoner's lily; 'He had the poison, and tried it upon dogs with good success.' Colonel Titus, one of Harbord's fellow French pensioners, came to his rescue, accusing Danby of diverting £200,000 out of the Exchequer for bribery – a great exaggeration – and of making a 'shameful peace' with France. 'His crime is great, and tends to the subversion of the nation, and so it is, when the king shall have no parliaments. Some fear the treasurer, and some love him. I do neither, and would impeach him!'[73]

Danby's defenders struggled on his behalf. Sir John Ernly vindicated his management of the Treasury and his role in foreign policy. Charles Bertie, the Lord Treasurer's secretary, also defended his fiscal stewardship, and asserted that 'he has not squandered the treasury in secret service'.[74] Danby's son, Peregrine, attacked Montagu directly: 'Montagu, in his discourse in France, has given the nation great discommendations. I have heard him say "the House of Commons had a company of logger-heads and boobies in it". For what my father is accused of, if proved, I would not spare him nor pardon him more than the greatest rascal that had done me the most injury.'[75] The debate continued well into the evening, and finally the Speaker put the question: 'That there is sufficient matter of impeachment against the Lord Treasurer.'[76] It is hardly surprising that determining the answer required a division. It was another very full House. Tellers counted 295 members, and when they finished it was apparent to all that the trick Montagu and his allies conjured had succeeded: 179 members voted to impeach Danby and 116 voted no. A sixty-three-vote majority was decisive: it broke Danby's grip on the Commons.

The House immediately appointed a committee to draw charges up against the Lord Treasurer, its membership overwhelmingly composed of his enemies. Now the issue would not be whether Danby could effectively manage Parliament, but rather could he keep his head on his shoulders?[77] The king's solicitor general, Sir Francis Winnington, reported the committee's articles of impeachment against Danby on Saturday 21 December. Heretofore a loyal supporter of the ministry, Winnington now abandoned it – a move that soon cost him his job.[78] Before voting, a number of Danby's supporters complained that the impeachment committee met secretly. Peregrine Bertie jeeringly said that 'the committee did sit in holes' to avoid transparency.[79] Lord Cavendish defended their procedure: 'Those who except against the committee, were not of the committee, who would only come to spy what we did. God forbid that the treasurer's life and estate should be in danger by what we did at the committee!' He followed this obvious falsehood by adding 'But we are in danger of our lives and estates, by his means. I would have him give an account of his actions to the Public.'[80] This wrangling went on some time, but eventually William Williams, chair of the committee, read out the articles. There were six. Danby had 'traitorously encroached to himself regal power' by dealing with Louis XIV without the knowledge of the secretaries of state. He had 'traitorously endeavored to subvert the ancient and well-established form of government of this kingdom' by raising an army with no intention of using it against France. He intended to use French money to enable the king to live without Parliament. He is 'popishly affected, and hath traitorously concealed . . . the late horrid and bloody plot'. He has 'wasted the king's treasure' to the tune of £231,602 on 'unnecessary pensions and secret services'. And finally, 'he hath by indirect means procured from his majesty for himself diverse considerable gifts and grants of inheritance'. A series of divisions followed to accept or reject these articles. Each one passed, none with a majority of fewer than 27 votes – a decisive statement.[81] The wheels had come off the Lord Treasurer's machine.

Shaftesbury and his allies won a great victory when they impeached Danby. Although he remained in office for the moment, these votes proved that his usefulness to the king was over. Charles would have to replace Danby with someone he could rely on to get his business done, and a certain diminutive earl thought he would be an excellent candidate. But the king was by no means prepared to surrender, as the events of the next Sunday hinted.

Royal chaplains held services in the king's chapel every Sunday. Although Charles II never distinguished himself by his piety, he nevertheless dutifully attended the liturgy. Royal duty demanded it, and courtiers knew that sitting in the Tudor chapel's pews – recently remodelled by the famous Christopher Wren – could be useful. Both men and women used the occasion to show off new clothes, gossip, and collect tidbits of political news. But the court chapel could also be a royal megaphone. Sermons preached there often carried royally approved messages, and frequently were published, amplifying their impact. This Sunday the preacher was Thomas Sprat, a royal chaplain. He had begun his career serving the duke of Buckingham, but had joined the king's squadron of chaplains. A well-regarded preacher, his text came from Paul's letter to the Galatians: 'It is good to be zealously affected always in a good thing.'[82]

Galatians is not frequently the subject of court sermons, but this Sunday the Court used it to send a message: the danger of zeal. Sprat warned that 'there are crept in among you deceitful teachers' who 'zealously affect you, but not well'.[83] Zealots 'are not those men too often found to be the greatest, and do not they think themselves the truest Zealots, who are most notoriously ignorant? Who make it their business, their pride, to express their blind zeal, not only without all knowledge, but oftentimes against it?'[84] Zealots create heresy; zealots encourage faction: 'That is one fatal error, when men imprudently, and uncharitably often, seditiously and mutinously sometimes' employ their zeal in the service of deceitful teachers.[85] Sprat named no names, but his implication was clear. The zealots at work in Parliament threatened the state and social order, 'when men unduly exercise their zeal . . . not only against evil persons; not only against some good persons; but against those who are the most venerable, and sacred'.[86] The sermon continued, alluding to the Bad Old Days of civil war and regicide, 'I would ask any man experienced in the world whether the greatest part of all the pretended zeal, of all sides, in our memories, has not too much in public, almost continuously . . . vented itself . . . detracting from superiors, or slandering of governors? Slandering? 'Twere well if they stopped there. Slander is an innocent thing, in comparison of those dire attempts in which a rage of zeal has engaged too many zealots against their governors.'[87]

The Reverend Sprat finished his sermon with a plea for moderation and obedience to the king, head of the Church. 'So therefore we are to temper . . . our zeal . . . to temper it with innocence, benignity, and charity; to employ it against sin, and disobedience, and schism, in unfeigned piety towards God, in unshaken duty to His vice-gerent [the king], in hearty obedience to his church.'[88] No one in the chapel royal that day could have missed the meaning of that sermon: the zealotry on display in Parliament threatened to return England to the chaotic years of division and civil war. King Charles, listening from his private closet high on the back wall of the chapel, no doubt ended the sermon with a hearty 'amen!' Afterwards, Dr Sprat enjoyed a series of promotions in the Church, becoming Bishop of Rochester in 1684. Virtue is its own reward, but unwavering devotion to the head of one's Church often offers more tangible compensations.

Sprat signalled the king's intention to fight, and Charles acted first by dismissing courtiers who had voted for the impeachment from their offices. The king supplemented royal pressure on individuals by a lobbying campaign, both privately and publicly. Publicly, Charles and James both increased their attendance in the House of Lords. The marquis of Worcester's heir, Charles, at eighteen perhaps the youngest member of the House of Commons, kept his father informed about what went on in the Lords: 'what with the king pressing them and the Prince [James] being present all the while the matter was debated' did good service for the Lord Treasurer.[89] On 23 December, MPs brought the charges against Danby into the upper House, and the Treasurer, who was present, proclaimed his innocence. Danby's enemies insisted that he leave the House, but a motion to that effect failed – no doubt at least in part because of the royal presence. But the vote triggered a formal dissent by no fewer than eighteen peers, including Buckingham, Winchester and, inevitably, Shaftesbury. These were the hardcore opponents of the Court, impervious to the king's disapproval – but they were at best a third of the usual attenders. Public pressure of this sort could be quite effective. Another example came a few days later, when on 27 December the opposition proposed that Danby be imprisoned. The royal pair once again in attendance, this motion also failed – and fifteen opposition peers duly entered their formal dissent.[90]

Charles busied himself behind the scenes as well. Throughout December, William Chiffinch, page of the backstairs and perhaps Charles's most influential servant, led a parade of visitors to Whitehall. Ever since Charles had taken up residence in Whitehall as king, the backstairs were used for clandestine purposes – more often than not, for the discreet visits of women targeted for seduction. The backstairs emerged right at the door to the page's lodgings and could be accessed from Charles's bedroom. Here, away from prying eyes, the king gathered support and information. Bishop Burnet gave an account of one of these meetings. 'I waited often on him in the month of December. He came to me to Chiffinch's . . .; and kept the time he assigned me to a minute. He was alone, and talked much and very freely with me. We agreed in one thing, that the greatest part of the evidence [of the plot] was a contrivance. But he suspected some had set on Oates and instructed him, and he named the earl of Shaftesbury.'[91] The king, indeed, was certain that the earl was behind it all: 'He fancied there was a design of rebellion on foot.'[92] Charles also used these meetings to gather information, and here Burnet disappointed him. 'I perceived the king thought I was reserved with him, because I would tell him no particular stories, nor name persons.'[93]

The upright Bishop Burnet gave Charles few weapons for his struggle, but he convinced others that the Popish Plot was a vehicle for the enemies of monarchy. And as December wore on, the king saw growing evidence that this was so. One incident was the case of Miles Prance. On 21 December constables arrested the Covent Garden silversmith on charges relating to the Godfrey murder. Prance was a member of the once-thriving community of Catholic artisans producing a variety of luxury goods in Restoration London. Miles supplied the queen, and had also made various liturgical items – chalices, patens and the like, for Catholic clergy. He knew a number of London Jesuits, and unfortunately had been overheard praising them as 'honest fellows'.[94] In late 1678 any connection, however casual, to the Jesuits was dangerous. Having been received at Somerset House regularly did not help. But the calamity that befell the young silversmith came thanks to a personal quarrel. Like many Londoners, Prance and his family took in lodgers, sometimes an economic necessity, and sometimes a very risky proposition. So it was with Prance's tenant, John Wren. Wren's rent was fourteen months in arrears and he was suspected of stealing a silver tankard from his landlord. Prance decided to turn him out of his house. Before he could, Wren denounced Miles, saying that he had been mysteriously absent from home over the weekend of Godfrey's death.

The constables escorted the protesting silversmith to Newgate. Shaftesbury soon learned of the arrest, and had the petrified young man brought before his committee, first ensuring that William Bedloe had a chance to see him. Bedloe, taking his cue, immediately identified Miles as one of the men he had seen with Godfrey's corpse at Somerset House. This Prance vehemently denied, provoking the committee to send him back to prison where he might think over the wages of obstinacy. Placed in one of the least salubrious cells in the prison, and in irons, he was 'left to chew upon it, whether he would venture his soul or his carcass'.[95] Within two days a miserable Prance decided that cooperation with Shaftesbury might be in order. The committee offered him a pardon in return for a confession and information about the murder. Alternatively, he could be tried on Bedloe's testimony. As Sir Roger L'Estrange put it later, Miles's choice was 'whether being innocent he would confess himself to be a murderer, and so escape; or deny it, and hang: but charity began at home, and he chose the perjury.'[96]

The day before his second appearance before the Lords committee, someone left a copy of Bedloe's testimony about Godfrey's death in his cell. The silversmith needed guidance before he recounted his story.[97] So instructed, he gave a performance that quite satisfied Shaftesbury – Prance served the very useful purpose of further supporting Bedloe, who thus far was the only person claiming first-hand knowledge of Sir Edmund Godfrey's supposed murder. Jailers delivered Prance to Shaftesbury's London house the next evening, and in a gruelling session lasting almost six hours he told his newly rehearsed story. He accused three Somerset House menials, Robert Green, Henry Berry and Lawrence Hill, of joining him in Godfrey's murder. His story differed in some details from Bedloe's – for example, he said that Berry had strangled Godfrey with a 'large twisted handkerchief' rather than Bedloe's deadly cravat. But the general outline was the same. Prance added more detail about the peregrinations of the corpse, as the murderers shuffled it from room to room in Somerset House, over several days, and later carried it via sedan chair, and then on horseback, to Primrose Hill. He also minimized his own role in the affair, saying that his role was to stand watch while the others did the strangling.

By Christmas eve, word of Prance's confession was the talk of London. Lord Herbert wrote to his father about 'one Prants, a silversmith . . . who has they say confessed so much as to confirm wholly Bedloe's testimony . . .'[98] In addition to interrogation by the Lords committee, on Monday 23 December a delegation of MPs from the lower House also turned up at Newgate and took its own version of Prance's story. The next day he went to Whitehall and told the same story to the king and Privy Council. By now, 'by the help of some illuminations in Aldersgate Street [where Shaftesbury's house stood] he began to see daylight' and added more detail, not only about the murder, but about the plot generally. He overheard Jesuits talking about a Catholic army of 50,000 men. One, Grove, passed on a juicy tidbit when in Prance's shop, 'to buy two spoons'. Grove said that Lords Belasyse, Arundell, Powis and Petre had papal commissions to lead the rebels. Quite why Grove chose to blurt out this highly secret information to a tradesman is a mystery. Prance said he could prove Grove's presence in his shop, because he noted the sale of the two spoons in his accounts.[99] He denied knowing anything of an assassination conspiracy against the king.

This was all excellent for Shaftesbury, who could now use Prance to confirm evidence from both Oates and Bedloe. He also had the names of Godfrey's alleged murderers, all three of whom swiftly joined Prance in prison. The lord's threats of hanging had been quite effective. Later, Sir Roger L'Estrange ruefully forgave Miles his perjury. Given the pressure from the Lords of 'a certain ambulatory committee' (because of its habit of meeting in various private houses to avoid scrutiny of its methods), what could Prance do? They could decide 'When and to what degree to squeeze, to pinch, to ease, to shackle, to comfort or to torture' their prisoners.[100]

Having made his statement, Prance returned to Newgate, taking up residence in more comfortable quarters, cherishing the promise of a royal pardon. On Christmas Eve he went with Lords Ossory and Monmouth on a tour of Somerset House, showing them the scene of the crime – though his vagueness about the layout of the place probably did nothing to enhance his credibility.[101] But he had the Christmas recess of Parliament to work on his story, and when the houses reassembled on 26 December both received his statement. Over the next few days, however, Prance thought about what he had done. Berry and Hill were locked up with him in Newgate, a daily reminder of the injury Prance had done them. Green was slightly more fortunate in that his jail was the Gatehouse, less infamous than Newgate. All three adamantly denied their guilt when examined by the king and Privy Council. During this interrogation, Prance confronted each of the accused, and the king specifically asked Miles 'Whether he would on his salvation declare all that he said to be true?' Prance replied, 'it was as true as God is true, and that he did upon his salvation affirm it'.[102]

In the solitude of his cell, these positive oaths worked on Prance's conscience. On 28 December he asked Captain Richardson, the warden, to request an audience with the king. Arriving by way of the backstairs and Mr Chiffinch, Prance retracted his entire story. He had never seen Bedloe before in his life; he knew the Somerset House three, but nothing whatever about Godfrey's death. 'Knows nothing of anybody' and 'Knows nothing in the world of all he has said', wrote Secretary Williamson in his notes.[103] Asking him why he had lied, Prance told the king he feared Shaftesbury's threats of hanging. The next day, Prance returned to the palace for a grilling by the entire Privy Council, and reaffirmed his innocence. This recantation threatened the entire edifice of the plot – Prance directly confirmed both Oates and Bedloe. There were no others. If his credibility was gone, then where was theirs?

It might be that Prance's dramatic reversal prompted the king's next decision: to end the parliamentary session. Ever since the session began in October, both houses were absorbed in the plot, and then the pursuit of Danby. No other public business had been done and, most importantly, no money was forthcoming to the Crown. Charles had hoped until mid-December that by cooperating in the pursuit of the plot he might obtain funds. The attack on Danby dashed that hope. The advent of Prance, and the clear evidence that Shaftesbury used him to further his narrative of the Popish Plot, probably determined Charles to move as he did. On Monday 30 December he appeared unexpectedly in the Lords, crowned and robed. The Commons joined the peers and Charles announced 'It is with great unwillingness that he is come to tell them that he intends to prorogue them. All of them are witness that he hath not been used well.'[104] Promising to disband the army, to continue investigating the plot and to defend Protestantism, he dismissed them from Westminster.

Although he did not say so, the king intended not simply to end this most unproductive session – he intended to end the Parliament altogether through dissolution. Parliament was to resume on 4 February, but Charles had had enough of this body. Perhaps a newly elected House of Commons would be more amenable. Perhaps with evidence that the plot was a fiction pushed forward by Shaftesbury and his allies – something that Prance's recantation would help prove – he might gain the advantage.

As Charles contemplated a dissolution, Miles Prance returned to prison and there was subjected to overwhelming pressure by Shaftesbury and the Lords committee. The conditions of his imprisonment radically worsened; he had no blankets or bedding and the jailors loaded him with irons. The unheated cell would have been agonizingly cold, and his diet miserable. Soon he seemed on the verge of madness: 'He lay in such torments, both of body and mind, that he spent his hours roaring and groaning and restlessly exclaiming and crying out "Not guilty! Not guilty! No murder!"'[105] Captain Richardson reported that his prisoner 'used much raving talk' and thought that he might be feigning insanity. On 10 January 1679 the Privy Council dispatched William Lloyd, the vicar of St Martin-in-the-Fields (and a former chaplain to the duke of York's daughter Princess Mary), to comfort Prance. Lloyd might well also have had another motive – to ensure that whatever Prance had to say would do no damage to the duke. Lloyd found Miles in a miserable state and succeeded in getting him some bedding. But neither the king nor the council could do much for the prisoner. The king could pardon Prance and order his release – though if he did Shaftesbury would seize upon it as proof of a royal attempt to shield the conspirators. The same day Lloyd journeyed to Newgate, one of Secretary Williamson's correspondents told him of the growing conviction that the 'zeal and activity of a great person' (presumably James) threatened to 'stifle the plot'.[106] So apart from kind words and a marginal improvement in his conditions, Prance could hope for little from the Court.

But Shaftesbury and his friends continued to ratchet up the pressure. Repeated visitations from MPs or members of the Lords committee threatened Prance with hanging, or worse, the full-blown agony of drawing and quartering. They threatened his wife and children with beggary – for a felon's goods were forfeit to the Crown. By 11 January 1679 the pressure broke the young silversmith. He retracted his recantation. Beginning with the same story he told after his arrest, he went further. In an obvious effort to ingratiate himself with his principal torturer, he invented a Catholic conspiracy to assassinate Shaftesbury. Naming five Catholic acquaintances, including the now safely dead William

Staley, they intended to kill the earl and so remove the papist's most dangerous enemy.[107] Jailors immediately moved Prance to a new cell, took off his irons and restored the comforts he lost when he defied Shaftesbury's narrative.

The king must have been greatly disappointed by Prance's buckling, though he could hardly have blamed him. But the fact that he had done so made new elections even more risky. It was what Shaftesbury himself had aimed for since 1675 or before. The earl had accomplished a great deal in two months: the Test Act eliminated Catholic peers from the Lords; the queen stood accused of treason and seemed likely to fall; and Danby's utility had been destroyed. Dissolving Parliament was risky for Charles, to be sure. It would be a roll of the dice. But it had to be done.

SIX

THE FIRST TRIALS
NOVEMBER 1678–JANUARY 1679

The first of the plot's unfortunate victims, William Staley, went to his death at Tyburn on Wednesday 27 November 1678. On that same day, while Parliament was still in session, Edward Colman stood trial before the Court of King's Bench. The spectacle unfolded in Westminster Hall, adjacent to the Houses of Parliament, and no doubt many members witnessed the proceedings in the cavernous old building. Two hundred and forty feet long and sixty-eight feet wide, the hall had witnessed many historic trials. Now it was Colman's turn. The hall housed both the court of Common Pleas and King's Bench, whose premises occupied one end of the building. Both courts lacked the dignity we might expect of such institutions; they were jerry-built of rather flimsy planks and panels, separated from each other by thin plank walls. The courts looked like temporary structures thrown up at short notice, and in fact they were. Periodically Westminster Hall became the site of grand events demanding the use of the entire building, coronation banquets in happy times or public trials like that of Charles I in January 1649. When that happened, the law courts were actually disassembled and stored for later reassembly.

On this Wednesday, King's Bench enjoyed all the attention, for spectators eagerly awaited Colman's trial. This would be the first time Oates and his fellow informant William Bedloe would testify before a court of law; their appearances before the Privy Council and Parliament were preludes. Now a life stood in the balance. Four judges presided from their bench elevated above the court. The Chief Justice, Sir William Scroggs, was the senior jurist, renowned for his hostility towards popery. The other three were Sir William Wilde, a Londoner whose legal career stretched back to the Interregnum, Sir William Dolben, appointed to the court only a month before, and Sir Thomas Jones, a choleric Welshman who 'when much offended often shewed his heats in a rubor of countenance set off by his grey hairs'.[1] All four judges had plenty of experience with capital cases, but few had presided over one as sensational as this.

Proceedings began when the clerk of the court ordered the crier to 'make proclamation'. 'Oyez! Our sovereign lord the king does strictly charge and command all manner of persons to keep silence upon pain of imprisonment!'[2] Maintaining silence in a courtroom jammed with excited spectators was no doubt a tricky business, but somehow the bailiff managed through most of the trial. The first order of business was seating a jury. Twelve substantial London gentlemen, including one baronet, Sir Reginald Forster, and a knight, Sir Charles Lee, came forward to swear an oath to render justice. Colman might well have known some of the jurors; seventeenth-century courts often preferred jurors with knowledge of a defendant's reputation, and London was, despite its size, a city where most gentlemen of standing knew (or knew of) one another. In any event, as each gentleman came forward to swear the oath, Colman raised no objection to their service – a right he might have exercised under the law.

Once sworn the jurors took a seat in their box, an austere set of benches intended to create a level of discomfort encouraging attention to the proceedings. The hard seats occupied by the jury discouraged dozing, although in this case there seemed to be little likelihood of that. The clerk then read out a lengthy indictment, alleging that Colman had plotted with French priests and papal agents to secure the dissolution of Parliament and, more seriously, that he had known of and willingly participated in the Jesuit assassination plot against the king.[3]

Colman stood at the bar of the court (defendants were not allowed to sit) and entered his plea: not guilty. All criminal defendants in England faced the court alone: the rules forbade a defence counsel, except on points of law. Nor were defendants allowed to put defence witnesses under oath when questioning them, while prosecution witnesses swore to the truth of their testimony. The king's prosecution spoke for his majesty, and the king could not lie – if defence witnesses contradicted the king's evidence under oath they would in effect be calling the king a liar. Even though in truth there was abundant evidence that Charles II could stretch the truth – at times out of all recognition – the legal principle stood. In an age that took oaths seriously this was an important disadvantage for Colman. The clerk then addressed the jury: Colman 'puts himself upon God and his country: which country you are. Your charge is to enquire whether he be guilty of the high treason whereof he stand indicted, or not guilty.'[4]

Sir George Jeffreys, the Recorder of London (the city's chief legal officer), opened the Crown's case, assisted by Sir John Maynard, a seventy-four-year-old sergeant-at-law and MP who had vigorously pursued Colman in the Commons. Jeffreys matter-of-factly rehearsed the charges, while his second, Maynard, followed with rhetoric intended to fire up the court: 'Gentlemen, the prisoner at the bar stands indicted for no less than an intention to murder the king, for an endeavour and attempt to change the government of the nation, so well settled and instituted, and to bring us all to ruin and slaughter of one another, and for an endeavour to alter the Protestant religion, and to introduce instead of it the Romish superstition, and Popery!'[5] Maynard referred to Colman's notorious letters to Louis XIV's confessors, Fathers Ferrier and de La Chaise, the documentary evidence proving the Crown's case. The fact that none of the prosecution's letters were dated after 1675 meant nothing: 'we apprehend that he had intelligence unto 1678' and that it was 'very exceeding probable' that Colman destroyed more recent letters.[6] Maynard also referred to Oates as 'the first man that we hear of that discovered this treason' and whose enlistment of Sir Edmund Godfrey ended in the magistrate's death: 'We know what followed, the damnable murder of that gentleman, in execution of his office, so hellishly contrived . . .'[7] Maynard also took care to exonerate the duke of York from Colman's act, claiming that he wrote his letters to France without the duke's knowledge or approval – although in fact James was indeed aware of the letters.

Next on his feet was Sir William Jones, the king's Attorney General. Jones, forty-eight, had earned a solid reputation as a barrister, although Bishop Burnet commented that he 'had a roughness in his deportment that was very disagreeable' and he deployed that abrasiveness to good effect in this trial.[8] Jones claimed that the plot had begun with the Counter-Reformation, led by the Jesuits. This scheme to overthrow the Protestant religion 'hath often received interruption, so that they have proceeded sometimes more coldly, sometimes more hotly', but they were now closer to success than ever. 'Whole troops of Jesuits and priests' worked to gain converts, but growing impatient, 'they knew the people of England had but one head [Charles II] and therefore they were resolved to strike at that'.[9] Jones described the 'most diabolical' and 'most wicked and horrible design' crafted by the conspirators: teams of assassins, foreign military intervention, Catholic uprisings. Colman knew of the design, he approved of it, and carried money to pay the would-be killers. The evidence would show him no less guilty than the assassins themselves.[10] In fact, the Attorney General maintained, as the anointed Secretary of State of the proposed rebel Catholic regime, Colman was more dangerous than most of the other accused plotters. His foreign connections damned him as well; Jones alluded to the infamous letters, which, he said, would show without a doubt how deeply engaged he was in treasonous plotting with France. Not mentioned, of course, was the inconvenient fact that half of the English political class eagerly dealt with French agents, both supporters of the ministry, and even more enthusiastically, the opposition.

Like Sergeant Maynard, Jones admitted that no correspondence dating after 1675 was found, but he had no doubt that the correspondence continued until 1678. Jones anticipated an objection to this line of argument – why had Colman not destroyed all of his letters? The answer: vanity. 'I believe that we owe this discovery to something of Mr. Colman's vanity: he would lose not the glory of managing these important negotiations about so great a design. He thought it was no small reputation to be entrusted with the secrets of foreign ministers.'[11] The claim that more letters had certainly existed was weak, but Jones's reference to Colman's vanity probably impressed the jury more, because in fact the defendant had a well-earned reputation for officiousness and preening self-confidence.[12]

Jones finished his presentation and Colman began his first exchange with Lord Chief Justice Scroggs. It did not go well. Colman wondered 'why a prisoner, in such a case as this is not allowed counsel but your lordship is supposed to be counsel for him'. This was in fact standard procedure in criminal trials; defendants relied upon judges to explain the finer points of the law. It was not fair, but it produced convictions. Certainly Justice Scroggs demonstrated in this exchange that he intended to show no tenderness towards the accused. Colman worried that rampant anti-Catholicism made a fair trial impossible. 'Another thing seems most dreadful, that is the violent prejudice that seems to be against every man in England that is confessed to be a Roman Catholic. It is possible that a Roman Catholic may be very innocent of these crimes.' Colman begged the judge to bear this anti-Catholic bias in mind, 'unless your lordship will lean extremely much on the other side, justice will hardly stand upright, and lie upon a level'.[13]

This plea for fairness did not exactly impress Scroggs. 'You shall have a fair, just, and legal trial; if condemned it will be apparent you ought to be so, and without a fair proof, there shall be no condemnation. Therefore you shall find we will not do to you as you do to us, blow us up at adventure, kill people because they are not of your persuasion; our religion teacheth us another doctrine, and you shall find it clearly to your advantage.'[14] Whether the prisoner at the bar found this speech to be a comfort may be doubted.

Colman asserted his innocence. Admitting his correspondence with the French in 1674 and 1675 he denied any subsequent intrigues: 'after that time I did give over correspondence'. Scroggs was not convinced. 'Can mankind be persuaded that you that had this negotiation in 1674 and 1675 left off just then . . . Do you believe there was no negotiation after 1675 because we have not found them? Have you spoke one word to that? Have you confessed, or produced those papers . . .? When you answer that, you may have credit, without that it is impossible, for I cannot give credit to one word you say unless you give account of the subsequent negotiation.'[15]

The assumption that Colman's intrigues with France continued beyond 1675 might be logical, but the Crown could present no evidence to prove it. From a legal perspective, this favoured the defendant – but Colman soon learned that in his case assumptions trumped evidence (or the lack thereof). And then his situation soon took a turn for the worse: Titus Oates, clad in full clerical garb to impress the jurors, advanced to testify. The Chief Justice warned Oates to stick to the truth. Colman, who knew very well that Oates lied with aplomb, must have taken heart when Scroggs said, 'here's a gentleman stands at the bar for his life, and on the other side the king is concerned for his life. You are to speak the truth and the whole truth, for there is no reason in the world that you should add any one thing that is false. Let him be condemned by truth. You have taken an oath, and you being a minister know the great regard you ought to have of the sacredness of an oath, and that to take a man's life away by a false oath is murder, I need not teach you that.'[16]

Oates solemnly acknowledged the Chief Justice's warning, and immediately launched upon his well-rehearsed farrago of lies. He first encountered Colman in November 1677, accompanied by Father John Keynes, at Colman's house. Although this was their first meeting, Colman asked Titus to deliver a packet of letters to the Catholic seminary in St Omer. Oates said he saw the letters opened at their delivery; one was a newsletter in Colman's hand, making disparaging comments about the king and the recent marriage of his niece, Princess Mary, to the Protestant Prince of Orange, a match that 'would prove the traitor's and tyrant's ruin'. The other letter, in Latin, was for Father de La Chaise, Louis XIV's confessor. Also in Colman's hand, it was a reply to an earlier missive from France. That letter offered £10,000 on the condition that it be employed 'for no other intent and purpose but to cut off the King of England'.

Here Oates navigated a tricky point. De La Chaise's letter was addressed to Father Richard Strange, the Jesuit provincial in London. Why, then, asked Scroggs, did Colman write the reply instead of Strange? Demonstrating his talent for invention, Titus replied that 'having run a reed into his finger, [he] had wounded his hand'. Moreover, his secretary, Edward Mico, was too sick to write. Given that Strange had already fled the country and Mico was at that moment dying in Newgate (he died six days later), challenging this story was unlikely.[17] Oates firmly asserted under questioning from Scroggs that although Colman did not sign these letters, they were in his hand.

Attorney General Jones then asked Oates for an account of the famous Jesuit 'consult' of April 1678. Colman was not present, Titus said, but he overheard him approving the plot afterwards. Additionally, he claimed, Colman had written a letter urging the plotters to bring the duke of York into their plans. Justice Wilde pressed Oates from the bench: 'You did say positively that Mr. Colman did consent and agree to what was consulted by the Jesuits, which was to kill the king . . .?'[18] 'I heard him say it "was well contrived".' Both Jeffreys, the prosecutor, and Scroggs leapt at this confirmation: 'Do the gentlemen of the jury hear what he saith?'[19]

The damning point thus reinforced, Attorney General Jones moved on to other parts of the Oatesian fantasy. 'What do you know of any rebellion to have been raised in Ireland?' Titus, who evidently saw every piece of correspondence written by London Catholics, had read a letter from Peter Talbot, the titular Catholic archbishop of Dublin. This described a plot to poison the duke of Ormond, the Lord Lieutenant, and raise a rebellion. The rebels would be armed with 40,000 black bills (agricultural implements), obsolete weapons whose ineffectiveness against soldiers armed with muskets can be imagined. He also heard Colman say that he had found a way to transmit £200,000 to Ireland to fund the rebels.[20]

Organizing rebellion in Ireland, poisoning the Lord Lieutenant and raising gigantic sums of money did not distract Colman from his English plotting, however. Titus said Edward tipped a messenger a guinea to hasten delivery of a letter to four unnamed Irish 'ruffians' charged with ambushing the king at Windsor. He also advocated sweetening the plotter's offer to Sir George Wakeman by £5,000. A mere £10,000 would not be enough to persuade the doctor to poison Charles, and Colman himself copied out letters urging contributions from English Catholics for the cause. 'By this means thousands of pounds were gathered,' said Oates – though no one asked what had happened to these thousands.[21]

Oates also knew that the pope intended Colman to be Secretary of State in the new Catholic government, having seen a copy of his commission lying around the chamber of the Catholic attorney, Richard Langhorne. Justice Wilde asked Titus if he had seen any other commissions there. 'A great many, I cannot remember, there was a commission for my lord Arundell of Wardour, the lord Powis, and several other persons. But this belongs not to the prisoner at the bar: I mention his commission.'[22] Having thus casually incriminated more innocents, Titus described his relationship with Langhorne, whose sons he had known in Spain.

Oates's tale told, Attorney General Jones invited Colman to question the witness. Colman challenged Oates. When first questioned before the Privy Council in September, Titus had told the king that he did not recognize Edward, 'and he is extremely well acquainted with me now, and hath a world of intimacy . . . I never saw Mr Oates since I was born, but at that time.'[23] The Chief Justice then prodded Oates, 'answer to what Mr. Colman saith'. He replied feebly, 'I would not swear that I had seen him before in my life, because my sight was bad by candle light, and candle light alters the sight so much, but when I heard him speak I could have sworn it was he, but it was not then my business.' And again he blamed the light: 'I cannot see a great way by candle light.'[24]

This testimony clearly annoyed Scroggs. What Oates could or could not see at that moment was irrelevant – he was revealing the plot to the king and Privy Council. Why did he fail to mention such an important conspirator as the man intended to be the papally appointed Secretary of State? Oates wriggled. Going into specifics with Colman present might divulge information he might use to escape. Besides, Titus claimed, he was exhausted: 'I was so weak, being up two nights, and taking prisoners, upon my salvation, I could scarce stand upon my legs.'[25] What, asked Scroggs, did he accuse Colman of at that examination? Again Oates prevaricated – he'd accused Edward of writing newsletters with unflattering expressions about the king, 'as near as I can remember, but I would not trust to my memory'. Again he excused himself on the grounds of fatigue.

The Chief Justice's scepticism was plain. Oates had just testified in great detail about Colman's complicity in every aspect of the plot – and yet he had not mentioned one of these lurid details when telling all to the Privy Council. Why? 'I being so tired and weak that I was not able to stand on my legs . . .'[26] Scroggs pressed his point: 'You was by when the Council were ready to let Mr. Colman go almost at large?' 'No,' said Oates, 'I never apprehended that, for if I did, I should have given a further account.' 'Why,' asked the Chief Justice, 'did you not name Colman at that time?' Oates responded with a non-sequitur: 'Because I had spent a great deal of time in accusing other Jesuits.'[27] Now Justice Wilde intervened, obviously concerned about Titus's failure to accuse Colman immediately. He asked how much time had passed between his accusations about Colman's 1675 letters and his later claims connecting him directly to the king's planned assassination. Again, Oates's response was less than reassuring – he had never accused Colman of involvement in the assassination attempt before the king and Privy Council at all. This part of the story he reserved for Parliament – more than a month after his first appearance before the council. 'How came you,' asked Scroggs, 'Mr. Colman being so desperate a man as he was, endeavoring the killing of the king, to omit your information of it to the council and to the king . . .?'[28] Oates took refuge in his poor memory:

'Why did you not accuse all those Jesuits by name?'

'We took a catalogue of their names, but those I did accuse positively and expressly we took up [arrested].'

'Did you not accuse Sir George Wakeman by name, and that he accepted his reward [for poisoning Charles]?'

'Yes, I did then accuse him by name.'

'Why did you not accuse Mr. Colman by name?'

'For want of memory, being disturbed and weary in sitting up two nights, I could not give that account of Mr. Colman, which I did afterwards, when I consulted my papers, and when I saw Mr. Colman was secured, I had no need to give a farther account.'[29]

Lacking the benefit of counsel, it was the defendant's job to cross-examine the witness. Colman focused on his first confrontation with Oates before the Privy Council. When examined Edward was close at hand in the council chamber, but Oates failed to recognize him. Why? 'I had the disadvantage of a candle upon my eyes, Mr. Colman stood more in the dark.' Colman objected that Oates claimed to have seen him several times in previous months, engaged in scheming with London's Jesuits: 'He names several places that he met with me, in this place and that place, a third and fourth place about business.' One wonders what the jury thought of Oates's reply to this, 'He was altered much by his periwig in several meetings, and had several periwigs, and a periwig doth disguise a man very much, but when I heard him speak I knew him to be Mr. Colman.'[30] Seventeenth-century periwigs were indeed likely to alter the wearer's superficial appearance, cascading as they did beyond the shoulders, and often coming in different colours. No one challenged Oates on this point, but it seems telling that he immediately tried to divert the court's attention.

When Justice Scroggs tried to pin Oates down with a direct question, 'How often had you seen Mr. Colman?', Titus responded with a complete non-sequitur: 'When the question was asked by my lord chancellor, Mr. Colman, when were you last in France? He said, at such a time. Did you see Father de La Chaise? He said he gave him an accidental visit. My lord chancellor asked him whether or no he had a pass? He said no. Then he told him, that was a fault for going out of the kingdom without a pass. Have you a kinsman whose name is Playford, at St. Omer? He said he had one ten years old [who is in truth sixteen]. That question I desired might be asked. Then the king bade me go on.'[31] This filibuster, utterly irrelevant, did not fool the Chief Justice, who noted that it failed to answer the original question: How many times had he met Colman?

Colman saw his advantage and pressed it. 'It is very strange Mr. Oates should swear now, that he was so well acquainted with me, and had been so often in my company, when upon his accusation at the council table, he said nothing of me more than the sending of one letter, which he thought was my hand . . . And he did seem to say there he never saw me before in his life.'[32] Sir Thomas Dolman, one of the Privy Council's clerks, supported Colman. Confronted with Colman before the board, Dolman said that Oates claimed 'that he did not well know him'. Scroggs, still keen to get to the bottom of Oates's vague assertions, intervened. 'Did he [Oates] add that he did not well know him by candlelight? But Mr. Oates, when you heard his voice, you said you knew him, why did you not come then, and say you did well know him?' Titus's response to this would not have done justice coming from a guilty schoolboy 'Because I was not asked.'[33]

At this point things looked promising for Colman: the star witness seemed at best unreliable, and for all of his bluster, his story barely held together. Scroggs addressed Sir Thomas Dolman:

'But, Sir Thomas, did he say he did not well know him after Mr. Colman spake? Was Mr. Colman examined before Mr. Oates spake?'

'Yes.'

'Mr. Oates, you say you were with him [Colman] at the Savoy and Wild House, pray, Sir Thomas, did he say he did not know him, or that he had seen Mr. Colman there?'

'He did not know him as he stood there [before the Privy Council],' replied Sir Thomas.[34]

Whether the prosecution found all of this helpful is doubtful: Oates had clearly failed to impress Chief Justice Scroggs, and Justice Wilde seemed troubled as well. But the Crown had not finished. Dolman retired from the stand and Sir Robert Southwell, his fellow clerk of the Privy Council, replaced him. A forty-three-year-old Irish Protestant, Southwell had every reason to fear Catholic plots. His family had suffered during the Catholic rebellion that shook Ireland from 1641, and although he had made a highly successful career in England, ably serving on diplomatic missions to Portugal and Brussels, his clerkship put him at the heart of English politics. His central role in the council's investigation of the plot worried him – by now it was clear that the ministry's enemies in Parliament hooped to charge men like himself with obstruction, if not actual collusion with the papists. Later, Southwell described his feelings at the time, 'during that interval I could have lived with more ease in a powder mill'.[35] For this reason, Southwell kept meticulous notes of his work on the plot should he be hauled before a parliamentary committee. And as a witness he had no desire to bend too far backwards for the defendant.[36]

Southwell's testimony dealt a serious blow to Colman's defence. When questioned by the Privy Council in Colman's presence, Sir Robert said that Oates declared that the defendant had personally paid Sir George Wakeman £5,000 (of the £15,000 promised) for poisoning the king. Southwell ignored the problem of Titus's inability to recognize Colman, and Scroggs seized upon his claim. 'This answers much of the objection against him [Oates] . . . he charged you expressly with it at the Council table.'[37] Colman defended himself by pointing out that the council clearly thought little of the charge: 'The charge was so slight against me . . . that the council were not of his opinion', and rather than sending him to Newgate – the destination of most of Titus's victims – he was placed in the hands of a council messenger, a much looser form of restraint.

But again Southwell undermined Colman's account. 'Mr. Oates gave so large and general an information to the Council, that it could not easily be fixed. Mr. Colman came voluntarily in on Monday morning (the day after his questioning) . . . hearing that there was a warrant against him. By reason of so many prisoners that were then under examination, he was not heard until the afternoon, and then he did with great indignation and contempt hear these vile things, as thinking himself innocent.' What worried Sir Robert was a possible accusation of negligence: 'Mr. Colman then made so good a discourse for himself, that though the lords had filled up a blank warrant to send him to Newgate, that was respited, and he was only committed to a messenger.'[38] The tide turned against Edward when the Privy Council examined his letters: 'several of these papers and declarations sounded so strange to the lords that they were amazed'. Before dismissing Southwell, the Chief Justice took care to reiterate Sir Robert's point for the benefit of the jury, 'he did charge you home then for being one of the conspirators, in having had a hand in paying of money for poisoning the king'.[39]

Oates had now done his worst against Colman, and until Sir Robert Southwell appeared, the defendant might have felt that Titus failed to damage him fatally. But Southwell's testimony, and Justice Scroggs's emphasis of it, must have shaken Edward. And there would be more prosecution testimony to come.

The court now turned to the Crown's second star witness, William Bedloe. Sir Francis Winnington, the Solicitor General, introduced the new witness, asking him to testify to his knowledge of Colman's part in the plot. Winnington's colleague, Attorney General Jones, took up the questioning. What did Bedloe know about Colman's commission from the pope? He was to be Secretary of State, said Bedloe – though he admitted that his information was second-hand. He never saw any actual document, but rather had been told by a prominent lay Catholic, Sir Henry Tichborn, of Edward's impending elevation to high office.

Bedloe launched into his tale. In April 1675 he said he had carried a large packet of letters to Father de La Chaise in France. Hanging around 'two French abbots and several English monks' in Paris, William overheard them talking about their plot: 'The king was to be destroyed and the government subverted as well as the Protestant religion.'[40] Prosecutor Jeffreys raised the issue of French money. How much was there, and what was it for? Dodging the issue of amounts, Bedloe turned up the drama. 'It was to carry on the design to subvert the government of England, to free England from damnation and ignorance, and free all Catholics from hard tyranny and oppression of heretics.'[41] Bedloe had an even better line in lurid prose than Oates. 'What did you hear Mr. Colman say?' asked Jeffreys. Bedloe replied, 'That he would adventure anything to bring in the Popish religion . . . if he had a hundred lives and a sea of blood to carry on the cause, he would spend it all to further the cause of the Church of Rome, and to establish the Church of Rome in England, and if there was a hundred heretical kings to be deposed, he would see them all destroyed.'[42]

Bedloe heard this hair-raising threat in Colman's London house in 1677, he said, prompting a challenge from the prisoner: 'Did I ever see you in my life?' Bedloe defiantly replied, 'You may ask that question, but in the stone gallery in

Somerset House, when you came from a consult, where were great persons, which I am not to name here . . . you saw me then.' Bedloe threatened to take the case into areas the Crown emphatically wanted to avoid – the queen's official lodgings at Somerset House and mysterious unnamed 'great persons' were elements of Lord Shaftesbury's preferred narrative, not the government's. Attorney General Jones hastily dismissed Bedloe, whose role in the trial ended forthwith.

The Crown then steered the case back to the approved story, focusing on Colman's letters. Several witnesses testified about the search for them. The Privy Council's servants found 'a great deal' of papers in Colman's study and desk, and one small wooden box hidden in his bedchamber's chimney. Southwell and Dolman, tasked with examining this mass of paper, took some time to work through them – there were 'three great bags' in addition to the contents of the hidden box. Witnesses verified that crucial documents were in Colman's handwriting.

Now the Crown turned to the contents of the seized documents. 'It will appear,' said Jones, 'if there were no other proof in this case, his own papers are as good as a hundred witnesses to condemn him.'[43] The clerk of court read Colman's 'long letter' to Father de La Chaise, dated 29 September 1675. In it Colman described his efforts since 1673 to advance the Catholic (and not coincidentally, French) cause in England. Parliament, Colman maintained, was the main threat, so preventing its meeting – or securing a dissolution – was his goal. This might be attained through the liberal application of French gold, to the tune of £300,000. For an additional £20,000, Colman claimed he could get the king to reinstate his brother as Lord High Admiral, an office James resigned when Parliament passed the first Test Act of 1673. Colman added that James approved of his proposals in words that seriously compromised the duke: 'His royal highness [James] was very sensible of his most Christian majesty's friendship and that he would labour to cultivate it with all the good offices he was capable of doing . . . that my Lord Arlington [who favoured war with France] and the Parliament were not only unuseful, but very dangerous both to England and France, that therefore it was necessary that they should do all they could to dissolve it.'[44]

The letter continued, digging an ever-deeper hole both for Colman himself and the duke: 'If we can advance the duke's interest one step forward, we shall put him out of the reach of chance forever . . . if he could gain any considerable addition of new power, all would come over to him as the only steady center of our government, and nobody would contend with him further. Then would Catholics be at rest, and his most Christian majesty's interest secured with us in England . . .'[45] Even more inflammatory language followed – Louis XIV could earn 'God almighty's glory, the salvation of his own soul, and the conversion of our poor kingdom, which has been a long time oppressed, and miserably harassed with heresy and schism.'[46] 'Colman's letters!' indeed. It was little wonder that Shaftesbury and his allies saw Colman's private diplomacy as a smoking gun in their campaign against the duke of York.

James certainly knew about Colman's dalliance with the French, and these revelations were highly problematic for him. When Colman wrote his letters, James was trying to undermine Danby, and he sought Louis's money to counteract the Lord Treasurer's own patronage. But by 1678 those efforts were ancient history; in three years factional infighting had moved on; now James and Danby found themselves in the same awkward boat, and Colman's letters threatened to swamp them both. The prosecution made an effort to throw the duke a lifeline, arguing that James knew nothing of his servant's correspondence, and James himself solemnly denied knowing what Colman had been up to.[47] One letter found in Colman's house, the prosecution said, was written in James's name without his permission. Sergeant Maynard threw a little dust in the eyes of the jury: 'Pray observe that he [Colman] takes upon him to prepare a letter, and that in the duke's name, but contrary to the duke's knowledge or privacy, for which when he had the boldness as to tell him of it, the duke was angry and rejected it.'[48] James no doubt wished that Edward Colman had never been born.

Having done their bit to shield James, the prosecution now brought out its final, and most damaging, evidence. 'My Lord,' the Attorney General said, 'I have but one paper more to read, and I have kept it till the last, because if we had proved nothing by witnesses, or not read anything but this, this one letter is sufficient to maintain the charge against him.'[49]

He read from one of the letters seized in Colman's house: 'We have here a mighty work upon our hands, no less than the conversion of three kingdoms, and by that perhaps the utter subduing of a pestilent heresy, which has domineered over a great part of this Northern world a long time, there were never such hopes of success since the death of our Queen Mary, as now in our days, when God has given us a prince who is become (may I say a miracle) zealous of being the author and instrument of so glorious a work, but the oppositions we are sure to be met with, is also like to be great, so that it imports us to get all the aid and assistance we can, for the harvest is great, and the labourers but few.'[50] For a courtroom full of Protestants convinced of the wickedness of Catholics, words like this – even praise for Bloody Mary! – were both shocking and chilling.

With that the prosecution rested. Now Colman had to defend himself, and not surprisingly he began by assaulting Titus Oates. Edward asked Oates to specify the days in April they were together, and the location of the Jesuit's meeting. Titus was vague: 'I cannot swear the particular day of the month, I cannot so charge my memory.' Oates then said that while Colman had not attended the 'consult', in August 1678 he approved the plan to murder the king: 'he did say it was a very good proposition, but he thought the reward too little'.[51] Pressed by Scroggs and Justice Wilde for the exact words that Colman had spoken, Titus again took refuge in vagueness, 'He did express his consent, but to say the very words, I cannot tell.'[52] Colman asked Oates exactly when in August he overheard these words, and Oates said 'I believe, I will not be positive in it, it was about the 21st day of August.' This, Colman said, was impossible: he was in the country for nearly all of August. Furthermore, Colman denied ever having known, or even seen, Oates or Bedloe before they accused him of treason.[53] Nor, said Edward, did the witnesses testify to the same fact – Oates said the conspirators planned to poison Charles, and Bedloe that the method was to shoot or stab him.

Chief Justice Scroggs erupted at this, 'No man shall be guilty if denial shall make him innocent! They swear to the fact of killing the king, both of them, and that's enough. If one saith you have a plot to poison, that is killing the king, and the other swears a plot to shoot or stab him that is to the killing the king also . . .!'[54] Colman protested, 'For treason (with submission to your lordship), I hope there is none in that [letter], though there are very extravagant expressions in it. I hope some expressions explain it, that it was not my design to kill the king.'[55]

The defendant's denial prompted another tirade from Scroggs. 'You are charged to have had a correspondency and agency with a foreign power to subvert our religion and bring in foreign authority and power upon us . . .! How can this be proved plainer than by your letter . . .?' Desperate now, Colman argued that he acted to 'make the king and the duke (as far as I thought in my power) as great as could be'. No one, Edward said, would give him £200,000 unless they thought he acted with James and Charles's approval. Scroggs had no intention of allowing Colman to hide behind the duke, much less the king: 'What a kind of way and talking is this? . . . You do seem to be a mighty agent, might not you for a colour use the duke of York's name to drive on the Catholic cause, which you was driven to by the priests mightily, and think to get 200,000 pounds advance money and a pension for yourself, and make yourself somebody for the present and secretary of state for the future? If you will make any defense for yourself, or call in witnesses, we will hear them. Say what you can, for these vain inconsequential discourses signify nothing.'[56]

Colman called a single witness to prove his alibi, his steward, Jerome Boatman. Boatman testified that his master had been in Warwickshire all of August, but when Scroggs asked him whether he had been in London at any point that month, Boatman admitted that Colman had been in London, but he could not pinpoint the days. This feeble testimony fell flat, and Colman seemed to realize it. 'If you have a mind to say anything more, say what you can,' said the Lord Chief Justice. Colman's brief reply, 'I can say nothing more than what I have said. Positively I say, and upon my salvation, I never saw these witnesses, Oates but once, and Bedloe never before', was redolent of defeat.[57] The defence rested.

Sir Francis Winnington then summed up the prosecution's case for the jury. He piled on the rhetoric: 'The cause before you, I dare adventure say, is a cause of as great a nature, and includes as great crimes as ever came to this bar.'[58] Sir Francis repeated the substance of Oates and Bedloe's testimonies and repeated some of the more inflammatory remarks from Colman's letters. Arriving at his peroration, he said, 'Therefore I hope, gentlemen, that when you meet with offenders that are guilty of such stupendous crimes, you will do justice upon them, which will be a great satisfaction to the king and all his good Protestant subjects.'[59] Sergeant Pemberton piled it on further: 'Gentlemen, you hear the crime is of the highest nature . . . to destroy our king, and take away our religion, and to enslave us all to the pope, and make us all truckle to the priests.' Pemberton credited the 'finger of God' for averting catastrophe – through his instruments, Oates and Bedloe. Combined with the plain language of Colman's letters, 'I think you, gentlemen, have such evidence as would satisfy any man.'[60]

Now it was the Chief Justice's turn to summarize the case for the jury. Scroggs focused on Colman's letters. They showed 'That which is plainly intended, is to bring in the Roman Catholic, and subvert the Protestant religion.' This assertion, undoubtedly true, Scroggs then linked to another proposition – subverting Protestantism, he said, required 'killing the king, as being the most likely means to introduce that, which, as it is apparent by his letters, was designed to be brought in'. This was rhetorical sleight of hand; Colman's hopes for a Catholic England, expressed in his correspondence, had no obvious connection to an assassination plot, though Scroggs pretended otherwise. But given the seventeenth-century Protestant's view of the inherent treachery of Catholics, it is little wonder that the jury found the judge's comments persuasive.

Scroggs's summation focused almost entirely on Colman's letters; he mentioned neither of the Crown's star witnesses by name: 'For the other part of the evidence, which is by the testimony of the present witnesses, you have heard them. I will not detain you longer now, the day is going out.'[61] This was hardly a ringing endorsement of the witnesses' wider story; the court clearly found Oates and Bedloe's tales less than decisive – and Scroggs practically ignored them.

The Chief Justice then turned the case over to the jury. 'Gentlemen, if your consultation shall be long, then you must lie by it all night, and we shall take your verdict tomorrow morning. If it will not be long, I am content to stay a while.' The jury wanted none of that: 'My lord, we shall be short.' Justice Wilde soberly intervened, 'We do not speak to you to make more haste, or less, but to take a full consultation, and your own time; there is the death of a man at stake, and make not too much haste.'[62] Wilde's caution had no impact: the jury departed the court and returned within minutes.

'Are you all agreed of your verdict?'

'Yes.'

'Who shall speak for you?'

'The foreman.'

'Edward Colman, hold up thy hand.'

'Is Edward Colman guilty of the high treason whereof he stand indicted, or not guilty?'

'Guilty, my lord.'

Colman, recognizing that his fate was sealed, nevertheless protested: 'I am a dying man, and upon my death, and expectation of salvation declare that I never saw these two gentlemen, excepting Mr Oates, but once in all my life, and that was at the Council table.'[63]

But for Scroggs the case was closed: 'Mr. Colman, your own papers are enough to condemn you.'[64]

The next day, 28 November, the court reassembled for sentencing. The clerk asked Colman, 'What canst thou say for thyself, wherefore judgment of death should not be given against thee, and an execution awarded according to law?' Edward again rehearsed his alibi and attacked Oates's testimony – but Chief Justice Scroggs rejected the argument: 'But as for what you say concerning Mr. Oates, you say it in vain now, Mr. Colman, for the jury hath given in their verdict, and it is not now to be said, for after that rate we shall have no end of any man's trial.'[65]

Scroggs then proceeded to pass sentence – not before speaking at some length. Even if Colman had played no part in an assassination plot, he argued, his attempts to convert England to Catholicism made him guilty. This line of argument implicitly conceded that Oates and Bedloe's testimony lacked credibility, though of course the judge did not say so. Scroggs urged Colman to confess fully 'Were I in your case, there should be nothing at the bottom of my heart I would not disclose.' In the end, Scroggs even sounded sympathetic, 'I have, Mr. Colman, said thus much to you as you are a Christian, and as I am one, and I do it out of great charity and compassion, and with great sense and sorrow that you should be misled to these great offenses under pretense of religion.'[66]

But the law was relentless: treason demanded exemplary punishment, and Scroggs pronounced sentence: 'You shall return to prison, from thence to the place of execution, where you shall be hanged by the neck, and be cut down alive, your bowels burned before your face, and your quarters severed, and your body disposed of as the king sees fit, and so the Lord have mercy upon your soul.'[67]

A prisoner convicted of treason could not, by custom, speak after sentencing. But Chief Justice Scroggs indulged Colman, who steadfastly maintained his innocence, provoking a debate with the Chief Justice over his letters. Justice Scroggs refused to believe that Colman's correspondence with France had ceased in 1675. 'I am sorry, Mr. Colman, that I have not charity enough to believe the words of a dying man; for I will tell you what sticks with me very much: I cannot be persuaded, and nobody can, but that your correspondence and negotiations did continue longer than the letters that we have found, that is, after 1675.'[68] Scroggs's doubts were no doubt well-founded, but he was asking Colman to prove a negative – the lack of letters dating after 1675 hardly proved that there *were* such letters.

In the end, the argument petered out, and after granting Colman permission to see his wife, cousin and a (Protestant) clergyman, he returned to his cell in Newgate. English justice acted swiftly. Six days later, on 3 December, he was bound to a sledge, and a horse dragged him from Newgate to Tyburn – a journey of not much more than a mile. We do not know exactly how many Londoners turned out to witness the execution, but no doubt many, probably thousands, did. Once there, he mounted the scaffold and faced the multitude.

Edward's last words proved disappointing for most of the spectators. He declared that he died a faithful Roman Catholic, and said that his Church was not 'at all prejudicial to the king and government'.[69] At this point, the sheriff interrupted him – unless he intended to confess his crimes and express contrition, Edward must be silent. Hoping to extract more information about the Godfrey murder, the sheriff asked if Colman had anything to say about it. Edward denied knowing anything about Godfrey's death; he was a prisoner when the magistrate disappeared. His public remarks ended, Edward spent a few minutes in prayer. The executioner then hoisted his victim, strangling him until he neared death – and then lowered him for the customary butchery. Colman was disembowelled and his remains quartered. The Crown at least spared the widow the humiliation of a public display of Edward's mangled body; he was buried – in unconsecrated ground – near St Giles-in-the-Fields. Mary Colman's life was also shattered by her husband's fate; she committed suicide not long afterwards.[70]

Many said that Colman had expected a last-minute reprieve, but it never came. The duke of York had favoured Edward, and he might have intervened on his behalf, but his brother was implacable. King Charles believed that Colman's private diplomacy was reason enough for his execution, and he knew a pardon would spark outrage. Shaftesbury would be delighted and the king shrewdly avoided further inflaming the situation. Not until 1929 did Edward Colman receive justice, when Pope Pius IX beatified him as a martyr.

Two weeks after Colman died, on 17 December, the second plot-related trial opened. Thomas Whitbread, William Ireland, Thomas Pickering and John Grove stood indicted for high treason. Unlike Colman, whose exalted connections had led to a trial in Westminster Hall, the proceedings took place at the Old Bailey. Located near St Paul's Cathedral, the Old Bailey and Newgate jail were near neighbours, conveniently so for the trial of London's accused felons. The old courthouse, like most of the rest of London, had burned down in 1666, and a new building opened in 1673. Unlike Westminster Hall, where trials at least occurred indoors, here proceedings were held in the open air. The courtroom was walled on three sides, with one open to a fenced yard. Judges, court officials and jurors sheltered in the roofed courtroom, along with favoured spectators, crowded into a balcony overlooking the court. Prisoners stood in the yard, in the open air, where they (theoretically) could not infect their betters with jail fever. Behind the prisoners crowded those spectators not lucky enough to get a ticket for the balcony.

Lord Chief Justice Scroggs, with Justices Atkins and Bertie, presided once again, and though the court and yard must have been filled with spectators, most of them shivered in the cold December air. All five defendants pleaded innocent and the clerk swore in a jury of twelve Middlesex gentlemen. The jury foreman was Sir William Roberts, whose family had been enthusiastic supporters of Parliament during the civil war – a man hardly likely to be unbiased against Catholics – much less Jesuits. The remaining jurors, a baronet, knight, eight men identified as 'esquires' – that is, high-ranking gentlemen – and a single plain gentleman, formed a company whose social status was notably higher than the typical jury. Their objectivity might well be questioned, despite their rank.

A long, and repetitious, indictment followed, as each defendant separately was accused 'falsely, maliciously, deceitfully, advisedly, devilishly, and traitorously they did consult and agree to put and bring our said sovereign lord the king to death and final destruction, and to alter and change the religion rightly and by the laws of the same kingdom established, to the superstition of the church of Rome . . .'[71] After repeating all of this four more times – once for each defendant – the prosecution finally got down to business. Sir Cresswell Levinz and Sir Samuel Baldwin opened for the Crown. Baldwin started with Jesuit conspiracies dating to the reign of Queen Elizabeth, nearly a century earlier, connecting them to the Gunpowder Plot, also supposedly a Jesuit operation, and now the assassination plot revealed by Titus Oates. Thomas Whitbread, after all, was the leader of the Jesuit mission in London, and treason, as English Protestants knew, was a Jesuit speciality. Baldwin repeated Oates's story of the April 1678 Jesuit 'consult' and various details he provided – Grove was to have £1,500 for murdering the king, while Pickering, who preferred spiritual over material rewards, would collect 30,000 masses for his soul. The conspirators had hired four Irish 'ruffians' to ambush the king, for the bargain price of £80 – English Catholics apparently had a very low opinion of the value of Irish labour.

After summing up the case against the defendants, the prosecution turned to its witnesses. First up was Oates. Having rehearsed his story repeatedly before any number of witnesses, Titus jogged briskly through his testimony adding some new details, the better to incriminate the defendants.[72] Oates claimed the conspirators added the bishop of Hereford and Dr Edward Stillingfleet to their hit list; and added a new wrinkle – a Jesuit scheme to raise a rebellion in Scotland. Disguised as radical Presbyterians, several Jesuits would be sent north to stir up opposition to the Crown.

Oates repeated the story about Sir George Wakeman's role in the plot, and his haggling over the price of his services as royal poisoner – raising his fee from £10,000 to £15,000. At Justice Scroggs's prompting, Oates pointed out and named all of the defendants at the bar, swearing that each of them had been directly involved in the assassination conspiracy. Oates testified that he had seen the defendant Grove and Pickering prowling around St James's Park, waiting to ambush the king. They carried 'screwed pistols which were longer than ordinary pistols, and shorter than some carbines'. The would-be assassins loaded these dangerous weapons with silver bullets, intentionally 'champt' – their spherical shape slightly flattened 'for fear . . . if the bullets were round, the wound that might be given might be cured'.[73] Why the plotters used silver bullets instead of humble leaden ones Oates left unexplained – though he assured the court he had seen them no fewer than three times, in May, June and August 1678. Having told the court about his own beating by Whitbread, who allegedly feared Titus had betrayed the plot to the king, Oates then repeated one of his favourite salacious details, that Whitbread had sentenced Pickering to 'twenty or thirty strokes of discipline' (on his bare bottom was the implication) for being a careless assassin. Presented with an easy shot at the king, 'he had at that time not looked to the flint of his pistol, but it was loose, and he durst not venture to give fire'.[74] Poor Pickering, beaten by his masters for his inept villainy, plaintively told Chief Justice Scroggs, 'My lord, I never shot off a pistol in all my life!'

Oates's story told, Father Whitbread began his questions, remarking upon the injustice of his situation: 'My lord, I am in a very weak and doubtful condition as to my health, and therefore I should be very loath to speak anything but what is true, and I know it is much harder to prove a negative, than to assert an affirmative; it is not a very hard thing for a man to swear anything if he will venture his soul for it, but truly, I may boldly say, in the sight of Almighty God before whom I am to appear, there have not been three true words spoken by this witness.'[75]

This heartfelt sally only led Justice Scroggs to reiterate his anti-Catholic tropes:

'Do you hear, if you could but satisfy us, that you have no dispensation to call God to witness a lie . . .'

'My lord, I do affirm it with all the protestations imaginable!'

'But if you have a religion that can give a dispensation for oaths, sacraments, protestations and falsehoods that are in the world, how can you expect we should believe you?'[76]

Scroggs finished this exchange with a typical example of his malevolent wit. He asked Whitbread, 'What, I warrant you, you are not Provincial of the Jesuits, are you?' 'I cannot deny that, my lord.' 'Then there are more than three words he [Oates] hath spoken are true.'[77]

Under further questioning, Oates accused a prominent Catholic gentleman, Sir John Gage, of receiving an officer's commission in the rebel army charged with the general massacre of Protestants following Charles's assassination. Titus, aided by Scroggs, wrangled with the defendants about his close relations with the accused. Grove denied anything but the slightest acquaintance, prompting the Chief Justice to ask 'What, don't you know Mr Oates?'

'My lord, I have seen him before.'

'Why this it is, ask a Papist a question and you shall have a Jesuitical answer!'

Grove admitted he had seen Oates perhaps two or three times, and further admitted he once lent Titus eight shillings. Not surprisingly, the only repayment the hapless Grove received was an accusation of treason. Oates claimed they drank together on a number of occasions, defaming Parliament and translating libels into French for the benefit of Louis XIV. Oates also casually threw in, for good measure, that over his cups Grove boasted that he and three Irishmen (such black hearts, the Irish) had started the fire that two years before burned down most of Southwark. For this Grove had collected £300 while his fellows pocketed £200 each.[78]

Next came John Fenwick. Oates said Father John was his confessor. 'I believe he never made any confession in his life,' Fenwick replied sardonically, allowing Justice Scroggs another opening for his mocking wit.

'Yes, he [Titus] hath made a very good one now. Were you of his acquaintance, Mr Fenwick? Speak home, and don't mince the matter.'

Fenwick testified that Oates had borrowed money from him too, claiming that he had not eaten for days, and of course he had never been repaid.

Fenwick and William Ireland both told the court that when Oates said he was in London at the Jesuit consult, he was in fact at St Omer, wearing out his welcome. Fenwick claimed that 'we can prove by abundance of witnesses' Titus's whereabouts in the spring of 1678, and could produce a deposition from residents of the college, sworn before local magistrates. Justices Scroggs and Atkins rejected this. 'You must be tried by the laws of England, which sends no piece of fact out of the country to be tried,' said Scroggs. Atkins added, 'Such evidence as you speak of we would not allow against you, and therefore we must not allow it for you.'[79]

Whitbread intervened – 'May this gentleman . . . produce any two witnesses that saw him in town at that time?' Oates responded with a list of names: Father

Warner, Sir Thomas Preston, Father Williams – all of whom were dead or had fled. The only other people who could testify to his presence in London, he said, were the defendants. Scroggs uncharacteristically admitted the force of Fenwick and Whitbread's argument: 'If you can prove this upon him, that he was absent, and not in England in April or May, you have made a great defence for yourselves, and it shall be remembered for your advantage when it comes to your turn.'[80] These words must have raised the hopes of the defendants, for they all knew that they could indeed call witnesses who would prove Oates's perjury.

When Titus had finished, Scroggs, solicitous as always, said, 'Let Mr Oates sit down again, and have some refreshment.'[81] Now it was Bedloe's turn. He began by saying he had been employed by the Jesuits for five years 'for the promoting of a design tending to the subversion of the government, and the extirpating of the Protestant religion . . .'[82] No heretic would survive in England. This prompted an outburst from Whitbread, quickly suppressed by the court, giving Bedloe the opportunity to smugly hammer home the Jesuit reputation for dissimulation, 'My lord, I am so well satisfied in their denials, that I cannot but believe they who can give a dispensation, and have received the sacrament to kill a king and destroy a whole kingdom, do not scruple to give a dispensation for a little lye to promote such a design . . .'[83]

Bedloe said he had carried letters to and from Jesuits in England and France, beginning in 1675. In 1676, he said, he saw an incriminating letter from Lord Belasyse among others. The following year he brought letters describing 'the consultation held in the gallery at Somerset house, all tending to the destruction of the Protestant religion and killing the king . . .' Here he turned coy, 'but I do not think fit to declare here who were the persons at that consultation'. But of course Bedloe's implication was clear – he meant the queen and duke of York. Then followed an account of his travels from Paris to Spain, still acting as postman for the Jesuits – following an itinerary identical to his European crime spree, where his path crossed Oates's the previous year.

None of this testimony implicated any of the defendants directly, but Bedloe was only getting started. In August he had heard about Grove and Pickering's part in the assassination plot, but this was hearsay evidence. At the end of August or early September, Bedloe said he had been present when Ireland, Grove and Pickering discussed the failure of the famous Irish ruffians to dispatch King Charles at Windsor. They talked about a new attempt, one that Grove eagerly pressed, saying that one who undertook such an endeavour 'had the glory to die in a good cause'.[84] Ireland protested that he had never seen Bedloe before, though he made little impression on the court. The other two defendants, Whitbread and Fenwick, emerged unscathed from Bedloe's account.

Father Ireland challenged Bedloe to bring a witness to support his testimony – excepting Titus Oates, that 'Knight of the Post', a term applied to professional false witnesses. The court would have none of this: 'You must be corrected for that, Mr Ireland. You shall not come here to abuse the king's evidence,' said Scroggs. 'Take off his credit as much as you can by proof, but you must not abuse him by ill language,' said Atkins.[85]

Ireland sparred with 'Captain' Bedloe over his alleged presence at Somerset House, demanding names of anyone who would affirm his testimony. Bedloe named two Jesuits, Fathers Lefevre and Perrare – sparking yet another Scroggsian intervention about the unreliability of Catholic witnesses '. . . we know very well what answers we are like to be put off with by men of your own persuasion at this time of day!' 'My lord, if nobody's oath can be taken that is of another persuasion than the church of England, it is hard,' remonstrated Ireland, but to no avail.

Scroggs challenged Ireland to produce the witnesses, an impossibility. Perrare had disappeared, and Lefevre had already fled, and was wanted by the Crown – return would be suicidal for both men. 'You keep such company as run away, and then you require him [Bedloe] to produce them, whom the king's proclamation cannot bring in,' triumphed Scroggs. Father Ireland found himself reduced to a feeble riposte, 'I keep none but honest company.'[86]

But Bedloe intended more: 'If your lordship pleases I have one thing more that is very material to speak . . .' This was a recent elaboration – in addition to killing the king, Bedloe said, the conspirators had also aimed to murder the earl of Shaftesbury, the duke of Buckingham, the duke of Ormond and his son the earl of Ossory. The addition of Shaftesbury and Buckingham to the list of targets was a transparent ploy to boost their credibility as champions of the opposition and anti-Catholic crusaders. Throwing in Ormond and Ossory was a bonus, offering the possibility of expanding the plot into Ireland, with its inexhaustible supply of papists who might easily be accused of any villainy. It seems unlikely that Bedloe colluded with Shaftesbury in this instance; adding Buckingham to the list of targets only detracted from the earl's significance. Nevertheless, the invention could not but assist the opposition.

Oates could not resist intervening, and he said that he had seen a letter signed by Whitbread, Ireland, Fenwick 'and others', describing a plan to assassinate

Ormond and raise a rebellion in Ireland. Interestingly, he had nothing to say about Shaftesbury and Buckingham, perhaps suggesting that his alliance with the opposition was still developing.

Unfortunately, Oates could not produce this letter – though he said a copy might be found in the Jesuit's letterbook, a book Whitbread said did not exist. Bedloe chimed in, claiming that he too had seen this book. Scroggs asked Whitbread to produce it 'and we shall see whether you cannot catch Mr Oates in something or other'.[87] The demand that Whitbread produce a non-existent book was typical of the Chief Justice's behaviour – as was his next remark: 'If a hundred witnesses swear it [that there was such a volume], they will deny it.'[88]

The Crown's star witnesses had now finished, and the prosecution introduced a devastating piece of evidence: a letter summoning William Tunstall, SJ, to a 'master consult' in London on 24 April 1678. Written by Father Edward Petre, now a prisoner in Newgate, the government found this document among the papers of another Jesuit, William Harcourt. While the letter says nothing about treason or assassination, its language seemed decidedly sinister: 'Everyone is minded also, not to hasten to London long before the time appointed, nor to appear much about the town until the meeting be over, less occasion should be given to suspect the design. Finally, secrecy, as to the time and place, is much recommended to all those that receive summons, as it will appear of its own nature necessary.'[89]

Although the letter did not mention any of the defendants, nor elaborate any specific details of a plot, it nevertheless proved highly effective, making it seem clear to the jury that there was indeed something very secret afoot. Under questioning, both Whitbread and Ireland denied knowledge of this letter – Ireland employing what contemporaries would have described as 'jesuitical' language to do so: 'It is none of my letter, my lord.' Scroggs pressed, 'Did you never hear of it before?' 'Not that I know of in particular,'[90] replied Ireland. In this both Jesuits surely perjured themselves, for of course there was a 'consult' on 24 April – only not about overthrowing the state and Protestantism. Of course the Jesuit mission routinely operated secretly; under laws dating to Queen Elizabeth's time their very presence in England was a capital offence. But the defendants were very poorly positioned to explain away the injunctions to be secret. The impression that this letter must have made on the jury could not have been good for the accused.

The Crown then presented the final piece of its case. The clerk brought forward the seals that Whitbread and his fellow Jesuits used on their correspondence – the ones Oates swore he had seen on 'commissions' appointing various conspirators to places in the prospective rebel army and forthcoming Catholic regime. Of course none of the commissions themselves could be produced – there were none. But these official-looking seals heightened the impression that the Jesuit operation was dangerously effective and widespread.

The defence now began, though not before Justice Scroggs surprised the jury with an intervention. Oates incriminated all five defendants, he said, but Bedloe only swore against three – Grove, Pickering and Ireland. The case against Fenwick and Whitbread, said Scroggs, lacked the statutory requirement of two witnesses to prove a treason charge. Although Oates's testimony might be enough 'to satisfy a private conscience', the law insisted upon two witnesses. For this reason, Scroggs ordered Whitbread and Fenwick's removal from the bar. This was not an acquittal, rather a temporary reprieve, and the two were returned to their cells.[91]

Father Ireland presented his defence first, hoping to prove that he was out of London in August, when Oates claimed he had been in the city plotting regicide.[92] Ireland said that he had travelled to Staffordshire, some 150 miles from London, with Lord Aston, John Aston and several others. John Aston was in town, and could testify that Father William spent all of August in the country.

'Call Mr. John Aston!' said the court crier. The crowded court waited expectantly for Aston to shoulder his way through the throng – and waited.

'It is a hundred to one if he be here, for I have not been permitted so much as to send a scrap of paper,' said Ireland. Even if he had, seventeenth-century criminal procedure did not allow the accused to compel witnesses to either attend a trial, or, if they did, to testify under oath. But had Aston showed, he might at least have raised some doubts about the prosecution's witnesses – he was, after all, a relative of Lord Aston, and a gentleman. But he was also a Catholic, and Lord Aston was himself under suspicion. Raising the family's profile by testifying on behalf of Father William would have required more courage than Aston possessed.

Unfortunately, Ireland had played into the prosecution's hands. They called a witness, Sarah Paine, who had been John Grove's maid. She testified that she had in fact seen Ireland in London in August, visiting her master's house. Father William's response was to call his sister and his mother, Eleanor, to contradict the Crown's witnesses. Ireland said that others had seen him in Staffordshire – but he had no good answer when Justice Scroggs asked 'Why did you not send for them before, to have them ready?'[93] And then Oates chimed in to hammer another nail into Father William's coffin – it was common practice among the Jesuits, he said, to postdate letters by several days. This made it possible to 'prove' an alibi – someone who dated a letter in Staffordshire on 16 August could not be in London on the same day. This, Oates said, Ireland had done – Titus said he saw a postdated letter by Ireland, dated from St Omer, even though the good father was in fact in London on that date. This letter, of course, did not exist – but Oates's word that it did was enough for the court, despite Ireland's protest that Titus had lied.

Ireland brought two more witnesses: a coachman named Harrison, who said he had carried Father William into Staffordshire, and Mr Charles Gifford, who testified that Ireland visited him at his home not far from Lord's Aston's, from 24 August to 9 September. The word of a coachman would not have made much impression on the jury, and while Gifford was a man of substance, he was also a Catholic, and Scroggs had already made clear to the jury his distrust of 'papist' testimony. Ireland's defence rested.

Grove and Pickering had even less to say in their own defence – both complained they had no time to call witnesses, an excuse Scroggs rejected, as he did their pleas for more time to bring witnesses forward, warning them not to delay the proceedings. 'Only you must tie up the jury, and they must neither eat nor drink till they give in a verdict,' said Scroggs. This practice was no small part of the reason for the swiftness of the average jury deliberation – a process rarely lasting more than half an hour. Beyond flatly denying the veracity of the prosecution's witnesses, Pickering and Grove had almost nothing more to say.

The last gasp of the defence followed. William's sister Anne, by dint of desperate pleading, brought forward a new witness, Sir Denny Ashburnham. Ashburnham represented Hastings, Oates's home town, in the House of Commons, and he came to speak of Titus's reputation. He had long known Oates, and the acquaintance had not been inspiring: 'I have known him from his cradle, and I do know that when he was a child, he was not a person of that credit that we could depend upon what he said.'[94] Here was, at last, a solid blow to Oates's credibility. And Ashburnham followed it up by introducing a copy of a perjury indictment lodged against Oates some years before. This case, never brought to trial, represented one of Oates's early brushes with the law – he falsely swore charges of pederasty – the irony – against an innocent man. This might have seriously undermined Oates's testimony, but Ashburnham hedged. He did not doubt that a conspiracy existed, 'and I would not speak anything against the king's witnesses when I myself was satisfied with the truth of the thing, and I do think truly that nothing can be said against Mr Oates to take off his credibility' but the indictment he brought in to court.[95] Understandably, the Parliamentarian (who Shaftesbury classified as 'twice vile') wanted to avoid being seen as a champion of Catholics, but he was acting with some courage. Indeed, he paid the price – losing his seat in the next election.[96]

Scroggs attempted to repair any damage that Sir Denny's testimony might have done by saying, 'Mr Oates's evidence, with the testimony of the fact itself, and all the concurring evidences which he produces to back his testimony, hath convinced [Sir Denny] that he is true in his narrative.'[97] To this Ashburnham agreed, badly denting any hope his original words might have given the accused.

Now the Chief Justice gave his charge to the jury. It was predictably hostile towards the defendants. Scroggs summarized Oates and Bedloe's testimony, emphasizing the fatal letter from Father Petre summoning a meeting of Catholic clergy for April 1678. He excused the witnesses' connection to the plot: 'It may seem hard, perhaps, to convict men upon the testimony of their fellow offenders, and if it had been possible to have brought other witnesses, it had been well. But in things of this nature, you cannot expect that the witnesses should be absolutely spotless. You must take such evidence as the nature of the thing will afford, or you may have the king destroyed, and our religion, too.'[98] The Chief Justice also dealt with Sir Denny Ashburnham's testimony about Oates's poor reputation. If the Crown's case rested solely upon Oates, 'those irregularities of his, when a boy' would have damaged his credibility. But Scroggs went on, oblivious to the colossal irony of his words. 'But when the matter is so accompanied with so many other circumstances, which are material things, and cannot be evaded or denied, it is almost impossible for any man, either to make such a story, or not to believe it when it is told . . . I am sure never a Protestant ever did, and, I believe, never would invent such a one to take away their lives.'[99]

Scroggs finished with an extended rant against Catholicism: '. . . they have debauched men's understandings, overturned all morals, and destroyed all divinity . . . If there can be a dispensation for the taking of any oath . . . it perverts and breaks off all conversation amongst mankind, for how can we deal or converse in the world when there is no sin but can be indulged, no offense so big but they can pardon it, and some of the blackest be accounted meritorious?'[100] He graciously admitted that perhaps *some* papists might be saved, 'but they can never hope to be so in such a course as this'. The Catholic Church might once have been Christian: 'They have some parts of the foundation, it is true, but they

1. Titus Oates. One of thousands of portrait engravings of the 'Protestant Hero', here depicted in the robes of a Doctor of Divinity (which he had no right to wear). This version, by a German engraver, demonstrates that Oates's fame spread well beyond England's shores.

2. William Staley dragged to Tyburn. Staley, son of a prominent Catholic goldsmith in London, was the first victim of the Popish Plot. Accused of wishing Charles II dead, he was arrested in a tavern on the dubious evidence of a pair of shady drinkers hoping for a reward. Convicted, Staley was tied to a sledge, dragged from Newgate prison to Tyburn, and there drawn and quartered.

S.ᵉ E.B.Godfree Strangled
Girald going to stab him.

3. The 'murder' of Sir Edmund Godfrey. The mysterious death of the London magistrate sparked a national panic. Godfrey had taken one of Oates's earliest depositions about a Catholic plot to murder the king. His disappearance and death were assumed to be the work of Catholics determined to silence him. The scene here is printed on a playing card, one of the many efforts of London entrepreneurs to profit from the excitement generated by the plot.

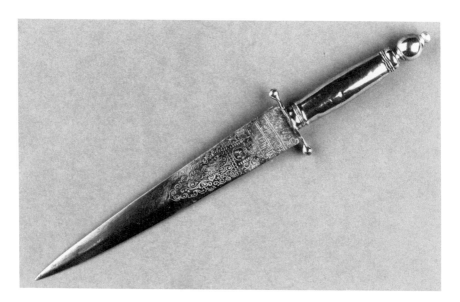

4. A 'Godfrey dagger'. London cutlers produced hundreds of these weapons and sold them to people who feared murder at the hands of sinister Jesuits. This is a particularly fine example, with a silver handle and engraved with the words MEMENTO GODFREY.

5. Every London artisan who could take advantage of the panic surrounding Sir Edmund Godfrey's supposed murder did. This silver medal depicts the magistrate being throttled with his own cravat. The reverse shows an ingenious double portrait: held one way it depicts the Pope; turned upside down, the image of his alter ego, Satan, appears.

6. 'Captain' William Bedloe. A Bristol-born counterfeiter, swindler, petty thief and jail bird, Bedloe's arrival in London provided the crucial second witness required to convict defendants of treason under the Act of 1351.

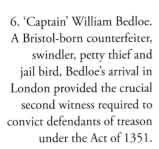

Capt: WILLIAM BEDLOE
Discoverer of the Popish Plott.

7. The Old Bailey. A number of the trials of accused plotters took place here. Located a short distance from Newgate prison, where many defendants were jailed, it replaced an earlier court building destroyed in the Great Fire of 1666. Its ground floor, containing the principal courtroom, was open to the air, allowing large numbers of spectators to witness trials.

8. Sir William Scroggs, Chief Justice of the Court of King's Bench. Derided by his enemies for his alleged 'low birth', Scroggs had been a royalist officer in the civil war, and afterwards entered the law. His royalist principles and close association with Lord Treasurer Danby earned him a knighthood and a judgeship. He rose to the place of Chief Justice just before the Plot began and so presided over many of the most important trials that followed. He was renowned for his quick wit, which he often deployed to the discomfort of those appearing in court before him.

King Charles the Second and Queene Catharine

9. Charles II and his queen, Catherine of Braganza. Depictions of the royal couple together are quite rare. Unlike his father, Charles I, who commissioned a number of family portraits, Charles II, whose indifference to his marriage vows was notorious, had little interest in such wholesome scenes. His apparent neglect of his wife encouraged attempts by opponents such as the earl of Shaftesbury to attack her, even accusing her of plotting Charles's death.

10. Anthony Ashley Cooper, first earl of Shaftesbury. Talented, unscrupulous and immensely ambitious, Shaftesbury's career was punctuated by radical shifts in pursuit of his own interests. A royalist officer in the civil war, he changed sides. During the Interregnum he courted Lord Protector Cromwell. After the Restoration he turned his undeniable talents to royal service as Chancellor of the Exchequer and Lord Chancellor. The loss of the latter office turned him into a determined enemy of the king and his brother James, doing all he could to deny James's right to succeed to the throne as Charles's heir.

11. James, duke of York. Depicted here in Roman armour evoking Mars, the god of war, this portrait was intended to glorify James's achievements as Lord High Admiral. James was the last member of the royal family to command a fleet in battle and he proved himself to be a brave and successful commander. His conversion to Catholicism, public knowledge of which came soon after this portrait was made, greatly complicated British politics. As Charles II's heir presumptive, James's religion seemed to be an existential threat to a Protestant nation.

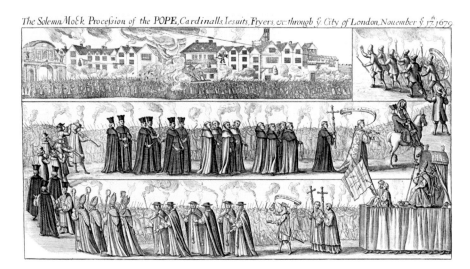

12. Anti-Catholic demonstration, London. Organized and paid for by supporters of the duke of York's exclusion from the throne, on 17 November 1679 – the anniversary of Elizabeth I's accession – hundreds of marchers dressed as Catholic bishops, monks, nuns and cardinals processed through London. The demonstration culminated in the burning of an over-life-sized effigy of the Pope. In order to add drama to the spectacle, organizers trapped live stray cats inside the effigy, which thus howled gruesomely as it burned.

13. Titus Oates and the Devil. By late 1679, the once universal credit enjoyed by Oates and his fellow informers had dwindled and scepticism of his charges became common, especially among those opposed to exclusion. Printers, always eager to seize a perceived market, obliged the sceptics with a flood of pamphlets, broadsides and ballads. This engraving makes Titus a client of the Devil, who promises to make him Grand Vizier of Hell after his conversion to Islam – an ironic nod to Oates's history as a Baptist, Anglican and Catholic.

14. More Plot kitsch. This stove tile is one of a set produced by London entrepreneurs depicting various moments in the plot. Here Sir William Waller, who made himself famous by conducting numerous raids on suspected Catholics, burns 'Popish trash' – rosaries, crucifixes, sacred images and the like. Waller's fame was tarnished by the numerous abuses he visited on his victims – often stealing their personal property and perjuring himself in court.

15. Reliquary of Oliver Plunket, Catholic Archbishop of Armagh. Seeking to boost the impact and credibility of their charges, Shaftesbury and his allies widened their net to include prominent Irish Catholics. Convicted of treason, Plunket was drawn and quartered on 1 July 1681. Fellow Catholics bribed the executioner, who turned the remains over to them. Ultimately Plunket's severed head returned to Ireland, where it is displayed in St Peter's church, Drogheda. Archbishop Plunket became St Oliver in 1975.

16. Titus Oates in the pillory, May 1685. James II's accession to the throne in February 1685 insured that Oates would pay for his lies. Convicted of perjury, he was sentenced to a severe flogging, life imprisonment and required to stand in the pillory five times a year for the remainder of his life. Luck intervened with the overthrow of James in 1688, and Oates was released. Though he tried repeatedly to reprise his career as Protestant hero, his toxic personality insured that he had small success.

are adulterated and mixed with horrid principles. They eat their God, they kill their king and saint the murderer. They indulge all sorts of sins, and no human bonds can hold them.'[101] Addressing the jurors, he finished, 'Let prudence and conscience direct your verdict, and you will be too hard for their art and cunning.'

The jury withdrew and returned only minutes later with their verdict: guilty. Their swift action earned the thanks of Justice Scroggs, always ready to skewer Catholics: 'You have done, gentlemen, like very good Christians, that is to say, like very good Protestants, and now much good may their thirty thousand masses do them.'[102] The foreman, Sir William Roberts, earned his reward a few months later, being elected unopposed as Middlesex's MP, while the other jurors enjoyed a brief popularity as stalwart defenders of Protestantism.[103]

The court asked each of the prisoners if they had any final words before it passed sentence. Father Ireland continued to object that he had not had time to bring in his witnesses, an argument immediately rejected. Thomas Pickering had nothing to say, and John Grove confined himself to a woeful 'I am as innocent as a child unborn.' Their final statements made, the king's executioner entered the court, bound the defendants, and Sir George Jeffreys, the Recorder of London, pronounced sentence, though first he advised them to consider the state of their souls: 'Thus I speak to you, gentlemen, not vauntingly, it is against my nature to insult upon persons in your sad condition. God forgive you for what you have done, and I do heartily beg it, though you do not desire I should, for, poor men, you may believe that your interest in the world to come is secured to you by your masses, but do not well consider that vast eternity you must ere long enter into . . .'[104] Jeffreys urged them to repent and lauded English justice, 'you have had the full benefit of the laws established in England, and those the best of laws, for such is not the law of other nations . . .' The defendants no doubt had other views.

Then the sentence: drawing and quartering, 'And the God of infinite mercy be merciful to your souls.'[105]

Father William Ireland and John Grove entered their 'vast eternity' a little more than a month later. The execution went on as usual: jailers bound Father William and Grove to separate hurdles, and they were dragged through the streets to Tyburn, where a large audience awaited the spectacle. From the scaffold, Ireland denied his guilt, prompting the sheriff to chide him for contradicting the king's court. His protest scotched, he asked God's blessings for the king and royal family, asked for the prayers of Catholics – of whom there were no doubt some in the crowd – and pardoned his enemies. One Catholic pushed through the crowd surrounding the scaffold and implored Father William to pray for him 'whither he was going' – paradise. He was rescued by the guards when the hostile crowd threatened to beat him.[106] London Catholics particularly venerated Father William; in the aftermath they scrambled for relics 'with keen rivalry to obtain from the executioner's underling bits of his clothes, and small portions of his flesh or little ribbons dipped in his blood'.[107] Afterwards witnesses credited these tokens with miracles. Grove, laconic as always, confined himself to a plain statement of his innocence, 'We are innocent, we lose our lives wrongfully; we pray to God to forgive them that are the causers of it.'[108] Thomas Pickering's date with eternity did not come until May, to the great annoyance of the House of Commons. On 27 April 1679, vexed by the delayed justice, the Commons addressed King Charles, urging him to carry out the execution. Charles answered, 'Gentlemen, I have always been tender in matters of blood . . . this is a matter of great weight, I shall therefore consider of it, and return you an answer.' But the pressure continued to grow, and finally, on 25 May, the king gave in. By this time, Pickering, a prisoner for some eight months, was more than ready to go. 'Arriving at the place of execution, he appeared to the spectators (after a manner very unusual to persons in his condition) with a countenance not only calm, sweet, and serene, but even cheerful, smiling, and pleased, solemnly protesting upon his salvation, he was innocent in thought, word, and deed, of all that was laid to his charge.' He prayed for his accusers, turned to the hangman, and uttered his last words, 'Friend, do thy office.'[109]

— SEVEN —
CONFOUNDING POLITICS
WINTER AND SPRING 1679

In February came more trials and executions. The latest defendants were connected with Queen Catherine's household. They were all low-ranking servants, but not surprisingly the queen worried about the possible consequences. On 4 February, Sir Robert Southwell wrote to his friend the duke of Ormond that 'The poor Queen has her frights and anxieties, not knowing what conclusion her concern may have, and just now those whom Prance did accuse about the murther of Justice Godfrey are going to their trial.'[1] Already accused by Oates and Bedloe, she worried what new 'revelations' might be forthcoming. The atmosphere worsened when someone anonymously posted a paper at Somerset House, the scene, it said, of 'the tragedy of Sir Edmund Godfrey by the Queen's servants'.[2]

On 10 February proceedings opened against Robert Green, Henry Berry and Lawrence Hill, accused of the murder of Sir Edmund Berry Godfrey. Green and Berry served in the queen's chapel, Green as a cushion-bearer (he was too feeble to do more than lay cushions on the pews) and Berry as a porter. Hill served Dr Gauden, physician to the treasurer of the chapel. Held at the Old Bailey and presided over by the inevitable Chief Justice Scroggs, there was an air of repetition about the trial. The foreman of the jury was Sir William Roberts, who served in the same role in the trial of Father Ireland and Fenwick, and Oates and Bedloe waited in the wings to trot out their incriminating fantasies. The trial opened in the midst of a scrum of spectators; the chill winter air drove many from the windy courtyard into the space reserved for the court and its officers. They crowded into the jury box, sheltered from the weather, until threats of £100 fines from the bench dispersed them.[3]

Titus Oates testified first, though in reality he could say nothing directly incriminating the defendants. He used his opportunity to boast of his relationship with Godfrey, who, he said, relied upon him for support and comfort – and to hint at obstruction from great persons 'whose names I name not now'.[4] The prosecution's case in fact depended on the testimony of the much-abused silversmith Miles Prance. Now over his previous qualms about fingering innocents, he testified that the three defendants plotted Godfrey's death along with a pair of Irish priests, one Girald (or Fitzgerald) and Kelly. The accused lured Godfrey into the queen's residence at Somerset House and strangled him there. No one seems to have wondered how Godfrey, a robust man in his prime, could be overpowered by this particular group. Berry and Hill were old men, mere 'bags of bones' as one observer put it.[5] Nevertheless, Prance swore that the defendants had done the deed. Afterwards, Sir Edmund's corpse endured a comically macabre journey through various rooms in Somerset House, until several days later it was smuggled out in a sedan chair, propped on a horse and finally dumped at Primrose Hill. 'Captain' Bedloe followed to bolster Prance's account – though like Oates he had not witnessed the murder himself. But the murderers had hired him (for a handsome £2,000) to help dispose of the body. Bedloe claimed that he accepted the offer, but deliberately stayed away from Somerset House on the day Godfrey was moved – though not before having a peek at the corpse by the light of a lantern days earlier.

Prance, then, was the only actual witness to the murder. Mounting an effective defence required solid alibis, not to mention an ability to overcome the bias of the judges, particularly Scroggs. When Sir Robert Southwell testified about Prance's uncertainty upon showing him around the scene of the crime (Prance had difficulty finding the Somerset House room where Godfrey's body was hidden), Scroggs intervened to claim the slip added to Prance's credibility. 'Here, saith he, I will not be positive, but having sworn the other things which he well remembered, positively, he is made the more credible for his doubtfulness of a thing which he does not remember, which a man that could swear anything would not stick at.'[6] Hill produced Mary Tilden, his master's niece, to testify that he was home on the evenings of Godfrey's death and removal, and Scroggs did his best to undermine her. He asked if she was Catholic – she was – and kept up a running commentary: 'You may say anything to a heretic, for a papist . . . It is apparent you consider not what you say, or you come hither to say anything that will serve your turn . . . You must know we can understand you through all your arts.'[7]

Scroggs continued his badgering of other defence witnesses; Green called Mr and Mrs Warrier, his landlords, who gave him an alibi that the Chief Justice found suspiciously exact. Warrier and his wife were with Green on the Saturday of Godfrey's disappearance, 12 October. 'Where were you the ninth of November last?' asked Scroggs. 'Truly,' answered Mr Warrier, 'I can't tell.' 'Why, how come you to remember what you did the twelfth of October, when you did not know where you were the ninth of November?'[8] The Warriers' testimony seemed to prove Green's alibi – until the judges managed to imply that the Saturday Mrs Warrier spoke of was 19 October, rather than 12 October. In fact, Mrs Warrier clearly meant 12 October, but Scroggs chose to misinterpret her words.

One defence witness refused to be intimidated. A Mr Ravenscroft stood up for Lawrence Hill, who he had known for thirteen or fourteen years as a loyal servant to his elder brother. 'What religion are you of?' asked Scroggs. 'My father and mother were Protestants.' 'But you are a papist, are you not?' 'I have not said I am a papist yet.' Justice Dolben intervened, 'In the meantime, I say you are one!' Ravenscroft answered defiantly, 'Do you so? Then pray go to Southwark and see.' This exchange forced the Attorney General to admit that Ravenscroft had in fact taken the oaths of Supremacy and Allegiance, marking him as a Protestant. Ravenscroft then testified that visiting Mrs Hill shortly after Prance's December arrest, he had found her distressed – rumours in the neighbourhood accused her husband of participating in the Godfrey murder. Returning the next day, Ravenscroft found that Hill was gone – arrested and taken to Newgate. To Ravenscroft, as he told the court, this convinced him of Hill's innocence. Mr Ravenscroft told the court that he believed in Hill's innocence – he had known that he was suspected, and yet did not flee: 'all that I say is, if flight be a sign of guilt, as no doubt it is, Adam, ubi es? And courageousness is a sign of innocency, then this man is innocent.'[9]

Ravenscroft's motive for testifying was to help, 'for I saw Hill's wife and Berry's wife were all simple people, without defense for themselves.' The attempt did little good. 'What is all this to the purpose?' sneered the Attorney General, 'Only this gentleman hath a mind to show that he can speak Latin.' 'I thank God I can speak Latin as well as any man in the Court,' rejoined Ravenscroft. Scroggs dismissed the witness with a contemptuous 'Well, this is nothing.'[10]

Henry Berry's defence focused on disproving Prance's account of Godfrey's disposal on Wednesday 16 October. He – joined by Bedloe – said that the murderers took Godfrey out of Somerset House in a sedan chair. But Berry brought four soldiers of the queen's guard to testify that no sedan chair left Somerset House that night. Scroggs suggested that the guards might have left their posts for a drinking bout, but they denied this. A dramatic moment followed. As Berry's witnesses left the courtroom, Mrs Hill shouted out, 'I desire

Mr Prance may swear why he den[ied] all this?' She was referring to Prance's December recantation of his evidence, a subject not yet discussed in the trial.

'Stand up, Mr Prance,' said the Chief Justice, 'that gentlewoman does desire to know what induced you to deny what you had said.'

'It was because of my trade, my lord, and for fear of losing my employment from the Queen, and the Catholics, which was the most of my business, and because I had not my pardon.'[11]

'I desire he may swear whether he were not tortured,' Mrs Hill insisted.

'Answer her.' Justice Dolben ordered the witness. 'Were you tortured to make this confession?'

'No, my lord, Captain Richardson hath used me as civilly as any man in England; all that time I have been there (in Newgate) I have wanted for nothing,' lied Prance.

'There are several about the court that heard him cry out,' Mrs Hill replied heatedly, 'and he knows all these things to be as false as God is true, and you will see it declared hereafter, when it is too late!'

'Do you think,' said Scroggs, without a trace of irony, 'he would swear three men out of their lives for nothing?'[12]

Their defence finished, the accused listened as the Attorney General summed up the Crown's case and Scroggs instructed the jury with his usual invective. 'And for priests being preachers of murder, and your sin, that it is charity to kill any man that stands in their way, their doctrine will make you easily believe their practice, and their practice proves their doctrine. Such courses as these we have not known in England till it was brought out of their Catholic countries, what belongs to secret stranglings and poisonings are strange to us, though common in Italy. But now your priests are come hither to be the pope's bravos, and to murder me for the honor of his holiness . . .'[13]

The jury returned its verdict after a short consultation; the members seem not to have even left their box. Guilty. 'Gentlemen,' pronounced Scroggs, 'you have found the same verdict that I would have found if I had been one with you and if it were the last word I were to speak in this world, I should have pronounced them guilty.' The courtroom erupted in applause. Afterwards, Miles Prance and William Bedloe split the £500 reward offered for Godfrey's murderers, and Prance received a £50 annual pension.

At their sentencing the following day, Berry, Hill and Green received an unexpected mercy from the court. The tipstaff, one of the minor officers of the court, had seized the defendants' coats, claiming them as his fee. The judges refused to allow this. 'But this seems a very barbarous thing, to take their clothes off their backs,' said Justice Wilde.[14] The garments restored, the judges sentenced all three to hang.

Lawrence Hill and Robert Green's execution, scheduled for 17 February, was delayed – parliamentary elections were scheduled for that day and the sheriff, who presided over the poll, could not preside over a hanging at the same time. So Hill and Green had a few more days to contemplate eternity. Hill went first, and after his death the executioner found a text in his pocket – his last words. He asserted that he died a Catholic and again claimed innocence, 'I call God, Angels and men to witness that I am wholly ignorant of the manner, cause, or time of the death of Justice Godfrey . . .' Furthermore, he accused those responsible for his condemnation: 'I cite all such as have had a hand in this bloody contrivance', specifically mentioning Chief Justice Scroggs, Godfrey's brothers, the jury and the witnesses who testified against him. Although the sheriff would have prevented him from reading this speech, enterprising publishers soon printed it. Green was less prolix: he asked for the people's prayers and rather pathetically denied – twice – ever laying eyes on Edmund Godfrey, alive or dead.[15]

Henry Berry's execution had to wait over another week, until 28 February. A Protestant, it was thought he might be more likely to confess his guilt and offer further information about the plot. The chaplain at Newgate, the rector of St Martin-in-the-Fields, Dr William Lloyd, and another Protestant minister, George Wilson, worked hard to obtain Berry's confession. Wilson later published an account. When he entered the condemned man's cell he found him kneeling and at prayer. After he urged Berry to confess and avoid damnation, 'there was a strict tribunal after this life, before which we must all appear'.[16] But Berry adamantly denied taking any part in Godfrey's death, 'he knew not anything of the fact for which he was condemned'. Berry admitted one sin: converting to Catholicism 'for interest sake'. This, he believed, was why he deserved death. With the execution scheduled only a few hours off, Wilson decided that further pressure for a confession was useless, and Berry's remaining time should be spent in prayer.

Newgate's chaplain, joining Wilson in the cell, made one last attempt. A full confession, he said, might bring a royal pardon – but with only an hour or so before his arrival at Tyburn, Henry must have known that the promise was an empty one. 'Come,' said the chaplain, 'tell me what thou knowest bout the murder and do not damn thyself.' Berry again denied all knowledge of the crime. The chaplain assured him that no absolution or indulgence from a priest, or even the pope, could save him. Berry agreed, yet still would not confess. The chaplain desisted and he and Berry returned to prayer. Soon the sheriff arrived to convey his prisoner to the gallows. Mounting the cart over which dangled a noose, and before a huge crowd, Berry offered prayers for King Charles, asked forgiveness for his false accusers and once more said that he was as innocent as a newborn infant. As usual, this claim triggered the intervention of the sheriff, who told him he could not allow the prisoner to 'defame an honourable court'. But Henry Berry had the last word; as the cart upon which he stood was pulled from under him, 'he lifted up his hands towards heaven and said, "As I am innocent, so receive my soul, O Lord Jesus." '[17] Yet again a plotter deprived the crowd of their much-anticipated confession. This was the seventh execution connected to the plot (counting the hapless William Staley), and every victim had steadfastly asserted his innocence.

The trial and executions of Godfrey's alleged killers occurred at a moment of acute political tension. King Charles hoped that a compromise could be hammered out with some of the more moderate opponents of the court. By mid-January this had been done. Led by Lord Holles, an eighty-year-old stalwart of the parliamentary Presbyterian cause, members promised Charles a loan and new taxes in a new Parliament in return for the dissolution, Danby's resignation and the disbandment of the army. Furthermore, Holles and his group promised that the Lord Treasurer's impeachment would be moderated.[18] Danby's experiment in royalist Anglican coalition-building, once so effective, now lay in ruins, and he himself worried that he might soon join the five 'Popish lords' in the Tower.

Charles dissolved the Cavalier Parliament on 24 January 1679 and summoned a new one to meet on 6 March. In the meantime he struggled to regain the political initiative. The agreement with Holles encouraged Charles, but a major difficulty soon emerged: the earl of Shaftesbury. Shaftesbury had nothing to do with the negotiations, and although he happily took credit for forcing the dissolution (altogether untrue), he had no desire to make life easy for Charles, Danby or York.

This was the moment that the trial of Samuel Atkins came on. One of Shaftesbury's pawns in his anti-York campaign, Atkins might be a useful weapon. He was arrested in November, accused of assisting in Godfrey's murder, and had lain in Newgate since then. Shaftesbury probably had no part in scheduling

Samuel's trial, which opened on 11 February, but it conveniently highlighted the duke's possible role in the plot. Atkins worked for Samuel Pepys, secretary of the Admiralty Board and a long-time associate of the duke of York's. While James no longer served as Lord High Admiral – a post he resigned when Parliament imposed a religious test on offices in 1673 – he continued to have considerable informal influence in naval matters. By dragging Atkins into the net, Shaftesbury hoped to blacken Pepys and his patron.

When the trial opened on 11 February, Atkins must have been terribly worried; the odds were hardly in his favour. The courts had convicted every defendant accused in the plot so far. Why should his fate be any different?

But at the start of the proceedings, Samuel might have perceived a glimmer of hope. He stood accused of being both a principal and an accessory to Sir Edmund Berry Godfrey's murder. But at the outset, the prosecution admitted it had no evidence that Atkins played a direct part in Godfrey's death. So the trial now focused on the lesser accessory charge. Unfortunately, accessory to murder was still a capital offence, so a conviction would bring Atkins to the gallows as surely as if he had personally squeezed the life out of Godfrey.

Sir William Jones, the Attorney General, laid out the prosecution's case. Atkins, he said, harboured a grudge against Justice Godfrey, 'that he was a man too active, and that he was in no sort to be permitted to live, for if he were he would be very prejudicial to some he was concerned for'. Jones meant, clearly, Secretary Pepys, and beyond him the duke of York.[19] The Attorney General proceeded to describe the alleged nefarious events in Somerset House on 12 October 1678. Atkins, he said, was among those scheming to dispose of Godfrey's body. Jones claimed that a Royal Navy officer named Charles Atkins (no relation to Samuel) and William Bedloe would prove the case.

Charles Atkins took the stand first. Claiming to 'have a great regard' for Samuel, Atkins told of visiting the Navy Office one day in October, hoping to borrow money. There Samuel told Charles that Godfrey 'had very much injured his master, and if he lived would be the ruin of him'. Samuel asked Charles to find a naval petty officer named Childs and to send him to Secretary Pepys. This he did, and later, while walking near a favourite tavern, Charles ran into Childs. Charles avoided directly accusing Pepys, who, after all, was an influential man. Childs 'told me nothing of Mr. Pepys, but he would have engaged me to join in the murder of a man'.[20] Charles indignantly rejected the offer. Later, he said, Childs offered him £100 to keep his offer secret, and threatened to kill him if he did not. Testimony concluded, Charles stepped down and the Attorney General rose to his feet.

'Now, my lord, because it seems a strange thing that Mr. Atkins, who says he is a Protestant, should be engaged in this business, we have a witness here to prove that he hath been seen often at Somerset House at mass . . . And that is this boy.' Justice Scroggs asked the witness his age – about seventeen, came the reply – and Justice Wilde asked him what the consequences of swearing falsely would be, 'I shall be damned,' the youth said. At this point Samuel intervened and questioned the witness, even though he was not yet sworn. 'What religion are you of, boy.' 'A Protestant.' 'Do you know me?' 'No.'

Clearly embarrassed, Attorney General Jones hastily withdrew his witness, and his fellow prosecutor, George Jeffreys, lamely allowed, 'My lord, I perceive it was a mistake; it was somebody else. We will proceed to other evidence.'[21] The Crown never produced this 'somebody', and moved quickly to its next witness, William Bedloe.

Jeffreys asked Bedloe to tell about Samuel's role in disposing of Godfrey's body. Now it was Bedloe's turn to undermine the prosecution's case. There had been seven or eight men in the room with Godfrey's corpse, one of whom he did not recognize, and who claimed that he was Mr Pepys's clerk. The room had been poorly lighted and looking at Samuel Atkins in the court, Bedloe averred that he could not be sure this was the same man: '. . . it is hard for me to swear that this is he. And now I am upon one gentleman's life, I would not be guilty of a falsehood to take away another's. I do not remember that he was such a person as the prisoner is; as far as I can remember he had a more manly face than he hath, and a beard.'[22]

Bedloe's show of concern for the truth was certainly novel; his lies had already condemned several to death. In this case we might assume that he doubted the strength of the Crown's case and preferred to avoid being caught up in its failure. Having done nothing to support the prosecution, Bedloe left the witness box, to be replaced by a Mr Ward. Ward testified that he and Sam had planned to meet on Saturday 12 October, the presumed day of Godfrey's death. But Samuel failed to keep his appointment, a lapse the prosecution suggested was because Samuel was busy assisting Godfrey's murderers. The implication ignored the fact that Ward could not say for sure just where Samuel had been that evening, and Atkins explained that the date, made some ten days earlier, had simply been forgotten. He also offered to bring witnesses to prove he was elsewhere.

Ward's evidence seemed a thin reed, and Samuel turned his appearance to his advantage. The witness was once Samuel's schoolmaster, and Samuel asked him to speak about his religion and upbringing. 'But now, my lord, this gentleman is upon his oath, who is a Protestant, and was my schoolmaster, I desire him to declare whether I was bred a Protestant, or no, and whether my friends were so, or no?' Ward confirmed Atkins's Protestantism, and went further, '. . . my lord, he was always a Protestant, and a very zealous one, too'.

The answer impressed Justice Scroggs. 'There is very much in that!'[23]

Having one of their witnesses hijacked by the defendant must have been mortifying for the prosecution, but there was nothing they could do. And here the Crown rested its case.

Now Samuel began his defence. He noted that he had done all he could to help Charles Atkins, his accuser – 'a man whom I have kept from perishing . . . I petitioned, solicited for him, and was instrumental in getting him out of prison, for a fact that I shall by and by tell you. And though this, my lord, may seem against me, yet by and by . . .'

No doubt to Samuel Atkins's bewilderment, Scroggs interrupted: 'Hold, you mistake, Mr. Atkins, he does you no mischief at all, for he saith no more than that he hath been discoursing with you about the plot, and you said Sir Edmundbury Godfrey had very much injured your master . . . and asked particularly of Mr. Child . . . All of which is nothing to the purpose.'

Atkins was confused: 'But I never had any such discourse with him my lord.'

'If you had, or had not,' replied Scroggs, 'it is no matter, you need not labor your defense as to anything he says.' Charles Atkins's testimony, the Chief Justice meant, did nothing to prove the charge against him.

'I protest before God Almighty, I know nothing of it!'

Sitting next to Scroggs on the bench, Justice Dolben asked, 'But what say you to Mr. Bedloe's testimony. Did you see the body of Sir Edmund Godfrey at Somerset House?'

'No my lord, I am so far from that that in all my life I was never in the house.'

'Then,' said Scroggs, 'call a couple of witnesses to prove where you were that Monday night, the 14th of October, and you need not trouble yourself any further.'[24]

Waiting in the court was Captain Vittles and several members of his crew. Vittles told the court that Samuel, in the absence of his hard-driving master – gone to Newmarket to attend the king and duke of York – had planned an outing. Vittles commanded one of the king's yachts, and Atkins hoped to impress a couple of 'gentlewomen' with a visit. On Monday 14 October, Samuel, along with his lady friends arrived at Vittles's vessel, anchored in the Thames. They arrived at about 4:30 p.m., and what followed was an epic drinking bout: '. . . and so about eight or nine o'clock we had drunk till we were a little warm, and the wine drinking pretty fresh, and being with our friends, we did drink freely, till it was indeed unseasonable – I must beg your lordship's pardon, but so it was. And at half an hour past ten . . . I put him [Sam] into the boat very much fuddled.'[25] The sailors landed a drunken Atkins at Billingsgate an hour later, to reel home and experience the luckiest hangover of his life. Bedloe, recalled, confirmed that the man he was told was Atkins was in Somerset House at 10:30 p.m., and stone-cold sober.

The prosecution's case lay in ruins, and it scrambled to control the damage to their narrative. Attorney General Jones conceded that the case had fallen flat, 'My lord, in this matter it is in vain to contend in a fact that is plain. But I would desire (because some perhaps will make an ill use of it) that they would be pleased to take notice, here is no disproving the King's evidence. For Mr. Bedloe did not at first, nor doth he now, charge him directly to be the man, so that whoever reports that the King's evidence is disproved, will raise a very false rumor.'[26]

Lord Chief Justice Scroggs enthusiastically joined in the whitewashing. The king's evidence remained solid, he said, and no blame could be cast on Bedloe – though he said nothing about the egregious Charles Atkins. The defence concluded and the jury considered its verdict. Without leaving the court they agreed Samuel Atkins was innocent. Justice Scroggs released the defendant with a cheery admonition to Captain Vittles, 'Well, well Captain, go you and drink a bottle with him.'[27] Atkins was the first person accused in the plot to be acquitted – his Protestantism was at least as important as his alibi, but for those pushing the plot it was a definite setback.

The failure of this indirect assault on the duke of York no doubt annoyed Shaftesbury and his friends, but they looked forward confidently to the new Parliament, where they could renew their assault. Elections were underway across the nation even as the most recent trials unfolded, and the atmosphere was highly charged. As the first general election in eighteen years, this would have certainly generated a high level of interest. But elections in the midst of public excitement about the plot ensured that these evoked comparison to those of 1640 and 1641 – an ominous sign for the court. More ominous still, constituencies where court candidates had routinely been selected without opposition now saw contests. Contested elections doubled – some 125 against only 58 in the last general election, held in 1661.[28] 'There was great dispute as to elections all over England at this time,' said Sir John Reresby, a Yorkshire ally of Danby's.[29]

Yet Charles and his advisors seemed unconcerned; perhaps they expected their negotiations with Lord Holles had sufficed to ensure a cooperative Parliament. They took few steps to exercise influence in the constituencies and the king signalled a desire to compromise. On 28 February the king ordered his brother James into exile, and though on 1 March he took the opportunity to reaffirm the illegitimacy of the duke of Monmouth, his eldest son, once again with a solemn statement entered into the Privy Council's records, Charles's brother could hardly have been much comforted.[30] By 4 March, James and his duchess were sailing to the Netherlands, ostensibly to visit Princess Mary and her new husband, William of Orange.[31]

The body that assembled in Westminster on 6 March was even more problematic than the last, though in his speech from the throne the king noted the steps he had already taken 'to unite the minds of all my subjects, both to me, and to one another'. He spoke longer than usual, and finished up with some wishful thinking: 'I will conclude, as I begun, with my earnest desire to have this an healing Parliament, and I do give you this assurance, that I will with my life defend both the Protestant religion and the laws of this kingdom, and I do expect from you to be defended from the calumny, as well as the danger, of those worst of men, who endeavor to render me and my government odious to my people.'[32]

Those endeavours soon began. Shaftesbury, the original psephologist, calculated that no fewer than 300 new members of the Commons would support the opposition.[33] The first test of Charles's command of the Commons was the election of a Speaker. Perhaps signalling his desire to conciliate his opponents, the king's candidate was Sir Thomas Meres – MP for Lincoln, and one whom Shaftesbury considered 'worthy'. In the last session, Meres had been a thorn in the government's side, an active member of the Plot committee and a vocal opponent of York's. These opposition bona fides notwithstanding, the house elected the previous speaker, Sir Edward Seymour, by acclamation. In the last session Seymour managed the king's business with some skill, but Danby resented his failure to rescue him from Montagu's attack in December, and he convinced Charles to support Meres instead. Sir Edward had greatly burnished his reputation in the House by his vociferous pursuit of the Popish Plot and Catholics in general, even advocating a blanket bill of attainder against accused plotters – an act that would deprive its targets of their right to a fair trial.

Informed of the Commons choice, the king balked. He refused to accept Seymour as Speaker – an exceptionally rare use of the royal prerogative, and one that sparked outrage in the House. The result was an immediate deadlock, both sides refusing to compromise. In an effort to seek a way out of the impasse, on 13 March Charles prorogued Parliament for two days. In the interim cooler heads prevailed and a compromise candidate, William Gleason, took the Speaker's chair – though Charles had reason to feel outmanoeuvred. Gleason, one of Shaftesbury's worthy men, was no great friend of the Court, and had even been involved in the attempted railroading of Samuel Atkins. Charles would probably have been better off accepting Seymour in the first place.[34] But the king seems at this stage to have been hoping that conciliating the opposition would smooth the way forward.

This apparent desire for compromise depressed Charles's supporters. 'It is very unhappy for a servant to serve an unconstant or unsteady prince, which was a little the fault of our master,' said Sir John Reresby, significantly understating the reality.[35] Charles did, though, support Danby even though the former Lord Treasurer's usefulness had ended in December. On 22 March he reiterated to both houses his belief in Danby's innocence – and announced that he would pardon him ten times over if necessary. The Lords, usually punctilious about printing the text of royal addresses, left this one out of their journal – and resolved to bring in a bill 'That Thomas Earl of Danby may be made forever uncapable of coming into His Majesty's presence, and of all offices and employments, and of receiving any grants or gifts from the crown, and of sitting in the house of peers.'[36] A committee including Shaftesbury, Monmouth and a number of their friends would draft the legislation. The following day Charles advised Danby to flee, an act that further enraged Parliament against him – and no doubt caused the earl and his friends more worries about an 'unconstant King'.

These setbacks notwithstanding, there were signs that scepticism about the plot had started to take root in some non-Catholic quarters. As early as 12 March the Lords gave Shaftesbury's Plot committee the authority to summon and question anyone daring to assert the innocence of those executed so far. For the most part these were friends and relatives of the accused, many Catholic. But a few more prominent voices were heard, and the plot's defenders intended to make examples of them. On Friday 21 March, Oates appeared at the bar of the Commons. He accused Danby of threatening him in the Privy Garden, and said that three members of the Commons – Edward Sackville, Henry Goring and Sir John Robinson – had abused him. Sackville, Oates claimed, had said, 'God damn him, it was no plot, and they were sons of whores who say that there is a plot, and that Oates was a lying rogue.' Goring supposedly said Mr Oates was a rascal, and a lying rogue, and he swore 'by God he believed not Mr. Oates, though the house did', and he called him a 'base, impudent fellow'.[37] Oates followed this up with complaints about his situation as the king's guest in Whitehall, 'I desire that I may be removed from Whitehall, and to make use of the liberty the law allows me . . . I have been baffled and abused, and hindered from serving my country.' He finished his complaint with the arrogant declaration, 'the King holds his crown by the same title I hold my liberty', a phrase that evoked a storm of criticism, implying as it did that Titus and his sovereign occupied the same moral plane.[38] Oates's arrogance grew daily, and as it did hostility towards him and his fellow informers grew. As Bishop Burnet put it, '. . . indeed Oates and Bedloe did by their behavior detract more and more from their own credit than all their enemies could have done. The former talked of all persons with insufferable insolence, and the other was a scandalous libertine in his whole deportment.'[39]

Edward Sackville rose to defend himself. A newcomer to the Commons at thirty-eight, this was his first session as a member, representing East Grinstead, a Sussex borough where his family had great influence. Sackville probably did himself no favours in his explanation: 'No man would think me guilty of so much folly as to say there was no plot, but I have said I believe not all Oates has said of it.' He also accused Oates of 'unbelievable' impudence and of slandering him as a rascal. This defence cut no ice with Thomas Pilkington, a London MP closely associated with Shaftesbury. 'The king and kingdom are obliged to Mr. Oates for his discovery, but if he be not upheld by encouragement, we may be lost. I would have every man that is an Englishman consider that if Mr. Oates has been abused, they who have wronged him may be made examples to deter others.'[40]

Not to be outdone by his fellow informer, William Bedloe appeared next, complaining that his guards were in fact spies and a threat to his life. With more freedom he claimed he could have arrested a hundred more priests, and he was still waiting for the £500 reward promised for the discovery of Godfrey's killers. Bedloe said he planned to use the money to reward poor people who assisted him in his priest-hunting work, though we might doubt his sincerity. He claimed Danby offered him a bribe, and was told by an unnamed 'great man' (York?) that he could decamp for Sweden, Jamaica, Switzerland or New England and be comfortably rewarded. But Bedloe had manfully resisted these efforts, 'I am ready to serve the kingdom in thralldom, as well as in liberty.'[41]

Over the next week the Commons further investigated Oates's claims against Sackville, Goring and Robinson. On Tuesday 25 March, Oates again appeared and accused Sackville of wagering £100 that Oates would soon be proved a rogue and a rascal. Titus once again demonstrated his winning charm when after the Speaker's reproof for affronting the king in the house the previous week, he gave the surly reply, 'I am sorry I gave offence to the house in what I said, but it was my conscience, and though I may not say it here, I will say it elsewhere, and believe it, too.'[42]

Titus's outburst gave some of the Crown's defenders an opening – Secretary Coventry, seconded by Sir John Ernly, one of Danby's friends, demanded that Oates be reprimanded more forcefully. 'Pray consider what this house will come to, if persons be permitted to speak here at this rate,' said Coventry. But the Reverend 'doctor' nevertheless had his defenders. William Garway, who would earn 300 gold guineas from the French ambassador for his work this session, argued, 'Mr. Oates is a passionate man, and none of the best mannered men, but no man can regularly censure Mr. Oates but he must debate the merits of the thing he has said.'[43]

The worst that Coventry could manage was a direction to the Speaker that Oates receive a rather gentle reprimand. Oates shrugged it off and brought eight witnesses, all testifying to Sackville's intemperate remarks in a Covent Garden coffee house. A Mr Ray told that Sackville had ardently averred 'That Mr. Oates, the main evidence against Berry, Hill and Green was perjured and that the Parliament were a pack of knaves and fools to take cognizance of two such perjured rogues as Oates and Bedloe, and that, to his knowledge, the Plot would prove a fanatical sectary plot to destroy the monarchy. And that Bedloe was a perjured rogue, and a highwayman, and he wondered that the House would take cognizance of him.'[44]

Shaftesbury's worthies were indignant. John Maynard, member for Plymouth, said 'The House of Commons voted this a plot, and the House of Lords also, and trial went upon this and clear evidence was the conviction of Colman. What is now before you? We are called "fools, and knaves, and rogues, and madmen" for believing it. I hope this gentleman will not continue among us, to be a companion of fools and knaves. Where did this gentleman do this? At a coffee house and taverns. It has been a great design, and general in the nation, to disgrace the evidence and the Parliament, and then the Plot was a foolish thing. It is a great charge upon this gentleman and deserves the severest censure that can be.'[45]

Brought to the bar, there was little Sackville could say – his tavern talk was, after all, mostly true, and it was hard to reject the word of eight witnesses, though he tried to temper his fault. 'I believe that there was a plot but not everything of the plot. I shall limit my discourse so for the future as not so much as to name Mr. Oates, nor anything of his former life.'[46] It was too little and too late. The House ordered that Edward Sackville, on his knees at the bar, be expelled from the Commons, imprisoned in the Tower, and that the king should be asked to take his commission as a lieutenant colonel in the army from him. Sackville's parliamentary career had lasted all of nineteen days, but unlike too many of Titus Oates's victims, at least he escaped with his life. In the end his stay in the Tower was brief, and his military career continued – in fact he received his reward (temporary, as it turned out) in the next reign, rising to the rank of major general.[47]

Sackville's fate proved that the plot's momentum continued, but the fact that its supporters believed such an example should be made of a sceptic suggests that there were fears that the wheels might fall off the juggernaut. The fate of the other two members Oates accused reinforces this view. Oates returned on 29 March, this time accusing Sir John Robinson, MP for Rye and Lieutenant of the Tower, of suppressing evidence of the plot revealed by one of his prisoners. Robinson, who Pepys had described years earlier as 'a bragging bufflehead', stoutly defended himself. 'I never was but in one Plot, and that was for the Restoration of the King' and after postponing further debate on the matter, the Commons followed up on 7 April with a committee composed mostly of members who heartily disliked Robinson. Although they never issued a report, the king dismissed him from his office, probably happy to replace a sixty-four-year-old governor with someone more active. These were dangerous times, and the Lieutenant of the Tower controlled an arsenal that might be vital if rebellion broke out.

Keeping the plot at the forefront of events was part of the opposition's strategy. On 24 March, Shaftesbury alerted the Lords to a new pamphlet, printed in

French and translated into English, that related unflattering information about Oates's life on the continent. This might well have been *A Letter from Amsterdam to a Friend in Paris*, published anonymously, most likely in London. It related some of Oates's earlier adventures, 'His debaucheries are notoriously knowne in and about Hastings I shall not defile my paper with them', although the author could not resist describing Titus's service as a naval chaplain. 'Sometime after he was embarked for Tangiers, he fell to his old tricks of sodomy in the ship and was taken *in flagranti*, to escape hanging, according to his demerit, he adventured drowning and stole away narrowly to shore in the cockboat.'[48] The author impugned Oates's intellect: 'an ignorant dolt that could not speak six words nor write three lines of true Latin. I must tell you the character the Spaniards gave of him: wee have a mean opinion of the English hereticks since so ignorant and ridiculous an animal could gain esteem among them.'[49] The pamphlet cited testimony from English merchants in Spain, who swore Oates was in Bilbao when he claimed to be in Madrid, and in St Omer when he claimed to be in London, plotting the king's death. The author's verdict was unsparing. 'I hope you are fully satisfied that the Plott is a diabolicall fiction of Oates: that he himself is a pure compound of lies forgeries and perjuries. I hear there is a statue preparing for him as preserver of the kingdom. I shall adorn it with an epigraph for his sake: 'Upon this fellow's testimony is grounded the whole machine of the Plott, others are brought in as buttresses to support a weak foundation . . .'"[50]

The pamphlet went on to attack Bedloe: 'A fiddler's son . . . well known over most parts of England, Low Countries, France and Spaine for debaucheries, cheats, robberies and rogueries.' Miles Prance, 'who hath sworn forward and backward several times in the case: hee is now for the plot, but I presume when the next fit comes he will swear against it.' And the latest informer, Stephen Dugdale, furthermore, was reported to be a gambler 'who used to imbezle his Lord's money and play several other cheats . . .'[51] The author finished with an obvious allusion to the plot's enablers, both in Parliament and outside it: 'But all this increases the difficulty of the . . . query: how the whole nation could be worked to such a temper as to believe it. This is soone answered if the time were seasonable: the successe of a plot doth not so much depend upon the composition as upon the management: there lyes all the art and wit.'[52]

The principal manager of the investigation at the moment was Shaftesbury. He and his committee visited the Tower to question the Catholic peers about this scandalous attack on their main witnesses. They learned it was the product of the defence's private investigation into Oates and Bedloe, though none of them admitted to a hand in publishing the information. The committee, determined to protect their informers, asked for, and received, broader powers to search for and prosecute those involved in these publications. Yet the appearance of sceptical accounts of the plot must have spurred the opposition to act before the kettle went off the boil.

In the first week of April Lords Powis, Belasyse, Petre, Arundell of Wardour and Stafford resumed centre stage. The Commons accused all five of 'Wicked plots, conspiracies, and treasons', including the assassination of the king, planning to raise a rebel army, and the murder of Sir Edmund Godfrey. On 7 April the impeachment managers presented these charges to the upper House, which debated when and how to try the lords. The next day, Shaftesbury, clearly orchestrating the process, suggested procedures for the upcoming trial. The House agreed that the five lords should be brought from the Tower, and kneeling at the bar of the house, hear the Commons charges against them. The House also ordered that the defendants should be allowed legal counsel – though their assistance could be used only in matters of law. That meant that the accused's lawyers would be barred from challenging witnesses or evidence. It was a common procedure in criminal cases, but it distinctly disadvantaged defendants.

On 9 April four of the five accused appeared at the bar. Some – probably not including Shaftesbury – might have detected the irony of their situation. All of them had supported the royalist cause during the civil wars, and all had suffered to one degree or another. Subjected to large fines, they were forced to sell portions of their estates during the Interregnum. Lord Petre and Viscount Stafford endured exile, and all five paid swingeing fines to the government. Lord Arundell of Wardour destroyed his own family's castle to prevent its seizure by parliamentary forces in the civil war. Lord Belasyse, a royalist officer during the war, was shot in the head in 1643 and again wounded and captured in 1645. All five of these peers had unquestionably served the Stuart dynasty with more than common devotion. But in the minds of many their Catholicism overrode their service.

One by one four lords kneeled at the bar, then rose to hear the Commons charges. The decrepit Belasyse, sixty-four and immobilized by gout, remained in his damp quarters, but he soon received a copy of the impeachment. The House ordered that the accused should be granted access to documents and testimony necessary for their defence, and appointed counsel for each man. Afterwards the four lords returned up the Thames to the Tower, a journey made more than usually harrowing by the attendance of a huge crowd of hostile Londoners. The next step was for the five lords to respond to the Commons charges. These responses came in on 15–16 April. Four of the five peers replied in much the same way to the charges against them: they were completely innocent. But they also argued that presenting a defence against the charges was impossible because they were so imprecise and general. The impeachment vaguely referred to meetings held by the plotters to conspire murder and rebellion 'for many years now long past'. How, the lords asked, could they find witnesses who might give them alibis for 'many years'? As Belasyse said of his own case, '. . . it is no way possible for him to be prepared with his just and lawful defence, by witnesses, to prove himself absent and in another place at the time of such meeting or consultation'. Furthermore, the charges were equally nebulous about the locations of these meetings held over 'many years'. An adequate defence against charges so vague, he argued, was impossible.[53]

William Lord Petre, who had been jailed twice during the Interregnum for royalist plotting, was the only one of the five who responded straightforwardly. 'This defendant further saith that he is not guilty of all or any of the matters by the said articles of impeachment charged against him; and, for his trial therein he humbly putteth himself upon God and his peers.'[54]

The House of Commons was not amused by these answers. Only Petre's was acceptable; the rest were 'argumentative and evasive, to which the Commons neither can nor ought to reply'.[55] A committee of the Lords considered the Commons objections, and as it was led by the ubiquitous Shaftesbury, agreed entirely with the lower House's complaint. The Lords ordered all of the peers but Petre to resubmit their answers. This they did, and by the end of April the stage was set for the peers' trial.

In the meantime, however, a much larger target hove into view. Since December there had been a relentless effort to tie the duke of York to the plot. His exile made keeping pace with developments difficult for him – the stories told by the growing cadre of informers evolved on almost a daily basis. Friends like Reresby tried to keep the duke informed, but it was not easy. James kept an anxious eye on events from abroad, but he must have been shocked when news came of his brother's apparent capitulation to his enemies. On 21 April the king entered the House of Lords, summoned the Commons and delivered a short speech: 'My lords and gentlemen I thought it requisite to acquaint you with what I have done now this day, which is that I have established a new Privy

Council, the constant number of which shall not exceed thirty.'[56] The president of this new Privy Council: Anthony, earl of Shaftesbury.

In addition to Shaftesbury, the new council included a number of his allies, men such as Lords Russell and Cavendish, vocal proponents of the plot in the Commons. Charles dismissed allies of Danby and James, though he did hold over a few of the more moderate members of the old Privy Council like Lord Chancellor Finch.[57] But the balance clearly had shifted to favour James's most implacable enemies, and the duke feared the consequences. '. . . in my mind all things tend to a Republike,' James wrote to his son-in-law the Prince of Orange. 'For you see all things tend towards the lessening of the king's authority, and the new modell things are put into is the very same as it was in the time of the Commonwealth.'[58] Would Charles offer up his brother as a sacrifice? James must have wondered.

The king's abrupt action suggests that he continued to think that compromise was possible – as with his earlier negotiations with Lord Holles, he might have felt that co-opting the opposition could work. Some thought that Charles's current favourite mistress, the Duchess of Portsmouth, had a hand in the experiment, hoping to shield herself from attack – as a French Catholic she was obviously in danger. Others, such as Sir William Temple, a diplomat closely connected to the Prince of Orange, believed the idea was the king's. Bishop Burnet thought it the fruit of Charles's natural indolence: 'The king was weary of the vexation he had been long in, and desired to be set at ease and at that time he would have done anything to get an end to the plot, and to the fermentation that was now over the whole nation.'[59] Reresby agreed – he encountered Charles at court not long after the new Privy Council was named: 'I was at the king's couchee. I wondered to see him soe chearfull amongst so many troubles; but it was not his nature to thinke much, or to perplex himself.'[60]

Whoever was behind the new Privy Council, Shaftesbury and his friends were justified in thinking that they now directed the course of events. They now had a foothold in both the Privy Council and Parliament, and it was not long before they set their sights on the duke. In an unusual Sunday sitting, on 27 April, the opposition fired the opening shots of what they expected to be the decisive campaign. The business of the day was 'to consider how to preserve the King's person from the attempts and conspiracies of the Papists'. A couple of members, probably allies of the duke, tried to obstruct the debate by introducing other items to the agenda, but they were shouted down with 'Several loud cries, "To the business of the day!"'[61]

The day's business was for member after member to rise and excoriate the duke of York, not hesitating to accuse him of direct complicity in a plan to murder his brother the king. Thomas Bennett, MP for Shaftesbury (both the borough, and, as it happened, the earl – for Bennett never deviated from his patron's positions), was typical. 'Colman's letters to the Pope, Cardinals, and French king's confessor were all penned and sent by the Duke of York's command . . . I do believe that this plot would not have been carried on without the duke of York's approbation . . . I would not sleep til something was done to secure the King's person and the Protestant religion!'[62]

William Lord Russell, the newly minted privy councillor, demonstrated how futile King Charles's accommodation of the opposition had been. 'If we do not do something related to the succession, we must resolve, when we have a prince of the Popish religion, to be Papists or burn. And I will do neither! . . . Therefore I desire that a committee be appointed to draw up a bill to secure our religion and properties in case of a popish successor.'[63] In the course of the long debate – during which Secretary Coventry was the only member who dared defend the duke: '. . . for the Parliament to make . . . a successor, I say it is against law and the government'.[64] Finally, John Hampden, the twenty-eight-year-old member for Buckinghamshire, proposed a resolution: 'That the duke of York being a papist, and the hopes of his coming to the crown have given the greatest countenance and encouragement to the present conspiracies and designs of the Papists against the king and the Protestant religion.'[65] This passed without any opposition – even from Coventry. It was left to John Colt, 'a hot disobliged and fierce-speaking man against the Court', to state the obvious implication of this resolution, 'If the duke be found to have a hand in the conspiracy, I know no reason but that the duke may be impeached, though absent, and then there is good ground for a bill to provide for a Protestant successor.'[66] Shaftesbury's allies Sir John Trevor and John Trenchard immediately called for an examination of the papers held by the plot-investigating committee and for a report, 'the effect of those which relate to the Duke's being concerned in the plot'.[67] Directly connecting James to the plot now topped the agenda as a means to deny his right to succeed Charles as king.

Two weeks later, in another Sunday session, the Commons returned to the subject. Some MPs argued that James be permanently banished; Thomas Pilkington, MP for London and one of Shaftesbury's 'worthies', proposed recalling James and impeaching him for high treason. His fellow London MP, Sir Thomas Player, who had long nursed a personal grudge against the duke, averred:

'I join with the motion that has been made for an eternal banishment of the duke of York . . . but yet, that it might go farther . . . therefore, besides the duke's banishment, I desire that he may be excluded from the crown of England, and all Papists whatsoever (as I am sure they may be) by law.'[68]

It was left once again to Secretary Coventry to defend the legitimate succession. 'The propositions I have heard moved today are the most ruinous to law and the property of the subject imaginable. Will any man give the Duke of York less law than the worst felons have, to banish and disinherit him without so much as hearing him?' Coventry argued that altering the succession would inevitably lead to civil war. 'Think, by putting the Duke of York by in the succession what you will entail upon your posterity! You will put him upon desperate and irrecoverable counsels . . . Pray run not upon these extremities before you have well considered of it!'[69] A handful of members seemed sympathetic to Coventry's arguments – one, Sir William Hickman, raised the very good point that while Parliament in Westminster might exclude James from the English Crown, there were two other nations over which they had no control: the Scottish and Irish: '. . . if you incapacitate the duke from succeeding in England, he may go into Scotland, and succeed there to that crown, and I believe that Ireland will go along with Scotland . . . and so you will entail a war for ever upon England'.[70]

Debate continued until darkness began to creep into the chamber, but the opponents of exclusion made no progress. The House divided on the question, with the 'aye's leaving the chamber. This revealed such a lopsided majority for exclusion that the few members left in the seats scattered 'and would not be counted, but yielded the question'.[71] The House appointed a committee composed of 'worthies' to draft a bill. Four days later the bill returned from committee and was read for the first time. On 21 May the bill came up for its second reading, and this time a division did take place – the exclusionists dominated, 207 to 128. After its third reading the bill was set to move to the Lords, where a more dramatic showdown could be anticipated.

In the meantime, the two houses wrangled over Danby's impeachment and the trial of the five lords.[72] The Commons and the opposition in the Lords wanted to try Danby first; the Lords refused. The Commons and the opposition peers wanted to exclude the bishops from all of the trials – doing them a favour by not forcing them to act as judges in capital cases. Surely clergymen should not be forced to shed Christian blood? Of course this argument had the benefit – no doubt obvious to all – of depriving the Court of a large block of reliable votes.

Their lordships refused over the protest of Shaftesbury and twenty-seven others.[73] The bishops would vote in the trials, though they would withdraw from the proceedings before any death sentences were passed. These disputes inevitably delayed progress on other business – even exclusion.

Hopes for excluding James soon received a major setback. On Tuesday 27 May the king appeared at Westminster wearing his crown and parliamentary robes – something he dispensed with when simply attending the Lords as a spectator, as he often did. Summoning the Commons to the upper House, Charles assented to two public bills and a private act – most importantly 'An Act for the better securing the liberty of the subject, and for the preventing of imprisonments beyond the seas', better known as the Habeas Corpus Act. Intended to prevent arbitrary imprisonment, the law allowed the courts to intervene and order a prisoner's release from jail if the judges thought an injustice had been done. Although ultimately the act would be an important defence of civil liberties, and remains in force today, unfortunately very few of those jailed because of the perjuries of Oates and his fellows received any benefit from its passage. This done, the king made a short speech: 'I was in good hopes that this session would have produced great good to the kingdom, and that you would have gone on unanimously for the good thereof. But, to my great grief I see that there are such differences between the houses that I am afraid very ill effects will come of them . . . Therefore, my lord chancellor, I command you to do as I ordered you.'[74] Whereupon Lord Chancellor Finch announced a prorogation until 14 August.

To say that this session of Parliament had been a disappointment for the Court would be an understatement. Elections for it had been tumultuous; more seats were contested in February 1679 than at any general election of the period, a sure sign of a political fever abroad in the land.[75] The elections had gone badly; not only had court candidates done poorly, but even after the Commons assembled, a number of MPs found themselves ousted from their seats by the committee of privileges and elections. The committee had heard over forty petitions from constituencies alleging irregularities in elections and a number of court supporters – like Sir John Reresby – had found themselves unseated. The agreement hammered out between the king, Danby and Lord Holles before the session opened proved to be a dead letter; Holles failed to deliver. The opposition drove Danby from office, the duke of York from the country, and began the process of trying both Danby and the five Catholic lords for their lives. Even the king's drastic remodelling of the Privy Council in April had failed to stem the tide – in fact it seems to have persuaded many, both at court and in the opposition, that Charles would give way – regardless of his repeated statements to the contrary. His actions suggested retreat, not advance. Emboldened, Shaftesbury led the charge to connect York directly to the plot and did everything in his power to heighten fears of a Catholic conspiracy. The culmination of the campaign, of course, was exclusion, and the testimony of the plot informers had been invaluable in advancing the cause.

But the session offered a handful of hopeful signs. Sceptics were emerging – three MPs had dared to challenge Oates's stories, and all three suffered for their temerity. But the fact that such comments were openly made must have heartened the plot's victims – those not already tried and executed, of course. Oates's swaggering insolence, both in and out of Parliament, also undermined the standing of 'the king's evidence'. The pious hero of Protestant England imagined by many was looking more like a greedy and petulant bully, cutting a wide path through London's taverns and coffee houses, offending and insulting wherever he went. 'Captain' Bedloe also did his share to tarnish the image of the informers, leading a riotous life in London to the scandal of many. More damaging information about the captain emerged in mid-April, at the trial of Nathaniel Reading before Justice Scroggs and the Court of King's Bench.

Nathaniel Reading was a lawyer, one of many who hung about Westminster cadging business from the litigants who swarmed the palace in term time. He was well known for his connections with Catholics and had served a number over the years. At the beginning of 1679 he approached Bedloe hoping to persuade him not to incriminate his clients, the lords in the Tower. Bedloe said Reading offered him a bribe – fifty-six gold guineas, unspecified 'great rewards', and a promise from Lord Stafford to hand over an estate in Gloucestershire after his acquittal. Bedloe arranged to meet Reading in his lodgings at Whitehall, taking care to have two witnesses in hiding to overhear the conversation. Afterwards, Bedloe went immediately to the Commons 'Secret Committee' investigating the plot and accused Reading of attempting to suborn him.[76]

Nathaniel Reading was tried for 'a trespass and misdemeanor' by attempting to 'lessen and stifle' the king's evidence. Proceedings began on 16 April. Reading claimed he was simply trying to prevent the effusion of innocent blood by persuading Bedloe to tell the truth. This might be true, or perhaps the possibility of a handsome reward from the accused Catholics was sufficient motivation. Perhaps it was a combination of the two. At all events, Reading's defence revealed much about Bedloe's character, none of it flattering. In his testimony Bedloe revealed that Justice Scroggs himself had some private doubts about his evidence – the Chief Justice had supposedly said 'That at this rate that Mr. Bedloe accuses men, none are safe, for he runs at the whole herd.'[77] Reading, testifying in his own defence, mentioned that Bedloe did not take this kindly, swearing 'in great expressions of passion' that 'it would never be well in England, till there was an honester man than the Lord Chief Justice'.[78]

The trial hinted at Bedloe's debauchery. Reading said he told Bedloe as a friend 'that he had not carried himself well, that he had been a very great scandal, abroad and at home, and that he would not do himself right' until he took spiritual advice from some of London's leading Anglican clergymen. This earned a contemptuous reply, 'They were all mercenary men that valued ten shillings above any man's soul.'[79] Bedloe also revealed that he had routinely colluded with Oates and a newly emerged informer, Stephen Dugdale, in crafting their evidence. According to Reading, Bedloe willingly offered to tailor his evidence against the lords for a price. Given the captain's history, the possibility cannot be discounted. Brazen dishonesty was Bedloe's stock in trade. Nathaniel said that he told the lords of Bedloe's offer and they rejected it.

While his defence undeniably cast Bedloe in the lurid glow of his dishonesty, unfortunately for Nathaniel Reading the captain had his two witnesses. One of these was Bedloe's servant, and thus beholden to him, and the other owed money to Reading, and was possibly prejudiced against him, but these objections cut little ice with the court and jury. The lawyer was duly found guilty, given a tongue-lashing by Justice Scroggs (who revealed no hint of distaste for Bedloe), and sentenced to pay a punitive £1,000 fine, a year in prison and an hour in the pillory.[80]

The 'king's evidence' emerged from this episode vindicated, but hardly undamaged. Cracks were appearing in the facade of the plot. More were forming.

— EIGHT —
TURNING POINT?
SPRING AND SUMMER 1679

In the spring of 1679, the duke of York, brooding on events in his Brussels exile, felt, understandably, discomforted. The earl of Shaftesbury remained at the head of the Privy Council and he and his allies in both houses of Parliament were losing no opportunity to heighten public fears of the plot. Both the Commons and the Lords had their 'secret' committees investigating every aspect of the conspiracy. Heavily populated with rabid anti-Catholics, these committees used their extensive powers to subpoena and jail suspects or material witnesses, pressuring their victims to broaden their accusations, aiming particularly at their leading targets: York, Danby, Queen Catherine and the five impeached peers. King Charles seemed supine, apparently doing nothing publicly to defend either his brother or his wife.

But there were growing signs of resistance to the informer's narrative. On 25 April, Titus Oates appeared before Shaftesbury's committee with a witness who he claimed would prove that Danby had offered him a reward if he could get Titus to withdraw his testimony against the former Lord Treasurer. This witness, Mr Lane, surprised Titus and the committee by denying any knowledge of Danby's attempted bribe – and went on to accuse Oates of slandering the king. Oates, Lane said, had called Charles a drunkard who surrounded himself with whores, pimps and rogues. Shaftesbury quickly shut the witness down, and rejected his testimony. An enraged Oates left the room to plot his revenge.[1]

It is possible that this Mr Lane was John Lane, a former servant of Oates's. Lane had been dealing with Thomas Knox, a gentleman in the household of Lord Dunblane, Danby's son. Knox hoped to do his master's father a service by undermining the credibility of both Oates and Bedloe. A few days after the abortive effort to upend Oates before the Lords, Knox, with Lane in tow, appeared before several London magistrates with a lurid tale: while in Oates's service Titus had repeatedly attempted to seduce him. His method was to send all of his servants to chapel each morning, except for his young footman, whose assistance he required 'to dress himself'. In fact Titus was more interested in undressing, to his servant's dismay. Lane had already quit Oates's service once, only returning after pleas from his mother, who badly needed financial support. The harassment continued and by the end of April, Lane was prepared to testify. Unfortunately, the magistrates whom Knox and Lane approached refused to take his deposition – they advised him to take his story to the Lords committee.

This advice could hardly have been welcomed by Knox and Lane: Shaftesbury was determined to protect his witnesses. And he did so – no sooner did word of Lane's accusations come to his ears than he instructed Sir William Waller and Edmund Warcup, a pair of London magistrates, to investigate. Both men worked closely with Shaftesbury and there was no question but that they would do his bidding. Before the day was out Knox and Lane were under arrest and in the Gatehouse prison. On 2 May they appeared before the committee for questioning, where Knox revealed his connection to Danby's family and admitted that he had organized Lane's testimony. For his part, Lane, thoroughly frightened by the prospect of an appearance in the pillory, recanted his story.[2] The unlucky pair went back to the Gatehouse where they would remain for weeks to come.

This attempt to destroy Oates's credibility failed – for the moment. But his victims continued working to expose him. Two important figures emerged to support accused Catholics: Elizabeth, countess of Powis, and Roger Palmer, earl of Castlemaine. Powis, whose husband lay in the Tower accused of treason, busied herself by supporting the many Catholics jailed on the word of the plot informants. She doled out money, food and words of comfort to many. Castlemaine had the misfortune to be married to (and humiliatingly separated from) King Charles's long-standing mistress, the duchess of Cleveland. He had converted to Catholicism in about 1662 and left England for two years, serving in the Venetian navy. After returning home, he took up the cause of Catholicism, writing a defence of English Catholics who had been accused of causing London's Great Fire. His stature as a Catholic writer ensured that when Oates began levying accusations, Castlemaine would be drawn in. Titus claimed that the earl was secretly a member of the Jesuit Order (and that he had been granted a divorce from his faithless wife). Furthermore he had approved of the plan to murder the king. This earned Castlemaine a three-month spell in the Tower between October 1678 and late January 1679. After his release the earl devoted himself to fighting on behalf of accused Catholics.[3]

Castlemaine played an important part in the next act of the plot: the trial of six Jesuit priests accused by Oates and Bedloe on 13 June. The defendants were Thomas Whitbread, the head of the Jesuit mission in London, and his colleagues, William Barrow (known to the court under his alias, Harcourt), John Caldwell (alias Fenwick), John Gavan, Anthony Turner and James Corker.[4] Four of them had been arrested early in the plot and strictly confined in Newgate ever since; Father Harcourt had eluded capture until 7 May, when a servant betrayed him. Whitbread's arrest almost sparked a diplomatic incident; he lived in the London home of the Spanish ambassador, a venue that should have been protected from arrests. But Oates bore Whitbread a particular grudge, as he had refused to allow him to join the Order. The other four brothers had laboured in the English mission for years. Whitbread became head of the mission only in 1677, though he had served in England since 1647.

The Jesuit mission in England inspired widespread terror and hatred; people credited them with almost superhuman powers. Masters of disguise, they ceaselessly plotted treason and murder, ever malevolent and cruel. Jesuits, it was said, disguised themselves as Quakers or as radical Protestant hedge preachers in Scotland in order to spread fear and discontent. As Titus Oates amply demonstrated – at least to the credulous public – no work of evil was beyond them. Hack writers and opportunist printers earned considerable sums catering to a fearful readership. In the winter and spring of 1679 titles like *The Horrid, Dreadful, Prodigious and Diabolical Practices of the Jesuits Discovered* and *The Jesuits' Intrigues* flew off the booksellers' shelves along with dozens of ballads and broadsides like *The Jesuits Character*. This ballad, sung 'to the Blacksmith's tune, Which nobody can deny', was typical of the genre:

The churches of God they make dens of thieves
They cajol the men and lye with their wives
When th'are to be hang'd none wish 'em reprieved . . .
Which nobody can deny!
Magnificent Houses, excellent wine
Their bread of the whitest, and linen so fine
With a cloak to the ground they always design
Which nobody can deny! . . .
To bloody revenge they still excite
For public hate and private spite

Are chiefly the Lectures they endite
Which nobody can deny! . . .
Princes and kings they design to slaughter
For which they are sometimes noos'd in a halter,
Belov'd as the Devil loves holy water
Which nobody can deny![5]

Inspired by such provocations, an excited mob of spectators crowded the Old Bailey on Friday 13 June, anxious to witness the comeuppance of the hated Jesuits. Presiding, as usual, was Justice Scroggs, aided by the other common law judges. This trial, unlike those that preceded it, would pit highly educated, eloquent defendants against the prosecution. Moreover, they had the support of Lord Castlemaine, who paid most of the expenses of the defence and who appeared in court throughout the proceeding, along with Lady Powis – an act of considerable courage considering the open hostility towards Catholics displayed by the crowd in the courtroom.

Before the trial began, one of the defendants, James Corker, petitioned the court for a respite. A Benedictine monk and one of the queen's chaplains, he was alleged to have helped draw Catherine into the plot. But he had not been informed of the date of his trial because of a clerical error, and had had no time to call witnesses or prepare a defence. The prosecution admitted that there had been some confusion over Corker's case, and Scroggs ordered his removal from the dock – he would be tried at a later date. This was truly a lucky escape – for Corker survived, but not without undergoing continued imprisonment and two more trials.[6]

After empanelling the jury the case began and from the start it was evident that the Jesuits were well prepared. Two of the defendants, Whitbread and Fenwick, argued that they should not be tried, as charges brought against them in December 1678 had been dismissed because only one witness, Oates, rather than the required two, testified against them.

Their invocation of precedents against double jeopardy demonstrated one of the defendants' advantages – the availability of legal advice. They would soon display another advantage – their training in debate and argumentation. The first witness against the defendants was Oates, whose testimony was less sure than in previous trials. He expressed uncertainty on a number of points – 'I cannot be positive', 'I will not be positive in it' – and was forced to explain away the fact that when confronted with Father John Gavan before the Privy Council months before, he had not recognized him. Titus's excuse was that Gavan had changed his appearance, 'he had gotten on a periwig and one asked me whether I knew him? I know him now, but truly then I did not well know him, because he was under that mask and I could not say anything against him then . . .'[7] He testified to seeing documents implicating the defendants in the plot. Significantly, he implied the duke of York's innocence – Whitbread, Oates claimed, had said 'That he hoped to see the black fool's head at Whitehall laid fast enough, and that if his brother should appear to follow in his footsteps his passport should be made too, or to that purpose, "he should be dispatched".'[8]

The Jesuits clearly rattled Oates, asking him a number of questions that revealed inconsistencies in his account. Titus appealed to the court, 'My lord, I beg this favour, that if the prisoners at the bar ask any questions, they may be proposed to the court, for they are nimble in their questions, and do a little abuse the evidence [that is, the witnesses]. They put things upon them that they never say.' Justice Pemberton agreed, directing Gavan to ask his questions to the court. 'I would do so my lord,' said Gavan, 'in whose honour I have more confidence than in whatsoever Mr. Oates says or does.' This brought a rebuke from Justice North: 'Do not give the king's witnesses ill words.'[9] Oates continued on the defensive, as Whitbread, Fenwick and Gavan quizzed him about discrepancies between his current testimony and statements he had made previously. He deployed the disguise dodge when Father Turner asked why Oates had failed to recognize him before the Council. 'You were then in a disguised habit and a nasty periwig, and I did not know you so well.'[10] Chief Justice Scroggs rescued Oates from his predicament, telling Whitbread 'I see your defence will be little else but captiousness, to disprove him in circumstances of time, place, persons, or numbers; now all these are but little matters to the substance.'[11]

His considerable ego no doubt bruised by the manhandling he received from the defendants, Oates left the stand. Making his debut in court was the next witness, Stephen Dugdale. Originally from Staffordshire, he had first appeared on the scene in December, testifying before the Privy Council with information about the plot. He incriminated Viscount Stafford, one of the five Catholic lords in the Tower, saying that the peer had told him of the plot in September 1678. He also said that his former master, the Catholic Lord Aston, headed a provincial outpost of the conspiracy. Aston joined the other jailed peers and Dugdale joined the ranks of Popish Plot informants.

Like the other principal witnesses in these trials, Dugdale was a fraud. He had been dismissed as Walter, Lord Aston's steward, after embezzling money from him, stealing the wages of the servants and pocketing rent paid by the tenants. A chronic gambler deep in debt, despite his light-fingered service to Lord Aston, he had ended up in the Stafford jail in November 1678. It was there that he saw the advantages of informing and volunteered his 'information'.[12] His breeding and education as a gentleman boosted his credibility; Bishop Burnet commented 'He was a man of sense and temper, and behaved himself decently, and had somewhat in his air and deportment that disposed people to believe him . . .'[13]

On the stand Dugdale told of reading letters from Whitbread to Father Ewers, Lord Aston's Jesuit chaplain. These described in some detail the plan to assassinate the king and raise a rebellion. Father Gavan was Dugdale's principal target in this testimony. He had the misfortune to meet the witness while visiting Lord Aston's estate, and Dugdale used the acquaintance against him. Gavan, he said, was one of the main organizers of the plot: he was 'a good orator and learned man, and a good scholar, to persuade people into the design'.[14] Gavan, he said, met in September 1678 with several other Jesuits at Tixall, Aston's home, where they discussed plans to kill King Charles. A confrontation between the witness and the accused ensued. Gavan protested he knew nothing of this meeting, and challenged Dugdale, 'Look upon me with confidence, if you can.' But Dugdale, a practised liar, radiated confidence, claiming to have been a pupil of Gavan's – which the priest denied – and even boasted that he gave the Jesuits £500 'to pray for my soul and for the carrying on the work'. Stephen claimed that Gavan had promised him sainthood as a reward, no doubt a rich irony for the defendants.

Dugdale also said he had read one hundred letters written about the plot by Father Harcourt. Harcourt admitted sending a handful of letters to Father Ewers, but never any about an assassination plot: 'I never did write any such letter, nor did I ever in my life seem to approve of any man's death or murder.' Harcourt also said that weeks before, testifying before the Commons 'Secret Committee', Dugdale had been unable to identify Harcourt's handwriting – he failed a simple test on this occasion. The MPs asked Harcourt for a writing sample and three of them wrote a few lines of their own. Dugdale could not identify Harcourt's hand then, though he now claimed to know it very well. The defendant's point did not persuade the judges. Scroggs trotted out the Jesuits-as-tricksters trope, 'You write more hands, as well as have more names, and can counterfeit your hands . . .'

Justice Pemberton piled on, 'You speak before your time, and your bare word goes for nothing.'[15] Rounding out his testimony, Dugdale said he had heard Father Turner approve the plot in Ewer's chamber at Tixall two years earlier – though Turner strongly denied being in Staffordshire at any time in the last four years. But if the Jesuits in the dock were unimpressed by Dugdale's testimony, Chief Justice Scroggs was satisfied: 'You deliver your testimony like a sober modest man, upon my word.'[16]

The next witness was Miles Prance, now fully committed to his new role as a perjurer, his qualms of conscience cast aside. His testimony focused on William Harcourt and John Fenwick, who, he said, had both discussed the plot with him in the course of doing business. His story seemed more than slightly preposterous: Harcourt commissioned an image of the Virgin Mary, intending to send it to fellow Catholics in Maryland (which the geographically challenged silversmith thought was 'in the Portugal's country'). When paying for this artefact at Prance's shop counter, Harcourt blurted out that there was a plot to murder the king. Fenwick he overheard talking about raising 50,000 Catholic rebels. In a subsequent conversation with Father John Grove, conducted over the purchase of 'two or three silver spoons to give away at a christening', Prance learned that Lords Powis, Belasyse, Arundell and Petre would lead this army. Grove insouciantly reassured Prance about the effect this massive rebellion might have on trade: 'I asked him, what shall we poor tradesmen do, if we have civil wars in England? O, said he, you need not fear having trade enough, you shall have church work enough, to make images, chalices, and crucifixes and vases and such like things.'[17] As both Ireland and Grove were now dead, recently drawn and quartered, neither could confirm Prance's rather unlikely story.

Next up was William Bedloe, who faced the awkward problem that in December he had denied under oath knowing anything about the guilt of Whitbread and Fenwick. This, he explained, was because at the time of the trial he was engaged in entrapping Nicholas Reading. Reading, who had recently endured the humiliation and violence of London's pillory, was working on behalf of the lords in the Tower, attempting to tamper with Bedloe's evidence. The story was an odd one – Bedloe claimed that Reading expected him to exonerate Whitbread and Fenwick as proof of his sincerity towards the lords. This convoluted explanation satisfied the court, and his testimony continued. He had nothing first-hand to say about two of the accused, Turner and Gavan, but Fenwick, Harcourt and

Whitbread were targets. All three, Bedloe said, had at various times spoken of the plot, and he had carried many messages for the Jesuits, all of which contained information about it. 'Mr. Harcourt is no stranger to my bringing of packets and portmanteaus over to him, from beyond the seas.' This sparked an exchange with Harcourt, 'He never brought but one in all his lifetime.' 'What!' exclaimed Bedloe, 'did I never bring but one packet? Have not I brought divers and divers portmanteaus?' 'You never brought a portmanteau in your life.' Bedloe repeated defensively, 'I have brought divers.' Harcourt replied, 'You know I never saw you but twice in my life before today, and when I met you at the Privy Council.'[18]

By Harcourt's account, he and Bedloe had met twice before the plot broke: five years earlier Bedloe delivered a packet of letters from Dunkirk, and on the strength of that brief meeting he soon returned with a hard-luck story and a plea for a loan of twenty shillings.[19] The priest gave Bedloe the money and never saw him again until after his arrest. Given Bedloe's track record with his creditors, this comes as no surprise.

But Bedloe continued spinning his tale, claiming that Harcourt had given Sir George Wakeman a bill of exchange for £2,000, a down payment for the king's poisoning. This Harcourt challenged the witness to prove – what merchant made this bill? A bill that large must appear in someone's accounts – who issued it? Bedloe could not say. Scroggs intervened to defend the witness, 'Do people take notice of every particular bill of exchange that they see, which they are neither to pay or receive?' John Fenwick reasonably asked, 'But what reason does he give your lordship, or the jury, to believe that there were such a bill, unless he does produce either the bill, or the person that paid it?' Scroggs replied, '[Does] it matter whether there were such a bill or no, or whether he had mentioned it or no?' Fenwick answered, 'But seeing he hath mentioned it, I say there is nothing of proof in it, but only his bare word.' This prompted the judge to shut down the argument altogether: 'Yes, there is his oath.'[20] Unfortunately for the accused the seventeenth century had great confidence in the value of an oath – all experience of humanity's capacity for lies notwithstanding.

The defendants had scored some points against Bedloe. His explanation for not accusing Whitbread and Fenwick in December was rather lame, his flustered response about his work as a Jesuit courier hardly inspired confidence, and the exchange over Wakeman's bill raised questions. But now the Crown offered damaging pieces of evidence: two letters found among Harcourt's papers. The first had been used in previous trials, where it also had a disastrous impact on the defence – it was the summons to the Jesuit 'consult' of April 1678. The letter mentioned 'the design' and enjoined 'secrecy as to time and place'.[21] Justice Scroggs, fortified by Oates's testimony, assumed that 'the design' was the assassination plot, a plan obviously requiring secrecy – but the defendants offered another interpretation. The meeting was one routinely scheduled triennially to settle the mission's affairs. In this case, Harcourt maintained, the main order of business was to select a brother for a trip to Rome to settle the affairs of the mission. The court rejected this argument, 'Look you, Mr. Harcourt,' said Scroggs, 'you say well, but we are not to be altogether disciples of yours, so as to have no sense of our own and to be imposed upon so weakly as this.'[22] Whitbread argued that the word 'design' was perfectly innocent: 'First, it is a very hard thing to bring so many men's lives in danger, merely upon the interpretation of a word, which may as properly signify one thing as another. Is it not proper for me to say, "I have a design to dine with such a man tomorrow, or the like?" ' 'It is true, now,' said Scroggs, 'but hearken . . .', at which point the Jesuit, no mean debater, interrupted: 'But that was the thing designed . . . choosing of an officer . . . and that it should be kept secret was as prudential a thing as possibly could be. Was it not proper here, because our profession was not publicly permitted in this kingdom and therefore that was the reason why secrecy was enjoined? And this, upon my salvation, was all that was ever intended or thought.'[23]

The judges had no sympathy for this argument, although Scroggs found himself forced to shift ground in the face of Whitbread's logic. Interpreting the meaning of the word 'design', which Whitbread effectively pointed out might mean anything was not the point: 'It is not one word alone,' said Scroggs, 'but the sense.'[24] Father Gavan added his own exposition reaffirming Whitbread – and proving Dugdale's point that he was an able orator. Justice Scroggs was uncharacteristically patient through all of this, but ultimately was not persuaded, 'I did never find, though you are as good at it as ever any I met with (for I never met with a priest that had much more understanding), but really you do not answer me.' Whatever the Jesuits argued, however, they could not prove a negative – and there was also Titus Oates's perjured account of the 'consult'. Again Scroggs pointed to the prosecution's evidence: '. . . this letter of your own, which cannot be denied, is an unanswerable proof. It does monstrously confirm Mr. Oates's testimony to be undeniable as to the meeting at the consult.'[25]

The second document was a letter found among Harcourt's papers, and the prosecution claimed it proved the existence of the papal commissions of various

Catholics as leaders of Oates's fantasy rebellion: Belasyse as lord general, Powis as treasurer and so on. The author of the document was an English Jesuit in Rome, Christopher Anderton. 'We are all here very glad of the promotion of Mr. Thomas Harcourt. When I writ that the patents were sent, although I guess for whom they were . . . because our patrons do not use to discover things or resolutions till they know they have effect.'[26] The dangerous word 'patents' immediately caught the judge's attention. 'What sort of patents?' demanded Scroggs. Whitbread answered: 'the patents appointing him provincial of the English mission'. 'But,' countered the judge, 'the letter says "patents" plural, and you are but one man.' Whitbread said that the Vatican used the plural form for individuals – as indeed did the English state, which routinely issued 'letters patent' to individuals. Unfortunately Whitbread neglected to make this latter point, and Oates was quick to repeat his claim that he had seen multiple patents in the spring of 1678.

This ended the prosecution's case; it was now the accused's turn – though before they could begin Oates intervened to ask that his witnesses – who would rebut those of the defence – be sworn. The court denied this request; the defence would be presented first. Oates's attempt to jump ahead of regular court procedure was significant – he knew very well that the defence would present witnesses who would damage, if not completely destroy, his credibility. His own witnesses were meant to salvage that credibility. If they were heard first, he might control the narrative more effectively.

Whitbread, the senior brother, began. 'I thank God, my lord, I am not afraid of death, but I should be very loth to die unjustly.' Oates, he said, was a perjurer, and he would prove it with witnesses. Moreover, he asked why, if such a plot existed, would he trust a man like Oates with the secret? 'Now I desire your lordship would be pleased to consider whether this were probable . . . and whether I ought not rather be sent to Bedlam than Newgate, for trusting a man such as he, whom by his own confession I never saw till that time.'[27] Although Oates 'was very zealous to be entertained among us', the mission rejected him both because they feared he was not a good Catholic and because he led an idle life. In order to be rid of him, the society outfitted him with a new suit, a periwig, and lent him £4 – which (naturally) he never repaid. 'But that I should be so . . . mad as at the first sight of such a man as this to trust him with such a great intrigue as this was, and to write in such a plain strange manner, and send by post to Mr. Dugdale . . . had been a madness.'[28] But Whitbread said his real defence rested on the witnesses he intended to call.

Before the first defence witness came to the stand John Fenwick intervened. 'Pray, my lord, be pleased to take notice that this man's evidence all along is, that he saw such and such letters from such and such persons. They have no evidence but just that they saw such and such letters, and how is it possible that a man who was turned away from St. Omer's for his misdemeanors, that I should show him all my letters?'[29] The government confiscated a thousand of Fenwick's letters, and yet there was not a word of treason in any of them. 'All the evidence that is given comes but to this: there is but saying and swearing.'[30]

Once again the court demanded that the accused do the impossible: prove a negative. Scroggs said, 'say you it is strange that they should not find one letter in all those numerous papers that were taken that contains any traitorous matter; but I say it is forty times more a wonder that one should be taken than for all the rest to be undiscovered.' 'For God's sake,' said Fenwick, 'where are the commissions signed, and monies paid?'[31] The only effective way to deal with the court's logic was to destroy Oates's credibility.

And so it was time for the defence's witnesses. The courtroom seethed with hostility towards them; the crowd outside the court jostled and shouted abuse at them as Lord Castlemaine, who had maintained them, ushered them in. Whitbread first asked that his witnesses testify under oath – thereby greatly increasing their credibility. But the court would not allow this – Scroggs and Justice North said no one accused in a capital case could swear to the truth of their evidence, although the Chief Justice did offer a small concession (which he would afterwards completely undermine): 'I will say this to the jury, that they are not sworn is because they cannot, but the jury is to take great heed of what they say, and to be governed by it according to the credibility of the person and of the matter.'[32] Father Gavan, demonstrating the depth of his scholarship, pointed out that the great common lawyer Sir Edward Coke had in his magisterial *Institutes of the Common Law* said that there was no law against swearing defence witnesses – though Justices Scroggs and North trumped the argument: 'You argue against the known practice of all ages', and 'There never was any man, in a capital case, sworn against the king.'[33] This question, resolved in the prosecution's favour – as they always were – set the stage for the first witness, a student from the Jesuit college at St Omer, Mr Hilsley.

Hilsley testified that Oates was in Europe in April 1678. The court lost no time asking Hilsley his religion – he was, not surprisingly, Catholic. Justice Pemberton, who had been brought up in a Parliamentarian household, displayed a snide anti-Catholic bias, saying 'Be not ashamed of your religion, do not deny that; your Provincial [Whitbread] there can give you a dispensation for what you say', and later added, 'he is a boy very fit to be made a Jesuit of'.[34] There followed a parade of some sixteen St Omer students, most of whom were in their late teens, along with a handful of older men in service at the college. All asserted that Oates had been at St Omer throughout the spring of 1678. Several witnesses testified that Oates was conspicuous in the college. Considerably older than the rest of the students, he had a separate table in the refectory. This distinction, possibly in deference to his age – or perhaps a means of keeping Titus away from impressionable young men – made any absences obvious. Oates made himself conspicuous in other ways as well – one student, Mr Palmer, recalled Oates mocking other students. On another occasion Oates almost came to blows with a student whose seat he demanded at a play. Another student, Thomas Billing, recalled a different quarrel that resulted in Oates being knocked down.[35]

Oates defended himself with a mixture of obfuscation, ad hominen attacks and more elaborate lies. He sowed confusion over whether particular dates were old style (the Julian calendar used in England) or new (the Gregorian calendar, used on the continent, ten days ahead). He declared that Jesuit witnesses were not credible: '. . . they have dispensations, and are bound by an implicit obedience to say what the Jesuits bid them . . .'[36]

The atmosphere in the court was tense – spectators jeered and laughed at several defence witnesses, prompting Scroggs to issue a sermon on English justice: the defence witnesses 'are good evidence and competent witnesses, I must tell you that, and no man must deny it, for though you [Catholics] deny heaven to us, yet we will not deny heaven to you, nor witnesses . . .' This prompted a 'great shout' in the court. The Chief Justice continued, 'You must pardon the people's shouting, for you have turned their hearts so that there is no living for a papist in England, I will maintain it', and here he was again interrupted by a loud demonstration from the audience before finishing 'You shall have all the justice that can be, and all the favor the law will allow', a promise the defendants might well have doubted.[37] That at least one of the accused doubted the court's sincerity was plain moments later when Father Gavan asked to be tried by ordeal – a method not used in England since the thirteenth century.

Gavan's request was quickly rejected, but Scroggs seized upon it as a means to further the anti-Catholic narrative: 'You are very fanciful, Mr. Gavan, you believe your cunning in asking such a thing will take much with the auditory, but this is only an artificial varnish. You may do this with hopes of having it take with those who are Roman Catholics, who are so superstitious as to believe innocency upon such desires, but we have a plain way of understanding here in England . . .'[38]

Father Whitbread pointed out discrepancies in Oates's testimony at earlier trials – and that as a perjurer his testimony in this case should be rejected. But the court countered that Titus had not in fact been indicted, much less convicted, of perjury. Therefore his testimony was good in law. Father Harcourt also attacked the informers, 'I say, my lord, these persons are known to be every one of them very bad and flagitious [i.e., villainous] persons, and that every one of them have undertaken this course merely to get a livelihood: they are men of desperate fortunes, they get a living by swearing false, they find that the best trade.'[39] John Fenwick called witnesses to shed light on William Bedloe's shady past – Captain Hill said that he was jailed in the Marshalsea Prison with him, where they both 'fed upon the basket' – that is they survived on charity. Bedloe had cheated a cutler of a silver-hilted sword and, said Fenwick, 'He was forced to run the country for many cheats, and was forced to borrow four or five shillings to redeem his boots.'[40] But the court refused to disqualify Bedloe – he had a royal pardon for his offences and therefore they did not exist in law. Scroggs allowed that Bedloe 'was a naughty man, he was with you in this plot', his partiality once again on display.

The defence rested and Sir Cresswell Levinz summed up the Crown's case, after which it called several witnesses to prove that Oates had in fact been in London in April 1678. Although their stories were not altogether persuasive, and it was later shown that two witnesses were coerced, this was enough for Justices Scroggs and North, who insisted, all suggestions to the contrary, that Mr Oates 'is still an upright and good witness'.[41]

Now that all the witnesses had been heard, the accused had the opportunity to make a statement. Jesuit eloquence was now on display. Addressing the jury directly, John Gavan again attacked Oates's credibility, '. . . to make credible witnesses there is required honesty of life, and truth in their testimony, for no man can be a good witness that is not an honest man.' As to the honesty of Mr Oates's life, the Jesuits thought Titus 'not a person of that diligence or fidelity to be entrusted by them; he was turned out of St. Omers'. 'Does that prove any dishonesty in Mr. Oates?' asked Scroggs. 'No, but I speak to his credibility.' 'Speak plain,' said the judge, 'how does it impeach Mr. Oates's evidence, that the Jesuits did not like him?' 'It might be ground of hatred and malice in him against them.'[42] Gavan also pointed out that Stephen Dugdale stole £300 from his master – a charge that Justice Scroggs refused to allow, because Gavan could offer no proof. 'You must not fall upon persons with no evidence!' The defendant finished, 'I do assure your lordship, as I hope to see the face of God, I am innocent of what is charged upon me. And God bless the king and this honorable court.'[43]

John Fenwick contrasted the virtuous defence witnesses with the mean and avaricious informers for the Crown. He dwelled on the implausibility of the informer's stories – Oates says 'he saw such and such letters from Mr. Whitbread. Now is it possible that a man that had no credit at all with us, that we should be such fools as to trust him with letters such as those, then your lordships must hang us twice – once for fools, and then for knaves.' Where is the evidence? Where are the letters? The 'commissions'? Evidence of money raised or paid? Where are the weapons? Months had passed since Oates emerged, thousands of letters and documents had been sifted through and none of them had a word to say about an assassination plot.[44]

Whitbread made the same point about the improbability of Oates's story, part of which was that Father Thomas had beaten Titus as punishment for disobedience: 'I thank God I don't look like a fighting man, nor I never did, but who can think I should be so mad, when I had committed such a secret to him, to beat him as he says? It is strange that such a plot should be discovered wherein so many persons of quality, honor and reputation are said to be concerned, and yet no footsteps of it appear.'[45] Father Harcourt reiterated this point, saying 'They only affirm such and such things without any reason, to persuade you to believe them, and it is easy to say, and so it is to swear it. So that all I have to say is this, since a negative cannot be proven I hope innocency will find some that shall defend it.'[46]

The defendants all passionately argued that Oates, Bedloe and Dugdale were corrupt liars. They hammered home the utter implausibility of their stories, and did so to good effect, bolstered by a display of Jesuit forensic skill, complete with Latin tags: 'Nemo repente fit nequissimus' [no one suddenly becomes wicked]. But the judges had the last word in their charge to the jury. The defence did not impress Chief Justice Scroggs: 'They defend their lives as they do their religion, with weak arguments and fallacious reasons.'[47] Nor was he persuaded by the sixteen boys from St Omer: 'because they are of a religion that can dispense with oaths, though false, for the sake of a good cause'. As the Catholic Church is 'bloody and inhuman' and it justifies murder and rebellion, he told the jury, 'I must leave it to you, to consider how far these young men, trained in such principles, may be prevailed on to speak what is not true.'[48]

Scroggs also defended the prosecution's witnesses, excusing Oates for his imprecision with regard to dates as 'a thing that no man can precisely charge his memory with'. As for Stephen Dugdale, embezzler and thief, 'Upon my word he hath escaped well, for I find little said against him, very little either as to the matter or manner of his evidence. They would have made reflection on him for his poverty, but I hope that they, whose religion is to vow poverty, will never insist on that for any great objection against any.'[49] About William Bedloe, Scroggs spoke not a word – suggesting that his utility as a witness was on the wane.

The jury retired and fifteen minutes later returned with its verdict: guilty, inspiring the audience to give 'a great shout'.[50] Few would have been surprised; so far not a single Catholic accused in the plot had been acquitted (Samuel Pepys's clerk Sam Atkins was Protestant). But the trial did allow the accused to highlight some of the inconsistencies and irregularities in the informer's stories. The support of Castlemaine was critical; he paid the expenses of the seminarians, and he took careful notes of the trial – notes that he would later use to write and publish a defence of the accused. The defendants themselves impressed many with their arguments – though in the end they could do nothing against the deeply held anti-Catholic prejudices arrayed against them.

The next morning the court reconvened, this time to try a Catholic layman, Richard Langhorne. Now in his mid-fifties, he had built a successful career advising Catholics, both lay and clerical. As the court learned in earlier trials, he established trusts to safeguard Catholic property, which legally was subject to confiscation if used for what English law defined as 'superstitious purposes' – income devoted, for example, to maintaining a priest or supporting a Catholic institution. Langhorne himself often served as a trustee, and he did a considerable amount of work for the Jesuits. As the Order's man of business he knew a great deal about its property – all of which was carefully concealed behind a screen of trusts and dummy ownership. Unfortunately for Langhorne he had crossed paths with Titus Oates on two fleeting occasions before the outbreak of the plot – once, in 1677, when Titus brought him a letter from his son Charles, then a student at the Jesuit college in Valladolid, Spain. Oates had recently been expelled and apparently offered to bring the message hoping to cadge some sort of charity from a prosperous attorney. The second meeting between the two men came later when Oates carried a letter from Langhorne to St Omer, thanking the fathers there for their help in finding a wayward son.[51] The next time Langhorne saw Oates was when he arrived at his chambers in October 1678, leading a troop of officers who proceeded to arrest him and ransack his office. Held as a strictly guarded prisoner in Newgate for nine months, his trial at last got underway.

As ever, the prosecution's case depended upon the testimony of Oates and Bedloe. Oates told of carrying letters from Spain and to St Omer noting that one of them contained suspicious words, though he was uncharacteristically vague about what they were. Much more damning was Langhorne's response when Oates, after the April 'consult', told him about the plan to kill the king, 'And when I did so, Mr. Langhorne lifted up his hands and his eyes and prayed to God to give it good success.'[52] He also saw 'several parchments' lying on a table in Langhorne's chamber. Of course any seventeenth-century barrister's office would have plenty of parchment lying about – but these documents were special. They were papal commissions appointing the principal leaders of the upcoming Catholic rebellion – the five Catholic peers in the Tower would be England's new Lord Chancellor, Lord Treasurer and generals in the rebel army. Only Lord Stafford missed out on an exalted post in the fantasy regime, 'As to my lord Stafford, I cannot give so good an account, but as I remember, he was to be a paymaster in the army, or some such office.'[53] Langhorne himself would be the army's solicitor general.

Oates said that Langhorne played a key role in raising money to support the plot, and that the barrister was grumpy about George Wakeman's holding out for more than £10,000 to assassinate the king. Wakeman, Langhorne supposedly said, 'was a covetous man . . . a narrow-spirited and a narrow-souled physician'.[54] Langhorne pressed Oates about timing, provoking Titus to ask for the court's protection, which Chief Justice Scroggs duly provided, 'All their defence lies in catches upon a point of time, in which no man living is able to be positive.'[55] But here Oates contradicted the story he told only the day before about his London trip in April 1678 – yesterday he swore he had been in London for five or six days, and today he said 'I was in England under twenty days'. Even Scroggs noted this discrepancy, though he did nothing to highlight it. Langhorne, who clearly knew his business as a barrister, then shifted the questioning onto an area that made Oates distinctly nervous: his checkered history. When, asked Richard, did Oates leave the Church of England? Did Oates have a benefice in the Church? Oates confessed that he had been vicar of Bobbing, Kent – a chapter in his life he certainly would prefer to skip. But Langhorne was relentless – why did Oates give up his living? Oates's response was shifty – first he refused to answer, but Scroggs pressed him and got the grudging reply, 'The air was not a good air in that part of Kent, and I had not my health, and that was one reason, and for other reasons best known to myself.' In fact Titus had hardly been a model clergyman – his flock accused him of being too drunk to perform a service, stealing their chickens, and of making 'very indecent expressions' about Christianity.[56] His departure was not voluntary, and, here, on the witness stand, he was not about to admit it. Having put Titus on the defensive, Langhorne rested his case, and the prosecution called William Bedloe.

Before starting his tale, Bedloe called the court's attention to a distinguished spectator, asking 'whether a known Roman Catholic may take notes of the evidence in such a cause?' The scribe in question was the marchioness of Winchester, daughter of the imprisoned Lord Stafford. Reflecting the casual misogyny of the times, Justice Scroggs refused to be bothered: 'She will do herself, nor nobody else any great hurt by what she writes . . . a woman's notes will not signify much truly, no more than her tongue.'[57] In this case Lady Winchester enjoyed the privilege of the under-appreciated – her notes would be very helpful in the composition of pro-Catholic accounts of the plot.

On this occasion Bedloe testified with his usual inventiveness. He told of how Edward Colman wrote letters concerning the plot, and then, accompanied by himself, they were brought to Langhorne's chambers, where he copied them in a book. Louis XIV's confessor, Father de La Chaise, received some of these letters and others went to various Catholic figures like the papal nuncio in Brussels. Jesuits in Salamanca, he said, were gathering a mixed force of Irish exiles and lay brothers – pretending to be pilgrims bound for Santiago de Compostela, they would instead sail for Britain, landing at Milford Haven in Wales. Lord Powis would meet them there and lead them on an expedition of fire and sword across the kingdom, slaughtering Protestants as they went.[58] All of these plans Langhorne dutifully transcribed in his letter book – a parchment-bound volume some three inches thick. The need to record every detail of this treasonous conspiracy so meticulously was a question that appeared to occur to no one.

Concluding his testimony, Bedloe carefully reserved the right to invent new lies if necessary. Asked by Langhorne if this was all he had to say against him, the 'captain' replied, 'I cannot say that, my lord, that this is all I have to say against him; things may occur to my memory hereafter, which do not now.'[59] Next a

Mr Buss, cook to the duke of Monmouth, testified – wholly irrelevantly – that in September 1678 he had overheard someone imply that there was a conspiracy. No one mentioned the defendant – nor was there any explicit mention of a plot – but the court instructed the jury to take this as proving the conspiracy 'in general'.

Langhorne now began his defence, first attempting to impeach Oates and Bedloe. The accused Jesuits had made the same effort the previous day and Richard now suffered the same rebuff: though Oates and Bedloe had themselves been active abettors of the plot, they had pardons – this, the court ruled, meant that they in effect had committed no crimes and therefore their testimony must stand. Langhorne tried a different tack: 'I desire to know whether they have not received any rewards or gratifications for the discovery they have made, and the service they have done? And whether they expect further rewards?' Of course, both Oates and Bedloe benefited handsomely from their perjuries, but neither could admit that – both claimed to be £700 out of pocket due to their heroic efforts. Justice Pemberton saw Langhorne's purpose immediately: 'Mr. Langhorne does suppose that the witnesses are corrupted and bribed. Do you think, Mr. Langhorne, that the king will bribe his witnesses?'[60]

Justice Scroggs challenged Langhorne to present proof that his accusers were bribed, otherwise he must pursue a different line of defence. 'Does your defence consist wholly of this sort of matter, objecting to the incompetency of the witnesses? Can you make no answer to the fact?' Langhorne's reply to this epitomized the nearly impossible situation of all the defendants in the plot. 'I must tell your lordship, my whole defence must run to disable the witnesses, for, my lord, I was committed to Newgate the 17th of October, and I have been kept there close prisoner . . . I never conversed with any friend or relation, nor knew anything of news, but only with some few persons sent by . . . the House of Commons or the Council. And I was never examined by any since I was committed. I never heard what was charged against me, and I could not foresee what these men would testify . . . therefore I can have no defence, unless it be by lessening their credit . . .'[61]

To that end, Langhorne called the St Omer students back to the stand – but not before an alarmed Titus Oates called out, 'My lord! Here are papists come into the court with their swords on!' 'They will not draw them here,' assured Scroggs – prompting the Lord Mayor, Sir James Edwards, to call out 'It is well enough, it is well enough Dr. Oates, you are safe enough here.'[62] Once again, the students and servants from St Omer testified that Oates was in Europe when he claimed to be in London. And once again the court accused the witnesses of being coached. One witness, Mrs Grove, kept a lodging house where Oates said he stayed when in London. She testified that Titus never slept there – eliciting his usual dodge, that he was in disguise. Mrs Grove's maid supported her mistress: Oates never lodged with them.

At this juncture Lord Castlemaine urgently interrupted the trial. A hostile crowd was assaulting Langhorne's witnesses: they 'are so beaten and abused without that they dare not come to give their evidence for fear of being killed'. Castlemaine said that the mob beat one of the witnesses so badly that he feared for his life. The court reacted strongly: '. . . it is by no means a thing to be allowed of. If your lordship let us but know them, and we will take care for the punishment of them, for we will show ourselves to be just and fair, and give them all the fair play that can be',[63] said Scroggs. It is unlikely that either the accused or his witnesses took much comfort in this statement. Appearing at all, at great personal risk and considerable expense, was an act of great courage – and, in a way, testimony to the reputation of the common law. In these trials, however, 'fair play' was a concept talked about much more than practised.

Langhorne's final statement before Scroggs summed up strongly denied Oates's charges, maintained that his witnesses spoke truthfully, and he pointed out the impossibility of proving a negative – Richard could never prove that documents had never existed. All of his papers had been seized and very thoroughly examined, and nothing resembling treason found. But Bedloe swore they existed, and the prosecution could argue that they were destroyed.

Scroggs's charge to the jury was similar to his remarks the day before. He harped on the unreliability of the St Omer witnesses – Catholic doctrine 'so false and pernicious, so destructive and so bloody' made all of their testimony suspect and he ignored testimony pointing to Oates's fabrications.[64] The Chief Justice ended with a passionate assertion of the reality of the plot: 'Here is a gentleman that stands at the bar, upon his life, on the one hand, but if Mr. Oates says true all our lives, and liberties, our king, and our religion are at the stake on the other hand. God defend that innocent blood should be shed, and God defend us also from Popery . . . Follow you your consciences, do wisely, do honestly, and consider what is to be done.'[65]

The jurors retired and soon returned with their verdict: guilty. Sentencing followed immediately, both of Langhorne and the five Jesuits – the usual gruesome fate reserved for traitors: hanging, drawing and quartering. 'After which there was a very great acclamation' from the audience, satisfied that Protestant justice had prevailed once again.[66]

All six of the condemned returned to Newgate, where they spent the following week preparing for death. Each man remained in a separate cell, although the court allowed them visitors in a jailor's presence. Among those who came were Shaftesbury and his ally Essex. They promised Gavan and Turner, the youngest of the prisoners, a reprieve in return for a full confession. They refused, determined not to condemn themselves with lies.[67] A hostile commentator noted that 'with a confidence usual to those of their persuasion, and especially of their society, they appeared outwardly not much concerned with thoughts of death . . .'[68] At about 9.30 on the morning of Friday 20 June the five Jesuits emerged from prison, watched by a huge crowd. Awaiting them were hurdles drawn by four horses each, accompanied by a strong guard on the watch for any attempts at rescue. In fact it was more likely that the brothers needed guards to protect them on their last journey. Whitbread and Harcourt wore black, the others were dressed in coloured coats, perhaps making a statement of unconcern about their fate. Jailors tied each man to a hurdle – two by two, with John Fenwick bringing up the rear alone on his. The procession then began, carrying the men to Tyburn, through an enormous press of spectators.

At Tyburn the constables placed the priests on a single large cart, tying their hands and fixing nooses around their necks. Jack Ketch, the executioner, busied himself with the fire intended to consume their vitals. Sir Richard How, the sheriff of London, stood by. A wealthy fishmonger and shipowner, How had the unpleasant task of presiding over the executions.[69] Each one of the Jesuits had spent time in the previous days preparing their last words – 'dying speeches' were held in high regard and eagerly anticipated. Most believed that a convict's last words revealed much about both himself and his crimes, and the usual form required confession and contrition. Part of Sheriff How's job was to encourage his charges to deliver what the people expected.

As the senior Jesuit, head of the English mission, Thomas Whitbread spoke first. Looking out over a vast and expectant crowd of spectators he said, 'I suppose it is expected I should speak something to the matter I am condemned for, and brought here to suffer . . . You all either know, or ought to know, I am to make my appearance before the face of Almighty God and . . . as I hope for mercy from his divine majesty, I do declare to you here present, and to the whole world, that I go out of the world as innocent and as free from any guilt of these things laid to my charge in this matter as I came into the world from my mother's womb.'[70] He said he rejected any kind of treason and assassination 'without any equivocation or mental reservation', and commended his soul to God.

Next came Father Harcourt, the oldest Jesuit, who said much the same thing, 'I am as innocent as the child unborn', blessing King Charles and Queen Catherine, 'the best of queens'. He finished by asking for the prayers of any Catholics present – and there were probably many there. Anthony Turner denied any knowledge of the plot, or even being in London when the infamous consult met. The sheriff's patience waned at this point, and he interrupted, 'You do only justify yourselves here. We will not believe a word that you say. Spend your time in prayer . . .'[71] Resuming – and ignoring Sir Richard's admonition, Turner again claimed innocence, though in addition to asking blessings for the king he also forgave his false accusers, 'from the bottom of my heart, as I hope myself for forgiveness at the hands of God'.[72] The youngest Jesuit, John Gavan, spoke eloquently next. Divine mercy depends upon complete confession, Gavan said, and 'now in this hour I do solemnly swear, protest and vow, by all that is sacred in heaven and on earth, and as I hope to see the face of God in glory, that I am as innocent as the child unborn of those treasonable crimes which Mr. Oates and Mr. Dugdale have sworn against me . . .'[73] He forgave his accusers, the judges and jury that condemned him, and blessed King Charles.

The last to speak was John Fenwick, and his declaration of innocence resulted in a debate with the sheriff, who accused Fenwick not only of the crimes for which he was convicted, but also of involvement in the Godfrey murder, a charge Fenwick strongly denied: 'Now that I am a dying man, do you think I would go and damn my soul?' How replied, 'I wish you all the good that I can, but I will assure you I believe never a word that you say.' But Fenwick persisted, 'I do again declare that what I have said is true, and I hope Christian charity will not let you think that by the last act of my life I would cast away my soul by sealing up my last breath with a damnable lie.'[74]

Each man then prayed privately for a time, after which the executioner pulled hoods over their eyes and whipped the carthorse into motion. Ketch afforded his victims a small mercy before the butchery began: he waited until all were dead. The quartering of five bodies must have taken some time, and it kicked off a mad scramble for souvenirs. Some dabbled their handkerchiefs in Jesuit blood for martyr's relics, some merely out of a gruesome desire to have some reminder of the day's excitement. One boy, a butcher's apprentice, went farther than most: when Ketch threw Father Harcourt's organs into the fire, he 'resolved to have a piece of his kidney which was broiling on the fire. He burn't his fingers much, but he got it . . .'[75]

The authorities put Langhorne's execution off, because Shaftesbury had persuaded him to give more information about the plot and other affairs of the Jesuit mission. Rumours circulated that the attorney held £20,000 (some said £80,000) worth of property in trust for the mission, property that could be seized by the Crown. Langhorne submitted a statement to the Privy Council on 3 July. This said nothing about an assassination plot and focused on Jesuit property – and was not enough to save him. Shaftesbury, as president of the council, insisted that the execution go ahead. The king allowed this – though he suppressed Richard's information, thereby saving the Jesuits' property.[76]

On 14 July, Langhorne went to Tyburn, carrying with him a printed copy of his last speech – one which Sheriff How refused to allow him to read. Speaking from memory, Richard denied the charges against him in detail, and like the Jesuits before him he forgave all involved in his trial and punishment. This speech soon circulated widely, and demonstrates that there were people in and around London entertaining doubts about the plot's reality. One correspondent, the Irish peer Lord Massereene, writing only days after Langhorne's death, griped about the spread of disbelief: 'The testimony of those who have evidenced against the plotters and . . . brought them to Tyburn is now I assure you more disparaged than ever, and the loss of Catholic blood regretted as if it were the precious blood of martyrs . . . the obstinacy of Langhorne, and a feigned speech which was called his (and which I am sure [was] printed before he uttered his real speech at the gallows) has done much mischief, and there are privy counsellors who affect the innocency of the sufferers.'[77] The refusal of all of the convicted plotters to confess clearly made a significant impact on public opinion.

Lord Massereene accurately described the conflict within the Privy Council. King Charles's attempt to co-opt Shaftesbury had clearly failed; his decision to prorogue Parliament on 27 May exemplified this. Charles and Shaftesbury clashed openly in council on 17 June. In early May a group of anti-Episcopalian extremists dragged the primate of the Church of Scotland, James Sharp, out of his coach near St Andrews and murdered him. An uprising by radical Presbyterians in Scotland soon followed. The question before the council was whether to send troops from England to suppress the uprising. Charles wanted to appoint his illegitimate son Monmouth to lead the expedition, while Shaftesbury – who some thought had engaged in secret communication with the rebels – opposed sending a force north. The council voted unanimously – except for its president – to raise troops. Shaftesbury insisted that Parliament must be recalled, no doubt hoping to increase pressure on the duke of York and keep the plot in the political forefront. This Charles refused to countenance. In the course of a bitter debate Shaftesbury told the king that without 'the rights and liberties' of an Englishman under a monarchy, he would prefer to live under a commonwealth.[78] As the word 'commonwealth' was poison to Charles, this tactless statement could only have increased the king's determination to sideline the earl.

In the face of these events, clearly Charles needed a new plan. Belying his reputation for sloth, at this moment the king acted vigorously, first of all to defend the queen. The five Jesuits met their fate at Tyburn on 20 June, and the next day the earl of Ossory told his father, the duke of Ormond, 'The king is very generous and just in resenting the aspersions laid on the Queen, and is thinking how he may save her from being named by those who I think absolutely accuse her.' Charles told the Privy Council he was convinced of Catherine's innocence and that he 'would not suffer her to be unjustly scandalized'.[79] By early July a new strategy emerged, in which Charles deliberately excluded Shaftesbury and his allies from his counsels – on 24 June, for example, he met privately in his bedchamber with several councillors to discuss the upcoming trial of Sir George Wakeman.

Full meetings of the Privy Council now convened only once a week. It met on 6 July at Hampton Court and Charles announced his decision to dissolve Parliament and call another to meet in the autumn. Shaftesbury protested that his opinion had not been sought and that he 'could not but discharge his conscience in representing the evil consequences of this resolution'. Charles replied that it was clear to him that this Parliament must go, and that it was his right to decide whether the council agreed or not.[80]

On 24 June, Ossory, who was his father's eyes and ears at court, reported that Charles 'minded nothing else'. The Wakeman trial, the king believed, amounted to an assault on the queen. The Privy Council called Oates, Bedloe, Prance and Dugdale and interrogated them. Prance and Dugdale had nothing very damaging to say, and the first two carefully hedged. Their positive statements against Catherine to Parliament and in earlier court cases notwithstanding, the council concluded that their information 'does not amount in the judgment of the law to fasten guilt upon her'.[81] The king was greatly relieved.

Most expected Wakeman's trial would end in the usual conviction: ''Tis not doubted but Sir George will be found guilty of endeavoring to poison the king, the evidence against him being very large and positive.'[82] But unlike all the other accused plotters, Wakeman had plenty of time to prepare. A newsletter written on 10 July noted that 'Dr. Wakeman doth not intend to be Colmanized.'[83] Held in the Gatehouse prison under conditions less strict than the prisoners in Newgate, he received news from the outside world. Thanks to Oates and Bedloe's account on 24 June to the Privy Council, Wakeman knew in detail what his accusers would say. He had more material assistance than previous defendants as well – the council sent its own officers to Bath to bring one of the doctor's key witnesses, an apothecary named Ashby, to town for the trial.[84]

On Tuesday 18 July the trial began at the Old Bailey, with Scroggs again presiding. All of the previous plot trials drew wide public interest, but this one riveted the nation. Wakeman's connection to the queen ensured that the courtroom was packed and every coffee house and tavern in the capital awaited the outcome with bated breath. All eyes were on the lantern-jawed royal physician – like his accuser 'Doctor' Oates, Sir George was no heart throb. Wakeman stood in the dock with three other defendants, William Rumley, William Marshal and James Corker, all Benedictine priests in the queen's service. Attached to Catherine's chapel at Somerset House, they had been jailed early on in the plot and unlike Wakeman they enjoyed few of the advantages he had in preparing their defence. Their part in the conspiracy was to have raised money to pay Sir George his handsome reward for murdering King Charles.

The indictment recited the now-familiar tale; Wakeman had agreed to poison the king for £15,000 in case the various other methods planned for his death failed. The empanelled jury included a new cast of characters; in previous cases some jurors sat in other plot trials. In this case none of the gentlemen chosen had served on a previous panel. It is difficult to know much about these men, although most are identified as gentlemen from in and around London. There are some interesting possible connections, though. The foreman, Ralph Hawtrey, later became a strong supporter of James II as MP for Middlesex. Another juror, Henry Hawley, might have been related to Francis Hawley, one of James's gentlemen of the bedchamber. John Bathurst might have been connected to Sir Benjamin Bathurst, who became James's household commissioner of revenue in 1682. Henry Hodges might have been related to Hugh Hodges, a London attorney and Tory MP. Perhaps there was some royal influence at work? This might well have been the case, though at least one juror, John Baldwin, had a notable connection with enemies of the dynasty. He served as secretary to the Parliamentarian general Lord Essex and was gentleman porter of the Tower until the Restoration, when the new government had dismissed him.[85]

Two prominent London lawyers presented the Crown's case. The junior counsellor was Sir Edward Ward, a forty-one-year-old barrister, the leading practitioner in the Court of Exchequer. The senior prosecutor was Sir Robert Sawyer, a former Speaker of the House of Commons. In the Commons the previous autumn he had helped draft an address to the king calling for Queen Catherine's removal from court – clearly he had no qualms about this particular prosecution.[86]

Stephen Dugdale testified first. He had nothing particular to say against any of the defendants, but the Crown intended his testimony to prove the existence of an assassination plot. He told of letters received and various conversations he had had with others, including Lord Stafford, about killing the king. He said he had agreed to participate in the regicide 'either to have taken his life away by shooting, or by stabbing, or some way'.[87] Chief Justice Scroggs actively questioned the witness – more even than Sawyer and Ward – and the tone of his questions was uncharacteristically sceptical. Either Dugdale spoke very quietly, or the noise in the packed courtroom made it difficult for the accused to hear what he said; Sir George and Corker complained and Scroggs had to repeat the gist of Dugdale's words. One of the letters, supposedly written by the recently executed Whitbread, openly described the plan to murder Charles and came to Dugdale through the regular post. All four defendants reacted incredulously – what sort of fool would entrust such a letter to the regular mail? 'No man living can believe it,' said Sir George.[88] Even Justice Scroggs found this implausible: 'You say it is strange, and indeed it is so, that such a design should be writ so in plain English in a letter . . .'[89] Father Marshal attacked Dugdale's testimony for its implausibility; the witness spoke of reading over a hundred letters over a two-year period, written by a number of different individuals, many of which dealt in one way or another with the plot. How likely was it, Marshal asked, that so many people knew of this plan? '. . . here is person after person, conspiring without end, and letters to this person, and letters to that person, and nothing is proved to be done upon it . . .'[90] And, Father Rumley asked, 'Where are these letters?' 'I burnt those letters which I kept . . . but in a multitude of letters it is hard to tell particulars, I tell you what I remember of them,' said Dugdale. This hardly satisfied the defendants,

'Methinks you might be more ready in your evidence, than upon every turn to say you cannot remember,' Rumley remonstrated.[91]

During Dugdale's testimony the accused asked for pen and paper – and surprisingly the court granted the request. Was this another sign of a changed attitude towards the defendants? The court had now given the defence an important tool – making notes increased their ability to keep track of the witnesses' numerous contradictions and lapses of memory. Because they could not begin their defence until after the Crown rested its case, it was vital that the accused could refer to their own notes.

Next on the stand was Miles Prance, sent there again to verify the existence of the conspiracy, but having nothing directly to say about any of the prisoners at the bar.

The Crown's case really depended upon Oates's testimony. In July 1678 he had allegedly seen a letter from Wakeman to a patient, Mr Ashby. It prescribed a course of treatment for an illness – a combination of milk and water from the mineral springs at Bath. And, by the way, the letter also mentioned that 'the queen would assist him in poisoning the King'. Oates did not explain why Sir George would have added such an extraordinary postscript to a routine prescription. Some days later, in the company of several priests, Oates said, he had attended a meeting at Somerset House, the queen's official lodgings. Oates had waited in an anteroom while the other priests went in, but he could clearly hear what went on: 'I did hear a woman's voice which did say that she would assist them in the propagation of the Catholic religion with her estate, and that she would not endure these violations of her bed any longer, and that she would assist Sir George Wakeman in the poisoning of the king.' He then gilded the lily: '. . . when they came out I desired that I might see the Queen, and so when I came in I had, as I believe, a gracious smile.' That Queen Catherine bestowed a gracious smile on Titus Oates might be one of the least likely things he said throughout the course of his many perjuries.

Having cast his aspersions on Catherine, Oates proceeded to Wakeman. He said he had heard several Jesuits offer Sir George £10,000 for the assassination, a sum the doctor rejected as too small. A £5,000 sweetener had brought Wakeman on board, however. Father Harcourt entered the agreement in an 'entry book'. Wakeman also signed a receipt for £5,000 in the same book. Oates hedged about the source of this payment, 'I cannot undertake to say who it was', but his conscience told him the money came from Mr Staley, the London goldsmith whose son was the plot's first victim. And of course Harcourt could hardly be questioned about this, having been executed a month earlier. And like most of the documents Titus spoke of, no such entry book had been found among the thousands of documents seized by the Crown.

Sir George demanded that the elder Mr Staley be called to confirm or deny Oates's words – though Scroggs rebuffed him: '[Oates] only says he believes Mr. Staley paid it.'[92] Titus much preferred to rest his case on the dead; he also rattled the bones of Edward Colman and Richard Langhorne for the jury – both had participated in organizing Sir George's bargain, he said. Now finished giving his evidence, Wakeman had the opportunity to question Oates. Sir George asked, 'Have not you said, before the king and council, that you never saw me in all your life, and that you did not know me?' Oates's rather feeble response was that at their initial encounter before the Privy Council it was dark and he was exhausted, 'being so ill for want of rest, in respect both of my intellectuals and every thing else; but now I have a proper light whereby I may see a man's face . . .' Wakeman pointed out that Titus had said virtually the same thing to excuse his inability to identify Edward Colman.[93] He also asked why, on that occasion, Titus had said nothing about Wakeman's part in the plot. '. . . can any one believe, that if such evidence had been given to the king and council against me . . . that I should not have been immediately taken into custody, but that I should have my liberty so long as I had?' Justice Scroggs pressed Oates on this question, and received an evasive reply, 'I can, by and by, give an answer to it', before quickly turning to the other defendants – probably to distract the court's attention.[94] The Pope intended Father Corker to be bishop of London, and Corker had written letters to raise money for carrying on the conspiracy. The Crown presented two letters in Corker's hand, although neither had any clear bearing on the conspiracy. These letters did nothing more than to allow Titus to claim he had seen other incriminating letters (which naturally were not in evidence, as they did not exist) in the same handwriting. Oates was even more vague about the other defendants, saying little more than that they knew something about the plot and had consented to it.

The Benedictines took turns pressing Oates about his imprecise dates; William Marshal protested that defending himself would be impossible if he had to account for all his movements over a period of weeks. The Crown's star witness remained evasive, but with some pressure from the Chief Justice – itself notable – Titus finally identified 14 or 16 August as the crucial date. Perhaps sensing that the court's deference to his tales had waned, Oates made a bid to be excused, 'My lord, I desire I may have leave to retire, because I am not well.' Scroggs denied the request.[95]

Now it was William Bedloe's turn. In early August 1678, while loitering in Father Harcourt's chambers, an aggravated George Wakeman had entered. The doctor protested that he had long been ready to act, but that the Jesuits were slow about his payment. Like Oates before him, Bedloe specifically incriminated Queen Catherine, claiming that Sir George had said, 'I find more encouragement from my good lady and mistress than from any of you all.'[96] Whatever promises he had made before the Privy Council in advance of the trial, the 'Captain' seemed intent upon dragging the queen into the plot.

Harcourt had mollified the disgruntled Wakeman by giving him a bill of exchange for £2,000, although Bedloe was more than a little reticent about the details. He could not remember who the bill was from – though he took care to say that it had been drawn at the queen's order. But as for the name of the goldsmith upon whom it was drawn, he could say nothing except that he thought 'he dwelt somewhere about St. Dunstan's church',[97] a claim he later widened to include the vicinity of Fleet Street. Later the same day, Bedloe ran into Wakeman on the street and asked him if he had received his money – he had, he said.

Bedloe's testimony against the other defendants was less detailed. One observer, the diarist John Evelyn, left his own impression of the prosecution. The Crown's witnesses left Evelyn unimpressed – most of their evidence was hearsay and not very persuasive. Oates, Evelyn thought, was 'a vaine, insolent man, puff'd up with the favour of the Commons'.[98] And even Scroggs made a surprising intervention. Sir William briefly summarized Bedloe's testimony with a decided slant in the accused's favour. 'I do not find, by the strictest observation I have made, that Mr. Bedloe . . . does say any great thing against any one of them . . .'[99] Sir Robert Sawyer leapt to his feet in consternation, saying that Bedloe had said much more – reminding Scroggs of Bedloe's account of his meeting with Father Harcourt and Sir George, when the defendant expressed his frustration at going unpaid. The Chief Justice called on Bedloe to repeat his account of that conversation, prefacing it with an uncharacteristically generous remarks about the accused. 'We are now in the case of men's lives, and pray have a care that you say no more than what is true upon any man whatever. I would be loth to keep out Popery by that way they would bring it in, that is by blood or violence. I would have all things go very fair.'[100]

Bedloe retold his story, still incriminating both Sir George and the queen, and Scroggs again attempted to undermine the witness, saying 'He says now quite another thing than he said before.' This prompted both of the king's counsels, Sawyer and George Jeffreys, as well as Justice North, to interject 'No! He said the same before.'[101] Bedloe persisted, claiming that Sir George did agree to kill the king. At this, Wakeman turned to his fellow defendants and despaired, 'There is my business done!'[102]

Wakeman called his witnesses first. Mr Chapman, a Bath apothecary, testified that he had seen Sir George's letter prescribing a course of mineral water for Mr Ashby, and that it contained not a word about regicide. Chapman provided lodgings for Ashby on his trip to Bath, and he supervised his treatment. In order to do so, in fact, he had torn off the relevant part of Wakeman's letter, which he presented to the court as evidence. Oates denied that the letter Chapman presented was the one he saw. Wakeman introduced two more witnesses, his servant Hunt, who wrote the letter at Sir George's dictation, and Elizabeth Hennigham, who had been present when the letter was written. Both testified that the letter was entirely innocent and contained nothing treasonous. Titus stuck to his story – there was another letter. Wakeman not unnaturally asked why should he write two prescriptions for the same person? Left unasked was perhaps a still more obvious question – why should one of these prescriptions randomly discuss a conspiracy to assassinate Charles II with his wife's encouragement? It is notable that Justice Scroggs intervened several times to emphasize yet another question: 'the question will be upon Mr. Oates's credit, how far the jury will believe him'.[103]

But Dr Oates's credibility soon suffered a more significant blow, when Sir Philip Lloyd, clerk of the Privy Council, mounted the stand. Lloyd highlighted the blatant contradictions in Oates's testimony before the council during the early days of the plot. On 30 September 1678, Oates told the council that he had seen a letter between two Jesuits implicating Sir George in a scheme to poison the king. The council summoned Sir George, who denied the charge and hoped that the king would give him an opportunity to vindicate his honour. The council decided not to arrest Wakeman on the strength of what amounted to hearsay, and asked Oates if he had any direct information about Sir George. Oates, Sir Philip said, 'did lift up his hands (for I must tell the truth, let it be what it will) and said, "No, God forbid that I should say anything against Sir George Wakeman, for I know nothing more against him."'[104] To this Titus responded feebly, 'I remember not one word of this.' Falling back on his earlier excuse of exhaustion, '. . . by reason of my being hurried up and down, and sitting up, I was scarce compos mentis'. This cut no ice with Scroggs, 'What, must we be amused with I know not what, for being up but two nights?'[105]

In his testimony before Parliament, shortly after this appearance before the Privy Council, Oates told of seeing the incriminating letter to Ashby, written by Wakeman. This stunned Sir Philip – if this were true, why had Titus said nothing of this at his earlier examination before the council? Why had he said, 'I know no more against him'? Again Oates protested his exhaustion, though Justice Scroggs responded, 'It did not require such a deal of strength to say "I saw a letter under Sir George's own hand."' Furthermore, said Scroggs, Sir George would have been arrested immediately had Titus mentioned the Ashby letter in the beginning. Oates, annoyed, retorted, 'To speak the truth, they were such a council as would commit nobody.' This petulance earned him a rebuke from the court, and a remarkably hostile remark from Justice Scroggs, 'You have taken a great confidence, I know not by what authority, to say anything of any body.' In no plot trial to date had Scroggs been anything but solicitous towards the Crown's witnesses. Clearly the winds were shifting.

The next important witness was Sir Thomas Dolman, whose task it was to rescue Oates's exhaustion dodge. Dolman, like Lloyd, was a clerk of the Privy Council, and he told the court of Oates's labours over two days, dragging Catholic clergy from their beds and ransacking their lodgings. 'Mr. Oates was in as feeble and weak a condition as ever I saw man in my life . . .'[106] Wakeman turned Dolman's appearance to his advantage, however, because it offered him the chance to give a detailed account of his first examination by the king and council in which he had denied any knowledge of a plot – though he admitted that he found the charges against him so absurd he did not treat them as seriously as he should have done. Then Sir George rehearsed his family's loyalty to the Stuarts, and recounted how the Protectorate jailed him for royalist plotting. Having done his best to use his record of loyalty make a favourable impression, Wakeman stood down and James Corker rose.

Father Corker impugned the credibility of Oates and Bedloe, saying they had led 'scandalous lives', provoking Justice Scroggs to ask for proof of this fact – though interestingly with much less vigour than he had done in other trials. 'If the jury know it of their own knowledge, I leave it to them – but you have proved nothing.'[107] Corker hammered away at the implausibility of the plot – who would believe that such a vast conspiracy, involving so many men well known for their virtue and past loyalty, could exist? 'It is not rational or probable that such vast whole armies should be raised, and foreign nations concerned in the Plot. All which, notwithstanding all the evidence that can be made out of this plot, is but only their positive swearing.'[108] Furthermore, when Oates, heading a posse of officers, burst into his lodgings to arrest Thomas Pickering, James Corker had remained unrecognized and unmolested. The authorities did not arrest Corker for another month – after Oates fingered him as the prospective Catholic bishop of London. Why did Titus not recognize him immediately? Why leave him at liberty? Corker called a witness, his housekeeper Ellen Rigby. Rigby testified that when the early morning raid on her house occurred, both Corker and William Marshal were sleeping. The officers had taken Pickering away, 'the company that came in never asked for you [Corker] and said they had nothing to do with you'.[109] Rigby also took an opportunity to strike a blow at Oates – she had seen him only once before the raid, when, about a year earlier, he had turned up begging a handout from Mr Pickering – who told her never to admit him to the house again.

Throughout Corker's defence Scroggs was uncharacteristically gentle, complimenting Father James for asking the jury to draw its own conclusions. William Marshal also noted the alteration in the Chief Justice's attitude, and claimed that it had saved him from despairing of his own case. 'But, my lord, since your lordship is pleased to fling forth some encouragement, and to hang out the white flag of hope . . . I shall now endeavour to make defense for my life as well as I can.'[110] Marshal argued that before his arrest there was no search being made for him and his name appeared in none of the informers' testimony. His arrest itself was a matter of chance – looking for a friend he walked into a house where a search party was at work. Why, he asked, would he walk into such a situation – an officer at the door, the house ablaze with lights? A guilty man would surely turn and flee. Unfortunately, Sir William Waller, who had been present at the raid, was still in court. He rose and said, probably untruthfully, that Marshal had wandered in unwittingly. Waller unhelpfully contradicted Marshal in a number of ways, denying his version of the arrest as well as his account of his first confrontation with Oates. Marshal said that Oates had not recognized him; Waller said that he had. Ordinarily a magistrate's word carried great weight with the court, and these almost certain perjuries dismayed Father William: '. . . my lord, what he says is to my great astonishment'.[111] Left to contemplate the dishonesty of Sir William, Marshal ended his defence.

The defendants all made final statements – Sir George and Father Corker vehemently denied the charges against them, and Father Marshal unleashed an eloquent plea of innocence. Not a single person convicted so far had made a dying confession – surely an indicator of innocence – '. . . if no credit be to be given to the protestations of men dying that have ever been judged sober and just, how can faith be reposed in the testimony of such living persons as know no God nor goodness?' No doubt looking at Oates and Bedloe as he spoke, he continued, '. . . may not he . . . who hath owned himself a villain in print, be thought false in his testimony, while preferment tickles him, rewards march before him and ambition beckons to him, which he greedily follows, though God and conscience tell him it is unjust? England is become now a mournful theatre, upon which such a tragedy is acted as turns the eyes of all Europe toward it . . .'[112]

This speech, with its implicit denunciation of English justice, goaded Justice Scroggs into another one of his anti-Catholic rants. 'Your doctrine is a doctrine of blood and cruelty, Christ's doctrine is a law of mercy, simplicity, meekness and obedience, but you have nothing but all the pride that ever a pope can usurp over princes, and you are filled with pride, and mad till you come again into the possession of the tyranny you once exercised here . . .'[113] If the audience was wondering whether the Chief Justice had gone soft on Catholics and favoured the defendants, their doubts were relieved; this violent rhetoric sparked cheers in the courtroom.

But soon those doubts returned – for in his summation for the jury, Scroggs spun the evidence favourably for the accused. First, he directed the jury to acquit Mr Rumley – only one witness swore against him and the law of treason required two. Second, Sir William declared that there could be no doubt but that there was a plot to assassinate the king and introduce Catholicism. But with respect to the defendants' questioning the prosecution testimonies' probability, 'that is well enough said'.[114] Several times Scroggs talked of the need to avoid injustices: '. . . we would not, to prevent their plots (let them be as big as they can make them) shed one drop of innocent blood . . . consider seriously, and weigh truly the circumstances and the probability of the things charged against them'.[115] Third, regarding Sir George Wakeman, Scroggs implied, without directly saying so, that Oates might have mistaken the physician's handwriting in the letter to Mr Ashly. There was also the alleged entry book in which Sir George's bargain was memorialized. This, the Chief Justice asserted, was all Oates had to say. But Sawyer, the prosecutor, intervened to note that Scroggs left out Oates's claim that he saw a commission appointing Sir George 'physician general' of the phantom Catholic army. Bedloe's evidence against Wakeman, Scroggs said, depended on his account of the conversation he had witnessed in Father Harcourt's lodgings – and he implied that Bedloe might be untrustworthy: 'Now if you believe this, then there are two witnesses against Sir George Wakeman.' The wording here is significant – in earlier trials Scroggs never allowed the possibility of disbelief to enter the court. The witnesses swore an oath, therefore all they said was presumed to be true. Here the judge introduced the possibility of disbelief – a notable assist to the defence. Finally, in the case of the other defendants, Scroggs downplayed the Crown's case, and highlighted the fact that both Oates and Bedloe had failed to recognize or arrest them when they had the chance early in the plot. He particularly scorned Oates's claim of exhaustion in Wakeman's first appearance before the Privy Council – 'It is wonderful to me; I do not know if a man be never so faint, could not he say "I saw a letter under his hand" . . .?'[116]

Chief Justice Scroggs emphasized the reality of the plot – but, he argued, 'that does not affect these men in particular'. The Crown's case depended upon the oaths of Oates and Bedloe – and Scroggs emphasized the defence's counter-arguments: 'Let us not be so amazed and frighted with the noise of plots as to take away any man's life without any reasonable evidence. If you are satisfied with the oaths of these two men, so. What Sir George Wakeman says about his not accusing him before the Council, and what these men say that he did not apprehend them . . . These men's bloods are at stake, and therefore never care what the world says, follow your consciences. If you are satisfied these men swear true, you will do well to find them guilty, and they deserve to die for it. If you are unsatisfied upon these things put together, and they do weigh with you, that they have not said true, you will do well to acquit them.' At this Bedloe erupted, 'My lord, my evidence is not right summed up!' 'I know not by what authority this man speaks,' replied Scroggs coldly.[117]

Now the jurors withdrew. Deliberations continued for a full hour – most unusual in a capital case, and unprecedented in all of the previous plot trials. At last the jury returned to the court with a verdict: Not Guilty.

Sir George and his fellow defendants were the first Catholics to have been acquitted in the course of the plot. Was this a turning point?

— NINE —
BATTLE ROYAL
JULY 1679–JULY 1680

London reacted to the acquittal of Sir George Wakeman and his fellow defendants with astonishment – and rage. Chief Justice Scroggs took most of the blame; he left London the day after the trial, hooted at by a mob. Someone punctuated the crowd's hostility with the corpse of a dog, hurling it into the judge's coach.[1] The Chief Justice bore continued abuse throughout his circuit, particularly in Gloucester and Bristol. None other than the duke of Buckingham insulted him in open court. Scroggs charged a local Grand Jury to enforce the laws against Catholics, and the duke scoffed that the judge was in fact 'a favorer of papists, and that he had private orders to assist and favor the papists all he could'. This earned Charles's former playmate an indictment for sedition.[2] Queen Catherine and her husband, on the other hand, were delighted. The acquittal 'has very much rejoiced the Queen,' wrote Lord Ossory. King Charles received the news with tears in his eyes and repeated his promise to 'remain steadfast in his justice and kindness to her'.[3]

In the immediate aftermath of the trial even Titus Oates seemed somewhat abashed – a newsletter of 24 July pronounced him 'somewhat indisposed' and a week or so later he requested permission from the king to 'retire for some time in the country for his health's sake'.[4] Rumours spread that Scroggs had received a £10,000 bribe, possibly from the Portuguese ambassador (who had unwisely called upon Scroggs to thank him for meting out justice), that various of the jurors were corrupt, and that one juror had since gone mad. Another story had a gentleman mistaken for one of the jury, being handed a piece of paper folded around fifty gold guineas. Like Justice Scroggs, the jurors endured the abuse of their neighbours. One, Alderman John Bathurst, was 'hissed off the Exchange', and several others began looking for new houses thanks to the hostility of their neighbours.[5]

The cascade of vituperative abuse that Chief Justice Scroggs experienced prompted him to make a public statement vindicating his proceedings in the

Wakeman trial and ordering its publication. He denounced the public demonstrations against him and his court. 'The people ought to be pleased with public justice, and not justice seek to please the people. Justice should flow like a mighty stream, and if the rabble, like an unruly wind, blow against it, it may make it rough, but the stream will keep its course.'⁶ Printers published and sold many libels such as *A Satyr against In-Justice: or, Sc – gs upon Sc – gs*. This gem, allegedly written by a woman named Jane Curtis, accused Scroggs of bribery: 'Some hungry priests he once did fell/With mighty stroakes, and them to Hell/ Sent furiously away, Sirs. Would you know why? The reason's plain,/They had no English nor French coyn/To purchase longer stays.'⁷

For these Scroggs had nothing but contempt and a warning, 'For those hireling scribblers . . . who write to eat, and lie for bread I intend to meet with them another way, for they are only safe whilst they can be secret; but so are vermin, so long only as they can hide themselves . . . Look to it, some shall be found, and they shall know that the law wants not power to punish a libelous and licentious press, nor I a resolution to execute it.'⁸

Did the king have a hand in the trial's outcome? We do not know – no hard evidence of tampering has ever been found. The selection of several jurors with ties to the duke of York is suggestive, and Justice Scroggs did not employ his usual bias from the bench, although he was still as ferociously anti-Catholic as ever. Certainly Shaftesbury suspected something. At a Privy Council meeting after the trial he announced that Sir Philip Lloyd and Justice Scroggs 'were no longer fit to serve either His Majesty or the nation'. Charles replied blandly, '. . . if men had proceeded according to their consciences he knew no fault they had done'.⁹

And although Sir George, who wisely moved to France after his release, was spared, Catholics still suffered. Throughout the summer of 1679 there were a series of trials – several presided over by Scroggs on circuit – of Roman Catholic clergy. Assize courts convicted priests in Cheshire, Yorkshire, Worcestershire and Wales among other places. These prosecutions did not relate directly to the plot – the accused were tried for violating draconian acts passed in Queen Elizabeth's reign. It was a capital offence under these statutes for any Catholic in orders to enter England. The law had been inconsistently, and recently quite rarely, enforced. But pressure to crack down on English Catholics had grown enormously since Oates's first revelations. In the summer of 1679 that pressure remained high. Charles ordered a stay of execution in several cases, but he allowed most of the convicted to hang. Like the five Jesuits before them, nearly all met their fate steadfastly, denying any knowledge of the plot and claiming that they had suffered for nothing but their religion. These trials no doubt satisfied the blood lust of many Protestants, but they also made a favourable impression on others, impressed by the fortitude on display at the gallows.[10]

Tightening the screws on English Catholics aided King Charles in his increasingly determined effort to counter Shaftesbury. At this stage, relations between the king and his erstwhile Lord President stopped just short of open war. Days before Wakeman's trial, the French ambassador reported that Shaftesbury had said '. . . we shall easily find the means by the laws of making him walk out of the kingdom'.[11] Charles, meanwhile, embarked on a systematic remodelling of local offices, dismissing magistrates who supported the earl's agenda, and appointing sympathetic sheriffs. Both men intended to influence the upcoming elections for the new Parliament, scheduled to open on 17 October. From July until September excitement grew. On 2 August, Henry Coventry, writing to the duke of Ormond, said 'Elections for Parliament employ men's brains and tongues very much', though he expected that in the end the new members would be much the same as those elected in the spring.[12] A few weeks later Ormond's friend Sir Robert Southwell noted everywhere he went 'a strange agitation in the spirits of the people, their minds warmed in a great part by contention and animosity in the elections . . .' 'Swarms of pamphlets' heightened tension between supporters of the Court and of Shaftesbury.

In the midst of this growing political tension, the king was taken seriously ill. In the last week of August he contracted a fever, attributed to over-exertion – thanks to a morning spent playing tennis and an evening hawking. Courtiers were alarmed by the severity of the king's fever. The physicians subjected the king to the full measure of seventeenth-century medical science. Doctors dosed Charles with a 'detoctum armarum' – a bitter-tasting distillation pronounced highly effective. If, as Bishop Burnet reported, this was 'Jesuit's bark' (quinine), the doctors were probably right.[13] No less (or more?) helpful was the 'gentle purge' he took. Composed of the dried sap of the flowering ash, or manna, tree, this sent him to the close stool sixteen times. Finally the doctors bled the king, taking eight ounces from an incision made in his foot.[14] Charles had recovered by the first week of September, though he remained quite weak. After the ministrations of the royal physicians this is hardly surprising. One of Ormond's friends, Lord Longford, saw Charles at Windsor, where he was resting. The king '. . . is brought very low, being so weak that he can but crawl up and down his chamber, yet he looks very cheerfully, though thin'.[15]

The most important consequence of this illness was that it brought Charles's brother hastening home from his exile in Brussels. James's arrival in the midst of an increasingly frantic parliamentary election season could do nothing but heighten tensions. His return brought home an important lesson: unless Parliament succeeded in denying him his crown, no exile could prevent him from returning to claim it. That realization added urgency to the exclusionist cause. This urgency generated resistance – a cycle of political conflict had begun, and no one knew when or how it might end. Both sides – supporters of the king and duke, and Shaftesbury's allies – seized upon whatever weapons came to hand. As Justice Scroggs had learned, libels and scurrilous pamphlets poured from the presses, satisfying a huge demand and repeating falsehoods on both sides. The Privy Council inveighed against attacks on the Lord Chief Justice, while London magistrates like Sir William Waller conducted raids on printing houses suspected of publishing pro-Catholic books and pamphlets. On 7 September, for example, Waller's posse confiscated no fewer than 1,500 copies of works defending the recently executed Jesuits and an edition of Richard Langhorne's 'memoirs'.[16]

Meanwhile, members of a new Parliament had to be chosen. In contrast to his attempt to co-opt Shaftesbury in the spring, and his passive attitude towards parliamentary elections then, Charles now acted more resolutely. The earl remained Lord President of the Privy Council, but rumours of his imminent dismissal were rife. In fact some thought he hoped to be sacked, expecting that it would increase his popularity.[17] When the king attended council meetings, his dislike for the Lord President was barely concealed, and for his part Shaftesbury's deference was superficial at best. For much of the summer Shaftesbury remained at home in Dorset, avoiding the council table altogether. Just before his illness, Charles, who was ordinarily not one to invite face-to-face conflict, summoned Shaftesbury to Windsor, intending a showdown. But the earl begged off, claiming illness, and the meeting never happened. Nor would it have made much difference; Shaftesbury continued campaigning for exclusionists around the country, and he made no bones about his plans for the upcoming Parliament: excluding James and installing a new queen.[18] He also intended to do what he could to advance the pretensions of Charles's illegitimate son Monmouth, who might be a substitute heir for James one day.

Further revelations about Catholic conspiracy could only assist exclusionists, so it is not surprising that as candidates vied for office more 'information' emerged. Robert Jennison, who had played a minor part in the Wakeman trial, returned for a repeat performance – although this time he hoped to put himself at centre stage. Appearing before the Privy Council on 7 August – with both the king and Shaftesbury present – Jennison told how in August 1678 the now hanged-and-quartered Father William Ireland, his cousin, had asked him to recommend four 'stout and courageous gentlemen' who might be trusted to assassinate the king. Jennison had told the same tale to Edward Warcup, a friend and client of Shaftesbury, the day before – thus ensuring that his revelations would receive maximum attention. Printed almost immediately afterwards, news reverberated around London coffee houses and taverns that the formerly anonymous 'four Irish rogues' contracted to kill King Charles now had names: Captain Levallyn, Mr Kerney, Mr Braball and Mr James Watson. Of course no one knew where these characters might be found, if they ever existed. But the new information revived the plot after the blow of the Wakefield acquittal, and that was enough for the present.

The truth, however, was very different – and sordid. Robert Jennison, identified in the Wakeman trial as the son of a substantial Catholic gentleman who enjoyed £1,000 a year from his estates, was a lawyer at Gray's Inn. Raised Catholic, he later became an Anglican, whether out of conviction or opportunism we do not know. But the rest of his family was steadfast in their faith; his older brother, Thomas, was actually a Jesuit and at the time of the Wakeman trial was imprisoned in Newgate. Robert visited his brother in jail, urging him to verify Oates's testimony through a false confession, an entreaty that Thomas vigorously rejected. Once parted, Thomas bitterly attacked Robert for lying about their cousin and aiding Oates and Bedloe, 'those two commissioners of hell', in their perjuries. Thomas despaired that Robert had 'justified Oates and Bedloe and by consequence taken upon you the blood of an innocent man, and a near relation, and of one to whose kindness you owe . . . much'. Robert, he lamented, had '. . . even outdone the malice of Judas, and those that crucified Christ . . . and conspired with the Devil to disappoint the design of Christ's passion, not only in the perdition of your own soul, but in hiding and driving truth from the nation'.[19] The only thing that would save Robert from the 'flames and torments of Hell', his brother said, was a full retraction of his testimony and the truth about Oates.[20]

Robert, however, had other ideas. If his brother refused to attach himself to Oates's band of informers, he would do so. The rewards would far overshadow whatever his conscience – or the Almighty – might throw at him. Very soon after his depositions appeared in print, he published his *Narrative*, reprinting all of his claims – he even included his brother's letter. Jennison dedicated this work to the earl of Shaftesbury, so famous for his 'Zeal for the preservation of the Protestant religion, and of His Majesty's person and Government'.[21] Even if this literary enterprise returned little but notoriety, there was at least one consolation to his irreparable break with his brother: Thomas was the heir to the family estate. If he went the way of Cousin Ireland, Robert stood to inherit £1,000 a year.

Jennison claimed that his book was meant to bolster the evidence of the informers, 'when some foil or damp was endeavoured to be cast upon them by the subtle contrivances of the adverse party'.[22] Promoters of the plot certainly made much of Robert's testimony; newsletters claimed that 'Mr. Jennison's father and sister doe confirm his testimony and when things are more ripe three persons of quality will come in with indeniable testimonies in vindication of those already given by Mr. Oates and Mr. Bedloe.'[23] These three persons failed to materialize, but in the meanwhile Jennison distracted attention from the growing scepticism about the plot. The same day that the printed record of Wakeman's trial emerged, another book appeared 'which endeavours to prove that there is noe plot and that Mr. Oates & etc. are rogues and that 2 or 3 years hence it will be noe more beleeved then it is beleeved that the Christians fired Rome in Nero's time'.[24] These works undoubtedly began to undermine the public's hitherto widespread belief in the plot. When Shaftesbury returned to London from his country estate in the first week of October, ready to organize his parliamentary campaign, someone told him 'the plot was dead . . .', though the earl stoutly denied it. 'If Mr Oates and all the witnesses known were dead yet he knew enough to prove the plot.'[25]

Reports of the plot's death were, in fact, premature.

A few days before Shaftesbury arrived in London, a new front against Catholic treason opened – this time in the north. A new informer named Robert Bolron turned up in London with another blood-curdling story. His master, a wealthy Catholic baronet named Sir Thomas Gascoigne, had plotted the king's death. On 10 May 1679, Gascoigne had offered Bolron £1,000 to 'pistol' King Charles. Robert, shocked, had refused – but promised to keep the offer secret. On reflection (long reflection, for he evidently kept his secret for several months), Bolron 'thought it a sin to conceal so wicked a thing', and so he found a magistrate and told his story. In late September he appeared before several justices and revealed Sir Thomas's wickedness. The Yorkshire JPs decided that Bolron should go to London to inform the Privy Council. With a letter of introduction (which he managed to lose on his way south) Robert proceeded to the city. Revealingly, rather than go directly to the council with his information, Bolron first visited Sir Robert Clayton. Sir Robert, who was about to assume the office of Lord Mayor of London, was a firm ally of Shaftesbury and there could be no doubt that Bolron went to him first to ensure maximum publicity – and possibly to coordinate his story.[26] Clayton took the Yorkshireman's deposition and sent him on to the council.

Bolron accused Sir Thomas and one of his neighbours, Sir Miles Stapleton, of engaging in the plot and soon messengers from the Privy Council rode north, arrest warrants in hand. They secured the knight and baronet, seized their papers and brought them protesting to London. Shaftesbury, still Lord President and newly arrived in town, naturally pursued Gascoigne and Stapleton vigorously. On Sunday 5 October, in the king's absence, the council spent most of its meeting debating the case. It seems likely that there was some resistance among the councillors. Sir Thomas, after all, hardly seemed the type to engage in desperate treasonous plotting: he was eighty-five years old, mostly deaf and lame. Sir Miles too seemed an unlikely villain, married as he was to the sister of the impeccably loyal earl of Lindsey.[27]

Robert Bolron, in turn, hardly qualified as a disinterested friend of justice and saviour of the king. He had managed Sir Thomas's colliery since 1674 – and in 1678 Gascoigne sacked him for embezzling funds. He made away with over £200 and stood in danger of prosecution for a felony. His information was a clear case of self-protection. Sir Thomas could hardly go after him as a close prisoner in Newgate – and, as Oates, Bedloe and Dugdale had all shown, informing could lead to fame and handsome rewards. Robert took care to find a corroborating witness as well. He induced a former servant of Gascoigne's, Lawrence Mowbray, to support his allegations, promising him money and the high life of a witness for the Crown. As long as Shaftesbury and his allies remained on the Privy Council the glaring deficiencies of men like Bolron and Mowbray could be glossed over, but there was no doubt that this new information provided only limited fuel to sustain public excitement.

As Lord President, Shaftesbury called an extraordinary meeting of the Privy Council on 16 October, where he continued pushing the Yorkshire narrative and made an intemperate speech denouncing the duke of York. Parliament was due to open the next day and clearly the earl intended to begin the session with all of his exclusionist banners flying. But King Charles had prepared a counter-move.

MPs and peers duly assembled at Westminster the following morning, and took the required oaths of allegiance and supremacy, a routine that prefaced every new Parliament. That done, and nothing else, the usher of the black rod called the Commons to attend in the Lords to hear a message from the king: Parliament was prorogued until 26 January.

The prorogation dashed Shaftesbury's hopes to use Parliament as a weapon in his war with the duke of York (and now quite clearly the king). And Charles landed another blow the following day. He dispatched a letter to the earl informing him that his presence would not be required in council that day. Of course this came as no surprise to Shaftesbury, and indeed he had courted dismissal for some time, thinking that once out of office he might garner more sympathy and support. He 'wondered not much to be dismissed' and piously claimed that he had never 'disserved' the king. The Privy Council assembled without its late president and Charles pointedly noted his reasons. Shaftesbury had called extraordinary meetings of the council in which the earl had discussed his brother and the king insisted that whether James remained in England or not was no business of the council. He then punctuated his displeasure by ordering Shaftesbury's name struck off the list of councillors.[28]

Shaftesbury was correct to think that his sacking would give him an advantage. As Sir Robert Southwell wrote to his friend the duke of Ormond, 'Those who in the prorogation of Parliament and the displeasure against the earl of Shaftesbury, joined together, and this just at the season when the Duke [of York] is here, exercise great license in their observations and discourse, imputing all misfortunes to one cause and magnifying the earl of Shaftesbury as the public martyr. This will doubtless furnish new fuel to the press, which has already afforded such flames as if all the beacons of England were set on fire.'[29] More than a few people at court agreed with this analysis, thinking that the king had played his hand badly. But Charles had had enough of the little earl, and wanted rid of him whatever the cost. As it happened, however, Shaftesbury soon had a new weapon to deploy – one given to him gratuitously by his own enemies.

In early 1680 London's prisons bulged with Catholics swept up in the raids and arrests that had begun in the autumn of 1678. Very few of those arrested had been fortunate enough to be bailed; most were condemned to remain in the Gatehouse, or worse, Newgate, until they came to trial. For those without means, jail was misery. Rations were execrable; those who could not pay extra for provisions ate cheap bread served from a common basket. There were no proper beds for many, no bedding for others. Vermin – fleas, lice and rats – shared accommodations with prisoners, and death from typhus was common. Before the outbreak of the plot Catholic clergy aided imprisoned co-religionists. But now many of those priests were themselves prisoners, had fled or were in hiding. Giving charity to prisoners now fell to lay Catholics. One of the busiest and most effective of these was Elizabeth Cellier. A Catholic convert, Cellier's husband was a Frenchman and she earned a living as a midwife. Many of Cellier's clients were Catholics, some of high rank, notably the countess of Powis, whose husband currently resided in the Tower, supposedly a leading figure in the plot.

Mrs Cellier regularly visited Newgate, where she brought money and food to unfortunate Catholics. During the spring of 1679 one of those – or someone who claimed to be – was a young man who called himself Thomas Willoughby. Jailed for debt, Willloughby persuaded Elizabeth that he was a worthy object of her charity. Willoughby, 'in irons and rags', told Elizabeth his sad story – he had inadvertently lodged in a house where counterfeiters operated and he had been arrested on suspicion. The disgrace of this had led his only means of support, an uncle, to cut ties with him. Having not eaten in two days, he said, 'he was in great danger of perishing there, and in very humble and religious words, begged my charity'.[30] This Elizabeth provided, giving him small sums over the next few months. In return, Willoughby acted as Elizabeth's eyes and ears in the prison, reporting to her on the numerous visits to accused plotters from men like Shaftesbury and Justices Waller and Warcup.

In the summer, Elizabeth paid Willoughby's debts of £5, thus securing his release, intending to use him as a messenger and general dogsbody. Thomas barely had time to begin serving the Catholic cause before he was again arrested, this time on an old charge of counterfeiting. Somehow this rather obvious red flag made no impression on Elizabeth Cellier, who again arranged his bail. Thomas was sprung from jail at last, and Cellier got his coat out of hock and gave him a pair of blue stockings and breeches, along with a 'grey hat tucked up, to prevent flapping around his ears . . .'[31] During the Jesuits' trial Willoughby ran errands, carried messages, called coaches for the St Omer witnesses and generally made himself useful. In the process he won Mrs Cellier's trust, and she introduced him to Lady Powis, who attended all of the plot trials and was anxious to do whatever she could to aid the defendants and derail the plot. Powis employed Willoughby as a messenger and tasked him with keeping tabs on some of London's better-known anti-Catholics. And the countess passed him farther up the lay Catholic hierarchy, to the earl of Peterborough. The earl, seeing Willoughby's potential as a tool against Shaftesbury, Oates and his friends, introduced him to the duke of York after James returned from Brussels. The duke, in turn, introduced him to his brother the king – although unlike Willoughby's other noble patrons Charles was sceptical. But he passed Willoughby on to Secretary Coventry and gave him a small amount of money.

Willoughby said that during the king's illness prominent exclusionists – including Shaftesbury – planned to seize power in the event of his death (or possibly even without Charles's demise). Monmouth, who had since been exiled by his father to the Netherlands for his growing alliance with Shaftesbury, would be installed as king. The proof of this conspiracy was in the form of documents found in the lodgings of Colonel Roderick Mansell. Having trouble finding a London magistrate willing to order a search of Mansell's rooms, Willoughby trumped up a search by informing customs officials that smuggled goods might be found in his rooms. When the search was conducted no contraband emerged, but the officers did find a packet of papers hidden behind Mansell's bedstead – just the kind of documents that Willoughby had told the king and duke might be found.

This was hardly surprising, since Willoughby had in fact written these papers himself and planted them. Whose idea was this 'Presbyterian Plot'? Many thought Lady Powis and her midwife friend had invented the conspiracy as a means of discrediting Shaftesbury and his henchmen. They might have; certainly they were no friends of the earl. He was, after all, clamouring for the drawing and quartering of the countess's husband. Both women denied any involvement – they eagerly accepted Willoughby's story of a Whig plot because they wanted to believe in it. And Thomas Willoughby, whose real name was Thomas Dangerfield, was fully capable of dreaming up the entire scheme himself.

Dangerfield, the son of a small-time Essex gentleman, was, at the age of twenty-five, a criminal of impressive dimensions. A petty thief before he entered his teens, he graduated to a variety of more serious offenses: robbery, horse theft and counterfeiting. At some point he abandoned a brief attempt at respectability, as an apprentice barber, and returned to his criminal pursuits. These were far flung – he operated in England, Scotland and on the continent – and although the authorities caught him several times and he spent many nights in one jail or another, he somehow avoided the gallows though he had committed enough capital crimes to stretch a dozen necks. By 1679, when he met Elizabeth Cellier, he had a brand on his hand, the fruit of an earlier run-in with the law, and very dim prospects.[32] He seized upon his new-found and high-ranking Catholic friends as a way out of his predicament, and it could well be that he intended his invented plot to be the start of a new, comfortable life, secure in the protection of none other than the heir to the throne.

But Dangerfield's plan, if that is what it was, quickly came unstuck. Colonel Mansell strongly denied the existence of any plot, and soon Thomas's reputation caught up with him. His criminal history badly damaged his credibility, and he found himself, on 22 October, once again enjoying the hospitality of Newgate's jailers. Mrs Cellier came to his rescue again, paying his bail. His freedom regained, Dangerfield paid a call to Cellier, warning her that he was about to be interrogated before the Privy Council. He also seems to have stolen a moment to plant another set of documents, incriminating Cellier and Lady Powis, at the bottom of a large tub full of meal.

Dangerfield's examination before the Privy Council on 27 October was a disaster. Although he attempted to make a good impression, arriving at Whitehall 'splendidly in habit' and accompanied by a liveried servant, the encounter quickly went awry.[33] Confronted with his record, he admitted that he had stood in the pillory and been jailed for counterfeiting. He said that he had considered 'trepanning' – killing – Shaftesbury and had taken notes for Lady Powis at the summer's plot trials. He reported having visited Lord Powis in the Tower on multiple occasions. Now convinced that Dangerfield had conspired with Catholics to subvert the plot, the council sent Thomas to Newgate, his home away from home, and ordered a thorough investigation.

The next day William Waller turned up at Mrs Cellier's house and arrested her.[34] She went to the Gatehouse, while Waller and a group of officers proceeded to ransack her home. 'All that night he and his crue kept their rendezvous in my house, tearing and pulling down the goods, and filling his own and his footmen's pockets and breeches with papers of private concern.'[35] The search revealed Dangerfield's planted documents, and so the 'Meal Tub Plot' was born.

On Saturday, 1 November, Dangerfield abandoned his career as an agent provocateur for Catholics and transformed himself into an anti-papist hero. He accused Cellier, Lady Powis, Lord Castlemaine, Lord Peterborough and an astrologer named John Gadbury of scheming to incriminate prominent exclusionists with a fake 'Presbyterian Plot'. And he added a new facet to the conspiracy: two of the jailed peers, Lords Powis and Arundell, had offered him

£2,000 to kill the king – an offer he said he rejected – but he did agree to murder Shaftesbury for £500. The accused who weren't already imprisoned were rounded up and charged with treason.[36]

The Privy Council spent the next several days investigating the conspiracy, and although King Charles remained sceptical, most of the council took the charges seriously. Robert Southwell informed his friend Ormond that examinations of a number of witnesses added credibility to Dangerfield's story: 'the truth of his information is more and more confirmed, how strong soever the infamy of the pillory rises up against him'.[37] The council, in the king's presence, questioned Mrs Cellier on 1 and 2 November. In her later account, Elizabeth described how she stood firm despite the hostility of some of those present, particularly the Lord Chancellor, Finch, who said that no one would believe her and unless she confessed all she would hang.[38]

Now the plot was anything but 'dead'. It gave Shaftesbury and his allies a perfect opportunity to increase pressure for opening Parliament. Even moderates like Southwell believed that only a Parliament could resolve the crisis: '. . . nothing but a Parliament can deal with the plot so as to bring things to a final determination and to quiet the minds of the kingdom upon this subject. For I perceive it is like a tumor that grows bigger and bigger, not likely as some have hoped by time to evaporate. It must absolutely be lanced or else it will never end.'[39] The taverns and coffee houses buzzed with news and rumours about the fresh revelations; scribblers filled the newsletters with garbled accounts of depositions and witness statements.

Magistrates like Waller redoubled their persecution of London Catholics; on 3 November, Waller seized two cartloads of Catholic books, 'habits, vestments, crucifixes, relics and many other popish trinkets'. Among the relics taken were some of the recently executed Jesuits, 'the hair of one of them, a peece of the Coates of another, & a peece of the rope that hanged one of them, also a handkerchief dipt in Colman's blood'.[40]

Shaftesbury worked to take advantage of the excitement. He affected indignation that no one on the Privy Council had informed him that Dangerfield planned to assassinate him, and he declared that he had only by chance escaped Dangerfield's dagger. Thomas said that he had been in the earl's company not once but twice, yet he did not get an opportunity to strike. Whether these encounters actually happened may be doubted – but they served the purposes of both men.[41] Temporizing as ever, King Charles opened a back channel to Shaftesbury only to find the earl in no mood to compromise – he would resume his seat in the council only if Charles assembled Parliament and abandoned the queen and his brother. Rumours circulated that Shaftesbury planned to assemble MPs before 26 January, the date set for the new session's opening.[42] If true, this would be little short of revolutionary – one of the key prerogatives of the Crown was the power to set the parliamentary calendar. Depriving Charles of that right would go a long way to undermining the monarchy.

The king was well aware of the danger of this new eruption. He rejected a suggestion in the Privy Council that an official narrative of the Meal Tub Plot be printed. A number of privy councillors, mostly those added along with Shaftesbury in the spring's abortive attempt to co-opt the opposition, urged the king to open Parliament early. Lords Essex, Russell, Cavendish and Sir Henry Capel argued that only a Parliament could deal with the popish threat. Charles refused even to discuss the matter.[43]

Having failed to get his way working through the Privy Council, Shaftesbury decided to apply pressure from out of doors. He circulated rumours that Charles had offered him the Lord Treasurer's wand, and a free hand in appointing any of the great officers of state. He said he had rejected these offers out of hand – he would not step foot in Whitehall until Charles expelled from court every Catholic, including the queen, his mistress the duchess of Portsmouth and the duke of York.[44] These extravagant claims angered the king, but Shaftesbury was unconcerned – they increased his standing with the public.

The earl also had a hand in organizing a gigantic anti-Catholic spectacle in the city. Queen Elizabeth's Accession Day, 17 November, occupied an important place in the Protestant calendar. Mythologized as popery's nemesis, the queen symbolized the titanic struggle against the antichrist. The Court's enemies knew they might use the occasion to advance their cause. Shaftesbury, joined by members of the Green Ribbon Club, planned to celebrate Elizabeth's accession in spectacular fashion. Meeting regularly in the King's Head tavern, the Green Ribbon Club served as Whiggery's nerve centre. Although Shaftesbury was not formally a member, many of his closest allies were.[45] With nearly 200 members, including many peers and MPs, the club strategized ways to attack the duke of York and Catholics at court and collected money to cover expenses. There had been similar processions in the past, but Shaftesbury intended to outdo them all.

At 3 a.m. church bells began ringing in the city and at 5 p.m. a vast procession began forming up.[46] At its head a man rang a hand bell, shouting 'dolefully' 'Remember Justice Godfrey!' Following him came an effigy of the martyred justice on a horse, propped up by one of his killers. Some forty men followed this, representing a variety of Catholic clergy: priests, bishops and friars. A priest in vestments 'embroidered with dead men's bones, skeletons, skulls, etc. giving pardons very freely to those who would murder Protestants' walked ahead of six mock-Jesuits who carried 'bloody daggers'. A figure imitated Sir George Wakeman, 'the Pope's chief physician with Jesuites powder in one hand and a urinal in the other'. A massive crowd, estimated at 200,000, packed the city's streets, windows and balconies, hooting and shouting at the gorgeously attired pseudo-Catholics. The men portraying the clergy demanded extra pay from the Green Ribbon Club to compensate them for the risk of injury posed by flying debris. Bravest of all must have been the two altar boys who stood in front of the Pope's effigy. This, the highlight of the procession, stood on a raised float with the boys sitting in front, swinging a pot of incense and bearing white silk banners. These had red crosses painted on them, 'and bloody daggers for murdering heretical kings and princes', and must have been a magnet for all sorts of missiles from the crowd.[47]

Lighted by 150 torchbearers and accompanied by musicians, the procession made its way to its destination: the statue of Queen Elizabeth at Temple Bar. Organizers had bedecked the queen with a crown of gilded laurel leaves, and provided her with a shield proclaiming 'THE PROTESTANT RELIGION' and 'MAGNA CARTA'. All of this was brightly lit so no one could miss the implication – and the crowd had no trouble making the connection between Protestantism and civil liberties. Left unspoken, but well understood, was its opposite: Catholicism went hand and hand with tyranny. There followed a fireworks display and a song from a figure representing the English people:

> See, yonder stands Queen Bess
> Who saved your souls from Popish thrall.
> O Queen Bess, Queen Bess, Queen Bess!
> Your Popish plot and Smithfield threat
> We do not fear at all
> For lo! Before Queen Besses feet
> You fall, you fall, you fall![48]

Afterwards the crowd threw His Holiness into a massive bonfire to rapturous applause. For the rest of the evening the city's streets hosted more bonfires and loud anti-Catholic abuse. The demonstrators took care to express their feelings outside Somerset House, the queen's official residence, though Catherine was at Whitehall, sheltered by her husband.

The king certainly disapproved of these demonstrations – though he allowed them to proceed. This might well have been a deliberate strategy on his part, for there was a growing unease in the kingdom. Massive crowds in the streets triggered bad memories of the disorder and crisis of the early 1640s – disorder that led to civil war – and Charles knew that many of his subjects would go to any length to avoid a return to those days. There were many, even at court, though, who thought the procession added irresistible pressure for the opening of Parliament. Southwell, writing to Ormond, said 'It is almost incredible what multitudes of people met on the 17th instant to celebrate Queen Elizabeth's night, and as strange that after all those squibs and bonfires they should all without confusion resort unto their beds . . .' Southwell attributed the peaceful ending to the confidence people had of the imminence of a Parliamentary session.[49]

Exclusionists (now abusively called 'Whigs') continued ratcheting up the pressure on Charles; the earl of Essex resigned his position in the Treasury; and rumours abounded in the city that a number of peers had met to plan a joint descent on the king to demand a Parliament. The success of the Accession Day extravaganza convinced Shaftesbury that a broader campaign might force the king's compliance, and so he began a systematic drive to drum up public petitions, first in London but soon throughout the kingdom.

In the meantime, an effort to ruin Titus Oates misfired when on 22 November John Lane, his former servant, accused Titus of sodomy before the Middlesex Grand Jury. Lane was almost certainly truthful; what we know of Titus's history makes the charge entirely credible. But persuading the gentlemen of Middlesex of the truth of the charge was a non-starter. The grand jurors refused to indict the worthy doctor, and Lane found himself under arrest. Three days later Oates hauled Lane and his friend Thomas Knox into King's Bench on a charge of 'retarding, obstructing, and . . . suppressing justice' by discrediting the king's evidence.[50]

Leading Whigs all turned out for the trial: Shaftesbury and seven other peers lent their presence to vindicate Oates's reputation. Both defendants suffered due to their connections: Knox to lord Danby (he had served Danby's son), and Lane to Lady Powis (she had arranged his bail from prison and sheltered him afterwards). Sir William Waller shouldered much of the prosecution's case, describing how in the spring of 1679 Lane had appeared before the Commons committee on the plot with information about his master. He accused Knox of organizing Lane's denunciation in an effort to help Danby. Thomas Dangerfield testified, at great length, that Lord Castlemaine had a hand in suborning witnesses and aiding Lane and Knox. Witnesses testified that Knox had helped Lane search for a London magistrate willing to take his deposition – a fruitless effort, which led, unfortunately for the accused, to being sent to Sir William Waller, Shaftesbury's tool. Waller of course had no desire whatever to hear Oates charged with a capital offence, and once he became involved inevitably Lane and Knox themselves became targets. The prosecution undeniably made it clear that the defendants had hoped to destroy Oates's credibility; Knox out of loyalty to Danby and Lane for hopes of reward – though if Oates had assaulted the young man, as is probable, Lane had personal reasons for revenge. The Crown made no serious attempt to refute Lane's story and the court simply accepted that his charge was false. The defence was little less than perfunctory; there were no witnesses and Mr Holt, arguing for Knox, could do little more than suggest that Thomas Dangerfield was not credible.

The jury did not even leave their box and 'laying their heads together agreed without delay, and without moving from the bar', delivered their verdict: guilty. There was the usual 'great shout' of glee from the audience and the Whig grandees adjourned for a triumphal dinner.[51] The court sentenced Knox to a 200-mark fine and a year's imprisonment and Lane earned a 100-mark fine, a year in jail and an hour in the pillory.[52] All in all it was a good day for Titus Oates and the earl of Shaftesbury.

Better things seemed on the horizon as well. On 27 November the duke of Monmouth returned secretly from his continental exile – without his father's permission. He spent the next two days laying the groundwork for a dramatic public re-entrance. At 2 a.m. on 29 November, to the joy of a well-prepared London mob, he entered the Cockpit, his former lodgings in Whitehall. By 3 a.m. church bells all over town were ringing and excited crowds were igniting bonfires in the streets. The celebrants forced passers-by to salute 'Protestant duke James' and by eight in the morning vendors were peddling broadsides and doggerel poetry praising their hero. The sudden appearance of these printed works made some, not least the king, suspect that his son's return had been carefully organized.[53] Southwell thought that Shaftesbury was behind the duke's appearance, and that he would join in the appeal for a new Parliament.[54] Lord Halifax, now a bitter enemy of the 'little earl', thought the same: Halifax 'thinks the business of the duke of Monmouth such a morris dance as that none but

Shaftesbury could have been adviser in it'.[55] Others feared that the duke of York, who had only just taken up his semi-exile in Edinburgh, would hasten back to London 'and then what next God knows'.[56] Civil war? The possibility seemed real to many at this moment.

The king, furious at his son's disobedience, sent messengers demanding his departure; Monmouth refused. The duke said he wanted nothing but to clear his name – he pointed to Thomas Dangerfield's Meal Tub revelations implicating him in a Whig conspiracy. But Charles knew well enough that this claim was specious; Dangerfield had already retracted those charges, claiming that he had invented them as part of a Catholic assault on leading Whigs. The real reason for his sudden reappearance was his determination to reinforce his alliance with Shaftesbury and, even more, to establish himself as the Whig candidate for the succession. It was hardly coincidental that at this moment a pamphlet purporting to prove Monmouth's legitimacy began circulating in London.[57]

Monmouth's behaviour was reckless, though given the fact that he took his cues from the earl of Shaftesbury this is unsurprising. Like the earl he seems to have confidently expected that Charles, who had always indulged and pampered his oldest child, would forgive him. But the king was implacable. After four or five peremptory commands to retire abroad, Monmouth moved out of Whitehall, though he remained close by, still in London, still begging a meeting with his father. Charles refused to see him, and he rebuffed his mistress Nell Gwyn's attempts to broker a reconciliation. Nell was well connected among prominent Whigs – she once described herself as 'the Protestant whore' – but despite Charles's fondness for her she made no headway. By 2 December the king's patience had evaporated. He dismissed Monmouth from all of his offices: captain of the Life Guard, Master of the Horse, Chief Justice in Eyre South of the River Trent, Lord High Chamberlain of Scotland and many others.[58] This left the duke facing a serious financial crisis – most of his income came from these sinecures – but he was determined to persist. It was a risky game, but he had the support of important people and he enjoyed the adulation of the multitude. If he could ride out the storm, existing on borrowed money, he might at last come home to a safe harbour as Prince of Wales.

How long the storm would last was the question. The king gave a positive hint when on 12 December he proposed a harsh proclamation aimed at Catholics – magistrates would compile a list of prominent recusants (those with £200 per year and up). These people would be invited to leave England, and if they refused they would lose one-third of their estates and be fined £20 for every week they refused to attend Protestant services. The proposal met with stiff resistance; some believed it impractical, even if it was desirable. But Charles insisted and a 'committee for suppressing popery' began work on the project. Within a week this body dispatched orders to London's magistrates demanding lists of Catholics, banned Catholics from Whitehall and offered a £10 reward for any Catholic discovered in the palace. The Privy Council ordered a crackdown on Catholics in foreign embassies, and prepared a proclamation allowing informers to collect rewards from Catholic estates.[59]

Heightened persecution accompanied this blizzard of proclamations. Justices Waller and Warcup continued their depredations in the city and hoped to enforce a proclamation expelling all Catholics from London. The duchess of Portsmouth dismissed a number of her Catholic servants and there were reports that the queen planned to reduce her household and close Somerset House.[60] Early in the new year seven priests stood trial, not charged with any connection to the plot, but rather for the Elizabethan crime of being in Catholic orders. Two of these, William Marshal and John Corker, had already been tried and acquitted along with Sir George Wakeman. This trial sparked some disagreement in the Privy Council; Sir William Temple argued against prosecuting priests without at least giving them a fixed date to leave the country. Lord Halifax strongly disagreed – telling Coventry that 'if I would not concur in points which were so necessary for the people's satisfaction, he would tell everybody I was a papist'. Furthermore, Halifax said, the plot 'must be handled as if it were true, whether it were so or not . . .'[61] Councillors like Halifax believed that any challenge to the reality of the plot was politically dangerous – that Sir William did not, however, suggests that the power of the narrative had begun to wane. Probably because of this, just before the trial began, Oates and Bedloe attacked Chief Justice Scroggs in an effort to forestall him from presiding. They accused Scroggs of defaming them at the Wakeman trial and several times since, and announced they would testify no more in his court.[62] Bedloe contributed the absurd information that a Te Deum mass had been sung in Portugal in gratitude for the Chief Justice.[63]

The Crown's star witnesses failed to remove Scroggs from the bench; he sat in his usual place in the Old Bailey when the case against the accused priests began on 17 January. The court agreed to delay the trial of David Keymish, whose health had broken down during his long imprisonment. The trial proceeded as many others had done: the Crown's witnesses were Dangerfield, Oates, Bedloe and Prance, and they all stood up and rattled off their usual litany of perjuries. The defendants fought bravely against their accusers; Lionel Anderson attacked the credibility of both Dangerfield and Bedloe, calling them 'rogues' to the consternation of the judges. But Anderson would not be silenced, ploughing ahead when Justice Scroggs asked him why Dangerfield was not a 'good witness'. 'My lord, a man pilloried twice, that hath broke prison once, and committed other heinous offenses . . .' He even called on the governor of Newgate, Captain Richardson, to confirm Dangerfield's bad character. Richardson certainly could have done so, but he demurred with a laugh saying 'I must not witness.'[64] Oates and Bedloe complained that the court was 'pestered with papists' and wanted them removed, a demand the judges rejected.[65] This was a small victory for the defence, but in truth all of the defendants were indeed Catholic priests. While the Crown's witnesses told multiple lies on the stand, that fact remained. The jury returned guilty verdicts against all six defendants, and they returned to Newgate under sentence of death.

The Parliament, so devoutly wished for by Shaftesbury, was due to open on 26 January, and Whigs busied themselves collecting signatures on petitions calling for no more prorogations. Shaftesbury's attendance at the trials of Catholics was an important part of his overall political strategy. Another was to puff up Monmouth, and a third was to put pressure on the king through an organized petitioning campaign. But not everyone cooperated; in the first week of January an unnamed 'sea captain' grabbed a petition lying on a table in the Amsterdam Coffee House and said that only 'fanatics' would sign such a document. In another incident, a group seized and burned in the street a petition with hundreds of signatures.[66]

These were signs of a growing reaction against Shaftesbury's tactics. Fears of renewed civil war grew; on 24 January, Secretary Coventry wrote 'Our fears and jealousies are as high as ever – I pray God they produce not such effects as they once did.'[67] Three days earlier the Privy Council heard Oates and Bedloe's complaints about Justice Scroggs. Most of Oates's allegations were trivial: one accused him of drinking excessively 'in the presence of a person of honor'. Who, Justic Scroggs asked, was this person? Shaftesbury, replied Oates. Scroggs replied that he had dined only once with the earl, at a banquet hosted by the Lord Mayor, 'And he said he might possibly at that time take a cup too much in Mr. Oates' judgment', which Titus seized on as an admission, only to have Scroggs, whose wit everyone was aware of, discomfit him: 'when His Majesty's health [a loyal toast] had passed, he began his Royal Highness' [James], which he supposed might be in Mr. Oates' judgment a cup too much'.[68] King and council vindicated the Chief Justice completely, and gave him permission to prosecute his detractors.[69] This could not but undermine the informer's credibility, and the results of the council's hearing were widely reported. And Charles seemed at last ready to take firm steps in other directions. On 26 January, to the impotent fury of the Whigs, he extended Parliament's prorogation, this time until April. A few days later Charles told the Privy Council that he had recalled his brother from Edinburgh. When the duke arrived back in London a month later, Charles ostentatiously met him as he and his duchess stepped off their barge at Whitehall steps, embracing them warmly.[70]

As James made his way south, Charles deployed a more serious weapon in his fight against Whiggery. The king ordered a new committee of privy councillors to comb through lists of magistrates in every county.[71] Justices of the peace associated with the Whigs who had supported Exclusion in Parliament, pushed for Whig petitions or were in any other way unreliable supporters of the royal brothers would be dismissed. This project involved Charles personally: he sat in on the committee's meetings, a clear sign of determination to act. Removing a gentleman from the bench was a serious step, rare and almost never done for political reasons. It signalled grave royal displeasure, and such a rebuke undermined a man's reputation in his community. Most JPs would think twice about hitching themselves to Shaftesbury's wagon if loss of office was the consequence. And there were practical reasons for the purge, too: loyal JPs could be invaluable in suppressing the petitioning movement that was shaping up all over the kingdom. They could crack down on political activity deemed disloyal, and it was obvious that the king planned further actions to impose his political will on the nation. This was decidedly not the passive, negligent monarch whom Shaftesbury counted on outmanoeuvring.

The purge of local government triggered the final departure from the Privy Council of most of the remaining Shaftesburyites: on 31 January, the same day that the committee to remodel the bench sat in both morning and afternoon sessions, Lords Russell and Cavendish, Sir Henry Capel and Henry Powle, acting on their patron's advice, went to the king. Confronting Charles, they jointly tendered their resignations. Charles accepted these resignations, probably with some relief. Afterwards, the earl of Ossory wrote that Charles 'spoke very contemptuously to me of the thing and them'.[72] The way these councillors made their departure, publicly and in a body, was an extraordinary affront to the monarch, 'unprecedented' as the council's secretary described it.[73] Secretary Coventry professed to be baffled by the councillors' actions: 'Their entry and exit have been both very remarkable, and neither very well comprehended by men of my small talent. We are full of fear and jealousies, and the effects of those passions. His majesty on the other side seemeth as resolved.'[74]

The court's offensive against its enemies ramped up in early 1680. The government prosecuted two London booksellers, Benjamin Harris and Francis Smith, for selling seditious books. The first, *An Appeal from the Country to the City*, was a Whig tract calling for a new Parliament, proclaiming the reality of the plot and painting a lurid picture of life under a Catholic monarch: '. . . behold troops of papists ravishing your wives and daughters, dashing your little children's brains out against the walls, plundering your houses and cutting your own throats by the name of heretic dogs'.[75] Written by Charles Blount, a member of the Green Ribbon Club, this screed had Shaftesbury's fingerprints all over it.[76] The other was a satire aimed at Chief Justice Scroggs, *Some Observations upon the Late Tryals of Sir George Wakeman*. This work, supposedly written by 'Tom Ticklefoot', one-time clerk to 'Justice Clodpate', attacked Scroggs for his conduct of the Wakeman trial. There was no doubt that 'Justice Clodpate' was Scroggs.[77] Blount escaped punishment, but Harris, who sold the work at his shop, was not so lucky. He was fined £500 and ordered to the pillory for an hour.

This verdict incensed many in the courtroom; clearly the spectators sympathized with the defendant. When the jury announced its verdict there was a storm of protest, prompting an indignant Justice Scroggs to lecture the audience: 'We had need to look about us, for if at such a time, and with such a base book, such clamorous noises shall be made, what shall become of us? . . . Would I knew some of the shouters, I would make them know, I would punish them.'[78] The demonstration increased the Chief Justice's hostility towards Harris – had not Justice Pemberton intervened, he would have added a public flogging to the printer's sentence. Paradoxically, Francis Smith got off much easier, despite the more personal nature of his attack on Scroggs. Absent from court because he was ill, Francis's wife appeared with counsel and declared her husband's remorse, throwing him on the court's mercy. The presiding judge, Justice Jones, accepted Smith's apology and promised to intercede with Scroggs, who, he said, was 'a person of that pity and compassion, that he loves no man's ruin . . .' For once this description was accurate – Smith escaped with nothing more than 'a small fine'.[79]

When Sir Thomas Gascoigne's trial began, on Wednesday 11 February, he had been jailed for some weeks. At his arraignment, on 24 January, the eighty-five-year-old gentleman, supported by his granddaughter, appeared confused – a condition worsened by extreme deafness. The clerk of the court had to come to the bar, stand next to the white-haired old baronet and shout the court's questions into his ear. When asked to enter a plea, he responded 'Gloria Patri, Filio, et Spritu Sancto, I am not guilty.' The court rejected this rather liturgical incantation, and Gascoigne then entered the more traditional 'not guilty' plea. He also demanded a jury of his peers – both by rank and residence. Unlike modern criminal trials, in which courts deliberately choose jurors with no personal knowledge of a defendant or the crime involved, the seventeenth-century theory was quite different. The court tried to seat jurors who knew the accused's reputation – a defendant's credibility and his reputation were inextricably linked. As Sir Thomas put it, 'I desire . . . I may have a jury of gentlemen, of persons of my own quality, and of my own country, that may be able to know something how I have lived hitherto.'[80] Chief Justice Scroggs, presiding as ever, granted this request, and the court waited three weeks while jurors travelled south from Yorkshire.

Only the day before the trial Robert Bolron, the Crown's principal witness, had given a pair of London printers exclusive rights to publish his *Narrative*. Bolron wanted to cash in no less than Oates and Bedloe and perhaps to influence the trial. Claiming to be a gentleman – stretching the definition of the term considerably – might enhance his credibility. This book revealed a plan to murder the king and a variety of details about Catholic strategies to protect their properties and sustain the faith. The latter information might well have been accurate – as Gascoigne's servant, Bolron might well have inside information about contributions made to Catholic causes, or property dedicated to Catholic use. Of an assassination plot, of course, there was no truth whatever. Bolron's narrative foreshadowed what he would tell the court.[81]

The trial began at 9 a.m. with Sir Thomas once again confused and unable to hear the court's proceedings. 'I cannot hear what is said,' he repeated several times.[82] Soon, though, a friend volunteered to relay the court's words to him and proceedings could begin. Empanelling a jury was the first step, and in previous plot trials one that went quickly. This time, however, the accused made extensive use of his right to challenge prospective jurors. Sir Thomas dismissed no fewer than ten men, and he seems to have excluded them on political grounds – any known to have signed a petition calling for Parliament earned his quietus. The

Attorney General, in a move unusual for these trials, rejected one potential juror, Nicholas Mauleverer. Nicholas was probably related to Sir Thomas Mauleverer, a Yorkshire MP who Shaftesbury noted as 'base' on his list of members.[83]

This voir dire was different from every previous plot trial, first because the jury pool was composed of Yorkshiremen rather than Londoners. But more notable is the role that politics seems to have played in the jury's construction. Gascoigne, by excluding known Whigs, defended himself against a politicized trial. The current reality was that political divisions permeated English society to an unprecedented degree. Sir Thomas – or his advisors, for given his age and deafness he might not have been the lead actor – was the first plot defendant who seems to have recognized that these divisions might work in his favour.

Robert Bolron testified first for the prosecution. In 1677, while managing Sir Thomas's coal mine, Gascoigne had lured him into treason. Robert swore what he called 'the oath of secrecy' and committed himself to 'extirpate and root out . . . Protestant doctrine, and to destroy the said pretended King of England . . .'[84] He overheard Sir Thomas scheming to protect his estate from confiscation in the event of discovery; he saw documents proving that his master sent money regularly south to the Jesuit mission in London; and he claimed that Gascoigne planned to endow a Catholic nunnery in Yorkshire after the king's death.

Lawrence Mowbray followed Bolron. A house servant of Gascoigne's, he told of a list of four or five hundred Catholics committed to join Sir Thomas's plot. Conveniently entitled, 'A List of them that are engaged in the design of killing the King, and promoting the Catholic religion', this list included Gascoigne's daughter, Lady Tempest, and a number of other prominent Catholic gentry in Yorkshire. Quite why Sir Thomas felt the need to advertise his treason in this way no one thought to ask, nor did anyone seem curious about why such an incendiary document might be left lying about for menial servants to peruse. Mowbray further said that each conspirator received a papal indulgence reducing their time in purgatory by 10,000 years.[85] Hiding behind a door, Mowbray heard Sir Thomas, a neighbour, Sir Miles Stapleton, and two priests discussing the plot, 'and they did unanimously conclude that it was a meritorious undertaking, and for the good of the church, and they would all venture their lives and estates in it'.[86]

The trial was not without an element of farce; poor deaf Sir Thomas could hear nothing of the witnesses' testimony, and everything Bolron and Mowbray said had to be repeated by his friend Mr Hobart, roaring into the baronet's ear. But Sir Thomas was by no means unprepared. He flatly denied all of the charges; there was no such thing as an 'oath of secrecy'. The list of 500 conspirators was 'an impudent lie', and 'it is all false he speaks, not a word of truth comes out of his mouth'.[87] Gascoigne intended to prove his innocence, calling no fewer than fourteen witnesses, almost all of whom were Protestants, to challenge the Crown's witnesses.

Mr Babbington, Gascoigne's attorney, told how he had orders from Sir Thomas to sue Bolron for a debt of £48, and another witness, Obadiah Moor, said that Bolron threatened revenge against Sir Thomas if the lawsuit proceeded. Robert said he would accuse Sir Thomas of harbouring priests (which was quite true) but, Moor said, in September 1678 Bolron specifically told him that Gascoigne had nothing whatever to do with the Popish Plot. By summer 1679, though, Bolron was loudly accusing Sir Thomas of offering him £1,000 to kill King Charles. Several other witnesses maintained the same thing. Several others noted that Bolron owed them money and skulked around Yorkshire in fear of arrest for debts. An innkeeper, William Batley, testified that he overheard Bolron persuading Mowbray to join him as a witness, promising him financial reward. Another witness, Matthias Higgringil, said Mowbray wanted revenge because he had been sacked for the theft of some of Lady Tempest's jewels.[88]

A high-status witness did much to undermine Bolron's credibility. Mr Pebles, Yorkshire's clerk of the peace, described at length his dealings with the informer at the previous assizes held in York. Robert, who had never met Pebles, introduced himself as the man who had accused Sir Thomas Gascoigne. He posed a legal question: if a man owes money to someone indicted for treason, is he obliged to pay it? Thinking, no doubt, of the £48 he owed, he obviously hoped he would be off the hook – but Pebles said that if the court convicted Sir Thomas, the debt would pass to the king. The conversation continued, with Bolron complaining of the two judges presiding over the assizes – they refused to see him, and they refused to offer him a guard for his protection. By this time Pebles wanted nothing but to get away; however Bolron followed him into the street demanding his help in arresting a gentlewoman 'greatly concerned in the plot'. Pebles refused even though Bolron threatened him, 'I can do you a prejudice if I will.'[89] Pebles made his escape, but soon after found himself arrested – accused by Bolron of taking bribes from Catholics seeking to avoid the Oath of Supremacy. There was no substance to this charge, of course – Yorkshire JPs investigated and found Bolron's accusation baseless.

Unfortunately for Robert Bolron, Justice William Dolben was one of the two judges he abused to Pebles and he was sitting right there on the bench. Not only did he intervene to confirm the clerk's story, but he pointedly asked Pebles about Bolron's reputation in Yorkshire 'Truly it is not very good in the country,' he replied – an understatement to say the least.[90]

Gascoigne completed his defence by showing that the money he sent to the London Jesuits was meant to support his ward, Mary Appleby, a Catholic currently living in France. The prosecution then summed up its case, trying to discredit the defence where it could. Three of the judges, Sir William Dolben, Sir Francis Pemberton and Sir William Jones, instructed the jury – Chief Justice Scroggs was absent, attending to other cases. Dolben's charge must have made the prosecution writhe. He stressed the 'improbability' of Bolron's evidence – why would Sir Thomas offer a part in his conspiracy to a man he was suing for debt? Why favour a man whose house you were about to seize? Justice Pemberton followed with a rather desperate attempt to salvage the witnesses' reputation: '. . . truly my brother Dolben hath rightly reminded you of that improbability . . . but then you must consider all the circumstances'. Those 'circumstances' might be found in the nature of Catholicism and Jesuit fanaticism. The testimony of Bolron and Mowbray might seem improbable and strange – but then papists do strange things: '. . . they put them upon all the immoralities and villainies that can be found out for the cause of religion, as they call it; nothing can seem strange that is testified against them'.[91] Justice Jones satisfied himself by simply noting that the case depended upon the witnesses' credibility, and as a Yorkshire jury the witnesses were 'better known to you than us'.[92]

This was indeed the case. After thirty minutes' deliberation the jury returned its verdict: not guilty. At almost the same moment, the court granted Lady Powis bail and released her.

The next day the king sacked Sir Francis Pemberton. Sir Francis had intervened on behalf of the Whig polemicist Benjamin Harris and his attempt to salvage the Crown's case in the Gascoigne trial marked him as too sympathetic to the Whig narrative. Reaction to the Gascoigne trial was swift, and it demonstrated the growing political divisions in the kingdom. 'Those who are zealously concerned in the prosecution of the plot are wonderfully dismayed . . .' Gascoigne's acquittal, the severe sentence imposed on Benjamin Harris and bail granted to Lady Powis 'makes the discontented shake their heads . . .'[93] Whigs convinced themselves that the Yorkshire jury was corrupt – some were, they alleged, tenants of Lady Tempest, while others spread a rumour that two jurors had recanted their verdict and wished to appear before the Privy Council.[94] Booksellers hawked Bolron's narrative but it competed with another pamphlet, *An Abstract of the Accusation of Robert Bolron*. This document ridiculed Bolron and Mowbray's testimonies and told of their shady Yorkshire past, taking a decidedly pro-Gascoigne line.

Attacks on the chief informers of the plot continued to grow; Whig magistrates issued warrants for the arrest of several 'who have taken the liberty to traduce and vilify Dr Oates, Mr. Bedloe and others of the king's evidence'.[95] City Whigs worked to rehabilitate the informers; Bolron was admitted as a freeman of the City and to the Company of Goldsmiths – though his involvement in their trade extended only as far as his personal interest in gold. The Goldsmiths feasted Bolron, Bedloe and Prance in an elaborate banquet 'where they had much discourse relating to the times'.[96] Duelling banquets punctuated the late winter and early spring of 1680; the day after the Goldsmith fiesta, Lord Mayor Clayton greeted King Charles and his brother at his home, 'where the bonfires, bells and loud acclamations of the multitude testified the joy and loyalty of the citizens of London'.[97] A week later Shaftesbury announced his intention to bring Monmouth with him to dine with the Lord Mayor – an invitation the Whig Clayton, who had far more prudence than the earl, declined to proffer.[98]

Tensions continued to rise from the top to the bottom of society. At court, Lord Cavendish ostentatiously cut the duke of York and the king ordered him out of Whitehall for it. Sir William Waller claimed to have uncovered a plan by fifty or sixty London apprentices to burn Oliver Cromwell in effigy, followed by a march through the streets and an assault on nonconformist chapels.[99] Whether such a plot existed may be doubted; Waller had an interest in stirring up fear and excitement. But it is clear that there were many in London, and more around the kingdom, who rejected the Whig narrative and whose belief in the plot had evaporated. The fact that many apprentices had masters with Whiggish and nonconformist sympathies was a bonus – a good reason for adolescent rebellion.

Spurring this particular bout of panic was one of Sir William's last acts as a magistrate – he was sacked early in April. His replacement on the bench was a very clear sign of the way the royal wind blew at this moment: Sir Roger L'Estrange. Sir Roger was a sixty-three-year-old stalwart of the royalist cause – sentenced to death by Parliament as a spy during the civil wars, he had spent time in prison and exile before returning home to take up his pen on behalf of a Stuart Restoration. His initial reward was an appointment as 'surveyor of the press' responsible for licensing new publications and for suppressing seditious literature. The job brought in an income, but with the rapid growth of the press, it was a frustrating one, and it ended in 1679 when the Licensing Act expired. Without his official government appointment, L'Estrange needed an income and he found it by churning out political literature. He was among the first authors who challenged the Oates–Bedloe narrative with his *History of the Plot*, published late in 1679. By the spring of 1680 he had become the leading public opponent of Titus Oates and the other informers, who responded with a deluge of libels accusing him of any number of malfeasances – most prominently of being a Catholic in league with the conspirators. Oates threatened Sir Roger in a personal encounter at Whitehall. Offended that L'Estrange had not doffed his hat to him, Oates announced ominously, ' "Squire L'Estrange," said he, "We shall have a Parliament" twirling his hat about, betwixt his finger and thumb, with a look and action not to be expressed.'[100]

L'Estrange was not intimidated. He was indefatigable; he gave as good as he got; and he was ready to undermine belief in the plot, using logic, ridicule and an appeal to common sense. 'But the world is so miserably divided betwixt some that will believe every thing, and others nothing, that not only Truth, but Christianity itself is almost lost between them, and no place left for sobriety and moderation. We are come to govern ourselves by dreams and imaginations, we make every coffee house tale an article of our faith, and from incredible fables we raise invincible arguments.'[101] These words resonated with many – as did Sir Roger's accessible style. 'And in some cases, I would wait a little for confirmation,' he recommended, 'without swallowing everything whole as it comes. Suppose my boy should come in and tell me it rains buttered turnips, I should go near to open the window to see whether it be so or no, and you would not blame me for doubting, either.'[102]

Now instead of a JP dedicated to harassing Catholics and uncovering Tory plots, Westminster had a magistrate no less devoted to disrupting Whiggish enterprises. The king awarded Sir Roger £100 from secret-service funds to assist him.[103] But the opposition was already pursuing a fresh countermove – this time from an unexpected direction. As attempts to gin up a plot based in Yorkshire and Staffordshire had largely failed, now Ireland would afford more exciting possibilities. Most English Protestants were well primed to fear Irish Catholic treachery. The Protestant government in Dublin ruled the Catholic majority there with a combination of legal discrimination, land confiscation and the occasional use of brutal violence. The regime kept Irish Catholics at bay, at the expense of occasional terrifying outbreaks of rebellion. The uprising that began in 1641, targeting Protestants, resulted in the deaths of thousands, and it remained fresh in English memories.

On 27 March, Shaftesbury, with an Irish priest named Edmund Murphy in tow, appeared before the Privy Council. The earl no doubt timed his appearance deliberately; the king was absent, attending the horse races at Newmarket. Shaftesbury and his witness delivered an account of a conspiracy against the Crown involving the Catholic Archbishop of Armagh, Oliver Plunket. Shaftesbury, in his usual histrionic style, was 'very zealous in searching into the bottom of it and says he will see the bottom of it though it should cost his life'.[104] The earl demanded that the council's clerks withdraw, so that his evidence might be revealed secretly. He also insisted that the Lord Lieutenant of Ireland, the duke of Ormond, be kept in the dark about the conspiracy. Secretary Coventry reported to Ormond that Murphy had a very bad reputation, but the council felt obliged to investigate, and asked Charles to return to town.[105]

Excluding Ormond from the investigation gave Shaftesbury's game away. The duke was among the most respected figures in Restoration politics, and he had a good relationship with both royal brothers. He was no great friend of Shaftesbury and his allies either. The earl hoped to accomplish a hat-trick – keeping the plot on the boil, toppling Ormond and advancing the exclusionist cause. Ormond's son, the earl of Ossory, reported regularly from Court and noted the spread of rumours designed 'to blast our reputations'. According to these reports, father and son had engaged with the Jesuits to facilitate a French invasion of Ireland.[106] An anonymous letter announced that 'there is a most horrid plot discovered in Ireland by very great persons of quality' and that the 'King and Council unanimously voted a damnable plot, and blank warrants are sent over to apprehend great men.' This letter credited Shaftesbury and his close friend, the earl of Essex, with leading the investigation.[107] That these stories were absurd mattered very little – the goal was to stoke English fears.

Acting on this information, the Privy Council sent a messenger along with another informer, a Catholic priest named Fitzgerald, on a mission to Ireland to arrest suspects and seize evidence. By 10 April, Ormond had pieced together the outlines of Shaftesbury's plan. At first bewildered by the sudden cessation of the mails from London, he had subsequently learned that it was because of suspicions that he was himself somehow involved in a plot. Discovering that the informer Fitzgerald was connected to Sir William Waller made Ormond smell a rat. The duke also saw the hand of 'a great man there', obviously Shaftesbury.[108] On 12 April a newsletter reported that the Irish 'treachery' was almost ready when Shaftesbury heroically revealed it, and that he had found another Irish informer ready to swear before the council.[109]

Ormond wrote contemptuously of the informers: one was 'a silly drunken vagabond that cares not for hanging a month hence if in meantime he may solace himself with brandy and tobacco'; Murphy was no less debauched; and the man Shaftesbury brought to the Privy Council was a known jailbird. They are 'such creatures that no schoolboy would trust them with a design for robbing of an orchard'. It was obvious to him that this 'plot' was simply a device to 'amuse the people'.[110]

Shaftesbury's posse spent most of April rooting around Ireland, searching for evidence to support their claims. They had little success. Ormond told of Fitzgerald's fruitless search for 'dangerous papers walled up in a ruinous abbey' in the west, and an extended trawl through Ulster had no more luck. But the Lord Lieutenant worried that he might lose his office. He would not go willingly, for he believed that the monarchy was under threat and he owed the king a debt of gratitude. Moreover, he resisted resignation because it would satisfy his enemies, 'giving them their will just when they would have it of me'.[111]

Once upon a time the old lackadaisical King Charles might well have sacrificed his loyal old servant (Ormond was now almost seventy and had served the Crown in one way or another for over forty years). But the old man need not have worried; Charles now believed himself engaged in a battle, and he would not deny himself an ally as experienced and competent as the duke. A marked sign of royal favour came soon; Charles appointed Lord Ossory to the Privy Council, 'which he did in the most obliging manner that could be . . .', and the duke of York added his own good wishes.[112] Now Ormond had an informant with access to every aspect of the investigation. Ossory showed the king his father's letters about Shaftesbury's informers and their delinquencies, and Charles said that he expected no serious information to emerge from their inquisition.[113]

The Privy Council's messengers and informers embarked for England on 23 April, 'with a cargo of witnesses such as they are. Yet they are the best any market in this kingdom will yet afford'. In the end the investigation rounded up ten shabby informers and the duke did not think these creatures' credibility would do much for Shaftesbury's schemes. He did worry that the rumours spread about by the Whigs would cause unnecessary alarm in Ireland, resulting in a slump in trade. Ormond's greatest concern was that the English government would try to force him to impose stiffer laws against the Catholic majority in Ireland. These, he believed, would backfire and might render Ireland ungovernable. He asked his son to use his new seat at the council board to head off any such suggestions.[114]

The boatload of informers arrived in London on 7 May, and the duke's expectations were realized. They appeared before a special session of the Privy Council and were questioned. The session was not a success, at least not for those interested in 'zealously pursuing' the Irish plot. The informers' thick Irish brogue baffled most of the councillors, and the clerks struggled to take down their inarticulate words. The council ordered that they be separated to prevent collusion, and kept from visitors, no doubt for the same reason. The council sent four of the informers back to Ireland with instructions to assist in the prosecution of Archbishop Plunket – an unwelcome development for Ormond, who detested them. Diplomatically he wrote to the Secretary of State of his doubts about the witnesses – one, Murphy, had broken jail and was charged with a capital crime, and the reputation of the others was bad: 'it may be suspected that they may hearken to an advantageous proposition from any hand'.[115]

The Irish plot was off to a rather rocky start, but Shaftesbury expected that eventually it would be a fruitful source of rumour and innuendo. In the meantime, however, setbacks continued. On 11 May, Elizabeth, countess of Powis, appeared before the Middlesex Grand Jury charged with complicity in the Meal Tub Plot. She had already been released on bail from the Tower, where she had been held for three months. Despite being charged with treason, she remained a lady of the queen's bedchamber, an obvious sign of favour. After a brief hearing, the jurors returned their verdict: *ignoramus*, 'we know nothing', that is, there was insufficient evidence against the countess to proceed to trial.[116] The court released Elizabeth, who resumed her advocacy of Catholics threatened by informers and politicians.

On 11 June it was Elizabeth Cellier's turn. Sir William Scroggs presided in the court of King's Bench, and the charge was treason. The Crown had two witnesses, as the law required: John Gadbury and Thomas Dangerfield. Gadbury testified first. In his early fifties, he had lived a very interesting life, beginning as a tailor's apprentice in Oxford. Gadbury had gained some education at Oxford in the mid-1640s, where he became particularly interested in astrology. For a time in the late 1640s and early 1650s he flirted with a variety of more or less radical political and religious groups, including the Levellers and the so-called 'Family of Love', whose antics included sexual license and sermons delivered in the nude. After the Restoration, however, Gadbury remade himself. He returned to the Anglican Church, associated with its more conservative clergy, and cast himself as a fervent supporter of the Crown. By the 1670s he had become one of England's leading astrologers, author of many almanacs and works of astrology. His conservative connections brought him into the orbit of the Court and he was often in the company of the countess of Powis, and more particularly, her friend and ally Elizabeth Cellier.[117]

Although Gadbury testified for the prosecution, he was not exactly helpful. Answering Scroggs's questions, he claimed to know nothing whatever about the Meal Tub Plot or Elizabeth Cellier's role in it. The astrologer recounted several conversations he had had with Cellier that the prosecution interpreted as sinister. Once, walking by Westminster Abbey on a rainy day, she remarked that the Abbey had once been filled with Catholic monks and she wondered if it ever would be again. This, the prosecution insisted, proved her knowledge of the plot – but Gadbury, in his testimony, interpreted her words differently. He took them as a wistful, and harmless, casual comment, and provoked laughter in the court when he added 'I only smiled to hear a woman's discourse.'[118] On another occasion, during the time when the king lay desperately ill at Windsor, she asked him if he thought Charles would die. This, the prosecution maintained, proved her desire to see Charles dead. But again Gadbury disappointed the prosecution – Elizabeth hoped Charles would recover. She wanted John to use his skill as an astrologer to make a prediction – something he refused to do, knowing very well that casting the king's horoscope was a capital offence.[119] Gadbury also said that Elizabeth had asked him to cast Thomas Dangerfield's horoscope, asking whether he was 'a person fit to be trusted'. Although no one mentioned it at the time, if this horoscope induced Cellier to trust Dangerfield, seventeenth-century astrology was seriously flawed.

Dangerfield took the stand next, and Cellier immediately challenged him as a no good witness due to his extensive criminal history. The midwife was very well prepared. Ralph Briscoe testified that he had seen Dangerfield burned in the hand for burglary at the Old Bailey. Elizabeth further accused Thomas of perjury and counterfeiting. She had copies of court records demonstrating several offences with which Dangerfield had been charged, and when he fell back upon his pardon – as Oates and Bedloe had successfully done in other trials – Elizabeth was ready. She produced a copy of the king's pardon (how? One suspects a helping hand in Whitehall) and noted that it did not grant a pardon for all of the felonies on Dangerfield's heroic record. Scroggs ordered Dangerfield to bring the original pardon to court while the case proceeded with a variety of witnesses who testified that Cellier had befriended and patronized Thomas, though none of them had any knowledge of the Meal Tub conspiracy. Those witnesses finished and the court waited for Dangerfield's return. The prosecutors, Sir George Jeffreys and Sir Creswell Levinz, must have been in agony as time stretched on. Justice Scroggs asked Mrs Cellier for any more proof of Dangerfield's villainy, and she obliged with records of his time in the Salisbury pillory and his outlawry for a felony. By the time Thomas did return to the courtroom, Scroggs was in a rage, convinced that the Crown's chief witness was a fraud and a rogue. Dangerfield produced his pardon, and on perusal it appeared that the word 'felony' appeared nowhere. He had been pardoned for perjury, but not for felonies (like, for example, counterfeiting and burglary).

The omission sparked a titanic outburst at Dangerfield from the Lord Chief Justice – who was hardly mild-mannered in the best of times. 'Such fellows as you are, sirrah, shall know we are not afraid of you! . . . It is notorious enough what a fellow this is, he was in Chelmsford jail. I will shake all such fellows before I have done with them!' Dangerfield protested feebly, 'My lord, this is enough to discourage a man from ever entering into an honest principle.' This was too much for Scroggs, 'What!? Do you with all mischief that hell hath in you, think to brave it in a court of justice? I wonder at your impudence, that you dare look a court of justice in the face, after having been made appear so notorious a villain!'[120]

Scroggs turned to the jury. Dangerfield was a no good witness, and Gadbury had proved nothing directly against Mrs Cellier. The result was obvious: they must return a not guilty verdict – which they immediately proceeded to do. Mrs Cellier fell to her knees and cried 'God bless the king and the duke of York!'[121] Scroggs then ordered Dangerfield to give security for his good behaviour – something he could not do, and so he ended his day once again behind bars.

Was the Chief Justice putting on a show designed to please the king? His conduct in this case no doubt boosted his stock at the palace, and he had the example of Justice Pemberton before him. But it is also likely that his rage at Dangerfield was not entirely manufactured. Scroggs had treated him with some respect in earlier trials, before written proof of his record had emerged. He had been hoodwinked by a jailbird and that must have been mortifying – the fact that unleashing a tirade and destroying Dangerfield's credibility publicly earned points with King Charles was a welcome bonus.

These failures in court continued with the trial of Roger, earl of Castlemaine, two weeks later. Oates had accused the earl as long ago as October 1678, claiming he was secretly a Jesuit priest with knowledge of the plan to kill the king. Oates had seen, he said, a divorce decree signed in Rome enabling Castlemaine's ordination. The earl suffered three month's imprisonment in the Tower before he was released on bail, and he used his time to write a furious attack on the informers and the injustices perpetrated on innocent Catholics, *The Compendium*. His courageous support for the accused, paying the expenses of witnesses from St Omer, and his outspoken defence of Oates's victims inspired a second assault. This time with support from Dangerfield, Oates accused Castlemaine of further crimes – coaching the St Omer witnesses, soliciting Dangerfield to murder the king and fabricating the Meal Tub Plot. Jailed again in November 1679, Castlemaine remained in the Tower, a close prisoner, for some seven months, despite repeatedly asking for his trial.

At last his day arrived, and in a packed and sweltering Old Bailey he prepared to face his accusers. Castlemaine introduced court records from Hastings showing that Oates had maliciously prosecuted William Parker on a charge of sodomizing a young boy. The court had acquitted Parker, who proved an ironclad alibi.[122] This, Castlemaine argued, demonstrated that Oates was unreliable and driven by vindictiveness – a claim the court rejected, noting that a jury's acquittal of a defendant did not necessarily make a perjurer of the king's witnesses. But the point had been made, and the prosecution tried hard to prevent the earl from even raising the issue. Notwithstanding Castlemaine's accusations, Oates testified once again behaving himself with his customary mendacious arrogance.

He was followed by Thomas Dangerfield, who must have stepped to the bar with apprehension after his savage treatment at the hands of Justice Scroggs. But the prosecution had had several weeks to prepare arguments defending Dangerfield's trustworthiness, and they were ready. So too was Castlemaine, who objected to Thomas's admission as a witness. Dangerfield, he said, had been indicted or convicted of no fewer than sixteen separate crimes – but in order to spare the court's time the earl introduced records proving only six of these, including theft and passing counterfeit guineas.[123]

Scroggs grudgingly accepted the Crown's argument that the king's pardon made Dangerfield a sufficient witness and allowed him to testify, but the jury had now heard ample evidence of his sordid past.[124] In his work for Mrs Cellier and Lady Powis, Dangerfield said he had encountered Castlemaine frequently, and had carried letters referring to Catholic conspiracies from the countess to the earl. Castlemaine was involved in producing the forged documents of the Meal Tub Plot; he had coached the students from St Omer; and he threatened violence when Dangerfield refused a reward for killing the king. In rebuttal, the earl called Mrs Cellier – who was loudly hissed at by the audience – and Lady Powis. Cellier contradicted Thomas's story about Castlemaine's anger – the cause, she said, was that Dangerfield had, without permission, gone to the five lords in the Tower and urged them to sponsor the publication of the last words of the executed five Jesuits, saying he had come from Castlemaine. The earl had not sent Thomas and was enraged at the unauthorized use of his name, threatening to have his servants kick him down the stairs if he ever showed his face at his house again.[125] Lady Powis testified that she had never in her life used Dangerfield to carry letters to the earl.

By this time the court had been in session six hours. The heat was oppressive, and the court wanted to conclude the trial. Justice Scroggs's charge to the jury rather half-heartedly summarized Oates's testimony, lingering on some of the discrepancies in his timeline. As for Dangerfield's testimony, Scroggs was openly hostile. 'You see how many crimes they have produced, a matter of six great enormous crimes; and by them you will see how far you ought to consider his testimony.'[126] Scroggs pointedly said that the Crown's case depended on two witnesses, and if the jury disbelieved one of them, an acquittal should follow. The jury took the hint and returned a verdict of not guilty. In a sign of the waning hold of the informer's narrative, the court erupted in applause, and Castlemaine afterward wrote, 'Truly, I must needs say that I found everybody extremely satisfied with my success, as I passed through the crowd to my coach.'[127]

This series of setbacks for Shaftesbury and the informers required a dramatic response, and the earl produced one three days later. The Middlesex Grand Jury, not ordinarily a venue for Whig grandees, was startled to find that the earl of Shaftesbury, Titus Oates and fourteen other peers and MPs were present for their session. They brought with them a petition, signed by hundreds, calling for a Parliament. This the judges refused to accept, knowing very well the king's position on such 'tumultuous petitions'. But even more shocking was Shaftesbury's next move: presenting an indictment of the duke of York as a popish recusant, and, for good measure, denouncing the duchess of Portsmouth, Charles's current favourite mistress, as a whore.[128] It was a bold move, typical of Shaftesbury. It demonstrated that he was at open war with the Court: insults such as these could neither be forgiven nor forgotten. But the earl had no interest in compromise; he was playing to the grandstand, doing his best to stir up excitement and increase pressure on the king.

Chief Justice Scroggs, at the king's command, hastily dismissed the Grand Jury before it could consider the indictments. This greatly disappointed Shaftesbury and his fellows, though they probably expected something of the kind. If their stunt kept the coffee houses and taverns buzzing, that was sufficient – it would lead, he thought, inevitably, to Parliament's opening. Then the earl would have the weapon he needed to finish the war.

On 1 July, only four days after Scroggs had scotched the latest attack on the duke of York by dismissing the Grand Jury, Charles delayed the opening of Parliament for the fourth time. The king, it now appeared, was winning.

— TEN —
COUNTER-ATTACK
SUMMER 1680–SUMMER 1681

The summer of 1680 unfolded with both parties grappling for advantage. Whigs continued gathering signatures on petitions asking for a new Parliament. The Court countered by organizing 'abhorrences'. These were counter-petitions condemning the Whigs for stirring up sedition and threatening the renewal of civil war. Unlike the Whig petitions, which drew signatures from a wide range of people, many of whom were nonconformist tradesmen, abhorrences came from the upper reaches of local society – lords and deputy lieutenants, magistrates, peers and regional grandees. While many men of rank signed the Whig petitions, the Court's strategy was to paint them as the work of a tumultuous rabble. For most of the summer of 1680 grand cavalcades of worthies bearing petitions and abhorrences crisscrossed England, Whigs in one direction passing Tories headed in another.

Keeping the plot alive was an essential element of Shaftesbury's strategy – it underlay many of the calls for Parliament's assembly. The Whig mantra was that only Parliament could properly investigate the conspiracy, and they pointed to the recent failed prosecutions as evidence of the Crown's misfeasance. The prosecution's case against Lord Aston, accused by Stephen Dugdale, fell apart in late June. Amid rumours of witness and jury tampering, the Attorney General asked for more time to prosecute, a request that Chief Justice Scroggs granted, though he also released Aston on bail.[1] The acquittal at a treason trial of Sir Thomas Gascoigne's daughter, Lady Elizabeth Tempest, in July added fuel to Whig complaints. The jury spared Lady Elizabeth, Sir Miles Stapleton and Mary Pressicks, all accused by Robert Bolron and Lawrence Mowbray. The one unfortunate victim was Thomas Thwing, Gascoigne's nephew. Sir John Reresby, present at the trial, believed Thwing's real offence was to be a Catholic priest. The jurors illogically judged him guilty, despite rejecting the testimony of the Crown's chief witnesses against the other defendants.[2]

These failures enabled the Court to put pressure on the principal informers. Thomas Dangerfield, thrown into the King's Bench prison on Scroggs's order, was assaulted by angry prisoners, and the Crown cut off his weekly allowance. Prominent London Whigs came to Dangerfield's rescue, raising 20 guineas and promising to sustain him until his release. Oates and Bedloe suffered a blow in early July – the king ordered a drastic reduction in their pensions. Titus and William had lived luxuriously on £10 a week, more than enough to live the life of a gentleman. The king reduced their payment to £2. The Privy Council ignored a petition for a restoration of their payments. Nor were the informers treated as sacrosanct by the wider public any longer. Mrs Cellier published an account of her ordeal, *Malice Defeated.* This pamphlet attacked Oates, Dangerfield and Shaftesbury with wit and courage – but without sufficient prudence, for no sooner had the work appeared than Elizabeth found herself indicted for libel. Sir Thomas Williams, the king's 'chemical physician', verbally assaulted Oates in the streets.[3] A few weeks later a lawyer named Christopher Osborn disrupted a service Titus was leading in the city. Osborn, who was 'fuddled' – that is, drunk – abused the Reverend Oates roundly, calling him a rogue and 'swearing dreadfully at him'. On the same day Dangerfield, now out on bail, drew his sword and attacked a man he thought was following him, 'cutting him twice or thrice about the head'.[4] More than ever the creators of the plot found themselves bound to Shaftesbury and the Whigs. The radical Whig sheriff of London, Slingsby Bethel, named Oates his chaplain. This was quite appropriate, since Bethel was no more a reliable Anglican than was Titus.

But the credibility of the plot informers got an unexpected boost in August. William Bedloe, who had accompanied the duke of Monmouth on a theatrical tour of western England, grew ill in his home town of Bristol. His illness, supposedly caused by 'overheating' on his ride from London, grew worse, and in his extremity he asked for Sir Francis North, the recently appointed Chief Justice of the court of Common Pleas. Sir Francis, who was in Bristol presiding over the assizes, came to Bedloe's sickbed. There the 'Captain' swore on oath to the full truth of all of his previous testimony. North carefully took down the details of this deathbed 'confession' and soon the news that one of the most prominent plot informers had confirmed, with his dying breath, the existence of the Catholic plot, spread throughout the nation. Seventeenth-century England put a great deal of weight upon a man's dying declaration, and Bedloe's gave a welcome boost to the plot narrative. The Whiggishly inclined drew a veil over the self-made Captain's sordid life; his end, as one newsletter put it, was a 'very good' one. Bedloe's celebrity earned him burial in the Lord Mayor of Bristol's own chapel and most of the city turned out for the service. Afterwards the city voted £200 to erect a funeral monument in the church.[5]

Bedloe's death did the credibility of the plot a temporary service, but it removed a crucial 'witness' from any further prosecutions and deprived plot-mongers of a fertile inventor of incriminating details. Some other fabulist would henceforth be required in order to keep the plot on the boil. A group of these were ready to hand – the informers rounded up by Shaftesbury in Ireland. They arrived in London on 16 September. Oates greeted them, treated them to a meal and delivered them to Lord Shaftesbury the next day. They were not a very impressive bunch – before introducing them to the earl, Oates had been forced to buy them new shoes, 'which they wanted very much'. This shambling group of witnesses did not inspire much confidence, 'I cannot hear that any of them is of any credit, some of them being abettors of Tories [Irish Catholic bandits] and receivers of them, others horse-stealers, but none, that I hear of, of any good note.'[6] Time would tell if these new informers, derisively called 'the tribe of the Mack Shams', would be worth the time and money (and footwear) lavished upon them.[7]

In the meantime, however, supporters of the plot could distract the nation's attention by the latest persecution of Elizabeth Cellier. On 11 September she stood trial once again in the familiar precincts of the Old Bailey, charged with libel. *Malice Defeated* had abused the king's witnesses, his courts, his government and the Protestant faith, the prosecution said. Witnesses testified that she sold the book (for a rather pricey two shillings a copy), and that she claimed authorship. Her defence was, frankly, rather feeble. She took refuge in the weakness of her gender: 'My lord, if I was a foolish vain woman, and did seem to speak some words about myself which I did not understand the consequence of . . .' Another witness, a printer named Mr Dormer, made it clear that Elizabeth was determined to publish her book whatever happened. Midway through printing it, a messenger from the Privy Council had arrived, ordering him to cease production. Dormer and Elizabeth had appeared before the council, which told them in no uncertain terms not to publish. Dormer had apologized and withdrawn, but Mrs Cellier went right out and found another printer.[8]

After this, Elizabeth could do little else but admit that she wrote *Malice*. She then attempted to demonstrate the truth of her charges, focusing particularly on claims that the jailers tortured prisoners in Newgate. Unfortunately, the prosecution could put Miles Prance on the stand. Knowing well what would happen if he told the truth, he lied and piously denied any mistreatment: 'Mr Prance, were you tortured in prison?' 'No, I never saw any such thing in my life.' How were you used?' 'Very well, I had everything that was fitting . . .'[9] As it happened, much of the testimony during this phase of the trial went for nothing – the courtroom was even more of a bear garden than in earlier trials, a packed and noisy mob of spectators anxious to see the infamous 'popish midwife' humbled. When preparing to consider their verdict, the jury complained that they could hear virtually none of the testimony.[10]

Whether they heard all of the evidence or not, the jury swiftly returned a guilty verdict. The court fined Elizabeth £1,000 and sentenced her to stand in the pillory for an hour on three separate days.[11]

A week after Cellier's conviction, the undersheriff of London and a strong guard of his subordinates conducted Elizabeth from Newgate to the maypole standing in the Strand. The court had chosen this venue because it was near Cellier's house and a highly visible location. It was early afternoon, a time of day that ensured maximum attendance. The authorities prepared for trouble; Mrs Cellier was widely hated by the London mob and there would certainly be a raucous crowd there. The undersheriff was right. Although she travelled in a closed coach, a multitude of jeering spectators lined the streets from Newgate to the Strand, raining missiles of every description down on the vehicle. The crowd was even bigger at the maypole and getting to the pillory itself must have been an ordeal.

Once Cellier stepped onto the raised scaffold built for the purpose, her arms and head were fastened into the pillory to the delight of the multitude. The constables burned several copies of *Malice*, pronouncing it a seditious libel. And then the fun began: rubbish, rocks, offal and rotten vegetables flew up from the crowd towards the helpless midwife.

Elizabeth had prepared herself as best she could. She carried a board in order to shield her face – though deploying it must have been difficult, with her arms pinioned. Under her gown she wore padding to protect herself. Stones, turnips and filth poured down on her along with the insults of an enraged mob of Catholic haters. One stone knocked her hood back, revealing the leather-covered iron cap she wore on her head. She fell twice, knocked down by stones, but the officers pulled her up again and the bombardment resumed with renewed vigour.

She withstood this abuse for a horrifying hour. The sheriff's men attempted to protect her, and took some blows themselves, but they could do little against the fury of the crowd. The undersheriff, sword drawn, arrested two or three obvious stone-throwers, but the mob rescued them. Once her hour had passed, the badly bruised midwife returned to Newgate, again running a violent gauntlet through the streets.[12]

Cellier could expect the same treatment in her next two trips to the pillory, and she understandably worried that she might not survive. She hoped for mercy, and after returning to jail she drew up a petition for the king. She said she was 'grievously bruised, and several officers [were] wounded in her defense', and she begged that her remaining pilloryings be suspended.[13] Her foot-boy had picked up several of the stones flung at her by the crowd, and she sent these along with her plea to demonstrate the danger she was in.

Charles sympathized with Cellier's plight, 'thinking it very cruel to have people's lives exposed in that manner for such a piece of justice'.[14] Unfortunately, Lord Chancellor Finch, to whom the king referred the petition, advised no action. The sentence imposed on Elizabeth could not be reversed legally, the Chancellor explained, and besides, her armoured clothing would be enough to protect her from the violence of the mob. Perhaps Finch still smarted from Cellier's defiance of his order not to publish *Malice* – in any event he had no empathy for the embattled midwife.[15]

And so another trip to the pillory, this time one set up at Covent Garden, was inevitable. On 23 September, protected as well as she could be beneath her clothing, she set off once again. This time the authorities tried something different – they used two coaches, hoping that the mob would be confused about which carried Elizabeth. The crowd probably just pelted both coaches as they slowly forced their way through the street bound for the pillory. At least Mrs Cellier could comfort herself in the knowledge that half of the dangerous (and odorous) trash thrown at her missed the target.

But once at the pillory there was no avoiding the crowd's fury. If anything, this experience was worse than the last. The market at Covent Garden was a relatively confined space – less capacious than the Strand, certainly – and it was packed. Knocked down by rocks twice, then stood back up by the officers, the violence of the assault actually toppled over the pillory itself, taking Elizabeth and two constables down with it. By the time her hour of torture ended Cellier was badly injured. Two surgeons examined her bruised body and certified that a third ordeal, scheduled a week later, would be fatal. The Lord Mayor then postponed her final appearance.[16]

Elizabeth's last appearance at the pillory took place about a month later, after the worst of her wounds had healed. This time the venue was Charing Cross, once again chosen for its visibility. The night before she suffered her final humiliation, she wrote the undersheriff to warn him that she had heard that people had stockpiled stones and bricks to throw at her. Her warning apparently had some effect, for although Cellier endured no less abuse than before, she at least survived. Apparently Lord Finch had been right.[17] Mrs Cellier's third pillorying seems to have attracted somewhat less attention than her first two. If so, it was largely because attention had turned to the new Parliament.

King Charles had repeatedly prorogued the Parliament originally scheduled to open in January 1680, to the fury of Shaftesbury and the Whigs. The latter had done all in their power to pressure Charles to relent; a substantial faction of councillors had urged the same thing. These men hoped that a session might reduce divisions. But Charles was not convinced. By October, however, he seems to have felt that the purges of local government, as well as his own ostentatious favour of abhorrers and none-too-subtle disdain for exclusionists, might make for a successful session. The government spent a considerable amount of time in September and October preparing the ground.

In late September the Reverend Oates fended off a new, and potentially disastrous, assault on his credibility. Simpson Tonge, Israel's son, appeared before the king at Windsor with important information about the plot. The elder Tonge had faded well into the background since the opening days of the plot; his mental instability had not worn well. His appearances before the Privy Council had been awkward and many concluded that Tonge bordered on insanity. Oates and Bedloe quickly overshadowed Israel, who, while still living in London, had played no part in the pursuit of plotters or their subsequent trials. Now his son emerged with a remarkable tale: Israel and Titus Oates had concocted the entire story of the plot out of whole cloth. He told, with considerable accuracy, how the pair had retired south of the Thames and holed up in an inn for several days, refining the details of their story. The king saw here an opportunity to overthrow the entire plot narrative – but he reacted with great caution. Keeping Simpson at arm's-length was important – there were councillors like Halifax and Finch, who strongly believed that any undermining the plot investigation was a gift to Shaftesbury and the exclusionists. Royal meddling would seem further evidence of the Court's popish sympathies. So Charles used his backstairs fixer, Thomas Chiffinch, to instruct an army officer, Captain Ely, to deal with the younger Tonge.

Ely brought Simpson quietly before Charles, and then he attempted to verify this new information by speaking to some of Israel's servants. Unfortunately, Ely's efforts to do this soon came to Oates's attention – someone blabbed, and Titus acted quickly to ward off the threat. On 22 September he brought two witnesses before the Privy Council. These two, a Mr Cooper and Mrs Fitzgarrett, accused Captain Ely of attempting to suborn Simpson Tonge and of offering them bribes – treats of food and drink in Cooper's case and 40 shillings for Fitzgarrett. When questioned, Ely said that he had paid Fitzgarrett on an order from Chiffinch. This caused a stir, because everyone knew that Thomas did nothing without the king's command.[18]

The Privy Council resolved on a closer investigation. Two days later Oates, Simpson and several witnesses appeared at the council board. It did not go well for young Mr Tonge. Oates brought witnesses who swore that Simpson was 'a rude fellow and a common thief, abandoned by his father for his debauchery'. Tonge contradicted himself in his testimony, first swearing that he had never written or approached the king. At this Captain Ely pulled out one of Tonge's letters to the king, and Simpson's credibility immediately evaporated. Now he said that Mr and Mrs Lane, parents of the pilloried John Lane, Titus's victimized former servant, had encouraged him. The council ordered Simpson to Newgate to await trial for libel and perjury.[19] The king, aware that Simpson's testimony would be rejected, had already hastened to drop him. 'The king knows Captain Ely, and remembers he brought Dr. Tonge's son to him at Windsor . . . Tonge's son left some papers with him [Charles] . . . but His Majesty found them very slight and immaterial, and would not afterwards see Tonge any more.'[20]

So Titus Oates's luck held still, and of course crafters of the plot narrative took advantage of his triumph. Over the next few days reports surfaced that Sir Roger L'Estrange, one of Oates's most persistent foes, had orchestrated Simpson's revelations. Others said that Mrs Cellier – presumably between public stonings – had lured him on. By 5 October a lurid tale was circulating in which Simpson planned to strangle his father and plant a note to suggest suicide, caused by his remorse over the deaths of so many innocents caught up in the plot.[21] Simpson Tonge sat in Newgate. He had in fact told the truth, but fate – and his own past – conspired against him. The king ran a significant risk in pushing Simpson's information, but he avoided any real damage by his hasty abandonment of the young man. This was hardly a courageous action, but perhaps under the circumstances it was an understandable one.

The opening of Parliament drew nearer, and Charles's servants prepared themselves. Titus was roaming the city's coffee houses, spreading rumours that the king intended to move Parliament from Westminster to the more reliable city of Oxford. This alleged outrage could only be countered by a demand to convene the Houses within the reliably Whig City of London. Councillors met regularly to prepare for the session, strategizing. They explored the possibility of peeling off some prominent Shaftesbury allies, such as Lord Cavendish.[22] They expected that the Whigs would make much of the 'McShams'. In late September, Shaftesbury received one of the Irish informers, Mr Burgh, who came to him for charity for himself and the rest of his tribe. The earl promised him that something would be done. Reports circulated that Whigs raised money for their support in coffee houses and at a dissenting chapel.[23] On 1 October, less than three weeks before the session was to begin, Secretary of State Leoline Jenkins wrote to a friend, 'You will hear of the caballing here towards the sitting of Parliament . . . One thing they will be certain to pursue with all eagerness, that is, the plot, and they will have new matter furnished out of Ireland.'[24] Jenkins said that Charles would co-operate and offer whatever safeguards against Catholicism that Parliament demanded – barring any change to the succession.

Charles delivered this message personally at Parliament's opening. With the Lords and Commons assembled before him – and the earl of Shaftesbury conspicuously absent – he read from a prepared speech. The king attributed his repeated delays in opening the session to diplomatic necessity. He needed time to conclude an anti-French alliance with Spain and the Netherlands. How many in his audience believed this is difficult to say. There were perhaps a handful of clueless backbenchers and maybe one or two unworldly bishops who took this seriously – but no one who had lived through the previous months of political turmoil could possibly have swallowed this excuse. Charles first proclaimed his desire to defend Protestantism, and said he would support any measures Parliament suggested, 'that may consist with preserving the succession of the crown in its due and legal course of descent'. He then urged continuing the investigation of the plot, saying, apparently with a straight face, 'I do not think myself safe, nor you neither, till that matter be gone through', and he also urged that the five lords in the Tower be brought to trial. He ended with a plea, more hopeful than realistic, for 'a perfect union amongst ourselves'.[25]

His speech done, Charles left the House of Lords, and MPs followed, headed for their own chamber, ready to demonstrate – or not – their concern for national unity. The signs were not good. Both houses spent the next couple of days swearing the oaths of allegiance. The Lords got down to business first. On Saturday 23 October the peers addressed Charles for a proclamation offering a pardon to any informers coming forward with information about the plot. The House established a new investigating committee, and not surprisingly Shaftesbury and his closest allies were on it. Shaftesbury dominated its proceedings from the start, although there were a handful of courtiers, like Lords Halifax and Arundell of Trerice, among its members.

On Tuesday 26 October the Commons ignored the king's warning about the succession. Lord Russell led the way: '. . . this Parliament must either destroy popery, or they will destroy us, there is no middle way to be taken, no mincing the matter'. He then proposed that steps be taken to 'quiet the just fears and apprehensions of the people and provide against a popish succession'.[26] The House resolved, without a division, to draft a bill excluding James, duke of York, from the throne. Even the privy councillors in the House, such as Secretary Jenkins, kept silent.

Thomas Dangerfield did his best to add momentum to the exclusionist cause. He appeared at the bar of the House the same day, and accused James of offering him money to advance the Meal Tub Plot (James himself admitted giving Thomas a small sum when they met) and of upbraiding him for not accepting a commission to murder the king (a blatant falsehood). He also accused the earl of Peterborough and the earl of Anglesey of conspiring to derail the prosecution of the five lords. Dangerfield's attack on Anglesey is a good example of the indiscriminate cluelessness of many of the plot informers. The earl, a Protestant Irishman, kept a nonconformist chaplain and was well known for his Puritan beliefs. He was an unlikely candidate for Popish Plotting.[27] Two privy councillors, Lawrence Hyde and Secretary of State Jenkins, declared Dangerfield perjured. Hyde pointed out that Thomas had said nothing of these things when under oath before the Privy Council. Now he accused the duke – but he was not under oath. Moreover, Jenkins said, no one could trust the word of a professional crook. Later the Secretary wrote that 'he spoke with great ease, clearness, and presence of mind but I cannot think that any that heard him believed one word he said'.[28] This was probably true among the minority opposing exclusion, but at this point believing in the plot had become a test of membership in the Commons.

Two sceptical members of the last Parliament had been expelled for daring to express their doubts, and on 28 October another member suffered for that alleged heresy. Mr Rowe, the official sword-bearer of the city of Bristol, swore that the previous October his MP, Sir Robert Cann, had denied the existence of the plot and said that there was instead a Presbyterian conspiracy against the monarchy. Cann's Bristol colleague, Sir John Knight, supported the allegation, provoking Cann to respond 'A jury of twelve men in Bristol will not give credit to Sir John Knight's testimony.' After these words Sir Robert muttered 'God damn me, it is true!' But alas he spoke these words in the hearing of William Strode, one of Shaftesbury's 'worthy' members. Strode piously informed the House of Cann's blasphemy, and an avalanche of denunciations followed from some of the House's 'worthiest' members. Sir Robert apologized to the House on his knees for swearing, but repentance did not satisfy his critics. The House resolved, again without a division or any argument, to expel Cann and imprison him in the Tower.[29]

Captain Thomas Bickley felt the wrath of the upper House at the same time. In a public meeting in Chichester he had said that 'Dr. Oates was a very bad man, and that it had been better if he had never been, and that he had contradicted himself two and twenty times in his testimony against the prisoners.' The peers summoned the captain to London intending some sort of exemplary punishment. It was clear that both houses would punish those who questioned the narrative – but it was also plain that more and more people were doing so. That meant that supporters of the narrative needed to press ahead even more vigorously, and Parliament was the best place to do it. As Thomas Bennett ('Shaftesbury's Bennett') put it, 'In Parliament it is a plot, and out of parliament it is none.'[30] Testimony could be orchestrated, there were no juries to convince or judges to deliver unwelcome charges.

Both houses relentlessly advanced the message. On 26 October a former servant of the Portuguese ambassador, Francisco de Feria, appeared in the Lords. Swearing on the book of Deuteronomy – he was born a Jew – he said that the ambassador had offered him 50,000 reales (about £10,000) to murder Oates and Bedloe. Later he expanded his hit list to include the earl of Shaftesbury. When De Feria asked how he should accomplish this, Ambassador De Melo had a novel suggestion: throw a 'hand granadoe' into the earl's coach. De Feria also told of the ambassador's ill-considered compliments to Justice Scroggs after the Wakeman trial, though nothing he said suggested an impropriety. He did, though, suggest that the queen and king might have surreptitiously intervened in the case.[31] The Commons heard the same story a few days later, and they appointed a committee, strongly exclusionist in tone, to report on steps taken against the plot since October 1678.

Shaftesbury also resumed his vendetta against Lord Castlemaine, presenting two witnesses who claimed that they knew him to be a Catholic priest. On the strength of these witnesses the Lords ordered Castlemaine's arrest – a fruitless gesture, since he had already left England in anticipation of further persecution.[32] Another target was Roger L'Estrange; the Lords committee summoned him three times to no avail, and now Shaftesbury presented testimony from Richard Fletcher that Sir Roger had told him he was a Catholic. The Lords then ordered L'Estrange's arrest and asked that he be sacked as a magistrate. Fletcher was certainly lying, but if perjury could remove L'Estrange from circulation Shaftesbury was more than content. Like Castlemaine, however, Roger fled, first to Edinburgh and afterwards to the Netherlands. In both cases Shaftesbury's accusations merely provoked his victims to expand their assaults on the plot.

The main focus of the attack in both Houses was the so-called 'Irish plot'. The McShams were busily, if somewhat incoherently, denouncing everyone Shaftesbury wanted denounced before his committee. The Lords ordered the arrest of the earl of Tyrone, accused of plotting a French invasion of Ireland in league with the Jesuits. They demanded the transfer of Archbishop Plunket from Dublin to London and he duly appeared to be made a close prisoner in Newgate. In the run-up to Gunpowder Day, Shaftesbury reported several times from his committee. The Lords spent nearly all of Thursday 4 November straining to understand the testimony of William Hetherington and Edmund Murphy, who said (apparently) that there had been an Irish Catholic conspiracy underway since 1673. Their testimony was peppered with headscratchers like 'magnipotent enemies' and denunciations of the duke of Ormond for treating them like 'jail birds or common vagabonds' – which most of them were. At least these informers gave value for Shaftesbury's money.[33] That few peers could actually understand them was something of an advantage – no one could question any discrepancies between what they said and their written depositions.

After 5 November the focus remained on the Irish plot. Ragged informers appeared in both the Commons and Lords several times over the next two weeks. But drivers of the plot explored other avenues as well. Robert Bolron, avatar of the Yorkshire branch of the plot, reappeared in the Lords. Bolron's tale was more elaborate than ever. In February 1677, he said, he took the 'oath of secrecy' that he had invented for the purpose of condemning Thomas Gascoigne. Now he embellished his account further: Sir Thomas and his priestly friends enlivened the ceremony by solemnly blessing an array of weapons, 'bullets, swords, guns and pistols'. At the same time, Robert said he received 30,000 years' remission of purgatory, with a promise of 50,000 if he repeated a 'litany for the intercession and conversion of England'.[34] He promised to provide a copy of this document upon request (it duly appeared in his printed *Narrative*). Bolron incriminated Lords Arundell of Wardour, Belasyse and Petre who had all pledged no less than £100,000 each to support the plot. Bolron said nothing about where these fabulous sums might come from. None of the peers he accused had anything like such wealth. Robert threw in the duchess of Portsmouth for good measure, accusing her of spying on behalf of Catholics.[35]

If Bolron's information did not add enough to the atmosphere of anti-Catholic frenzy, on 9 November Shaftesbury reported to the peers a new pending horror. He had witnesses who would prove that Mrs Cellier schemed to burn the entire Royal Navy![36] The fire-bug/midwife, so these informants said, planned to hire a brigade of arsonists. They would fan out among ships at anchor and set them alight. The general opinion was that arson was a Catholic speciality; that Catholics started the Great Fire of London was gospel for many. For them, destroying the fleet would be simple. The House ordered Elizabeth's indictment on a charge of high treason. Again. Shaftesbury's animus against Mrs Cellier seemed almost as virulent as his hatred for the duke of York.[37]

While the upper House entertained itself with these fantastic stories (and little else), the Commons did double duty. They listened to the claims of the Irish informers and other tales of popish perfidy, but simultaneously, and with startling speed, they worked on a new exclusion bill. On 26 October the House resolved to proceed with a bill, by 4 November it received its first reading and its second two days later (members having taken 5 November off for an anti-Catholic sermon about the Gunpowder Plot). Secretary Jenkins strove mightily to derail the juggernaut. 'This bill reflects upon the nation, as if when the duke came to the crown there would be a change of religion. I hope that five hundred members of Parliament will resolve not to change religion, though the duke come to the crown . . .'[38] The Secretary's words had no impact whatever, and the bill proceeded without even a division. On 11 November the bill was completed, passed (again without a division) and sent to the Lords.

The Lords took up the bill on Monday 15 November. The peers filled the House; one hundred answered the roll. The king was also present. Before the debate began, Thomas Dangerfield came to the bar and reiterated his charges against the duke of York, as well as several lesser figures: Lord Peterborough, Lady Powis and Mrs Cellier. This performance, orchestrated by Shaftesbury, was clearly designed to make the danger of James's accession seem more acute than ever.

The debate lasted well into the evening. Leading the charge against the duke was Shaftesbury, and his principal opponent was Lord Halifax. King Charles listened intently, and made his views crystal clear, nodding approvingly at opponents of the bill and scowling elaborately at those supporting it. At one point, while his son Monmouth spoke with dubious sincerity of his concern for the king, someone heard Charles say, 'It is the kiss of Judas he gives me.'[39] Charles fortified himself with food and drink delivered from Whitehall as the debate wore on. At last the House voted, and the result no doubt gratified Charles as much as it infuriated Shaftesbury. The peers decisively rejected the bill 63–30, provoking twenty-five to enter a formal protest into the *Journal*. Obviously, Charles's performance at the debate influenced many peers. He had clearly and repeatedly signalled opposition to any parliamentary tampering with the succession. In the end most of the peerage stood by the duke. Among the privy councillors, only two of any significance, Lords Sunderland and Anglesey, voted for the bill. In Anglesey's case it was possible that the charges levelled against the lord by the Irish informers intimidated him.[40]

Exclusion's second rejection only heightened Shaftesbury's determination to continue his attack on the duke. Pursuing the plot became more imperative still. The next target: the five imprisoned Catholic lords. It is noteworthy that many of the informers Shaftesbury's committee produced took care to implicate the Tower lords, and in the days immediately before the rejection of the bill, preparations began for the first trial: William Howard, Viscount Stafford, would be the first defendant. The Lords set his trial for 30 November, and the Commons were told to prepare their case. In the meanwhile, the Lords ordered conditions for the prisoners to be tightened: they were forbidden to communicate with each other. Plot supporters granted the privilege of collusion to themselves alone.[41]

The Catholic lords had been jailed for two full years, and attempts to get bail had repeatedly failed, even in the case of Lord Belasyse, who was in such poor health that he rarely left his bed. The others, Lords Powis, Petre, Arundell of Wardour and Stafford, all endured bouts of illness while confined. Parliament almost launched their trials in 1679, but a royal prorogation mothballed the prosecution. Now, however, the exclusionists planned an elaborate show trial that would keep the plot narrative alive a while longer. Some believed that Stafford was first in line because he was considered the easiest mark, a man who had few close friends, and who often quarrelled with his family. Moreover, his introverted personality suggested that he might conduct a weak defence.[42] Others thought that Stafford was first simply because the evidence against him, such as it was, was stronger than that against the other four peers.

The trial took place in Westminster Hall. The hall could accommodate several thousand spectators, but preparations took several weeks, directed by Sir Christopher Wren, the king's Surveyor General. The courts of Chancery, King's Bench and Common Pleas and over fifty shops were removed and a team of carpenters set to work creating a courtroom.[43]

The result of their labours was a transformed Westminster Hall. Workmen laid an elevated wooden floor, built long benches for the peers to sit on and created boxes for witnesses and the prosecutors. At one end of the hall stood a throne, representing the king – although the carpenters built an enclosed cabinet for Charles's use on the upper right side of the hall (the queen had her own on the left) – Westminster Hall was cold in December. Woolsacks (actually filled with straw) for the judges stood below the throne, with a chair placed for Lord Chancellor Finch, who would preside. Workers built a bank of theatre-style benches on both of the hall's long walls for MPs (and their guests – admission to the trial would be highly sought). Finally, the builders added a large gallery overlooking the courtroom for the use of foreign ambassadors and other distinguished spectators.

The model for this trial was the earl of Strafford's impeachment in 1641. Ironically the accused's own father, the earl of Arundell, had presided then. Now Arundell's fifth son would experience impeachment from the other side of the court's bar. At nine on the morning of 30 November a solemn procession formed at Lord Finch's house in Queen street, near Covent Garden. All of the king's judges, the Garter King of Arms, the Common's sergeant-at-arms, staggering under the weight of the mace, and the Lords usher of the black rod, carrying the much lighter white-painted wooden wand, symbol of Finch's authority as lord steward. Finch and his attendants travelled by coach to Westminster. Entering the House of Lords, he found the peers waiting, wearing their red parliamentary robes. Before proceeding to the hall, the bishops present reserved their right to attend the trial, but having done so, they left the chamber – it was not fit that clergymen should be obliged to pass a death sentence in case of conviction. This formality done, the peers processed two by two through Westminster, a long red line of aristocrats formed up by rank, from the junior baron to the senior duke, the king's cousin Prince Rupert. They filed into the hall and took their seats, again by rank and seniority. Behind and above them a huge crowd watched breathlessly as a gentleman laid an executioner's axe on a table, its blade turned away from the prisoner at the bar. Eighty-six peers attended the trial, as did the king, watching from the heated comfort of his cabinet.

Sir John Reresby observed the trial and described it as 'the most solemn thing I ever saw'. He believed that it came at a critical moment; the once universal acceptance of the plot narrative had ended, 'it being doubtful at that time whether there were more that believed there was a plot to take away the king's life by the papists, or not'.[44] Just as Shaftesbury intended, Stafford's trial would highlight and restore the narrative's credibility.

Escorted by the Lieutenant of the Tower, Stafford kneeled at the bar. Lord Finch commanded him to rise, and the trial began. 'You are prosecuted,' he told Stafford, 'and pursued by the loud and dreadful complaints of the Commons' and 'In this so great and weighty cause, you are to be judged by the whole body of the house of peers, the highest and noblest court in this, or perhaps any other part of the Christian world.'[45] John Maynard, MP for Plymouth and an eminent lawyer, opened the prosecution. He was no stranger to the setting; nearly forty years before he had been one of Lord Strafford's prosecutors. Now seventy-six, he still had plenty of energy and decades of trial experience – he had already appeared as a prosecutor in earlier plot trials. Joining him were several other prominent barristers: Sir Francis Winnington, Sir William Jones, a former Attorney General, and George Treby, the Recorder of London. All three of these barristers strongly supported exclusion, and five other MPs, all noisy Whigs, acted as their assistants.

The first day's witnesses focused on proving the existence of the plot in general, and not Stafford's supposed role in it. On Wednesday 1 December testimony centred on the viscount's alleged actions. With Bedloe dead, the prosecution needed another witness, and now it turned to Stephen Dugdale. He said that Stafford, visiting his master Lord Aston's country house in September 1678, offered him £500 to murder the king. He also said he saw letters mentioning the plot from Stafford to Father Evers, Aston's chaplain – though as in every other plot trial the prosecution entered no such letter into evidence.[46] Oates followed Dugdale, and told the familiar story – he had delivered a papal commission to Stafford naming him paymaster of the fantasy Catholic army. He cited conversations with now-dead fellow plotters such as John Fenwick speaking about Stafford's role in the conspiracy. After Titus concluded, a new witness appeared: Edward Turbervile. Raised Catholic, Turbervile had spent some time in the French army, was cashiered (or deserted) and had approached Lord Stafford in Paris, looking for a handout. Stafford, said Edward, had solicited the king's murder during one of those meetings, something Turbervile refused to do. Questioned by Stafford, Turbervile was vague on details. He could not describe the place where this conversation occurred. He initially misstated the year he met Stafford, and had to correct himself. Asked by Finch why he had said nothing about Stafford's treason for almost five years, he rather feebly replied, 'I had no faith to believe that I should be safe if I did it, but my brains might be knocked out . . .'[47] According to Bishop Burnet, however, Bishop William Lloyd, who was virtually chaplain to the plot, had converted Turbervile months before and kept him in his own house. During that time Lloyd pressed his guest for any information about the plot he might have – and he 'protested he knew no particulars'.[48]

After the prosecution's witnesses stood down, Stafford launched his defence with a rambling speech. Suffering from a heavy cold, many in the courtroom could not hear him and several times Lord Finch urged him to speak louder. Stafford rejected the doctrine of 'king killing' so cherished by Protestants; murdering heretic princes was contrary to the Church's teaching. He also argued that he had never been convicted of recusancy, and asked how under the law he might be taken to be a papist. It seems unlikely that the argument that he had never *officially* proved to be a Catholic went very far with his peers, but he did make a point when he said that he had had ample time to flee the country when Oates revealed his story.[49] He said he never laid eyes on Turbervile, and that his contact with Dugdale was limited to fleeting encounters as a guest in Lord Aston's house. The court spent much of the second day of the trial wrangling over whether Stafford could have copies of sworn depositions made by Oates, Dugdale and Turbervile. The prosecutors resisted stridently, no doubt fearing the possibility of contradictory testimony. The viscount won a partial victory on this; the Lords gave him access to the witnesses' testimony entered into the Lords *Journal* – but he failed to get copies of depositions made before magistrates outside of Parliament. Nor did he succeed in his request for an extra day to prepare his defence. The trial, said their lordships, would resume the next day at 10 a.m.

On Thursday morning Stafford presented his witnesses. His first target was Stephen Dugdale. William's daughter Isabella, the dowager marchioness of Winchester, and a widowed kinswoman testified that Dugdale's current testimony contradicted what he swore in the Wakeman trial – placing Lord Stafford at a conspiratorial 'consult' at Tixall in August 1678. Now he said the meeting occurred in September – because Stafford could prove an alibi for all of August.[50] Three servants of the marquis of Worcester proved that Stafford visited their master's house at Badminton in Gloucestershire in August, over 80 miles from Tixall. The viscount's page, a boy named Nicholas Furnese, contradicted Dugdale's account of Stafford's offer of £500 for the king's death. This supposedly happened when Dugdale and Stafford were alone in the peer's bedroom. But Nicholas's account differed. He said he was present throughout Dugdale's visit, and the only topic of conversation was who was likely to win a foot race scheduled for later in the day. The Commons managers asked Furnese about his religion, and he admitted that he was Catholic, doing nothing to aid his credibility before a room full of Protestant peers. Other witnesses described Dugdale's turpitude as Lord Aston's steward – his reckless debts and gambling, his embezzlement of his master's money, his cheating of the servants. Several witnesses said that Stephen offered them money to swear against Lord Aston and other local Catholics – 'he told me he could furnish me with money, and put me in a way to get money if I would come in as evidence against my lord Stafford,' said an upholsterer named William Robinson.[51] A barber named John Morrall told how Dugdale offered him £100 to join him as a witness, despite Morrall's protest that 'he knew no more than my Lord Mayor's great horse did' about the plot.[52]

Stafford worked to undermine Oates's credibility by pointing out various contradictions in his testimony and calling several witnesses, most of whom were his servants. The impact that this testimony had was mixed. John Evelyn, who was present, said Stafford's witnesses were 'very slight persons' who 'in truth they rather did my lord injury than service'.[53] Reresby, on the other hand, speaking of the Crown's witnesses, wrote 'They seemed so positive in this and other dangerous evidence that myself . . . knew not what to believe, had the evidence been men of any credit, but there were such incoherences, and indeed contradictions . . . towards the latter end of the trial, that . . . I was satisfied at last of its untruth.'[54] Evelyn was particularly harsh regarding Oates, 'such a man's testimony should

259

not be taken against the life of a dog'.[55] From this point forward Sir John disbelieved Oates altogether, and began rethinking his earlier belief in the plot. He wondered how it was that someone so intimately involved in the conspiracy, connected to many of the accused, had never managed to produce a single document proving its existence. By now Evelyn had seen Oates in trials and around London enough to have conceived a very negative opinion of him. Titus was 'so slight a person, so passionate, ill-bred and of impudent behavior' that he could not imagine the Jesuits would trust him with such 'high and dangerous secrets'.[56]

On the third day Stafford had not yet called all of his witnesses when Shaftesbury rose to call for an adjournment. Weary peers called 'Adjourn! Adjourn!' and so the day ended with Stafford's defence incomplete. The case resumed at ten the next morning.[57]

With high political tensions in full view Shaftesbury intervened to discredit one of Stafford's witnesses, and Lord Wharton, one of the most radical of the Whigs, did his best to prevent the entry into evidence of one of Oates's contradictory statements to the Privy Council. A fair trial was not what these noble lords wanted.[58] When the prosecutors took their turn, they called witnesses with obvious Whig biases. These included Stephen College, the joiner Shaftesbury had hired to create the effigy of the pope burned on 17 November.[59] One witness claimed that a defence witness had threatened to 'dong my brains out' with a pot.[60] And so it went. Two women testified that Dugdale had burned a number of papers, and the prosecutors said this was why nothing incriminating Stafford (or anyone else) had been found.[61] But the prosecution called no witnesses to defend Oates's reputation, suggesting something important – shares in Titus's enterprise seemed to be falling fast.

The court reconvened on Saturday 4 December. That day and on Monday 6 December the defence and prosecution summed up their cases, making their final arguments. Some observers thought that Stafford skilfully summarized his case, although Evelyn thought he spoke 'without any method and confusedly'.[62] But under the circumstances Stafford performed well. Unlike his accusers he had no legal training or experience, nor was he allowed legal counsel of his own. As Bishop Burnet put it, he 'urged every particular very strongly'.[63] He faced a team of barristers whose experience could hardly be matched. Their final argument demonstrated why they commanded such high fees at the bar, highlighting every possible weakness in Stafford's case and eliding artfully over their own. Titus

Oates, his credibility tottering, played a minor role in their argument, while Dugdale, vouched for by peers, MPs and ministers, still maintained his and thus bore a larger burden of proof.

On Tuesday 7 December eighty-six peers, still in their red parliamentary robes, returned to Westminster Hall to render judgement. Lord Finch put the question: 'Is William lord viscount Stafford guilty of the treason whereof he stands impeached, or not guilty?'[64] Following long-standing tradition, each lord stood, covered his heart with his right hand and declared his verdict. The roll began with the junior baron, Richard, Lord Butler of Weston, a younger son of Ormond who had received his peerage in 1673. 'Not guilty, upon mine honor,' said the baron. And the process continued, climbing the noble hierarchy, until the king's first cousin, Prince Rupert, cast the final vote: 'Guilty, upon my honor.' Thirty-one peers voted to acquit and a majority, fifty-five, voted guilty. Stafford, standing at the bar, saw an officer of the court turn the blade of the axe towards him.

Finch then said, 'My lord Stafford, I have but heavy tidings for you . . . their lordships do find you guilty of the treason whereof you are impeached.' Stafford, who surprised many by his resolution, responded, 'God's holy name be praised, my lords, for it.'[65] The peers then returned to their House, where they debated the sentence – some peers argued for a merciful beheading, but the judges said that the only form of execution prescribed by law was hanging, drawing and quartering.[66] And so the Lords returned once again to Westminster Hall, where Finch gave what Bishop Burnet described as 'one of the best speeches he ever made'. 'My part . . . which remains, is a very sad one, for I never yet gave sentence of death upon any man, and am extremely sorry that I must begin with your lordship,' said Finch, before wondering how a man of such lineage and loyalty to the Crown could become a part of a plot to murder the sovereign. He urged repentance and confession on Stafford and then began the ritual of sentencing: 'And now, my lord, this is the last time I can call you my lord, for the next words I am to speak will attaint you.' He followed this with the usual horrifying description of drawing and quartering, 'And God Almighty be merciful to your soul.'[67]

After passing sentence, Finch assured 'my lord Stafford' – a mistake, for he was now plain William Howard – that the Lords would petition the king for a simple beheading. Emotion overcame William, who thanked the House with tears in his eyes. Lord Finch then broke his white wand of office, symbolizing the end of the proceedings, and the prisoner returned to the Tower to await death.

The trial, political as it was, served Shaftesbury's purpose. It was an impressive spectacle and it kept the kingdom's attention focused on the Catholic threat. Evelyn wrote, 'the trial was carried on from first to last, with exceeding gravity, and so stately and august appearance I had never seen'.[68] The peers voted along mostly partisan lines, and it was notable that two of the three members of the Howard clan in the Lords voted to convict – testimony, perhaps, to the ill-feeling Stafford had created among his relatives over the years.

Two days after Stafford's conviction, Bishop Burnet and Henry Compton, bishop of London, visited the condemned in his cell. Any hope the prelates had of a conversion faded quickly, as Stafford remained true to his faith. And if they hoped for a confession they were wrong; Stafford passionately maintained his innocence, and he did so again when Burnet visited him the next day. Still hoping to survive, Stafford offered to reveal more information, and on Saturday 18 December he returned to the bar of the Lords. To the great disappointment of the Whig peers, he talked not about Oates's conspiracy, but the role he once played in seeking a toleration for Catholics. And when he spoke of Shaftesbury's role in those negotiations – the earl had indeed been involved – the House immediately shut him down. It was extremely inconvenient for anyone to remind the world that the earl of Shaftesbury had not always been the scourge of popery he pretended to be.

Bishop Burnet wrote that this attempt to mediate between Stafford and the Lords backfired on him. Shaftesbury accused him of attempting 'to blast him' and he 'so railed at me, that I went no more near him'. On the other side, the duke of York thought that Burnet sought to use Stafford against him, 'which was the beginning of the implacable hatred he showed on many occasions against me'.[69]

Stafford returned to the Tower to await his date with the executioner. James hoped that his brother the king might yet spare him, but he realized that pressure to sign the death warrant would be immense. From his semi-exile in Edinburgh, the situation looked ominously like 1640 when England had teetered on the verge of civil war. Then his father, also under great pressure from inside and outside Parliament, had allowed the earl of Strafford's execution, an act he later bitterly regretted.[70] Reresby noted that Charles II, present throughout the trial, 'seemed extremely concerned at [Stafford's] hard and undeserved fate'.[71] But the king signed the warrant on 18 December and fixed the date of the execution for 29 December. One more controversy intervened before Lord Stafford's final scene. The warrant ordered his beheading only – there would be no drawing and quartering. This prompted the two radical Whig sheriffs of London and Middlesex to protest. Slingsby Bethel and Henry Cornish petitioned the Lords demanding the full grisly punishment, and some Whigs in the Commons, notably Lord Russell, agreed.[72] The peers rejected the petition: Stafford would escape the worst.

An immense crowd, thousands strong, waited in the cold outside the Tower gate on Wednesday 29 December. Stafford would be the first peer of the realm executed for treason since the civil war.[73] At about 10 a.m. Bethel and Cornish, accompanied by a train of mounted gentlemen, rode to the Tower's gate and demanded the body of 'William, late viscount Stafford'. Captain Cheeke brought the former lord to the gate and turned him over to the sheriffs. They proceeded to the scaffold, built to make the spectacle visible to all, and Stafford, supporting himself with a cane, mounted the stairs. Attending him was a servant and two Catholic priests, one of whom served as chaplain to the Spanish ambassador. Already present was the executioner, masked and holding a covered axe. Mr Ketch had already placed the block and laid out a seven-foot-long piece of black cloth for his victim to lie upon. William asked Ketch if he had been paid for his clothes – it was the executioner's prerogative to take them, but he often received cash, avoiding the humiliation of a public stripping. Ketch said he had not. There followed a rather unseemly squabble: Stafford's man produced a purse containing £5. Mr Ketch thought this insufficient for the clothes of a nobleman, and Stafford added two guineas to the purse. The execution proceeded.

Stafford then pulled out his last speech. 'By the permission of Almighty God I am this day brought hither to suffer death, as if I were guilty of high treason. I do most truly, in the presence of the eternal, omnipotent, and all-knowing God, protest, upon my salvation, that I am as innocent as it is possible for any man to be . . .'[74] One witness said 'he seemed fearless of death' and noted that he read his speech 'in a cheerful unconcernedness'.[75] He acknowledged his sins, reaffirmed his Catholic faith and denied that the Church sanctioned regicide or rebellion. He denied knowing anything whatever of an assassination plot, said he had never laid eyes on Titus Oates before his trial, and that his conversation with Stephen Dugdale was never more than an innocent discussion of a foot race. Stafford forgave his accusers and his judges, and asked the audience to pray for the king. He ended saying, 'I beseech God not to revenge my innocent blood upon the nation, or on those that were the cause of it, with my last breath. I do with my last breath assert my innocency, and hope the omnipotent, all-seeing, just God will deal with me accordingly.'[76]

William then prayed privately for a few minutes, though he had to fend off the unwanted attentions of a Protestant minister, answering him 'in a great passion, Sir, what have you to do with my religion?' He then distributed a few personal items, a watch, his rings, crucifix and his cane, to his waiting friends. His servant helped him remove his coat and periwig, and he donned a silk cap into which he pushed his hair. Mr Ketch asked William if he wanted to give a sign before he delivered the blow; Stafford said 'No sign at all. Take your own time, God's will be done.' Stafford lay down, placed his head on the block, and the blow fell. 'The people gave a mighty shout,' said a witness. The blow was not altogether clean; Ketch had to finish the job with a knife. Afterwards he stood and displayed William's head to the crowd: 'Here is the head of a traitor!' Another 'mighty shout' rose from the mob.[77]

Ketch and his assistants placed the former viscount's body in a waiting coffin. Plain and adorned only with the letters W.S. and the date 1680, officials buried it in the Tower's chapel. To the annoyance of some, the grave was near the communion table. But William might at least have taken some comfort in the knowledge that his mortal remains rested in good company: close by lay the bones of Sir Thomas More and John Fisher, also martyred for their Catholic faith.

Printers were selling copies of Stafford's last speech by two o'clock on the afternoon of his death, and his words circulated widely; there was even an Edinburgh edition. Not surprisingly, this provoked a flood of hostile replies: *The late Viscount Stafford found more guilty by his pretended innocency in his last speech*; *Animadversions upon the speech of William (late) Lord Stafford*; *No faith or credit to be given to papists*, among many others. These attacks were the more necessary because Stafford had seriously undermined the plot narrative. As Reresby wrote, 'The lord Stafford was beheaded on Tower Hill, where he absolutely denied the crimes for which he suffered, and after so convincing a manner that all that saw him believed it.'[78]

Stafford's trial and execution advanced Shaftesbury's cause, but as a counter-attack against the Court it fell short. Part of the reason for this was the growing distaste for some of the principal leaders of the plot narrative. Thomas Dangerfield's credibility had by now declined to almost nothing. The only defenders of Dugdale's reputation were the most extreme exclusionists. William

Bedloe was dead, and shortly before Stafford's execution Israel Tonge died, a mostly forgotten half-mad crank.[79] And Titus Oates, already on shaky ground, as his appearance at Stafford's trial suggested, could not refrain from alienating all and sundry. Reresby tells the story of encountering Oates at the table of Peter Gunning, Bishop of Ely, the day after Christmas. Oates abused the duke of York, and he also slandered the queen mother, Henrietta Maria, as well as Queen Catherine. The company allowed Titus to run on 'after a manner which showed himself both a fool and a knave' for fear of appearing in his next 'narrative' of the plot, but finally Sir John opposed him, provoking Titus to storm out of the bishop's house in a rage. Gunning told Reresby that Oates constantly behaved this way, and no chiding from him had ever made the slightest impression.[80]

In the days after Lord Stafford's conviction, Parliament thrashed about in a carnival of rage and frustration. The Commons spent several days demanding ever more draconian action against Catholics; some wanted them prohibited from coming any closer than twenty miles from London. Some wanted to confiscate Catholic estates. Some wanted to expel all Catholics from England. Sir William Jones, who had led the prosecution in the Stafford case, demanded that Parliament expel Catholics from Scotland too – ignoring the fact that the English Parliament had no jurisdiction north of the Tweed. John Trenchard wanted to go farther still: 'The papists are still so insolent, that you must not only suppress them, but extirpate them, or they will extirpate us!'[81] Privy councillors and other supporters of the Court sat on their hands throughout these extravagancies. They knew the temper of the House very well. A defence of James or any hint of moderation about Catholicism would bring down the wrath of the House.

Then the Commons went on an impeachment binge. Justice Scroggs, once a hero, was now very definitely a goat. The House accused him of an array of judicial sins and threw in moral turpitude to add piquancy: Sir William, 'by his frequent and notorious excesses and debaucheries, and his prophane and atheistical discourses doth daily affront Almighty God, dishonor his majesty, give countenance and encouragement to all manner of vice and wickedness, and bring the highest scandal on the public justice of the kingdom'.[82] Joining him in the dock were three other judges, Sir Thomas Jones, Sir Richard Weston and Sir Francis North. The Commons charged them with intimidating grand juries, imposing excessive fines, making arbitrary rulings and generally favouring Catholic defendants while oppressing Protestants.[83] The House resolved to impeach the earl of Tyrone for planning a Franco-Jesuit invasion of Ireland and then it impeached Edward Seymour, its former speaker – supposedly for embezzling Naval funds, but really because he spoke against exclusion in the House.[84] It impeached a hapless Anglican minister, Richard Thompson, for a two-year-old sermon in which he allegedly disparaged the plot.[85]

On 15 December, Charles appeared before the House of Lords. The lower House attended at the bar, and the king expressed his frustration that the session had accomplished so little. He reiterated his rejection of exclusion, while promising once again to accept limitations on a Catholic successor. MPs returned to their House and began a debate in which most of the speakers continued to insist upon exclusion as the only remedy to the Catholic problem. The House resolved to bring in a bill banishing 'all considerable papists from the king's dominions'. Completely ignoring the king's rejection of exclusion, they also resolved that 'as long as the papists have any hopes of the duke of York's succeeding the king in the kingdoms of England and Ireland . . . the king's person, the Protestant religion and the lives, liberties, and properties of all his majesty's Protestant subject are in apparent danger of being destroyed'.[86] The House of Commons had doubled down.

The Commons spent the next three weeks pursuing their impeachments, finding new popish enormities to denounce and refusing to consider any new taxes to support the government. When the new year began, the stand-off intensified. Charles, responding to yet another address aimed at his brother, wearily repeated what he had said many times before: 'He is sorry to see their thoughts so wholly fixed upon the bill of exclusion . . . His Majesty is confirmed in his opinion against that bill, by the judgment of the house of Lords, who rejected it.'[87] Charles's message provoked a series of inflammatory resolutions on 7 January – yet another insisting on exclusion, one refusing to grant supply without exclusion and another proclaiming that any who advised the king to reject exclusion were 'promoters of popery and enemies to the king and kingdom'. Just to be sure Charles knew exactly who those enemies were, the House helpfully listed them: Lords Halifax, Worcester, Clarendon and Feversham, Lawrence Hyde and Edward Seymour – all prominent opponents of exclusion.[88] All of these passed with no dissent; privy councillors made no effort to impede them.

The Commons proceeded to pass several more furious resolutions: that Catholics had started the great London fire of 1666 (they didn't) and that the duke of York's pernicious advice caused Monmouth's dismissal from office (it did not – Charles had plenty of his own reasons). The House wanted Monmouth reinstated (he was not). Finally, any who advised the king to prorogue Parliament 'is a betrayer of the king, the Protestant religion and of the kingdom of England, a promoter of the French interest, and a pensioner to France'.[89] In response, Charles now played a high card: on 10 January he prorogued Parliament, and on 18 January he dissolved it.

The Commons resolutions were fine rhetoric, but they could not alter the king's power to determine when to terminate its session. The king sweetened this bitter pill by calling for a new Parliament to assemble on 21 March. But again, he played another winning card: this Parliament would not meet in Westminster, but in Oxford. The change of venue provoked outrage from exclusionists, but Charles was well within his rights. He had good reason for the change as well. London was a hotbed of Whiggery, and radical Whiggery at that. Oxford, on the other hand, was a royalist Anglican stronghold.

It was now winter, and the wind blowing from Whitehall felt especially cold to supporters of the plot. Keeping the flame of the plot alight as the nation prepared for new elections was imperative. In February, though, a new possibility emerged. Like many of the recent informers with tales of Catholic perfidy, this one came from Ireland. Edward Fitzharris, the second son of an Irish baronet, had served briefly in the French army but had returned to England in 1672. Granted a commission in the duke of Albemarle's infantry regiment, the Test Act of 1673 cut short his career. As a Catholic he had no choice but to resign. Fitzharris drifted around London afterwards, earning a precarious living on handouts until the opportunity to profit by informing arose.[90]

He was not particular about who he informed against, provided there was money in it. Fitzharris had connections at court – a relation served the duchess of Portsmouth – and evidently he played a role in a shadowy attempt by the king to buy the support of a prominent (but very poor) Whig peer, Lord Howard of Escrick. His court connections seem to have inclined him to offer his services to supporters of the duke of York, and he hatched a plan he hoped would substantially elevate his standard of living. In a variant of the Meal Tub Plot – he wrote a seditious pamphlet, *The True Englishman Speaking Plain English in a Letter from a Friend to a Friend.* Of course, Fitzharris was no Englishman, but that did not matter, as he intended to plant the document on a prominent Whig. Friends at court would reward him for undermining someone in the enemy camp. He joined forces with Edmund Everard, a shady informer who worked both sides of the plot – giving evidence before Shaftesbury's Plot committee, but also receiving occasional payments from the king's secret-service fund.[91] Everard arranged for Fitzharris to appear before a magistrate; he would then incriminate his target, triggering a search. The seditious pamphlet would come to light, and Fitzharris would be launched upon his lucrative career as an informer. But then his plan went awry. When Edward came before the magistrate, Everard turned on his erstwhile friend and revealed the plan. Fitzharris ended up in Newgate, charged with treason.

Word that someone with court connections had hatched another 'sham plot' was ambrosia for London's Whigs. Fitzharris soon received distinguished visitors in the shape of Sheriffs Cornish and Bethel. They convinced Edward of the wisdom of changing sides, and he cooked up a new story, entirely satisfactory from the Whig point of view. Fitzharris claimed that in 1672 both the duke of York and the queen had connived in a plot to overthrow Charles and impose Catholicism in England. Perhaps for variety's sake, he added a few new names to the roster of plotters: the marquis Monteculi, ambassador of the duke of Modena (the duchess of York's brother), and Hortense Mancini, the duchess of Mazarin. Hortense had once been a royal mistress, but the couple had fallen out due to her incorrigible promiscuity (with both sexes). Fitzharris added expertise in poisoning to her sexual talents.[92] Adding Mazarin to the mix supplied the spice of foreignness – Italians were notoriously prone to poison – as well as the tang of sex. Edward also claimed to know the details of Sir Edmund Berry Godfrey's death, 'and the same was done much in the manner as Prance had related it'.[93]

Soon, however, the Court got wind of the Fitzharris threat. Using Edward's phony pamphlet as a pretext, on 26 February 1681 the king ordered his transfer to the Tower for 'several dangerous and treasonable words'.[94] Charles intended to keep Fitzharris on ice – sequestered from Whig blandishments. Edward's dreams of the wealth and easy life of an informer now became a nightmare, and the young Irishman himself would soon be a political bone snarled over by Whigs and Tories.

While Edward Fitzharris contemplated the costs of freelance conspiracy, the kingdom conducted parliamentary elections. A torrent of propaganda poured from presses up and down the nation. Whigs maintained that Parliaments, liberty and Protestantism depended on their triumph; Tories countered that 'fanatics' (nonconformist dissenters) threatened a resumption of civil war. The king cleaned House during this period, dismissing several councillors he considered soft on exclusion: Lords Sunderland, Salisbury, Essex and Sir William Temple. He rejected a petition from sixteen peers asking for Parliament to be held in Westminster rather than Oxford.[95] Charles had another high card up his sleeve: his cousin Louis XIV secretly promised a subsidy of almost £400,000 over three years. The king knew that he would not need parliamentary taxation as long as England remained at peace. With this knowledge he could face a new assembly with confidence.[96]

Across the country elections to the Commons were much the same as they had been for the last Parliament. There remained a clear majority for exclusion in the lower House, though its prospects among the peers were no rosier than they had been the previous December. Charles arrived in Oxford a week before the session opened to great fanfare – a welcome change from Whig-dominated London. Joyful royalists filled the streets and every window along Charles's route, shouting 'Let the King live, and the devil hang up all Roundheads!'[97] Not long after this triumphant reception, Shaftesbury and many of his fellow Whigs staged their own public entry into Oxford. They rolled into town in coaches escorted by dozens of armed horsemen, as though they expected an ambush – perhaps they did. Tensions were at such a pitch that violence seemed near at hand. The grandeur of Shaftesbury's entrance was somewhat tarnished by the presence of Titus Oates, Stephen College, Thomas Dangerfield and a motley crew of informers, all there to lend their own special dignity to the proceedings.

On Monday 21 March peers and commoners piled into the dining hall at Christ Church college – the largest public space in town. There, in his crown and robes, seated under a portrait of another determined English monarch, Henry VIII, Charles II addressed his Parliament. He began by scolding the last Parliament (many of whose members stood before him now, re-elected). He spoke of the Commons 'strange unsuitable returns' to his offers of compromise, and said that many 'perhaps may wonder more that I had patience so long, than that at last I grew weary of their proceedings.' He said he wanted to forget the past, and hoped that 'I might not have any new occasions given me to remember more of the late miscarriages'.[98] Calling another Parliament so soon after the shipwreck of the last, he said, offered proof of his continued faith in the institution, and he once again offered to consider any proposals to secure Protestantism. But he would not move on the big question: 'What I have formerly and so often declared touching the succession, I cannot depart from.'[99] There would be no exclusion, ever.

MPs took two days to swear their oaths of supremacy and allegiance, and the House considered no fewer than twenty-six cases of disputed elections. Having so many petitions forcefully demonstrated the depth of England's divisions – long gone were the days of genteel, uncontested elections. These formalities behind them, MPs demonstrated the impact of Charles's speech. Members simply ignored the king. First, over the objections of Secretary Jenkins, the House voted to publish their votes – a clear example of the rising importance of the political press. Members wanted the ability to make their case publicly and this was a powerful way to do so. Having provided themselves with a public megaphone, the next order of business was all too predictable. Sir Nicholas Carew, the member for the Surrey borough of Gatton, stood up and said, 'I move, that for the preservation of the Protestant religion, and the king's person, a bill be brought in to prevent a Popish successor.' So much for forgetting 'late miscarriages'. Brushing aside Secretary Jenkins's protests, the House passed the resolution without a division.[100]

The Lords created a new Plot committee, manned by the usual suspects – leading Whigs along with a sprinkling of councillors for window dressing. The peers heard a plea for bail from the earl of Danby, immured in the Tower now for almost two years, and a petition from Scroggs for a speedy trial. Neither man got his wish. On Friday 25 March the Commons attempted to snatch the bone that was Fitzharris out of the court's jaws. It accused Edward of high treason and ordered Secretary Jenkins to carry the impeachment to the Lords. This Jenkins refused to do; as the king's Secretary of State he saw his appointment as a messenger as a calculated insult to the king. Whigs reacted furiously; Jenkins was, they claimed, offering a calculated insult to the House of Commons. In the end, after a good deal of Whiggish huffing and puffing, Jenkins withdrew his remarks and the hotheads agreed to spare the Secretary the humiliation of begging the House's pardon on his knees.[101]

The ploy failed, however. When on Saturday Jenkins presented Fitzharris's impeachment to the Lords, the Attorney General rose and announced that Edward had already been indicted in the common law courts and the king had ordered his prosecution there. This led to a long debate ending with a vote to allow the common law trial to proceed. The bone would stay in the Tower. Twenty Whig peers including Shaftesbury entered a formal protest against the decision.[102] The Commons petulantly resolved that the peers' rejection of their charge was a 'denial of justice' and threatened the common law courts with prosecution for 'a high breach of the privilege of Parliament'.[103] The same day MPs resolved to proceed with a new exclusion bill.

But the bill was not to be. On Monday 28 March the king arrived unexpectedly at Christ Church. He had smuggled his crown and robes into his sedan chair, and he put them on just after his arrival. The usher of the Black Rod commanded the Commons attendance, and Charles gave his shortest parliamentary speech, 'My lords and gentlemen, that all the world may see to what a point we are come, that we are not like to have a good end, when the divisions at the beginning are such: therefore, my Lord Chancellor, do as I have commanded you.' With this, Chancellor Finch rose and announced, 'It is His Majesty's royal pleasure and will, that this Parliament be dissolved.'[104]

When the disconsolate Parliamentarians scattered from Oxford the end of the Popish Plot was in sight. It had for several months already been a marker of partisanship. Its most fervent believers invariably supported exclusion and the Whigs. Royalists – or Tories as they now were called – mostly rejected the entire story as a fiction aimed at undermining the monarchy. King Charles, who had publicly encouraged the pursuit of plotters, now openly spoke of his disbelief. In April, Charles had a conversation in his bedchamber with Sir John Reresby: 'His discourse was generally of the impossibility of such a thing as the Popish Plot, and the contradictions of which it was framed.'[105] When Oates visited Whitehall in late March, he had a bodyguard bristling with blunderbusses and other arms – clearly he did not think himself safe so close to the Court.[106]

The king was implacable on the subject of Edward Fitzharris, though as with much else relating to the plot his course would be tortuous. On 28 April the Crown sought an indictment for treason against Edward from the Middlesex Grand Jury. The jurors balked – wondering aloud if they could act given the impeachment that the Commons had voted in March. It might not have been a coincidence that these objections arose from a jury whose foreman was Michael Godfrey, brother of the late lamented Justice Godfrey (and probable concealer of his suicide). The judges in the court of King's Bench insisted that the jury had no cause for concern and directed that they consider the indictment, which in the end the jury returned.[107]

When on Saturday 30 April, Fitzharris appeared before the King's Bench, he found a new Chief Justice presiding – Sir Francis Pemberton. The king had dismissed Scroggs, perhaps because as a prominent target of the Whigs he had become a distraction. Charles did not humiliate the judge, at any rate, granting him a handsome £1,500 pension, giving his son a knighthood and promoting his son-in-law to a judgeship.[108] But Pemberton would preside over the last two major plot trials, those of Fitzharris and Oliver Plunket.

Fitzharris had an impressive group of Whig lawyers by his side when the proceedings began. They included Sir William Jones, still famous for his prosecution of Lord Stafford, and several others who had been involved in plot prosecutions, including a former speaker of the Commons, an ex-Attorney General and the Recorder of London. These attorneys first did what they could to delay the trial, claiming they needed more time to prepare their case.[109] The Attorney General opposed this, and the court agreed, saying that the defence had already had three days to draft their plea.[110] Fitzharris's lawyers and the prosecution wrangled for hours on two separate days in early May over the court's jurisdiction. The defence claimed that a parliamentary impeachment trumped a case in King's Bench, although the prosecution argued that the Lords' rejection of the Commons impeachment meant there was in fact no impeachment at all. The judges also squashed Fitzharris's effort to divert attention to new 'revelations' in the Godfrey case. Edward asked for Lords Essex, Salisbury, the Lord Mayor and Sir Robert Clayton, to whom he would reveal all. Justice Pemberton sharply replied that he had already examined him about the Godfrey case, 'We asked you ten times, whether you had any more to say, and you said no!' Fitzharris responded feebly, 'My lord, I was in confusion and consternation; I scarce knew what your lordship said to me.'[111] In the end, the court ruled that it could try the case. A last desperate effort by Fitzharris succeeded, at least temporarily: he asked for time to bring a witness over from Holland. The trial was put off until 9 June.

The Fitzharris trial began with a struggle over the role of Anne, the accused's wife, in the trial. Mrs Fitzharris had loyally supported her husband throughout his legal ordeal – advising him and acting as a messenger and intermediary with lawyers and supporters. She now asked the court's permission to stand beside Edward in the dock. The prosecution objected that she would be acting as counsel for the defence – a privilege not granted to those charged with treason. Anne made a spirited reply, insisting 'I will not be removed.' The court overruled the prosecution and allowed her to stay on condition that she remain 'modest and civil'.[112]

Assembling a jury proved to be a struggle. London's sheriffs subpoenaed prospective jurors, and the prosecutors suspected that those called were chosen for their Whig sympathies. The Attorney General told the judge that the pool included three dissenting ministers 'and I know not how many fanatics'.[113] The fact that one of those in the pool was John Wildman, a Whig whose radicalism shaded into republicanism, was telling. Unusually, the Crown challenged five potential jurors, the defendant only one.[114]

The prosecution's case revolved around Fitzharris's sham pamphlet. The Crown took Edward's intended trap for a prominent Whig, *The True Englishman Speaking Plain English,* at face value. It was meant to spark a rebellion and end with the murder of both the king and his brother. The prosecution's first witness was Edmund Everard. Edmund said he had known Fitzharris in Paris, and that they reconnected recently in London. Everard swore that Fitzharris had approached him and asked his help in drawing up his libel. Edward supposedly told his friend that he worked in the French interest, aiming to destabilize a heretic nation. As a patriotic Protestant Englishman (or at least a facsimile thereof), Everard decided he would lay a snare for a false traitor. He arranged a later meeting with Edward and had a witness, a Mr Smith, concealed in his room to overhear their conversation.[115] After a second meeting, this time with none other than Sir William Waller, former terror of London Catholics, listening at the keyhole, Everard sprang his trap. Soon Fitzharris was in Newgate. This elaborate fiction prompted an outburst from Anne Fitzharris, 'I am sorry [Edward] kept such a rogue as you are company!' Only Edward's desperate promise that Anne would speak no more prevented her being thrown out of the court.[116] Smith followed Everard on the stand and confirmed his account, and then Waller testified to what he had heard in the second meeting. He must have known that he was doing a service to the court, an unfamiliar role for him. But perhaps he hoped to regain his lost magistracy or some other mark of royal favour. In any event, he followed Everard's script perfectly. Of course he knew the practice of perjury of old and he lied convincingly enough.

Fitzharris's witnesses contradicted the prosecution's testimony. The first was Titus Oates. He was in a doubly novel position: as a defence witness and a truthful one, at least in part. He told of an encounter with Everard at the Oxford Parliament. Edmund told him that Fitzharris's libel was part of a plan to ensnare leading Whigs. Titus added that Everard told him that the Court was behind the conspiracy.[117] Several other prominent Whigs followed Oates, attempting to undermine Everard's credibility.[118] When the final witness finished, 'Doctor' Oates appealed to the court for permission to leave – '. . . the crowd is so great I cannot stand'. This gave the Attorney General an opening for a joke at Titus's expense: 'My lord, that may be part of the Popish Plot, to keep Mr. Oates here, to kill him in the crowd.'[119] Titus had clearly fallen far to be treated so sarcastically in public by officers of state. Fitzharris called other witnesses to prove that he had been working for the Court, but they were not very helpful.

He then appealed to the jury, 'I hope, gentlemen of the jury, you will consider these are great persons that I have to do with, and where great state matters are at the bottom, it is hard to make them tell anything but what is for their advantage. And so I am left in a sad condition.'[120] Truer words were never spoken, though they did Edward Fitzharris precious little good. After half an hour's deliberation the jury returned and delivered a guilty verdict.

Edward, unique among the victims of the plot, had played both sides and managed to lose all around. His initial sham plot ended in his arrest by Everard and Waller, and his attempts to wriggle out of that predicament by turning on the Court led him into even further danger. From Reresby's account, Edward's fate was sealed by the king himself. Charles was not by nature a persecutor. But by the spring of 1681 he had come to the conclusion that in order to see off the challenge presented by his enemies there could be no compromise. Edward Fitzharris in any event was no innocent victim: he had tempted his own fate, and the king would lose no sleep over his demise.

The king, on the other hand, might have been troubled at the fate of Oliver Plunket, who had been tried in the same court the previous day. The Crown had attempted to try the titular primate of Ireland the previous winter, seeking an indictment from the Middlesex Grand Jury. But the company of 'McShams', whose testimony formed the basis of the charges, performed so poorly that the jurors refused to indict. Now, however, after months of Lord Shaftesbury's patronage, new wardrobes and English roast beef, these witnesses were ready for a repeat performance.[121]

The prosecution accused the archbishop of raising money to field an army of 60,000 Catholics whose mission was to massacre Ireland's Protestants. A charge of this sort carried deep resonance with English Protestants, who still vividly remembered the Irish rebellion of 1641. The English took the bloodthirstiness of Irish Catholics as a given – even though in the person of the mild-mannered Plunket that savagery hardly seemed evident. As Archbishop of Armagh, in fact, Oliver had been conspicuous in his cooperation with the government and had earned the respect of the viceroy, the duke of Ormond and his predecessor, the earl of Essex.[122] But that was then. Now, Plunket stood before the court of King's Bench, packed with the usual jostling crowd of spectators, liberally sprinkled with disreputable perjurers imported from Ireland. Sir Francis Pemberton, who needed little urging to display his anti-Catholic prejudices, presided.

The prosecution's witnesses told of a conspiracy dating back to the mid-1660s, even before the Pope named Oliver archbishop. In addition to the native-born

Catholics who were to make up the majority of the rebel army, the French promised an invasion force. One of the witnesses, a friar named Duffy, threw in the Spanish as well as the French.[123] No one seemed to wonder why France and Spain, perpetual enemies, should combine to invade Ireland. One witness, Father Murphy, seems to have suddenly developed a conscience. Although he had incriminated Plunket in detail before the Grand Jury, now, under oath, he refused to repeat his earlier story. He had not heard anything directly from Plunket himself about the plot, only through the archbishop's officers. Murphy's memory also seemed faulty; now he could not recall what he had said before the Grand Jury. Confronted with this sudden amnesia, Justice Pemberton assumed that the priest had been suborned, 'I see the papists in England have been at work with you.'[124] But apart from this misstep, the prosecution's witnesses had learned their stories well. Plunket protested that the witnesses against him had grudges related to discipline he had imposed upon them as archbishop and that some were convicted criminals. But the court refused to consider these complaints, because Plunket had no written records to demonstrate convictions or discipline. That, Oliver pointed out, was because he had been allowed no time or resources to bring records or witnesses over from Ireland. Plunket denied all of the charges against him, and said he had never been to most of the locations his enemies placed him in. He lived, he said, a very modest life with a single servant in a thatched cottage – the idea of his leading such an elaborate conspiracy was quite absurd.[125]

Plunket could do very little to defend himself beyond flatly denying the charges and raising questions about the witness's credibility. Only one witness, Paul Gormar, appeared for the archbishop. The best he could offer was to say that he never heard that Oliver had plotted anything, and that 'I thought you did more good in Ireland than hurt . . .'[126] Plunket's own defence was pitiable. All he could say was '. . . there is not one word of this said against me is true, but all plain romance. I never had any communication with any French minister, cardinal, nor other'. It took the jury fifteen minutes to render a guilty verdict.

On Wednesday 15 June, Plunket returned to court to receive his sentence. He again proclaimed his innocence and protested the unfair treatment he had endured – the worthlessness of his accusers, his inability to bring over witnesses and the absurdity of the charges themselves.[127] Justice Pemberton took the opportunity to parade his rabid anti-Catholicism before passing sentence. Catholicism was '. . . a false religion, than which there is not any thing more displeasing to God, or more pernicious to mankind in the world'.[128] The tirade over, Oliver pointed out that 'divers people here' (several names come readily to mind) had offered to save him in return for testimony against others. And he defended his faith, responding to Pemberton's crocodile statement, 'I am sorry to see you persist in the principles of that religion.' They are, said the archbishop, 'those principles that even God Almighty cannot dispense withal'.[129]

Justice Pemberton then passed the usual sentence, and Plunket returned to Newgate to await execution. Queen Catherine and the French and Spanish ambassadors asked for clemency to no avail. Even the earl of Essex, one of Shaftesbury's close allies, asked Charles to grant a pardon. He told the king that he knew the archbishop to be innocent – which provoked a furious Charles to respond, 'Then, my lord be his blood on your conscience. You might have saved him if you would. I cannot pardon him, because I dare not.'[130]

Perhaps the greatest indignity Plunket experienced in the end was that he suffered on the same scaffold as Edward Fitzharris. On 1 July horses dragged the two men to Tyburn tied to separate hurdles. Plunket reiterated his innocence in his final speech, and blamed his death upon 'those merciless perjurers, who did aim for my life'.[131] He forgave them, and blessed the king and royal family. Fitzharris made a speech of his own, declaring his innocence and asking that his body not be quartered but given to his wife, his most loyal supporter, after execution.[132] Both men suffered with fortitude. Plunket received his reward some 300 years later, being canonized by the Catholic Church in 1975. His severed head is currently displayed in a fine reliquary in Drogheda, Ireland.[133] It seems unlikely that Fitzharris avoided quartering, and any heavenly reward due to him could only come by virtue of God's grace.

On the day after Jack Ketch practised his art on these two unlikely partners in death, the king arrested Anthony Ashley Cooper, first earl of Shaftesbury, on a treason charge. Shaftesbury joined the five popish lords in the Tower. With its most powerful supporter incarcerated and in danger of his life, the Popish Plot was effectively over.

EPILOGUE

Shaftesbury's imprisonment marked the last act of the plot. With the political spearhead of the plot in jail much of the force behind the plot's narrative evaporated. Furthermore, by avoiding a new Parliament, King Charles denied the opposition a platform. There remained, however, some loose ends.

Sir Miles Stapleton, accused with Sir Thomas Gascoigne in the Yorkshire branch of the plot, stood trial in York on 18 July. Robert Bolron and Lawrence Mowbray testified against him as they had against Gascoigne, and to the same effect – a swift acquittal, despite the valiant efforts of Justice Dolben to extort a guilty verdict out of the jury.[1] London and provincial jails still held a number of Catholic priests, and over the course of the summer several were tried and convicted for being in orders (not as plotters) – but the king reprieved most of them, a sign that he no longer feared a public outcry.[2]

Indeed, the Court had the opposition on the run. Shaftesbury remained in the Tower through the summer and autumn of 1681. Charles ordered that he be held close prisoner throughout this period, although he was allowed visits from his family. The king brusquely denied a request from Oates to visit in order to provide 'spiritual comfort'.[3] The judges refused a petition for bail in October, and Shaftesbury finally appeared before the Middlesex Grand Jury on 24 November. Arrayed against him were some of the same Irish informers he had patronized in the Plunket case; they swore he had planned treason during the Oxford Parliament. Fortunately for the earl, the sheriffs were still Whigs, and they packed the Grand Jury with like-minded men. They threw out the indictment. Whigs everywhere rejoiced; London crowds lit bonfires in celebration and within a few days the earl left the Tower on bail.

Shaftesbury's brush with the law seems to have made no impression. From the spring of 1682 he began planning overt treason. The prospect of Tory control of the city of London pushed him to plan, in league with a number of radical

Whigs like John Wildman, open rebellion and, in the end, the murder of both Charles and James. By November 1682 the authorities were closing in; spies in the radical camp fatally compromised the conspiracy. Shaftesbury fled to Holland and died there only two months later, in January 1683, probably of liver failure. In Shaftesbury's absence plotting continued. The plan involved a number of Whig grandees – Monmouth, Lord Russell, the earl of Essex, Lord Howard of Escrick, Lord Grey of Wark, the earl of Stamford and Algernon Sidney. They planned to ambush and kill Charles and James as they returned from the races at Newmarket on 1 April 1683. Joining them was a motley collection of radical ex-soldiers and malcontents with whom they met secretly in the late winter and spring of 1683. The attack did not come off – the royal brothers returned to London earlier than expected. Before another attempt could be made, one of the conspirators, a nonconformist Londoner named Josiah Keeling, appeared before the Privy Council and betrayed his fellows. Some, like Monmouth and Lord Grey, fled. Authorities captured Russell and Essex; Howard of Escrick turned king's evidence in return for a pardon. Essex cut his own throat with a razor before his trial; a jury convicted Russell in July. Fortunately for him, King Charles allowed Russell the mercy of a swift beheading, something the Whig lord had wanted to deny the unlucky Lord Stafford.[4]

After checkmating the Whigs, Charles II ruled a one-party state. He purged Whigs from office and the Court, and he remodelled local government, calling in borough charters and issuing new, Tory-friendly ones. Booming trade and French largesse filled his treasury, and there was no need for anything so troublesome as a Parliament. Having exerted himself so vigorously to save his brother's right to the Crown, Charles reverted to his former state of charismatic indolence. He went to the races at Newmarket, he pottered among his chemicals, he dallied with his mistresses, he doted on Charles, his youngest illegitimate son, born in 1672, whose mother was the duchess of Portsmouth. But he knew the importance of maintaining a connection with his subjects: he continued the arduous practice of 'touching for the king's evil' until the end of his reign – in the crisis years surrounding the plot, in fact, he touched thousands. One historian estimates that no less than two per cent of the entire population of England passed through the royal hands.[5]

On Monday 2 February 1685, Charles, whose health had been quite robust since his last bout of fever in 1679, suddenly took ill – at this distance in time it is difficult to know for sure what the malady was. A team of over-attentive doctors bled and blistered him with a highly toxic preparation made of crushed beetles. Charles endured this torture for four days. On 5 February the king lay near death, and his brother ushered Father James Huddleston into the bedchamber. Huddleston, Charles's comrade on the flight from Worcester, had the honour of receiving the king into the Catholic Church. He had proven the Whigs right in at least one thing: he was, at heart, a papist. Charles died on 6 February.

James now became king, and for the creators of the Popish Plot nemesis was at hand. James wasted no time prosecuting the principal informers. Stephen Dugdale was already dead; he had expired in 1683, killed by alcohol and venereal disease. Of the surviving main informers, Thomas Dangerfield received judgement first. Arrested in March 1685 he stood trial in May and the court convicted him for libelling King James. The judges fined him £500 and directed that he be flogged and pilloried twice. Unfortunately for him, after his second trip to the pillory he got involved in an argument with a London attorney, Robert Francis. Dangerfield spat at Francis, who struck him in the face with his cane. The blow proved fatal.

Miles Prance stood trial for perjury in June 1686, was convicted and sentenced to a fine of £100, an appearance in the pillory and a public flogging. A timely return to the Catholic Church earned him the support of Queen Catherine, who successfully begged King James to omit the whipping. Three years later, when times once again turned against English Catholics, Prance fled to Europe and vanished.

Titus Oates, the malevolent inventor of the plot, found himself in deep trouble even before Charles's death. Jailed in 1684 he was convicted on a charge of 'scandalum magnatum' (libelling a peer – in this case the duke of York). He was fined a mind-boggling £100,000, a sum that would comfortably support over a thousand families for a year. Not having any such fortune, Oates went to jail until he could pay – effectively a life sentence. But Charles's death resulted in another prosecution, this time for perjury. The result was another conviction, a trip to the pillory – where he got much the same treatment as Elizabeth Cellier – a whipping, and a life sentence.

Oates's situation improved, marginally, after 1688, but his toxic personality ensured that he would never be far from trouble and scandal. Released from prison in December 1688, he attempted to revive his fortunes, petitioning Crown and Parliament for favour. He did manage to get a £40 pension, though he only kept it until 1692. Deprived of this lifeline, he sought refuge in marriage, despite his homosexuality. His wife was Rebecca Weld, daughter of a wealthy London merchant. She brought with her a fortune thought to be £2,000. Oates had spent it all within six months of the wedding. In 1698, Titus changed his religion again, joining a Baptist congregation in London. He proved somewhat popular there, preaching frequently about the horrors of popery. But he found it impossible to avoid alienating those around him. His boorish behaviour by no means mellowed with age. In 1699 he barged into the funeral of a woman against whom he held a grudge, mounted the pulpit and began a sermon that ended the service in chaos. In 1702 he assaulted a woman with his cane after she rebuked him for blasphemous speech. He finally died, regretted by absolutely no one, in July 1705.

Oates did, at least, outlive his great white whale, James Stuart. James began his reign with more power and promise than any member of his dynasty. His brother had subdued the Whigs; royalist Anglicans – Tories – ensured his succession. The first major challenge of his reign came when the duke of Monmouth, in exile since the Rye House plot unravelled, attempted to overthrow his uncle. In the summer of 1685 he landed in the west of England with a small force, expecting to rally support among the gentry and aristocracy. Many did rise in arms to support him, but the overwhelming majority were poorly armed and untrained yokels, many of whom were dissenters. At Sedgemoor in Somerset, James demolished this ragged force with a trained professional army, captured Monmouth and shortly afterwards had him beheaded. Mr Ketch badly botched the execution of his most illustrious victim, taking five frantic swings of the axe to do his work.

The collapse of the rebellion gave James confidence that God favoured his cause – and for him, that meant the One True Church. Over the next three years his policies favouring Catholics gave rise to a growing fear that what the Whigs had predicted might well come true: a forcible return to Rome. That James probably had no such intention made no difference. In October 1687, James's queen, Mary of Modena, announced her pregnancy and the prospect of a Catholic dynasty stretching indefinitely into the future loomed. The pregnancy bolstered his faith in God's grace, and James redoubled his efforts to favour his co-religionists, often in a ham-fisted fashion typical of a man trained in the authoritarian ways of the Royal Navy.

In June 1688 the queen gave birth to a healthy son, James Francis Edward, and the extension of the Catholic dynasty seemed assured. The prince's birth was for many the final provocation, and Tories, who James could not believe would abandon him, did exactly that. By late September, James realized that his Protestant son-in-law was preparing to intervene. William wanted above all to protect his wife Mary's interest in the English Crown, but he also feared that England under James would become a satellite of his mortal enemy, Louis XIV.

Facing imminent attack, James hastily reversed his pro-Catholic policies. But it was too late. William and some 15,000 mostly Dutch troops landed in Devon, wafted there by what the rebels called a 'Protestant wind'. It looked as though the mid-century civil wars were about to resume. In the end, however, they did not. James found himself betrayed and deserted on all sides. Significant parts of his army deserted to William. His daughter Mary had chosen her husband's side in the conflict and a fresh blow fell when Anne, James's second daughter, threw her support to the invader as well. James's spirit broke. He sent the queen and Prince James ahead to France, and followed a few days later. James would live under his cousin Louis's protection for the remainder of his life. He continued to hope for a second restoration, and there were a few moments in the 1690s in which the prospect glimmered before him. But they never materialized, and the exiled court lived on, bitter and increasingly threadbare. In 1697, Louis recognized William III as the lawful king of England, a desperate blow to James's dwindling hopes. He died in September 1701.[6]

At least seventeen Catholics, lay and clergy, died as traitors on the scaffold between November 1678 and July 1681. Others perished in prisons around the country before they came to trial. The lies of Titus Oates and his fellows had thrown the lives of English Catholics into turmoil and seriously damaged the Catholic mission in England. But it recovered, given a considerable boost after James II's accession. Even his overthrow did not provoke a wave of persecution as severe as that of the plot itself. And although England remained fiercely anti-Catholic – legal discrimination against Catholics endured until 1828 – never again would the kingdom be gripped by such a panic.

The Popish Plot's impact on Catholics faded, but its political legacy endured. Had the fantasies of Israel Tonge and the lies of Titus Oates not been so politically useful the plot might have been a much less significant matter. But politicians – initially Lord Treasurer Danby, but then, devastatingly, the earl of Shaftesbury – seized upon it as a means to advance their interests. Danby failed, but Shaftesbury for a time succeeded brilliantly. Ancestral English fears of Catholicism contributed to the widespread acceptance of outlandish stories, and this suspension of disbelief was further enabled by the vigorous growth of a popular press. Ideology as much as the pursuit of profit led to the publication of hundreds – thousands – of broadsides, ballads, pamphlets, poems, satires and books on one side of the debate or the other. Most of them were credulous acceptances of the informer's tales, but eventually they spurred a counter-attack. The plot greatly encouraged the spread of political discourse in England – much of it puerile, but many publications were serious contributions. And while many of them served to stoke political passions, they at least helped to move English political conflict from the battlefield, as in the 1640s, to the bookstalls.

Shaftesbury's success came at a price, of course, to innocent lives. Some have seen the earl as a valiant fighter against the incipient absolutism of the Stuarts. Perhaps, though, he demonstrated more than once a flexible attitude when sufficient power and rewards were dangled in front of him. And he had no compunction whatever in sending innocents to their death. But in the end this ruthlessness had a positive effect. It gave rise to the first political parties, and this was a matter of lasting importance. Whigs and Tories despised and hated one another, and were often willing to use underhanded tactics up to and including judicial murder to gain an advantage. But unlike their fathers and grandfathers, the Roundheads and Cavaliers of the 1640s and 1650s, the time for civil war was past. And the parties provided a way for political disagreements to be negotiated without recourse to violence. For that we might have to thank Titus Oates, William Bedloe, Thomas Dangerfield and the earl of Shaftesbury.

NOTES

LIST OF ABBREVIATIONS

AM	Additional Manuscripts, British Library
CJ	Journals of the House of Commons
CSPD	Calendar of State Papers, Domestic
HMC	Reports of the Historical Manuscripts Commission
HoL	*The History of Parliament: The House of Lords, 1660–1715*, Ruth Paley, ed., 5 vols. (Cambridge, 2016)
HoP	*The History of Parliament: The House of Commons, 1660–1690*, Basil Duke Henning, ed., 3 vols. (London, 1983)
KJV	the Holy Bible, King James Version
LJ	Journals of the House of Lords
ODNB	*Oxford History of National Biography*
TNA	The National Archives, Kew, England

PROLOGUE

1. Bishop Burnet, *History of My Own Time*, O. Airey, ed. (Oxford, 1900), 2:170–72; see also his account a few pages earlier re Carstairs.
2. John Warner, *The History of English Persecution of Catholics and the Presbyterian Plot*, T.A. Birrell, ed., John Bligh, trans., *Publications of the Catholic Record Society*, vol. 48 (London, 1953), p. 220.
3. CSPD March–December 1678, pp. 523, 532–33, 537, 541, 548, 571. The best account of the trial is *The Tryal of William Staley, Goldsmith* (printed by Robert Pawlet, London, 1678). Another account is *The Tryal and Condemnation of Mr. Will. Staley for High Treason* (London, 1678). See also *A True Relation of the Execution of Mr William Staley* (London, 1678); *The Behaviour of Mr William Staley in Newgate After Condemnation* (London, 1678); Samuel Smith, *An Account of the Behaviour of Fourteen Late Popish Malefactors Whilst in Newgate* (London, 1679); and *Survey of London, Vol. 36: The Parish of St. Paul Covent Garden*, F.H.W. Sheppard, gen. ed. (London, 1970); Burnet, *History*, 2:171–72.

CHAPTER 1: POLITICS AND POPERY, 1675 TO SUMMER 1678

1. ODNB, 'Andrew Marvell'; Nigel Smith, *Andrew Marvell: The Chameleon* (New Haven, CT, 2010).
2. CSPD 1677, p. 691.
3. Andrew Marvell, *An Account of the Growth of Popery and Arbitrary Government in England* (London, 1678), p. 1.
4. Ibid, pp. 73–74.

5. Ibid, p. 120.
6. Ibid, p. 155.
7. ODNB, 'Thomas Osborne'.
8. ODNB, 'Roger L'Estrange'; the best full-length biography is G. Kitchin, *Sir Roger L'Estrange* (London, 1913).
9. Gazette no. 1288, p. 2; CSPD March–December 1678, p. 1.
10. CSPD March–December 1678, pp. 313–14.
11. Ibid, pp. 305, 313–14.
12. Ibid, pp. 372–73.
13. Sir Roger L'Estrange, *An Account of the Growth of Knavery* (London, 1681), p. 23.
14. Hester Chapman, *Great Villiers* (London, 1949), p. 148.
15. AM 28053, f. 123, for one of his clandestine Paris trips, taken in September 1678.
16. Guy de la Bédoyère, ed., *The Letters of Samuel Pepys, 1656–1703* (Woodbridge, 2007), p. 29.
17. W.D. Christie, *A Life of Anthony Ashley Cooper, First Earl of Shaftesbury*, 2 vols. (London, 1871), vol. 2, app. 3, p. xliv, quoted in ODNB.
18. Samuel Pepys, *The Diary of Samuel Pepys, Robert Latham and William Matthews*, eds, 11 vols (Berkeley, CA, 1970–83), vol. 4, p. 251.
19. Quoted in K.H.D. Haley, *The First Earl of Shaftesbury* (Oxford, 1968), p. 417.
20. Quoted in ODNB.
21. Haley, *Shaftesbury*, pp. 412–21.
22. TNA, SP 29/401/ff. 231–32, for Shaftesbury's submission; Ibid, f. 261, for the bill.
23. Haley, *Shaftesbury*, pp. 436–37, 443–45.
24. A full account of the penal laws can be found in J.A. Williams, 'English Catholicism Under Charles II: The Legal Position', *Recusant History* 7 (1963), pp. 123–43.
25. A sample of these proclamations may be found in *Tudor Royal Proclamations*, P.L. Hughes and J.F. Larkin, eds., vol. 2, pp. 488, 515; vol. 3, pp. 13, 86; and idem, *Stuart Royal Proclamations*, vol. 1, pp. 245, 329.
26. Pepys, *Diary*, vol. 3, 1662, p. 202.
27. John Evelyn, *Diary* (London, 2006), pp. 516–17.
28. John Miller, *Popery and Politics in England, 1660–1668* (Cambridge, 1973), pp. 9, 11, 12, on London, see pp. 21–23; Philip Jenkins, 'Anti-Popery on the Welsh Marches in the Seventeenth Century', *Historical Journal* 23 (1980), p. 276; John Bossy, *The English Catholic Community, 1570–1850* (Oxford, 1976), ch. 8, 'How many Catholics?', esp. pp. 188–89.
29. Discussion of the Catholic gentry may be found in C.H. Aveling, *The Handle and the Axe: The Catholic Recusants in England from Reformation to Emancipation* (London, 1976), chs. 6 and 8; Bossy, *Catholic Community*, chs. 5 and 7; see also Sally Jordan, 'Gentry Catholicism in the Thames Valley, 1660–1780', *Recusant History* 27 (2004), pp. 217–43; and John Callow, 'The Art of Death and Life in Recusant Lancashire 1600–1754', *Recusant History* 26 (2003), pp. 598–615.
30. See the rolls of convicted and suspected recusants in the London Municipal Archive, MR/R/R/001; 003.
31. Miller, *Popery*, p. 40.
32. See Bossy, *Catholic Community*, for a description of the governance of the mission.
33. For the London mission, see E.L. Taunton, *The History of the Jesuits in England, 1580–1773* (London, 1901), p. 438.
34. For the Jesuits in general, see J.C.H. Aveling, *The Jesuits* (New York, 1981); the figures presented here are drawn from T.M. McCoog, 'The Society of Jesus in England 1623–1678: An Institutional Study' (University of Warwick PhD dissertation, 1984), app. vi, pp. 475–76; for the Benedictines see David Lunn, *The English Benedictines, 1540–1688: From Reformation to Revolution* (London, 1980).
35. Edward Cook, ed., *Memorabilia, or, The most remarkable passages and counsels collected out of the several declaration that have been made by the King, His L. Chancellors and keepers, and the speakers of the honourable House of Commons in Parliament since His Majesty's happy restauration, Anno 1660 till the end of the last Parliament 1680* (London, 1681), p. 34.

36. Bossy, *Catholic Community*, pp. 282–84. For examples of Catholic assertiveness, see below.
37. For Swale see Aveling, *Jesuits*, pp. 190–91; for Worcester, see ODNB, sub 'Edward Somerset, second Marquess'. Worcester claimed to have spent over £900,000 on the Crown's behalf in his lifetime.
38. Robert Bolron, *The Narrative of Robert Bolron* (London, 1680), p. 17.
39. Williams, 'English Catholicism', p. 123.
40. Archdiocese of Westminster Archives, Stafford Papers; fragmentary notes by Stafford of conversations held about securing toleration, probably written in 1681.
41. John Evelyn, *The Diary of John Evelyn*, E.S. de Beer, ed. (London, 2006), p. 372; ODNB, sub 'Sir Samuel Tuke'.
42. *The History and Proceedings of the House of Commons*, vol. 1: 1660–1680 (London, 1742), pp. 132–63.
43. Jordan, 'Gentry Catholicism', p. 221.
44. Bernard Basset, *The English Jesuits: From Campion to Martindale* (New York, 1967), p. 168.
45. Evelyn, *Diary*, p. 582.
46. Jenkins, 'Anti-Popery', p. 278.
47. Robert Bolron, *The Papists Bloody Oath of Secrecy* (London, 1680), p. 17.
48. Folger Library, Newdigate Newsletters, no. 120, 15 December 1674; no. 121, 17 December 1674. For the trial, see the Old Bailey Online, http://www.oldbaileyonline.org/browse. jsp?id=t16741212-1&div=t16741212-1£highlight.
49. Archdiocese of Westminster Archives, Diocesan Mss., vol. 34, p. 395.
50. See Andrew Barclay, 'The Rise of Edward Colman', *Historical Journal* 42 (1999), pp. 109–31.
51. Ibid, p. 126.
52. For one example of the province's management of a bequest, see Archdiocese of Westminster Archives, Diocesan Mss., vol. 34, p. 395.
53. John Trappes-Lomax, 'Letters From School: Francis and Michael Trappes at the English College Douai 1676–77', *Recusant History* 24 (1999), pp. 455–71.
54. Elizabeth cap. 2; for the operation of this process in general, see P.A. Hopkins, 'The Commission for Superstitious Lands in the 1690s', *Recusant History* 15 (1979), pp. 265–82.
55. The details have been described in Thomas McCoog, 'Society of Jesus', pp. 330–33.
56. For the Travers case, see Thomas McCoog, 'Apostasy and Knavery in Restoration England: The Checkered Career of John Travers', *Catholic Historical Review* 78 (1992), pp. 395–403; see also idem, 'Richard Langhorne and the Popish Plot', *Recusant History* 19 (1989), pp. 499–508.
57. T.A. Birrell, 'William Leslie, Henry Howard and Lord Arlington 1666–67', *Recusant History* 19 (1988), pp. 469–83.
58. LJ, 11:478–79.
59. Charles II, *A Proclamation Commanding All Jesuites and Popish Priests to Depart this Kingdom* (London, 1663).
60. Charles II, *A Proclamation for Banishing All Popish Priests and Jesuits, and Putting the Laws in Speedy and Due Execution against Popish Recusants* (London, 1666).
61. McCoog, 'Society of Jesus', p. 148.
62. Examples include: Richard Baxter, *The Certainty of Christianity Without Popery* (London, 1672); William Prynne, *Philanax Protestant, or, Papists Discovered* (London, 1663); Pierre du Moulin, who died in 1658, was reprinted frequently in the 1670s, e.g. *The Monk's Hood Pull'd Off* (London, 1671).
63. See Commons Journal; the bill is mentioned in Newdigate newsletter 240 (19 October 1675); Folger Shakespeare Library, Washington, D.C.
64. Miller, *Popery*, pp. 136, 142.
65. John Gerard, 'The Jesuit Consult of April 24th 1678', *The Month* 102 (1903), pp. 314–15.
66. Anonymous, *An Answer to the Letter From Amsterdam* (n.p., 1678), p. 9.

CHAPTER 2: HAND 'GRANADOES', SUMMER 1678

1. https://www.british-history.ac.uk/london-hearth-tax/london-mddx/1666/st-giles-cripplegate-barbican-south. Accessed 11 February 2019.
2. https://www.british-history.ac.uk/vch/middx/vol8/pp117-135. Accessed 12 February 2019. For Tonge's biography, see ODNB.
3. John Warner, *A Vindication of English Catholics* (1681), pp. 192–93.
4. *The Jesuit's Morals* finally saw the light of day in 1679, by which time Tonge's fame made anything he wrote saleable, if not readable.
5. Israel Tonge, *Journall of the Plott*, reprinted in *Diaries of the Popish Plot*, Douglas Green, ed. (New York, 1977), p. 4.
6. ODNB, 'Titus Oates'; Jane Lane, *Titus Oates* (London, 1949).
7. See ODNB, 'Thomas Pride'.
8. W.G. Moss, *The History and Antiquities of the Town and Port of Hastings* (London, 1824), p. 108.
9. Warner, *Vindication*, p. 192.
10. See ODNB, 'Matthew Medbourne'; Henry Howard, 6th duke of Norfolk.
11. Lane, *Titus Oates*, p. 45.
12. Bishop Burnet, *History of My Own Time*, O. Airey, ed. (Oxford, 1900), 2:425.
13. Ibid.
14. Warner, *Vindication*, p. 193.
15. ODNB, 'William Bedloe'.
16. Quoted in Lane, *Titus Oates*, p. 58.
17. Warner, *Vindication*, p. 46.
18. Roger L'Estrange, *The Shammer Shamm'd* (London, 1681), p. 40.
19. Tonge, *Journall*, p. 12.
20. Ibid, p. 7
21. TNA, SP 29/409/143, 19 July 1678.
22. Tonge, *Journall*, p. 11; for Petre see HoL 4:124–29.
23. Burnet, *History*, 2:158.
24. Tonge, *Journall*, pp. 11–13; Burnet, *History*, 2:158.
25. Roger L'Estrange, *Brief History of the Times* (London, 1687), part 2, pp. 15–16.
26. Ibid, p. 18.
27. Warner, *Vindication*, pp. 196–97.
28. For James's own account of these events, see James Clarke, *Life of James II* (London, 1816), vol. 1, pp. 516–18.
29. Tonge, *Journal*, p. 34.
30. Ibid, p. 35.
31. Ibid, pp. 42–43.
32. CSPD March–December 1678, p. 418.
33. Tonge, *Journall*, p. 48.
34. AM 38015, f. 278.
35. Titus Oates, *A True and Exact Narrative of the Horrid Plot and Conspiracy of the Popish Party* (London, 1679).
36. Much later Sir Roger L'Estrange called attention to all of these details in *Brief History of the Times*, part 2, pp. 4–13.
37. Tonge, *Journall*, pp. 48–49.

CHAPTER 3: GODFREY DAYS, SEPTEMBER–OCTOBER 1678

1. Quoted in Alan Marshall, *The Strange Death of Edmund Berry Godfrey* (Stroud, 1999), p. 76.
2. CSPD March–December 1678, p. 448. The Powder Plot was the infamous 1605 attempt by disgruntled Catholics to blow up James I and Parliament.

3. CSPD, p. 451.
4. Bishop Burnet, *History of My Own Time*, O. Airey, ed. (Oxford, 1900), 2:163.
5. Ibid.
6. Quoted in Marshall, *Strange Death*, p. 96.
7. Burnet, *History*, 2:164; Marshall, *Strange Death*, p. 97.
8. Marshall, *Strange Death*, pp. 100–13; Burnet, *History*, 2:164–65; *A True and Perfect Narrative of the Late Terrible and Bloody Murther of Sir Edmundberry Godfrey* (London, 1678).
9. CSPD March–December 1678, p. 467.
10. James Clarke, *Life of James II* (London, 1816), vol. 1, p. 546.
11. LJ, 13:293.
12. Ibid, 294.
13. CJ, 6:517–18.
14. LJ, 13:297.
15. Sir John Dalrymple, *Memoirs of Great Britain and Ireland* (Dublin, 1773), p. 47.
16. Sir John Pollock, *The Popish Plot: A Study in the History of the Reign of Charles II* (Cambridge, 1944), pp. 103–04.
17. William Lloyd, *Funeral Sermon* (London, 1678), pp. 1–2, 3, 19, 20–21, 24–25, 29–30, 34.

CHAPTER 4: THE INVESTIGATION, AUTUMN 1678

1. LJ, 13:298.
2. Sir Roger L'Estrange, *L'Estrange's Case* (London, 1680), p. 2.
3. CJ, 9:518.
4. Ibid, 9:519.
5. Ibid, 9:520.
6. Ibid, 9:518–21.
7. ODNB, 'Richard Langhorne'.
8. LJ, 13:301–02.
9. Roger L'Estrange, *Brief History of the Times* (London, 1687), part 3, p. 3.
10. Gilbert Dolan, 'Chapters in the History of the English Benedictine Missions', *Downside Review* 17 (1907), pp. 144–48.
11. ODNB, sub 'John Huddlestone'.
12. ODNB, sub 'Richard Langhorne'.
13. Thomas Jordan, *The Triumphs of London, Performed on Tuesday October XXIX 1678* (London, 1678), pp. 1–2.
14. Ibid, p. 3.
15. Ibid, p. 14.
16. Ibid, p. 20.
17. LJ, 13:309–10.
18. W.D. Christie, *A Life of Anthony Ashley Cooper, First Earl of Shaftesbury*, 2 vols. (London, 1871), p. 279; James II, *Memoirs*, part 1, p. 505.
19. LJ, 13:307.
20. Ibid.
21. LJ, 13:313–30.
22. See Thomas McCoog, 'Richard Langhorne and the Popish Plot', *Recusant History* 19 (1989), pp. 499–508.
23. LJ, 13:315.
24. Ibid, 313–30.
25. Ibid, 311.
26. Ibid, 332.
27. CJ, 6:530.
28. CSPD March–December 1678, p. 503.
29. K.H.D. Haley, *The First Earl of Shaftesbury* (Oxford, 1968), p. 472.

30. Anchitell Grey, *Greys Debates of the House of Commons, 1667–1694*, 10 vols. (London, 1769), 6:138.
31. Ibid, 147.
32. Ibid, 142.
33. Ibid, 148.
34. Ibid, 146.
35. Ibid, 140.
36. Thomas Lamplugh, *A Sermon Preached Before the House of Lords on the fifth of November* (London, 1678), p. 31.
37. John Tillotson, *A Sermon Preached November Fifth 1678 at St. Margaret's Westminster* (London, 1678), p. 28.
38. Ibid, pp. 24–25.
39. Ibid, pp. 43–44.
40. Walter Thornbury, 'St. Sepulchre's and its Neighbourhood', in *Old and New London: Volume 2* (London, 1878), pp. 477–91 (courtesy of British History Online).
41. Aaron Baker, *Achitophel Befool'd* (London, 1678), p. 2.
42. Ibid, p. 7.
43. Ibid, p. 12.
44. Ibid, p. 15.
45. Ibid.
46. Grey, *Debates*, 6:151.
47. Ibid.
48. CSPD March–December 1678, p. 495.
49. Ibid, pp. 503, 507.
50. ODNB, 'William Bedloe'; John Warner, *Persecution* (London, 1953), p. 215.
51. L'Estrange, *Brief History*, part 3, pp. 5–7.
52. Bishop Burnet, *History of My Own Time*, O. Airey, ed. (Oxford, 1900), 2:160.
53. L'Estrange, *Brief History*, part 3, p. 3.
54. LJ, 13:345.
55. Grey, *Debates*, 6:172.
56. Ibid, 173, the oaths of Supremacy and Allegiance, written to be impossible for a conscientious Catholic to take.
57. LJ, 13:349.
58. Ibid, 13: 350.
59. Ibid.
60. Ibid.
61. Ibid.

CHAPTER 5: KNAVISH TRICKS: ATTACKING QUEEN CATHERINE, THE TEST ACT, AND THE FALL OF LORD DANBY, NOVEMBER–DECEMBER 1678

1. CSPD March–December 1678, p. 519.
2. Ibid.
3. Anchitell Grey, *Greys Debates of the House of Commons, 1667–1694*, 10 vols. (London, 1769), 6:193.
4. Ibid, 199.
5. Ibid.
6. K.H.D. Haley, *The First Earl of Shaftesbury* (Oxford, 1968), pp. 199, 276–80.
7. HoL, 4:458–59.
8. Grey, *Debates*, 6:211.
9. Ibid, 212.
10. ODNB, 'Joseph Williamson'.

11. Grey, *Debates*, 6:216.
12. Ibid, 218.
13. Ibid, 218–19.
14. Ibid, 228.
15. Bishop Burnet, *History of My Own Time*, O. Airey, ed. (Oxford, 1900), 2:168.
16. Grey, *Debates*, 6:241–44.
17. Ibid, 244.
18. Ibid, 247–50.
19. See Mark Kishlansky, *Parliamentary Selection* (Cambridge, 1985).
20. Grey, *Debates*, 6:254.
21. CJ, 9:543.
22. Add Ms 61903, p. 77.
23. John Evelyn, *The Diary of John Evelyn*, E.S. de Beer, ed. (London, 2006), p. 591.
24. Grey, *Debates*, 6:287, note.
25. Burnet, *History*, 2:173.
26. ODNB, 'Catherine of Braganza'.
27. CSPD March–December, p. 539.
28. Grey, *Debates*, 287.
29. Ibid, 288.
30. Ibid.
31. Ibid, 289.
32. Ibid, 290.
33. Ibid.
34. Ibid, 291.
35. Ibid, 292.
36. Ibid, 293.
37. Ibid, 296–97.
38. Ibid.
39. Grey, *Debates*, 6:298.
40. LJ, 13:386–87; Peterborough quoted in HoL, 4:167.
41. LJ, 13:388.
42. Ibid, 389.
43. Ibid.
44. Ibid, 391.
45. Ibid.
46. Burnet, *History*, 2:165.
47. LJ, 13:392.
48. Ibid, 393; see also HoL, 3:383.
49. LJ, 13:393 [pronouns changed].
50. Ibid.
51. Ibid, 394.
52. Burnet, *History*, 2:171.
53. Quoted in Haley, *Shaftesbury*, p. 487.
54. CSPD March–December 1678, pp. 562–64.
55. J.H. Jesse, *Memoirs of the Court of England* (London, 1855), 3:170.
56. Quoted in Henry Sidney, *Diary of the Times of Charles the Second*, R.W. Blencoe, ed. (London, 1843), 1:67, f. 1.
57. HoP, 1:340.
58. ODNB; some sources say the money was to be an annual pension of £4,000.
59. Grey, *Debates*, 6:337–38.
60. Ibid, 345.
61. Ibid.
62. Ibid, 346.
63. Ibid, 346–47.

64. Ibid, 347.
65. Ibid, 348.
66. Ibid.
67. Ibid.
68. Ibid, 349.
69. Ibid, 349–50.
70. Ibid, 350.
71. Ibid.
72. Ibid, 350–51.
73. Ibid, 352–53.
74. Ibid, 354.
75. Ibid, 355.
76. CJ, 9:560.
77. Ibid.
78. HoP, 3:746.
79. Grey, *Debates*, 6:370.
80. Ibid.
81. CJ, 9:561–62.
82. KJV, Galatians 4:18.
83. Thomas Sprat, *A Sermon Preached Before the King at Whitehall December the 22 1678* (London, 1678), p. 2.
84. Ibid, p. 16.
85. Ibid, pp. 25–26.
86. Ibid, p. 27.
87. Ibid, pp. 27–28.
88. Ibid, p. 46.
89. HMC Beaufort, p. 80.
90. LJ, 13:434, 441.
91. Burnet, *History*, 2:171.
92. Ibid, 173.
93. Ibid, 174.
94. ODNB, 'Miles Prance'.
95. Roger L'Estrange, *Brief History of the Times* (London, 1687), part 3, p. 26.
96. Ibid, 3:14; also quoted in Haley, *Shaftesbury*, p. 492.
97. L'Estrange, *Brief History*, part 3, p. 27.
98. HMC Beaufort, p. 80.
99. CSPD March–December 1678, pp. 586–87.
100. L'Estrange, *Brief History*, part 3, p. 74.
101. LJ, 13:437–38.
102. CSPD March–December 1678, p. 592.
103. Ibid, pp. 592–93.
104. LJ, 13:447.
105. L'Estrange, *Brief History*, part 3, pp. 66–67.
106. CSPD January 1679–August 1680, p. 15.
107. L'Estrange, *Brief History*, part 3, pp. 69–70.

CHAPTER 6: THE FIRST TRIALS, NOVEMBER 1678–JANUARY 1679

1. See HoP, sub 'Wilde, Jones' (quoting Roger North).
2. William Cobbett, *Cobbett's Complete Collection of State Trials*, Thomas Howell, ed., 21 vols. (London, 1809–16), 7:1.
3. Ibid, cols. 3–5.
4. Ibid, col. 5.
5. Ibid, cols. 6–7.

6. Ibid, col. 7.
7. Ibid, col. 8.
8. Burnet quoted in ODNB, 'Sir William Jones'.
9. Cobbett, *State Trials*, 7, col. 9.
10. Ibid, col. 10.
11. Ibid, col. 13.
12. Andrew Barclay, 'The Rise of Edward Colman', *Historical Journal* 42 (1999), pp. 109–31.
13. Cobbett, *State Trials*, 7, col. 14.
14. Ibid.
15. Ibid, col. 15.
16. Ibid, cols. 15–16.
17. Ibid, cols. 16–17; information on Strange, ODNB, on Mico, www.00cities.org/micogenealogy/edward.html.
18. Cobbett, *State Trials*, 7, col. 19.
19. Ibid.
20. Ibid, col. 20.
21. Ibid, col. 22.
22. Ibid, col. 23.
23. Ibid, col. 25.
24. Ibid.
25. Ibid.
26. Ibid, col. 26.
27. Ibid.
28. Ibid, col. 27.
29. Ibid.
30. Ibid.
31. Ibid, cols. 27–28.
32. Ibid, col. 28.
33. Ibid.
34. Ibid.
35. AM 38015, f. 279.
36. See ODNB, 'Sir Robert Southwell'.
37. Cobbett, *State Trials*, 7, col. 29.
38. Ibid.
39. Ibid, col. 30.
40. Ibid.
41. Ibid, col. 32.
42. Ibid.
43. Ibid, col. 35.
44. Ibid, col. 37.
45. Ibid, col. 45.
46. Ibid, col. 46.
47. John Miller, *James II: A Study in Kingship* (Hove, 1978), pp. 88–89.
48. Cobbett, *State Trials*, 7, col. 55.
49. Ibid.
50. Ibid, col. 56.
51. Ibid, col. 58.
52. Ibid.
53. Ibid, col. 59.
54. Ibid.
55. Ibid.
56. Ibid, col. 60.
57. Ibid, col. 61.

58. Ibid.
59. Ibid, col. 64.
60. Ibid, col. 65.
61. Ibid, col. 70.
62. Ibid.
63. Ibid.
64. Ibid.
65. Ibid, col. 73.
66. Ibid, col. 74.
67. Ibid, col. 75.
68. Ibid, col. 76.
69. Ibid, col. 78.
70. ODNB, 'Edward Colman'.
71. Cobbett, *State Trials*, 7, 82–83.
72. Ibid, col. 93.
73. Ibid, col. 95.
74. Ibid col. 96.
75. Ibid, col. 100.
76. Ibid.
77. Ibid.
78. Ibid, cols. 102–03.
79. Ibid, col. 105.
80. Ibid, col. 106.
81. Ibid.
82. Ibid.
83. Ibid.
84. Ibid, col. 110.
85. Ibid, col. 111.
86. Ibid, col. 113.
87. Ibid, col. 114.
88. Ibid.
89. Ibid, cols. 118–19.
90. Ibid, col. 119.
91. Ibid, col. 120.
92. Ibid, col. 121.
93. Ibid, col. 123.
94. Ibid, col. 128.
95. Ibid.
96. See HoP, sub 'Denny Ashburnham'.
97. Cobbett, *State Trials*, 7, col. 129.
98. Ibid, col. 131.
99. Ibid, col. 133.
100. Ibid, cols. 133–34.
101. Ibid, col. 134.
102. Ibid, col. 136.
103. HoP, 3:339–40.
104. Cobbett, *State Trials*, 7, col. 138.
105. Ibid, col. 141.
106. Folger Library, Newdigate Newsletters, no. 737.
107. John Warner, *The History of English Persecution of Catholics and the Presbyterian Plot*, T.A. Birrell, ed., John Bligh, trans., *Publications of the Catholic Record Society*, vol. 48 (London, 1953), pp. 238–39.
108. Cobbett, *State Trials*, 7, cols. 142–43.
109. Ibid, cols. 143–44.

CHAPTER 7: CONFOUNDING POLITICS, WINTER AND SPRING 1679

1. Bodleian Library, Carte Ms 39, f. 13.
2. Folger Library, Newdigate Newsletters, no. 746.
3. William Cobbett, *Cobbett's Complete Collection of State Trials*, Thomas Howell, ed., 21 vols. (London, 1809–16), 7, col. 161.
4. Ibid, col. 167–68.
5. John Warner, *The History of English Persecution of Catholics and the Presbyterian Plot*, T.A. Birrell, ed., John Bligh, trans., *Publications of the Catholic Record Society*, vol. 48 (London, 1953), p. 240.
6. Cobbett, *State Trials*, 7, col. 192.
7. Ibid, col. 197–99.
8. Ibid, col. 204.
9. Ibid, col. 207.
10. Ibid.
11. Ibid, col. 209.
12. Ibid, col. 210.
13. Ibid, col. 218.
14. Ibid, cols. 222, 225.
15. Ibid, cols. 226–27.
16. Ibid, col. 227.
17. Ibid, col. 230.
18. See HoL, 3:374; K.H.D. Haley, *The First Earl of Shaftesbury* (Oxford, 1968), pp. 496–97; Andrew Browning, *Thomas Osborne, Earl of Danby and Duke of Leeds, 1632–1712*, 3 vols. (Glasgow, 1944–51), 1:312.
19. Ibid, 237.
20. Cobbett, *State Trials*, 7, col. 238–40.
21. Ibid, col. 241.
22. Ibid, col. 242.
23. Ibid, col. 245.
24. Ibid, cols. 245–46.
25. Ibid, col. 247.
26. Ibid, col. 248.
27. Ibid, col. 250.
28. HoP, 1:106.
29. Sir John Reresby, *Memoirs of Sir John Reresby*, Andrew Browning, ed. (Glasgow, 1936), p. 169.
30. John Miller, *James II: A Study in Kingship* (Hove, Sussex: 1978), p. 91.
31. James Clarke, *Life of James II* (London, 1816), vol. 1, pp. 541–42.
32. LJ, 13:449–50.
33. HoL, 1:195.
34. HoP, 'William Gleason'.
35. Reresby, *Memoirs*, p. 174.
36. LJ, 13:471.
37. Anchitell Grey, *Greys Debates of the House of Commons, 1667–1694*, 10 vols. (London, 1769), 7:9–10.
38. Ibid.
39. Bishop Burnet, *History of My Own Time*, O. Airey, ed. (Oxford, 1900), 2:196.
40. Grey, *Greys Debates*, 7:10.
41. Ibid, 7:12.
42. Ibid, 7:63.
43. Ibid, 64. For the bribe, see HoP, Garway.
44. Ibid, 50.
45. Ibid, 51–2.

46. Ibid, 51.
47. HoP, 'Edward Sackville'.
48. Anonymous, *A Letter from Amsterdam to a Friend in Paris* (London?, 1679), p. 2.
49. Ibid, p. 5.
50. Ibid, pp. 7–8.
51. Ibid, 8–9.
52. Ibid, p. 10.
53. LJ, 13:517–18.
54. Ibid, 524.
55. Ibid, 535.
56. Ibid, 530.
57. See Edward Raymond Turner, 'The Privy Council of 1679', *EHR* 30 (1915), pp. 251–70.
58. Quoted in Burnet, *History*, 2:210, f. 1.
59. Ibid, 210.
60. Reresby, *Memoirs*, p. 182.
61. Grey, *Greys Debates*, 7:137.
62. Ibid, 138–39.
63. Ibid, 147.
64. Ibid, 146.
65. Ibid, 150–51.
66. Ibid, 151.
67. Ibid, 152.
68. Ibid, 240.
69. Ibid, 242–43.
70. Ibid, 248.
71. Ibid, 260.
72. Parliamentary Archives, Joint Committee book, HL/PO/JT/1/1 ff. 6–9.
73. LJ, 13:594.
74. Ibid, 595.
75. HoP 1:106; see also the table on pp. 107–24.
76. Cobbett, *State Trials*, 7, col. 259ff.
77. Ibid, 271.
78. Ibid, 291.
79. Ibid, 292.
80. Ibid, 309.

CHAPTER 8: TURNING POINT? SPRING AND SUMMER 1679

1. HMC Ormonde, n.s. 5:68–69.
2. William Cobbett, *Cobbett's Complete Collection of State Trials*, Thomas Howell, ed., 21 vols. (London, 1809–16), 7:785; Folger Library, Newdigate Newsletters, no. 781.
3. ODNB, 'Roger Palmer earl of Castlemaine'.
4. Ibid, 'Thomas Whitbread', 'William Barrow (alias Harcourt)', 'John Caldwell (alias Fenwick)'.
5. *The Jesuits Character* (London, 1679).
6. ODNB, 'James Corker'.
7. Cobbett, *State Trials*, 7, cols. 325–26.
8. Ibid, cols. 323–24.
9. Ibid, col. 330.
10. Ibid, col. 333.
11. Ibid, cols. 333–34.
12. AM 38847, ff. 248–52; ODNB, 'Stephen Dugdale'.
13. Bishop Burnet, *History of My Own Time*, O. Airey, ed. (Oxford, 1900), 2:190; quoted in ODNB.
14. Cobbett, *State Trials*, 7, col. 335.

15. Ibid, col. 339.
16. Ibid, col. 337.
17. Ibid, col. 343.
18. Ibid, col. 346.
19. Ibid, col. 347.
20. Ibid, col. 349.
21. Ibid, col. 350.
22. Ibid, col. 351.
23. Ibid.
24. Ibid, col. 352.
25. Ibid, col. 353.
26. Ibid, col. 355.
27. Ibid, col. 357.
28. Ibid, col. 358.
29. Ibid, cols. 358–59.
30. Ibid, col. 359.
31. Ibid.
32. Ibid, col. 359.
33. Ibid, col. 360.
34. Ibid, col. 361.
35. Ibid, cols. 366, 370.
36. Ibid, col. 362.
37. Ibid, cols. 379–80.
38. Ibid, col. 383.
39. Ibid, col. 386.
40. Ibid, col. 392.
41. Ibid, col. 403.
42. Ibid, col. 407.
43. Ibid, col. 408.
44. Ibid, col. 409.
45. Ibid, col. 410.
46. Ibid.
47. Ibid, col. 412.
48. Ibid, cols. 412–13.
49. Ibid, col. 414.
50. Ibid, col. 418; Newdigate Newsletters, no. 798, 16 June 1679.
51. ODNB, 'Richard Langhorne'.
52. Cobbett, *State Trials*, 7, col. 428.
53. Ibid, cols. 428–29.
54. Ibid, col. 431.
55. Ibid, col. 432.
56. Jane Lane, *Titus Oates* (London, 1949), p. 25; quoting Burnet.
57. Cobbett, *State Trials*, 7, col. 437.
58. Ibid, cols. 437–38.
59. Ibid, col. 442.
60. Ibid, col. 446.
61. Ibid, cols. 447–48.
62. Ibid, col. 448; on Edwards see John Burke, ed. *A Genealogical and Heraldic History of the Extinct and Dormant Baronetcies of England, Scotland and Ireland* (London, 1841), p. 180.
63. Cobbett, *State Trials*, 7, col. 463.
64. Ibid, cols. 481–82.
65. Ibid, cols. 484–85.
66. Ibid, col. 490.

67. Thomas McCoog, 'Richard Langhorne and the Popish Plot', *Recusant History* 19 (1989), p. 500.
68. Anonymous, *The Behaviour, Last Words, and Execution of the Five Grand Jesuits and Popish Priests* (London, 1679), p. 2.
69. HoP, 'Sir Richard How'.
70. Cobbett, *State Trials*, 7, cols. 491–92.
71. Ibid, col. 494.
72. Ibid, cols. 494–95.
73. Ibid, col. 495.
74. Ibid, col. 501.
75. John Aubrey, *Brief Lives*, Kate Bennett, ed. (Oxford, 2015), p. 32.
76. McCoog, 'Richard Langhorne and the Popish Plot', *Recusant History*, 19 (1989), pp. 499–508, Newdigate Newsletters, no. 803, 26 June 1679.
77. AM 29910, f. 114.
78. HMC Ormonde, n.s. 5:136.
79. Ibid, 5:140.
80. Ibid, 4:530; see Raymond Turner, 'The Privy Council of 1679', *English Historical Review*, 30 (1915), pp. 251–70, here p. 269.
81. HMC Ormonde, n.s. 4:527.
82. Newdigate Newsletters, no. 812, 17 July 1679.
83. HMC Kenyon, p. 113.
84. John Kenyon, 'The Acquittal of Sir George Wakeman: 18 July 1679', *Historical Journal* 14 (1971), p. 700.
85. See the biographies in HoP.
86. See ODNB, 'Sir Edward Ward', 'Sir Robert Sawyer'.
87. Cobbett, *State Trials*, 7, col. 603.
88. Ibid, col. 610.
89. Ibid.
90. Ibid, col. 609.
91. Ibid, col. 611.
92. Ibid, cols. 621–22.
93. Ibid, col. 624.
94. Ibid, col. 626.
95. Ibid, col. 631.
96. Ibid, col. 632.
97. Ibid.
98. John Evelyn, *The Diary of John Evelyn*, E.S. de Beer, ed. (London, 2006), pp. 596–98.
99. Cobbett, *State Trials*, col. 641.
100. Ibid, cols. 641–42.
101. Ibid, col. 642.
102. Ibid, col. 642.
103. Ibid, cols. 646–49.
104. Ibid, col. 652.
105. Ibid.
106. Ibid, col. 656.
107. Ibid, col. 659.
108. Ibid, col. 660.
109. Ibid, col. 671.
110. Ibid, col. 664.
111. Ibid, col. 669.
112. Ibid, col. 677.
113. Ibid, col. 679.
114. Ibid, col. 682.
115. Ibid, col. 683.

116. Ibid, col. 685.
117. Ibid, col. 686.

CHAPTER 9: BATTLE ROYAL, JULY 1679–JULY 1680

1. Folger Library, Newdigate Newsletters, no. 813, 19 July 1679; John Kenyon, 'The Acquittal of Sir George Wakeman: 18 July 1679', *Historical Journal* 14 (1971), p. 707.
2. HMC LeFleming, p. 162.
3. HMC Ormonde, n.s. 5:158.
4. Newdigate Newsletters, no. 815, 26 July 1679; no. 820, 7 August 1679.
5. Ibid, nos. 816, 818, 820.
6. William Cobbett, *Cobbett's Complete Collection of State Trials*, Thomas Howell, ed., 21 vols. (London, 1809–16), 7, col. 703.
7. [Jane Curtis,] '*A Satyr Against In-justice, Or, Sc–gs upon Sc–gs*' (London, 1679); cited in ODNB, 'Sir William Scroggs'.
8. Cobbett, *State Trials*, 7, col. 703.
9. HMC Ormonde, n.s. 4:533.
10. For a selection of last words spoken by several priests, see Archdiocese of Westminster Archives, Diocesan Mss., vol. 34, pp. 507, 511, 515, 526.
11. Quoted in W.D. Christie, *A Life of Anthony Ashley Cooper, First Earl of Shaftesbury*, 2 vols. (London, 1871), p. 367.
12. HMC Ormonde, n.s. 5:166.
13. Bishop Burnet, *History of My Own Time*, O. Airey, ed. (Oxford, 1900), 2:242.
14. HMC Ormond n.s. 5:193–94.
15. Ibid, 197.
16. Newdigate Newsletters, no. 832, 9 September 1679.
17. HMC Ormonde, n.s. 4:535
18. Ibid, 537–38.
19. Robert Jenison, *The Narrative of Robert Jenison* (London, 1679), pp. 18, 19.
20. Ibid, p. 20.
21. Ibid, p. 5.
22. Ibid.
23. Newdigate Newsletters, no. 828, 30 August 1679.
24. Ibid, no. 817, 31 July 1679.
25. Ibid, no. 844, 4 October 1679.
26. Robert Bolron, *The Narrative of Robert Bolron* (London, 1680), p. 20; HoP, 'Sir Robert Clayton'.
27. HMC Ormonde, n.s. 5:221; Newdigate Newsletters, nos. 841, 846.
28. Ibid, 5:545–46.
29. Ibid, 546.
30. Elizabeth Cellier, *Malice Defeated* (London, 1680), pp. 5, 7.
31. Ibid, 12–13.
32. ODNB, 'Thomas Dangerfield'.
33. Newdigate Newsletters, no. 855, 30 October 1679.
34. See Rachel Weil, 'If I did say so, I lyed': Elizabeth Cellier and the Construction of Credibility in the Popish Plot Crisis', in Mark Kishlansky and Susan Amussen, eds., *Political Culture and Cultural Politics in Early Modern England* (Manchester, 1995), pp. 189–209.
35. Cellier, *Malice Defeated*, p. 18.
36. HMC Ormonde, n.s. 4:552–58.
37. Ibid, 556.
38. Cellier, *Malice Defeated*, p. 18.
39. HMC Ormonde, n.s. 4:556.
40. Newdigate Newsletters, nos. 858, 862.

41. Ibid, no. 863, 17 November 1679.
42. HMC Ormonde, n.s. 4:557–58.
43. Ibid, 5:238.
44. Ibid, 4:559–60.
45. J.R. Jones, 'The Green Ribbon Club', *Durham University Journal,* 18 (1956), pp. 17–20; David Allen, 'Political Clubs in Restoration London', *Historical Journal* 19 (1976), pp. 561–80.
46. Anonymous, *The Solemn Mock Procession of the Pope, Cardinalls, Iesuits, Fryers &c. Through ye City of London* (London, 1679).
47. Ibid; Jones, 'Green Ribbon Club', p. 19.
48. Anonymous, *Solemn Mock Procession.*
49. HMC Ormonde, n.s. 4:561.
50. Cobbett, *State Trials,* 7, col. 766.
51. Ibid, col. 812; HMC Ormonde, n.s. 4:561.
52. A mark was a unit of account, not an actual coin. It was worth two-thirds of a pound, or 13 shillings and 6 pence.
53. HMC Ormonde, n.s. 5:244, 245.
54. Ibid, 4:562.
55. Ibid, 563.
56. Ibid, 5:245.
57. Ibid, 4:562.
58. Anna Keay, *The Last Royal Rebel: the Life and Death of James Duke of Monmouth* (New York, 2016), p. 237.
59. HMC Ormonde, n.s. 5:252, 255–57.
60. Newdigate Newsletters, no. 878, 25 December 1679; no. 880, 29 December 1679.
61. Quoted in Cobbett, *State Trials,* 7, cols. 811–12.
62. HMC Ormonde, n.s. 4:572.
63. Newdigate Newsletters, nos. 887, 888, 15 and 17 January 1680.
64. Cobbett, *State Trials,* 7, col. 837.
65. Ibid, col. 860.
66. Newdigate Newsletters, no. 882, 3 January 1680.
67. HMC Ormonde, n.s. 5:266.
68. CSPD January 1679–August 1680, p. 376.
69. Newdigate Newsletters, no. 891, 24 January 1680.
70. Ibid, 280.
71. HMC Ormonde, n.s. 5:269.
72. Ibid, 274.
73. Ibid, 270.
74. Ibid, 271.
75. Charles Blount, *An Appeal from the Country to the City* (London, 1679), p. 2.
76. ODNB, 'Charles Blount'.
77. Anonymous, *Some Observations on the Late Tryal of Sir George Wakeman* (London, 1679).
78. Cobbett, *State Trials,* 7, col. 932.
79. Ibid, 937; Newdigate Newsletters, no. 897, 7 February 1680.
80. Cobbett, *State Trials,* 7, col. 963.
81. Robert Bolron, *The Narrative of Robert Bolron, of Shippon Hall, Gent., Concerning the Late Horrid Popish Plot* (London, 1679).
82. Cobbett, *State Trials,* 7, col. 965.
83. Ibid, 966; Newdigate Newsletters, no. 900, 14 February 1680; HoP, 'Sir Thomas Mauleverer'.
84. Cobbett, *State Trials,* 7, col. 969.
85. Ibid, col. 1001.
86. Ibid.

87. Ibid, 7, col. 1002.
88. Ibid, cols. 1020, 1022, 1024.
89. Ibid, col. 1026.
90. Ibid, col. 1027.
91. Ibid, col. 1043.
92. Ibid.
93. HMC Ormonde, n.s. 4:579.
94. Newdigate Newsletters, no. 900, 14 February 1680; no. 904, 23 February 1680.
95. Ibid, no. 904.
96. Ibid, no. 910, 8 March 1680.
97. HMC Ormonde, n.s. 5:288.
98. Ibid, 291.
99. Ibid; Newdigate Newsletters, no. 916, 25 March 1680.
100. Sir Roger L'Estrange, *L'Estrange's Case in a Civil Dialogue Betwixt 'Zekeiel and Ephraim* (London, 1680).
101. Sir Roger L'Estrange, *A Further Discovery of the Plot* (London, 1680), p. 7.
102. Ibid, p. 3.
103. ODNB, 'Sir Roger L'Estrange'.
104. CSPD 1680, p. 424; Newdigate Newsletters, no. 920, 1 April 1680.
105. HMC Ormonde, n.s. 5:295–96.
106. Ibid, 297.
107. Ibid, 302.
108. Ibid, 5:298.
109. Newdigate Newsletters, no. 924, 12 April 1680; no. 925, 15 April 1680.
110. HMC Ormonde, n.s. 5:302–03.
111. Ibid, 304.
112. Ibid, 305.
113. Ibid, 308.
114. Ibid, 312–13.
115. CSPD January 1679–August 1680, pp. 478, 480.
116. John Warner, *The History of English Persecution of Catholics and the Presbyterian Plot*, T.A. Birrell, ed., John Bligh, trans., *Publications of the Catholic Record Society*, vol. 48 (London, 1953), p. 421.
117. See ODNB, 'John Gadbury'.
118. Cobbett, *State Trials*, 7, col. 1046.
119. Ibid, col. 1048.
120. Ibid, col. 1053.
121. Ibid, col. 1054.
122. Jane Lane, *Titus Oates* (London, 1949), p. 27; Cobbett, *State Trials*, 7, cols. 1094–95.
123. Roger, earl of Castlemaine, *The Earl of Castlemaine's Manifesto* (London, 1681), pp. 49–50.
124. Cobbett, *State Trials*, 7, col. 1083.
125. Ibid, cols. 1103–04; Castlemaine, *Manifesto*, p. 72.
126. Cobbett, *State Trials*, 7, col. 1110.
127. Castlemaine, *Manifesto*, p. 81.
128. HMC Ormonde, n.s. 5:339; J.P. Kenyon, *Robert Spencer Earl of Sunderland* (London, 1958), p. 49.

CHAPTER 10: COUNTER-ATTACK, SUMMER 1680–SUMMER 1681

1. Newdigate Newsletters, nos. 952, 953, 26 and 28 June 1680.
2. William Cobbett, *Cobbett's Complete Collection of State Trials*, Thomas Howell, ed., 21 vols. (London, 1809–16), 7, cols. 1180–81.
3. Newdigate Newsletters, nos. 948, 956, 963, 17 and 28 June, 20 July 1680.
4. Ibid, no. 980, 9 September 1680.

5. Ibid, nos. 975, 976, 24 and 26 August 1680. The city evidently thought better of its generosity – no monument seems to have been built.
6. CSPD September 1680–December 1681, p. 24.
7. HMC Beaufort, 185.
8. Cobbett, *State Trials*, 7, cols. 1192–93.
9. Ibid, col. 1199.
10. Ibid, col. 1203.
11. Ibid.
12. Newdigate Newsletters, no. 984, 18 September 1680.
13. CSPD September 1680–December 1681, p. 30.
14. Ibid.
15. Ibid, p. 33.
16. Newdigate Newsletters, nos. 986, 988; 23 and 28 September 1680.
17. Ibid, no. 998, 22 October 1680.
18. CSPD September 1680–December 1681, p. 35.
19. Ibid, p. 40.
20. Ibid, p. 39.
21. Newdigate Newsletters, nos. 987, 991, 992, 25 September and 5 and 7 October 1680.
22. CSPD September 1680–December 1681, p. 40.
23. Ibid, p. 43.
24. Ibid, p. 47.
25. LJ, 13:610.
26. Anchitell Grey, *Greys Debates of the House of Commons, 1667–1694*, 10 vols. (London, 1769), 7:357–58.
27. AM 17018 ff. 153, 157; ODNB, 'Arthur Annesley, earl of Anglesey'.
28. CSPD September 1680–December 1681, p. 68.
29. Grey, *Greys Debates*, 7:381, 385.
30. Ibid, 357.
31. LJ, 13:624.
32. Ibid, 13:627.
33. Ibid, 13:634.
34. Ibid, 13:649.
35. Ibid.
36. Ibid, 13:656.
37. Ibid, 13:676.
38. Grey, *Greys Debates*, 7:425.
39. Ronald Hutton, *Charles II: King of England, Scotland and Ireland* (Oxford, 1989), pp. 395–96.
40. Ibid, p. 396; HoL, 1:199–200.
41. LJ, 13:663.
42. ODNB, 'William Howard Viscount Stafford'.
43. https://www.parliament.uk/about/living-heritage/building/palace/westminsterhall. Accessed 5 July 2021.
44. Sir John Reresby, *Memoirs of Sir John Reresby*, Andrew Browning, ed. (Glasgow, 1936), pp. 205–06.
45. Cobbett, *State Trials*, 7, col. 1297.
46. Ibid, cols. 1344–45.
47. Ibid, col. 1355.
48. Gilbert Burnet, *History of My Own Time*, O. Airey, ed. (Oxford, 1900), 2:270.
49. Cobbett, *State Trials*, 7, cols. 1359–60.
50. Ibid, cols. 1352–53.
51. Ibid, cols. 1400–01.
52. Ibid, col. 1402.
53. John Evelyn, *The Diary of John Evelyn*, E.S. de Beer, ed. (London, 2006), p. 624.

54. Reresby, *Memoirs*, p. 206.
55. John Evelyn, *Diary* (London, 2006), p. 625.
56. Ibid, p. 626.
57. Cobbett, *State Trials*, 7, col. 1441.
58. Ibid, cols. 1437, 1441.
59. ODNB, 'Stephen College'.
60. Cobbett, *State Trials*, 7, col. 1460.
61. Ibid, cols. 1463–65.
62. Evelyn, *Diary*, p. 624.
63. Burnet, *History*, 2:274.
64. Cobbett, *State Trials*, 7, col. 1552.
65. Ibid, col. 1554.
66. LJ, 13:705.
67. Cobbett, *State Trials*, 7, cols. 1556, 1558.
68. Evelyn, *Diary*, p. 627.
69. Burnet, *History*, 2:278.
70. James in a letter quoted in ibid, 2:275, n. 5; see also James Clarke, *The Life of James II* (London, 1816), p. 640.
71. Reresby, *Memoirs*, p. 206.
72. Cobbett, *State Trials*, 7, cols. 1562–63.
73. Newdigate Newsletters, no. 1026, 30 December 1680.
74. Cobbett, *State Trials*, 7, col. 1564.
75. CSPD 1680–81, p. 111.
76. Cobbett, *State Trials*, 7, col. 1567.
77. Ibid, col. 1568; CSPD 1680–81, p. 111.
78. Reresby, *Memoirs*, p. 209.
79. Newdigate Newsletters, no. 1024, 24 December 1680.
80. Reresby, *Memoirs*, pp. 208–09.
81. Grey, *Greys Debates*, 8:132.
82. CJ, 9:698.
83. Ibid, 688–92, 697–99.
84. HoP, 'Edward Seymour'.
85. CJ, 9:693–94.
86. Grey, *Greys Debates*, 8:161.
87. CJ, 9:699.
88. Ibid, 702.
89. Ibid, 703–04.
90. ODNB, 'Edward Fitzharris'.
91. ODNB, 'Edmund Everard'.
92. See Susan Shifrin, ' "Subdued by a Famous Roman Dame": Picturing Foreignness, Notoriety and Prerogative in the Portraits of Hortense Mancini, Duchess Mazarin', in *Politics, Transgression, and Representation at the Court of Charles II* (New Haven, CT, 2007) pp. 141–74.
93. Edward Fitzharris, *The Examination of Edward Fitzharris, Relating to the Popish Plot* (London, 1681), p. 11.
94. CSPD, 1680–81, p. 184.
95. HoL, 1:201.
96. Hutton, *Charles II*, p. 401.
97. Quoted in ibid, p. 400.
98. LJ, 13:745.
99. Ibid.
100. CJ, 9:708; Grey, *Greys Debates*, 8:295.
101. Ibid, pp. 305–08.
102. LJ, 13:755.
103. CJ, 9:711–12.

104. LJ, 13:757.
105. Reresby, *Memoirs*, p. 224.
106. Newdigate Newsletters, no. 1060, 2 April 1681.
107. Cobbett, *State Trials*, 8, cols. 247–49.
108. ODNB, 'Sir William Scroggs'.
109. Cobbett, *State Trials*, 8, cols. 253–56.
110. Ibid, cols. 260–66.
111. Ibid, col. 280.
112. Ibid, col. 332.
113. Ibid.
114. Ibid, cols. 333–36.
115. Ibid, cols. 342–44.
116. Ibid, col. 347.
117. Ibid, col. 362.
118. Ibid, cols. 363, 365.
119. Ibid, cols. 372–73.
120. Ibid, p. 378.
121. Burnet, *History*, 2:291–92.
122. ODNB, 'Oliver Plunket'; Burnet, *History*, 2:292.
123. Cobbett, *State Trials*, 8, cols. 463–64.
124. Ibid, col. 469.
125. Ibid, col. 482.
126. Ibid, col. 488.
127. Ibid, cols. 490–91.
128. Ibid, col. 492.
129. Ibid, col. 494.
130. Burnet, *History*, 2:292 and f. 3.
131. Cobbett, *State Trials*, 8, col. 496.
132. Ibid, col. 396.
133. ODNB, 'Oliver Plunket'.

EPILOGUE

1. William Cobbett, *Cobbett's Complete Collection of State Trials*, Thomas Howell, ed., 21 vols. (London, 1809–16), 8, cols. 501–26.
2. See, for example, the trial of Father George Busby at the assizes in Derby in the summer; ibid, cols. 525–50.
3. Newdigate Newsletters, no. 1099, 16 July 1681.
4. See ODNB, 'Rye House Plotters'.
5. Anne Keay, *The Magnificent Monarch: Charles II and the Ceremonies of Power* (London, 2008), p. 118 and appendix 1.
6. Most of the biographical information contained in the epilogue has been drawn from the invaluable articles found in the ODNB.

SOURCES AND FURTHER READING

This is a book that depends very heavily on printed primary sources, supplemented with archival materials and decades of reading and teaching about seventeenth-century Britain. It was conceived and written as a narrative history, and for this reason I have kept the textual references to a minimum. In proceeding in this fashion, I was following the model of J.P. Kenyon's wonderful *The Popish Plot* (Heinemann, 1972), the book that inspired me to become a Restoration historian. Our accounts of the plot differ in a variety of ways, but if anyone thinks my own comes anywhere near Kenyon's, I will be very pleased.

My background reading for this study spans many different genres and historical fields, and in the following I hope to introduce readers and students of British history to published works and source materials I have drawn upon, and that they might find interesting for further exploration. For general readers who desire deeper insight into the world of the late seventeenth century, for example, I can recommend Ian Mortimer's *The Time Traveller's Guide to Restoration Britain* (Pegasus, 2017) and Peter Earle's *The World of Defoe* (Atheneum, 1977). Robert Bucholz and Joseph Ward's *London: A Social and Cultural History* (Cambridge University Press, 2012) also provides a broad social history of the metropolis. Another valuable survey of Stuart London is Margarette Lincoln, *London and the 17th Century: The Making of the World's Greatest City* (Yale University Press, 2021). A book that focuses on the relationship between the monarch and the City of London is Christine Stevenson's *The City and the King: Architecture and Politics in Restoration London* (Yale University Press, 2013).

On the court and high politics, readers might start with Tim Harris's *Restoration: Charles II and His Kingdoms, 1660–1685* (Oxford University Press, 2005). Kevin Sharpe's *Rebranding Rule: The Restoration and Revolution Monarchy, 1660–1714* (Yale University Press, 2013) is full of valuable insights into Restoration politics. There are many biographies of Charles II to choose from;

two of the best are Antonia Fraser, *Royal Charles* (Dell, 1980), and Ronald Hutton, *Charles II: King of England, Scotland, and Ireland* (Oxford University Press, 1989). James II's life has been told by John Miller, *James II* (Yale University Press, 2000). Anna Keay has written two books that reveal much about Charles II's court: *The Magnificent Monarch: Charles II and the Ceremonies of Power* (Continuum, 2008) and *The Last Royal Rebel: The Life and Death of James, Duke of Monmouth* (Bloomsbury, 2016). The importance of women in the king's life – and the political and cultural life of his reign – may be glimpsed in *Painted Ladies: Women at the Court of Charles II* (Yale University Press, 2001), edited by Catharine MacLeod and Julia Marciari Alexander. A magnificent volume displaying the sumptuous nature of the court is *Charles II: Art and Power* (Royal Collection Trust, 2017), edited by Rufus Bird and Martin Clayton.

There are many books relating to Parliament and Parliamentary politics in this period. In 1961 J.R. Jones published *The First Whigs: The Politics of the Exclusion Crisis* (Oxford University Press); some historians have disputed elements of Jones's argument, but it remains an important book. K.H.D. Haley's biography of the little earl is still the best, *The First Earl of Shaftesbury* (Oxford University Press, 1968). Mark Kishlansky's *Parliamentary Selection: Social and Political Choice in Early Modern England* (Cambridge University Press, 1985) is an excellent account of how elections worked, and how the struggle over exclusion transformed them. For the House of Lords, see Paul Seaward et al., eds., *Honour, Interest and Power: An Illustrated History of the House of Lords* (Boydell and Brewer, 2010).

For more specialized readers, I have found the work of the History of Parliament Trust in documenting the lives of every member of both Houses throughout Charles's reign to be invaluable. Not only do these volumes give a complete history of each session of Charles II's Parliaments, but browsing through the biographical articles on members is fascinating: *The House of Commons 1660–1690*, ed. Basil Duke Henning (3 vols., Secker and Warburg, 1983) and *The House of Lords, 1660–1715* (5 vols., Cambridge University Press, 2016). The Trust makes the text of the volumes related to the Commons available online at https://www.historyofparliamentonline.org.

The diaries and memoirs of important Restoration figures are of great interest and were used extensively in *Hoax*. Premier among these, though alas it does not cover the years of the plot, is Samuel Pepys's *Diary* (11 vols., University of California Press, 1970–83). Pepys was endlessly fascinated by everything around him and his diary brings the period alive. If readers cannot muster the time for the complete diary, Claire Tomalin's outstanding biography of Pepys is a satisfactory substitute: *Samuel Pepys: The Unequalled Self* (Vintage, 2002). Rather more staid, but highly interesting nevertheless, is John Evelyn's *Diary*, ed. E.S. de Beer (Everyman, 2006). Evelyn, like Pepys, knew everyone – and he kept up his diary for many years longer than Pepys. Gilbert Burnet's *History of My Own Time*, ed. Osmond Airy (2 vols., Oxford University Press, 1897–1900), is a first-hand account of Restoration politics by an insider – not always accurate, but still valuable.

Restoration culture represented a determined backlash against the Puritanism of the preceding decade. The theatres, closed during the Interregnum, reopened and women mounted the public stage for the first time. Restoration comedies were bawdy, filled with sexual innuendo, adultery and farce. William Wycherley's *The Country Wife* (1675) is a good example of the genre, in which a London rake gains access to the wives of gentlemen and City merchants by feigning impotence. One of King Charles's favourite plays was *The Rover* by Aphra Behn, one of England's first female playwrights.

The expiration of the Licensing Act resulted in an explosion of political literature, much of it dreadful hackery, but some marked by exceptional wit and literary merit. For the latter, see John Dryden's *Absalom and Achitophel* (1681), a long satirical poem that fixed the character of Shaftesbury, Monmouth and other leading Whigs as immoral schemers for decades to come. Dip into the works of Roger L'Estrange to read the work of a master of satire. If you are Whiggishly inclined there is no shortage of reading material. One of the more prolific writers was Henry Care, whose *Weekly Pacquet of Advice From Rome* was eagerly snapped up every time it appeared. Anyone interested in a dive into the literature of the time can do so thanks to Early English Books Online – which includes virtually every book published in English before 1700. It may be found at https://www. proquest.com/eebo/index. Satires, sermons, ballads and broadsides – thousands of them – are readily available here.

For the Catholic community in Restoration England, the best place to begin is John Miller's *Popery and Politics in England, 1660–1688* (Cambridge University Press, 1973). More recently Fr. Thomas McCoog S.J. has written *Pre-Suppression Jesuit Activity in the British Isles and Ireland* (Brill, 2019), and has helped fill in the story of the embattled Jesuit mission in England under the Stuarts. Alexandra Walsham's *Charitable Hatred: Tolerance and Intolerance in England, 1500–1700*

(Manchester University Press) shows the clash between faiths in England across the Tudor and Stuart period.

There are many works dealing with the mass of the people from whom rogues such as Titus Oates and William Bedloe emerged. Alan Marshall's *The Strange Death of Edmund Godfrey* (Sutton, 1999) and his *Intelligence and Espionage in the Reign of Charles II, 1660–1685* (Cambridge University Press, 2003) both illustrate the seamy underworld of Restoration London. Richard Greaves's *Secrets of the Kingdom: British Radicals from the Popish Plot to the Revolution of 1688* (Stanford University Press, 1992) reveals much about the shadowy underworld of British plotters. Robert Hutchinson's *The Audacious Crimes of Colonel Blood* (Weidenfeld and Nicolson, 2015) is a biography of a Restoration adventurer as colourful as any of those involved in Oates's plot. A fascinating glimpse into the world of crime and criminals may be found at the Old Bailey Online, a searchable website that includes records of all the criminal trials held at the Old Bailey between 1674 and 1913: https://www.oldbaileyonlined.org.

In writing this book I used manuscript material from a number of important archives and libraries, most importantly the National Archives, the British Library, the Bodleian Library and the Folger Library. Even without the global pandemic restricting access to collections, there were a number of essential published primary sources: accounts of the key trials of the accused plotters may be found in William Cobbett's *State Trials*, volumes 7 and 8. Actually edited by Thomas Bayly Howell instead of the crusading journalist Cobbett, these volumes collect various contemporary accounts of the trials. Some scholars have questioned the accuracy of some of the printed transcripts, but as Kenyon argued long ago, they are the best sources we have, and, moreover, many of them were licensed by the court. The volumes published by the Historical Manuscripts Commission have also been crucial, as they contain many letters and papers of key participants. Some contemporaries, such as Bishop Gilbert Burnet, John Evelyn, Sir John Reresby and Roger North, wrote memoirs giving insight to the period. Parliamentary proceedings can be followed in the printed journals of both Houses, and debates in the Commons are printed in Anchitell Grey's *Debates of the House of Commons*. Nearly all of these may be found online. Detailed references to these sources will be found in the notes.

ACKNOWLEDGEMENTS

This book has taken far too long to write, and it has tested the patience of a very long list of people, beginning with Heather McCallum at Yale University Press and continuing right down to my nearest and dearest, my wife Sue and sons Charles and Henry. I think the dog might have suffered somewhat, too, though she is not as articulate as my family.

Writing a work of history is never easy, but in the midst of a global pandemic it becomes even harder. Libraries and archives on both sides of the Atlantic shut down, forcing me to depend on online and printed sources more heavily than I would otherwise have done. But without the assistance of some of those institutions – even during lockdown – this work would have been impossible. I benefited greatly from staff at the British Library, the Archives of the Archbishopric of Westminster and the Parliamentary Archives in London, the National Archives at Kew, the Bodleian Library in Oxford and the Folger Library in Washington, D.C. The resources made available by the Institute for Historical Research at the University of London have been invaluable, as have the online resources of the History of Parliament Trust. With libraries closed everywhere, the opportunity to use material provided by the Hathi Trust has been equally important.

Friends and colleagues in the field and at my home institution, Louisiana State University, have encouraged me greatly along the way. I will not list them all for fear of unjustly leaving some out – the roster would be a long one if I attempted it. But I must thank Darlene Albritton, our department administrator, who keeps us all up to the mark – and who deals with querulous academics with aplomb. Thank you all.

Apart from the long-suffering Heather McCallum, I owe a debt of gratitude to members of her team at Yale University Press: Katie Urquhart, Felicity Maunder and Lucy Buchan, who have shepherded this book through production.

ACKNOWLEDGEMENTS

And I owe particular thanks to Richard Mason, my copyeditor, who ably transformed my colonial English into proper British prose.

I have been fortunate over the years to have some outstanding graduate and undergraduate students, upon whom I've tried out ideas, or perhaps more accurately, inflicted unwarranted tedium upon. Connie Evans, Jeff Hankins, Keith Altazin, Heather Thornton, Kim Rush, Amanda Allen, Erin Halloran, Libby Taylor, Jennifer Tellman and Jess Payne all enlightened and challenged me on their way to their doctorates, and five more, Caroline Armbruster Reich, Alex Whitley, Tristan Rimmer, Matthew Flanders and Ben Haines, are well on their way to join them. I have taught thousands of undergraduates, and I think a few of them learned something. I know I have from them.

INDEX